THE CRISIS OF NEOLIBERALISM

The Crisis of
Neoliberalism

Gérard Duménil

Dominique Lévy

HARVARD UNIVERSITY PRESS

Cambridge, Massachusetts

London, England

Printed in the United States of America

First Harvard University Press paperback edition, 2013

Library of Congress Cataloging-in-Publication Data

Duménil, Gérard.
The crisis of neoliberalism / Gérard Duménil and Dominique Lévy.
p.   cm.
Includes bibliographical references and index.
ISBN 978-0-674-04988-8 (cloth:alk. paper)
ISBN 978-0-674-07224-4 (pbk.)
1. Global Financial Crisis, 2008–2009.   2. Neoliberalism—United States.
3. Capitalism—United States.   I. Lévy, Dominique.   II. Title.
HB37172008.D86   2010
330.973—dc22   2010006788

Contents

THE CRISIS OF NEOLIBERALISM

Introduction

From the Subprime Crash to the Great Contraction

The crisis that began with the subprime loan crash of August 2007 in the United States will remain a distinctive milestone in the history of capitalism. From its onset, the financial turmoil took unexpected proportions. The shock gradually unsettled the fragile financial structure that had been built during the previous decades and destabilized the real economy. By September 2008, it became evident that capitalism was entering into a deep and lasting crisis, a Great Contraction, reminiscent of the Great Depression.

The Crisis of Neoliberalism

Neoliberalism is a new stage of capitalism that emerged in the wake of the structural crisis of the 1970s. It expresses the strategy of the capitalist classes in alliance with upper management, specifically financial managers, intending to strengthen their hegemony and to expand it globally. As of 2004, when our book *Capital Resurgent: Roots of the Neoliberal Revolution* was published by Harvard University Press, this strategy appeared successful, based on its own objectives, the income and wealth of a privileged minority, and the dominance of a country. The contemporary crisis is an outcome of the contradictions inherent in that strategy. The crisis revealed the strategy's unsustainable character, leading to what can be denoted as the "crisis of neoliberalism." Neoliberal trends ultimately unsettled the foundations of the economy of the "secure base" of the upper classes—the capability of the United States to grow, maintain the leadership of its financial

1

institutions worldwide, and ensure the dominance of its currency—a class and imperial strategy that resulted in a stalemate.

A New Social Order—A Multipolar World

The crisis of neoliberalism is the fourth structural crisis in capitalism since the late nineteenth century. Each of these earthquakes introduced the establishment of a new social order and deeply altered international relations. The contemporary crisis marks the beginning of a similar process of transition. Not only is financial regulation involved, but a new corporate governance, the rebuilding of the financial sector, and new policies are now required. The basic tenets and practices of neoliberal globalization will be questioned, and production has to be "re-territorialized" in the United States to a significant extent. Accordingly, countries such as China, India, or Brazil will become gradually less dependent on their relationship to the United States. It will be, in particular, quite difficult to correct for the macro trajectory of declining trends of accumulation and cumulative disequilibria of the U.S. economy once the present Great Contraction is stopped.

In any event, the new world order will be more multipolar than at present. Further, if such changes are not realized successfully in the United States, the decline of U.S. international hegemony could be sharp. None of the urgently required tasks in the coming decades to slow down the comparative decline of the U.S. economy can be realized under the same class leadership and unchecked globalizing trends. The unquenchable quest for high income on the part of the upper classes must be halted. Much will depend on the pressure exerted by the popular classes and the peoples of the world, but the "national factor," that is, the national commitment in favor of the preservation of U.S. preeminence worldwide, could play a crucial role. The necessary adjustment can be realized in the context of a new social arrangement to the Right or to the Left, although, as of the last months of 2009, the chances of a Left alternative appear slim.

It is important to understand that the contemporary crisis is only the initial step in a longer process of rectification. How long this process will last depends on the severity of the crisis, and national and international political strife. The capability of the U.S. upper classes to perform the much needed adjustment and the willingness of China to collaborate will be crucial factors. A crisis of the dollar could precipitate a sequence of events that would alter the basic features of the process.

In the coming decades, the new social and global orders will have to confront the emergency situation created by global warming. These issues lie beyond the limits of the present study, whose focus is on the crisis. Stronger government intervention and international cooperation will also be required in these respects that add to the necessity of the establishment of renewed configurations beyond the wild dynamics of neoliberal capitalism.

Abstracting from the updating of some of the series, the last changes to the present text were made in October 2009, and there is obviously more to come. It would be unrealistic, however, to expect a final outcome in the near future. The book covers the causes of the crisis, its outbreak, and the first phase of the contraction of output around the globe, as well as the perspectives for the coming decades. The viewpoint is analytical, not normative.

The Strategy of the U.S. Upper Classes in Neoliberalism: The Success and Failure of a Bold Endeavor

Two very distinct categories of phenomena are involved in the analysis of the contemporary crisis: the historical dynamics of capitalism, on the one hand, and financial and macro mechanisms, on the other hand. The interpretation of the crisis lies at the intersection of these two sets of processes, and the difficulty is to do justice to both and account for their reciprocal relationships.

Neoliberalism should be understood as a new phase in the evolution of capitalism. As such, it can be described intrinsically—its basic mechanisms and contradictions. The reference to a most recent phase raises, however, the issue of *previous* phases. The comparison with earlier periods reveals the traits proper to the new period. The analysis of the social, political, and economic trends that led to the establishment of neoliberalism is also telling of the nature and fate of this social order. Symmetrically, the notion of a crisis of neoliberalism implies a possible transition to a new phase, and the nature of the society that will prevail in the wake of the contemporary crisis is a major component of the investigation here.

NEOLIBER-ALISM ↓ NEW PHASE

Thus, some preliminary questions must be answered. What is a phase of capitalism? How are such phases established? How do they disappear? What are the specific features of neoliberalism as such? The goal of the first chapter is to interpret the rise and fall of neoliberalism under U.S. world hegemony in the broader context of the historical dynamics of capitalism. The proper financial crisis and, later, the sharp contraction of output in the United States and around the globe define a second set of issues. There are two important facets of these mechanisms. One relates to the

Q's:

5

1

dramatic expansion of financial activity and financial deregulation. A degree of technical complexity is involved here, given the astounding capability of the financial actors to innovate (as in securitization, derivative markets, etc.). Macroeconomic mechanisms define a second ensemble of

2

VARIABLES

factors. The main variables of concern are consumption and investment, foreign trade, and the internal and external debt of the U.S. economy. And the two sets of mechanisms, financial and macro variables, can be adequately understood only in relation to each other. For example, the growth of the domestic debt, a basic component of the U.S. macro trajectory, relied on the new financial devices that made it possible. This is the focus of Chapter 2, which sketches the overall framework of analysis and conclusions concerning the analysis of the financial crisis and the contraction of output.

The purpose of Chapters 1 and 2 is to summarize the overall argument and, more fundamentally, to introduce a number of basic notions and mechanisms discussed in the rest of the book in a more detailed manner, and for which empirical evidence is provided.

1

The Historical Dynamics of Hegemony

The present chapter focuses on hierarchies among classes and countries, more specifically, neoliberalism as a class hegemony and the global dominance of the United States in neoliberal globalization. The sequence of formation, climax, and crisis of neoliberalism is interpreted as an episode in the history of the rise and fall of such social and international configurations. Neoliberalism appears as the latest of three social orders, which jointly constitute modern capitalism, that is, capitalism since the turn of the twentieth century. The rise and fall of each of these social orders can be dated to the occurrence of major crises, or "structural crises," such as the present one. The historical dynamics of international hegemonies are, somehow, distinct, although the two categories of phenomena are obviously interrelated. For example, the crisis of neoliberalism adds to the threat pending on U.S. hegemony.

Neoliberalism as Class Hegemony—Imperialism in Neoliberal Globalization

Neoliberalism is a multifaceted phenomenon, the outcome of a whole set of converging historical determinants, and it is difficult to precisely determine its beginnings. Actually, the earliest expressions of the new trends were evident from the end of World War II when the basic features of the postwar society and economy were defined. Various developments surrounding the crisis of the dollar in the early 1970s, such as the floatation of exchange rates, or the policies enacted during the dictatorships in Latin America in the 1970s, can be considered early manifestations. Simplifying to some extent, one can contend, however, that neoliberalism was first established in the United States and the United Kingdom at the end of the 1970s, a crisis decade, a few years later in continental Europe, and then around the globe. The year 1979, when the Federal Reserve decided to raise interest rates to any level allegedly required to curb inflation, is emblematic of the entrance into the new period.

A central thesis in *Capital Resurgent: Roots of the Neoliberal Revolution* is that the overall dynamics of capitalism under neoliberalism, both nationally and internationally, were determined by new class objectives that worked to the benefit of the highest income brackets, capitalist owners, and the upper fractions of management. The greater concentration of income in favor of a privileged minority was a crucial achievement of the new social order. Income statement data make this apparent. In this respect, a *social order* is also a *power configuration*, and implicit in this latter notion is "class" power. National accounting frameworks add to this observation that a large and increasing fraction of U.S. capital income comes from outside of the United States. Not only class relations are involved, but also imperial hierarchies, a permanent feature of capitalism.[1]

The new configuration of income distribution was the outcome of various converging trends. Strong pressure was placed on the mass of salaried workers, which helped restore profit rates from their low levels of the 1970s or, at least, to put an end to their downward trend. The opening of trade and capital frontiers paved the way to large investments in the regions of the world where prevailing social conditions allowed for high returns, thus generating income flows in favor of the U.S. upper classes (and broader groups that benefit to some extent by capital income). Free trade increased the pressure on workers, the effect of the competition emanating from countries where labor costs are low. Large capital income flows also derived from the growing indebtedness of households and the government. Extreme degrees of sophistication and expansion of financial mechanisms were reached after 2000, allowing for tremendous incomes in the financial sector and in rich households. The crisis, finally, revealed that a significant fraction of these flows of income were based on dubious profits, due to an increasing overvaluation of securities.

Besides the comparative interests of social classes, the leading position of the United States, economically, politically, and militarily, must also be considered. The political conditions underlying the dominance of the

United States in the decades preceding the crisis are well known. Two major factors are the fall of the Soviet Union and the weakness of Europe as a political entity. Neoliberalism corrected for the earlier decline of the leadership of the United States in the 1970s, at least vis-à-vis Europe and Japan. The U.S. economy is still the largest in the world in terms of gross domestic product (GDP), with a leadership in fields as important as research and innovation, both in production and financial mechanisms. As a consequence, the dollar is acknowledged as the international currency.

The international neoliberal order—known as neoliberal globalization— was imposed throughout the world, from the main capitalist countries of the center to the less developed countries of the periphery, often at the cost of severe crises as in Asia and Latin America during the 1990s and after 2000. As in any stage of imperialism, the major instruments of these international power relations, beyond straightforward economic violence, are corruption, subversion, and war. The main political tool is always the establishment of a local imperial-friendly government. The collaboration of the elites of the dominated country is crucial, as well as, in contemporary capitalism, the action of international institutions such as the North Atlantic Treaty Organization (NATO), the International Monetary Fund (IMF), the World Bank (WB), and the World Trade Organization (WTO). Economically, the purpose of this domination is the extraction of a "surplus" through the imposition of low prices of natural resources and investment abroad, be it portfolio or foreign direct investment. That countries of the periphery want to sell their natural resources and are eager to receive foreign investment does not change the nature of the relations of domination, just as when, within a given country, workers want to sell their labor power, the ultimate source of profit.

The same notion, hegemony, is used here to refer to both class hierarchical relationships, as in neoliberalism, and imperialism internationally. No distinction is made between *hegemony* and *domination* as in approaches of Gramscian inspiration. The notion emphasizes a common aspect within class and international mechanisms. In each instance, a class or country leads a process of domination in which various agents are involved. In neoliberalism, the upper fractions of capitalist classes, supported by financial institutions, act as leaders within the broader group of upper classes in the exercise of their common domination. Similarly, the United States acts as leader within the broader group of imperialist countries.

There are important implications to the notion of joint, though un-equal, domination by a group of upper classes or advanced countries. The common domination is based on cooperation but also rivalry. At the top of a social hierarchy, various groups are involved and support the project of a more narrowly defined leadership. Such hierarchical alliances can be denoted as "compromises," as the leader adjusts its demands to some of those emanating from its followers but finally prevails over them. The same is true concerning the comparative positions of the various countries within the group of imperialist powers. A compromise at the top also prevails in the exercise of a joint domination internationally, but discipline is imposed by the hegemonic power (as in Athens's Delian League).

In the determination of real and financial trends in contemporary capitalism, these two components—class and international hegemonies—have interacting effects. The present crisis manifests the contradictions of a historical trajectory jointly fashioned by these two strands of factors typical of what can be denoted as "neoliberalism under U.S. hegemony."

A Historical Perspective: Modern Capitalism

The definition of neoliberalism as the latest phase of capitalism raises the issue of previous periods and the overall periodization of capitalism (Box 1.1). What were the previous phases of capitalism? In what respect is neoliberalism distinct? The investigation here uses the notion of modern capitalism, meaning capitalism after the corporate, financial, and managerial revolutions, that is, from the turn of the twentieth century to the present, and neoliberalism is described as the third and most recent phase of modern capitalism.

The dawn of the twentieth century was marked by the emergence of a new institutional framework of capitalist relations, the set of institutions typical of modern capitalism. (In this analysis, a special emphasis is placed on the United States where the corresponding social and economic transformations were stark.)

1. *Capitalism in the late nineteenth century.* During the last decades of the nineteenth century, the size of enterprises increased in parallel to the sophistication of their internal technical and organizational processes. The

Box 1.1
Periodizing Capitalism

There is no single periodization of capitalism. History refers to a set of distinct phenomena, linked within a network of reciprocal relationships but also manifesting important degrees of autonomy. Analysts have based periodizations on, among other things, institutional transformations, long waves, technical change and profitability trends, competitive patterns, policy frameworks, or social and political relations. Rudolf Hilferding, for example, advanced the concept of "finance capital," to account for a feature of the new phase of capitalism in the early twentieth century (what the present study denotes as "modern capitalism"), on the basis of the transformation of the relationship between the financial and industrial sectors. An important literature focused on the notion of "long waves," originally articulated by Nikolai Kondratieff, with several decade-long phases of expansion and stagnating growth, separated by major crises. In the 1960s, Paul Baran and Paul Sweezy coined the concept of "monopoly capitalism," based on a new pattern of competitive mechanisms. In the United States, important research has been devoted to "managerial capitalism," another crucial aspect of the metamorphosis of capitalism. In previous work of the authors, the history of capitalism, from the late nineteenth century to the present, is described by reference to three categories of phenomena: (1) relations of production and class patterns; (2) configurations of power among classes, or social orders; and (3) the trends of the profit rate.[1]

There are important reciprocal relationships between such periodizations, although there is no unambiguous chronological overlap in the definition of periods.

---

1. R. Hilferding, *Finance Capital: A Study of the Latest Phase of Capitalist Development* (1910; London: Routledge and Kegan Paul, 1981); N. D. Kondratieff, "The Static and Dynamic View of Economics," *Quarterly Journal of Economics* 34, no. 4 (1925): 575–583; I. Wallerstein, "Globalization or the Age of Transition? A Long-Term View of the Trajectory of the World-System," *International Sociology* 15, no. 2 (2000): 250–268; G. Arrighi, *The Long Twentieth Century: Money, Power and the Origins of Our Times* (London: Verso, 1994); P. Baran and P. Sweezy, *The Monopoly Capital* (New York: Monthly Review Press, 1966); A. D. Chandler, *The Visible Hand: The Managerial Revolution in American Business* (Cambridge, Mass.: Harvard University Press, 1977).

development of transportation and communication allowed enterprises to expand nationally and internationally. Simultaneously, monetary and financial mechanisms underwent a thorough process of transformation and expansion, with the dramatic development of banks, loans, and fiduciary money.

The major depression that struck the U.S. economy during the 1890s, originally known as the "Great Depression" prior to the greater one in the 1930s, played a central role in the establishment of this new framework. The previous decades had witnessed the rise of trusts, pools, and cartels in an attempt to confront rising competitive pressures. The crisis of the 1890s was blamed on excess competition and increased the incentive to seek protection against cutthroat competition. The loose agreements between enterprises, which remained independent entities, to share markets or profits were prohibited by the Sherman Act. The act, passed in 1890, was the first federal legislation pertaining to competition.

2. *Three revolutions.* The historical framework used here distinguishes between nineteenth-century capitalism and capitalism after the major revolution in ownership and management (relations of production) accomplished at the turn of the twentieth century. Three components of this revolution—the corporate, financial, and managerial revolutions—can be distinguished. The *corporate revolution* refers to firm incorporations. In the wake of the crisis of the 1890s, the new corporate laws enacted in New Jersey (simultaneously to the passage of the Sherman Act) and rapidly extended to other States,[2] gave a general impetus to a dramatic wave of incorporation around 1900. The rapidly expanding banking system was the engine of the *financial revolution,* as large banks financed these new corporations in a complex relationship, actually a mix of support and dominance. Within this new framework arose a third transformation, the *managerial revolution,* in which the delegation of management to a salaried managerial personnel—supported by a subordinate clerical personnel—reached new heights (notably, though not exclusively, in relation to the organizational arrangement in the workshop known as "Taylorism"). This was a major step in the separation between ownership and management. Although the managerial revolution occurred at the turn of the twentieth century, this separation and the corresponding sophisticated management are fundamental features of modern capitalism in all of its phases. ("Managerial capitalism" is used here in reference to only the first postwar decades.)

3. *Capitalist classes and financial institutions: Finance.* The three revolutions allowed for the establishment of a bourgeois class less connected to individual enterprises. The ownership of the means of production was supported by the holding of securities. This was the outcome of the expansion of what Marx had called "money capitalists," lenders, and shareholders.[3] The combination of the corporate and financial revolutions with the emergence of large corporations backed by financial institutions introduced new types of relationships in which the power of the upper fractions of capitalist classes relied heavily on financial institutions (Box 4.1). This concentration of capitalist power within financial institutions and the importance of securities in the ownership of the means of production gave the domination of capitalist classes in modern capitalism a strong *financial* character. For this reason, this book uses the term "Finance" to refer to the upper fractions of capitalist classes and to financial institutions in any social arrangement in which these fractions of capitalist classes control financial institutions (as is generally the case in capitalism). Finance, as used here, is not a separate industry. Instead, it combines class and institutional aspects.

This notion of Finance applies only to modern capitalism. Prior to the three revolutions, there was obviously money capitalists besides "active capitalists" (entrepreneurs), as well as a financial sector in the economy. But a new institutional configuration was built at the turn of the twentieth century, with big capitalist families holding large portfolios of shares and bonds, potentially diversified among various industries, and with a financial sector playing a major role in the financing of accumulation and the exercise of the prerogatives attached to ownership. The notion of Finance is crucial to the analysis of neoliberalism. The power of capitalist classes and financial institutions in this social order cannot, however, be separated from the progress of management—notably, though not exclusively, financial management—which gained considerable importance. Thus, the early twentieth century marked the culmination of social trends already under way during the nineteenth century, whose emblematic figures were the rentier bourgeois class, a "leisure class" as in Thorstein Veblen's terminology,[4] and the new managerial classes.

4. *A tripolar class configuration.* Central to the analysis here is the observation that modern capitalism coincided with the establishment of new class patterns more complex than the simple distinction between capitalists and production workers. Besides traditional middle classes of small

1. Capitalist classes

2. Managerial classes

3. Popular classes

⭐ Diagram 1.1

peasants, shopkeepers, and craftsmen, modern capitalism saw the expansion of managers and clerical personnel.

The outcome of these social trends was not the formation of a single homogeneous intermediate class, the new middle class, in between owners and production workers, blurring class boundaries. Instead a sharp polarization occurred within these groups, meaning a new hierarchy among wage earners, a division between leading and subordinated categories. The phrase "managerial and clerical personnel" is meant to capture this dual pattern. ("Clerical" must be taken here in a broad sense, including notably commercial tasks or maintenance.) Managerial personnel define the leading category, and these clerical personnel, the subordinated category.

As a result of the gradual transformation of production and clerical labor during the latest decades of modern capitalism, it became gradually more relevant to consider jointly clerical personnel and production workers. This is a helpful simplification that reduces intermediate classes to managerial classes. The book uses the threefold pattern as in Diagram 1.1.

None of these classes is homogeneous. It is often useful to distinguish between the upper fractions and the remainder of the groups, as is traditional within capitalist classes. One can separate between the holders of a large portfolio of shares, the owners of small- or medium-size firms, and a truly petty bourgeoisie. But similar hierarchies are also typical of managerial classes. Last, the merger between production and clerical workers defines more a trend than a mature outcome and, in contemporary capitalism, the coexistence of heterogeneous categories is still a basic feature of these groups.

Power Configurations and Their Class Foundations

Neoliberalism is the latest of the three social orders that jointly constitute modern capitalism. There are class foundations to such social arrangements. For this reason, they can be denoted as "class power configurations." The first and third—respectively, from the turn of the twentieth century to the New Deal, and since the early 1980s—can be called a "first" and a "second financial hegemony." Financial hegemony, as used here, refers to the fact that capitalist classes—actually Finance, the upper fraction of capitalist classes and financial institutions—benefit from a rather unchecked capability to lead the economy and society in general, in accordance with their own interests or what they perceive as such. This is, somehow, a "normal" situation in modern capitalism, and the capitalism of the first postwar decades, from the New Deal to the late 1970s, during which this power was diminished, stands out as an exception. The social order that prevailed during those years is often called a "social democratic" or "Keynesian compromise," but this terminology is not unproblematic.

1. *The first financial hegemony.* A striking aspect of the first decades of the twentieth century was the combination of a free-market economy, both domestically and internationally (with the gold standard), and the dramatic progress of organization within corporations.[5]

As stated in the previous section, central aspects in the establishment of modern capitalism, during the first decades of the twentieth century, were the emergence of a bourgeois class more or less separated from the enterprise, and new financial institutions that were tightly connected to nonfinancial corporations. The access of the bourgeoisie to this new institutional configuration did not destroy all earlier segments. Instead, it involved the elimination of some fractions of the upper classes, the survival of others, or their transformation. In this new power configuration, the upper fractions of capitalist classes were able to dominate the economy and society, both nationally and internationally. The power of management within large corporations was already significant during the first decades of the twentieth century, and there was an increasing emotion among capitalist classes concerning their capability to control corporations. It is certainly possible to refer to the prevalence of a compromise between Finance and the upper fractions of managerial classes. It was the Great Depression, the New Deal, and World War II that signaled the end of this epoch.

2. *The postwar compromise.* The second period stretches from the New Deal and World War II to the end of the 1970s. There were three main facets to the overall transformation of social hierarchies during these

decades. They account for the diversity of terms used to designate the period.

A first set of features typical of the first decades after World War II were an enhanced managerial autonomy vis-à-vis capitalist classes, with a management of large corporations favorable to investment and technical change, the greater state intervention in the economy (regulation, in particular financial regulation, and development and macro policies, notably low real interest rates, and stimulative monetary and fiscal policies). This managerial autonomy, built on the basis of the managerial trends typical of modern capitalism in general but under the new political circumstances, is at the origin of the reference to managerial capitalism that culminated in the 1960s or 1970s (Box 5.1). The Keynesian revolution in the management of the macroeconomy can be understood as one component in this broader set of managerial aspects. Another feature was the existence of significant limitations placed on foreign trade in order to protect national economic development, and restrictions on capital mobility (the free movements of capital among countries), as within the Bretton Woods agreements of 1944. This framework of international relationships defines the other aspect of the proper Keynesian features of the postwar decades, although all the measures Keynes advocated were not implemented. Actually, the Keynesian revolution was so important that it must be placed on the same footings as the three revolutions at the turn of the twentieth century. This fourth revolution was much delayed, as evident in the Great Depression.

The second facet of the postwar compromise involved the increase in purchasing power, policies in favor of full employment, and the establishment of the so-called welfare state, that is, the gradual commitment of the state to provide for the health, retirement, and education of popular classes.

These two first sets of aspects are distinct. Their combination accounts for the variety of terms—"managerial," "Keynesian," or "social democratic compromise"—phrases that may appear more or less relevant depending on the countries considered.

The third aspect of this period was the containment of financial (or capitalist) interests. It is already implicit in the two first aspects above. Three major components can be distinguished: (1) a financial sector targeted to the growth of the real economy, and not to the "administration" of capitalist collective interests as in neoliberalism; (2) a lesser concern vis-à-vis shareholders (that is, a management aiming at accumulation instead of capital income), low real interest rates, and a "not-too-performing" stock market; and (3) possibly diminished profits that would result from higher labor costs.

In terms of class relationships, the power configuration in the postwar compromise must be interpreted as an alliance between the managerial and the popular classes under the leadership of the former. Capitalist classes were far from being eliminated and not fully excluded from the compromise, but private management, policies, and strong state intervention manifested social interests significantly distinct from those of the capitalist classes as, later, narrowly expressed in neoliberalism. One alternative interpretation, also in terms of a social compromise, is the existence of a compromise between capital and labor, as in Fordism. This perspective is formally faithful to a Marxist framework, since only two classes are implied. The viewpoint in the present study is distinct. Reference is made to an alliance between managers and the popular classes, increased managerial autonomy, and the containment of capitalist interests.

The features of the postwar social order differed significantly internationally. They were less accentuated in the United States than in Europe and Japan. Nonetheless, the limitation of capitalist interests was an important aspect of the first postwar decades in most countries of the center. Paradoxically, the theory of managerial capitalism, which most explicitly stresses the crucial role of managerial classes, developed in the United States, while other countries in Europe, Korea, and Japan pushed the containment of capitalist interests and the preeminence of managerial classes to the most advanced degrees (as in nationalization, planning under the aegis of governments, policies aiming at full employment, or a financial sector in the service of the productive economy). In Europe, as a result of the coexistence of state and private sectors, the notion of mixed economies was preferred to managerial capitalism.

Again, a major crisis destabilized these social patterns: the structural crisis of the 1970s. The crisis was the consequence of the downward trend of the profit rate and the cumulative inflation rates in which economic tensions were expressed. It created the conditions for the imposition of neoliberalism, whose emblematic figures were Margaret Thatcher and Ronald Reagan.

3. *Neoliberalism as a second financial hegemony*. Neoliberalism did not halt the trends typical of the three revolutions of the late nineteenth

century, nor did it reverse the fourth one, the revolution in the control of the macroeconomy, although the targets of macro policy were redefined. The transformation was, however, broad and radical. A first aspect was a new high management or, equivalently, corporate governance. Neoliberalism released the freedom of enterprises to act, the alleged return to a "market economy" (a euphemism for unbounded capitalist dynamics, domestically and internationally). In line with this ideology of the market, neoliberalism promoted deregulation in every field, particularly of financial mechanisms. It imposed strong macro policies aiming at the protection of lenders by the imposition of price stability, and the opening of trade and capital frontiers.

Ideology was not the engine of the neoliberal revolution. The relationship to class hierarchies is all too obvious. Each of the above achievements was consistent with the interests of the upper classes, that is, the maximization of high incomes. The purchasing power of workers was contained, the world was opened to transnational corporations, the rising government and household debts were a source of large flows of interest, and financialization allowed for gigantic incomes (wages, bonuses, exercised stock options, and dividends) in the financial sector. The hegemony of the upper classes was deliberately restored, a return to financial hegemony. A neoliberal ideology emerged, the expression of the class objectives of neoliberalism. This ideology was a crucial political tool in the establishment of neoliberalism.

IDEOLOGY
OF THE
MARKET

The dramatic social transformation realized during neoliberalism would have been impossible if an alliance had not been made between capitalist and managerial classes, in particular their upper fractions. This shift in alliances can be denoted as the "neoliberal compromise." Depending on the country, the adhesion of the managerial classes to the neoliberal project was more or less easy or difficult to achieve, given specific power configurations and the features of the postwar compromise in each country. In the United States, it was easier than in Europe. There were also significant differences based on the fields of activity, finance, engineering, and so on. But the thorough alignment of management and policies to neoliberal objectives would have been impossible in the absence of such a compromise.

This interpretation of history confers a prominent role to the position of the managerial classes in social transformations, but the alliance after World War II, between the managerial classes and the popular classes, was

Compromise
to the Right $\left\{\begin{array}{l}\text{1. Capitalist classes}\\[1em]\text{2. Managerial classes}\end{array}\right.$

$\left.\begin{array}{l}\\ \\ \\ \text{3. Popular classes}\end{array}\right\}$ Compromise
to the Left

Diagram 1.2

made possible only by the political conditions of the period and the popular pressure resulting from a strong national and international worker movement. Managerial classes are not, however, merely passive actors in history. They played a central role in both the establishment of the New Deal and postwar compromise, as well as in the return to financial hegemony in neoliberalism.

The substitution of the compromise between the capitalist and the managerial classes in neoliberalism, for the earlier compromise between the managerial and the popular classes during the postwar decades, provides class foundations to the traditional distinction between the Right and Left political orientations as suggested in Diagram 1.2.

Overall, the historical sequence of social orders is the expression of the temporary outcomes of successive rounds of class struggle—the engine of history—where the three agents above interact. The outcomes of these confrontations were, however, highly dependent on specific economic circumstances, such as technical-organizational change, the trends of the profit rate, and the maturity of the institutional framework in charge of the stability of the macroeconomy (notably, monetary policy).

Structural Crises: Profitability and Financial Hegemony

The three phases in the history of modern capitalism were punctuated by the occurrence of lasting and deep crises, denoted here as "structural crises." They are the crisis of the 1890s, the Great Depression, the crisis of the 1970s, and the crisis of neoliberalism culminating in the Great Contraction.[6] Structural crises are the combined outcomes of the internal contradictions of each social order and class struggle. They mark sharp breaks in the history of capitalism but do not change underlying evolutions (Box 1.2). The entire historical pattern can be summarized as in Diagram 1.3.

Box 1.2
A Direction in History

The succession of distinct phases in the history of capitalism, separated by structural crises, does not interrupt the course of history. Such major breaks do not generally determine the trends of social change but, rather, <u>stimulate underlying transformations</u>. They create conditions favorable to changes whose logic is the expression of more profound and, correspondingly, less obvious historical dynamics. <u>The three revolutions—financial, corporate, and managerial</u>—at the turn of the twentieth century, later supplemented by the Keynesian revolution (the centralized management of the macroeconomy) and financial stability, can be considered successive steps in the establishment of the institutional framework still typical of contemporary capitalism. Marx described these historical dynamics of capitalism in reference to the "dialectics of productive forces and relations of production."[1] A process is at work manifesting the gradual "socialization of production," meaning the development of organizations such as large enterprises and central institutions, and networks allowing for the sophistication of the social division of labor in each country and internationally.

(continued)

A central issue is whether history will repeat itself, the contemporary crisis triggering the entrance into a new phase. With the usual provisos concerning the unpredictable character of future developments, the answer given here is "Yes."

The profit rate is an important variable in the analysis of structural crises. (These historical trends in the profit rate are presented in Figure 21.1;

Diagram 1.3

(continued)

Just as the movements of tectonic plates manifest themselves in earthquakes, the lack of joint harmonious evolution between the various components of social change results in major perturbations as the whole system suddenly adjusts to the new configuration when social and political conditions are met. Together with profitability trends and the unchecked ambitions of the upper classes, the tensions that follow from this lack of synchronism are basic expressions of what can be denoted as "internal contradictions." The transition from the earlier framework of the late nineteenth century to modern capitalism was realized at the cost of a several-decades-long, stepwise, and painful process of which the Great Depression was an "unfortunate side effect." The progress of technology and organization, both in a broad sense, is the force that moves the social tectonic plates. Disruptions, expressed in structural crises, require the establishment of new social orders. The engine is always social struggle. Thus, with a startling regularity, history repeats itself along a succession of three- or four-decade-long intervals that mark the progression of underlying tendencies.

---

1. Karl Marx, *A Contribution to the Critique of Political Economy* (Moscow: Progress Publishers, 1970), Foreword.

see also Box 21.2). The crises of the 1890s and 1970s were both the outcomes of downward profitability trends. Conversely, the Great Depression and the crisis of neoliberalism are not linked to the downward trend of the profit rate. In both instances, the profit rate was undertaking a slow process of restoration. Neither an upward nor a downward trend of the profit rate can be considered a determinant of the contemporary crisis. This does not mean, obviously, that the profit rate is not relevant to the present analysis in some respects.[7]

The Great Depression and the contemporary crisis have in common that they both marked the culmination of a period of financial hegemony. The Great Depression can be denoted as "the crisis of the first financial hegemony." Such a denomination directly expresses its common aspects with the crisis of neoliberalism, itself "the crisis of the second financial hegemony." Both were consequences of the exercise of hegemony, class, and international hegemonies, the boundless expansion of the demands of the upper classes that pushed economic mechanisms to and, finally, beyond the frontier of sustainability.

A common feature of structural crises is their multiple facets and their duration. It is, for example, difficult to tell exactly how long was the Great Depression or how long it would have lasted had not preparation for the war boosted the economy. The macroeconomy collapsed into the Depression itself from late 1929 to 1933. A gradual recovery occurred to 1937, when output plunged anew. The war economy, then, thoroughly changed the course of events. The same was true of the crisis of the 1970s. The new course of events, in the transition to neoliberalism, prolonged the crisis under new forms during the 1980s, with the financial crisis that followed the deep recession at the beginning of the decade. Most likely, the same will be true of the contemporary crisis. Once positive growth rates prevail in the wake of the contraction of output, this will mark the entrance of a new phase, but certainly not the resolution of the tensions that led to the crisis. A lot will remain to be done. Will positive growth rates be decent growth rates? When will the disequilibria of the U.S. economy be solved? How will the government debt be paid? Will the dollar support international pressures? The establishment of a new, sustainable, course of events will be a long and painstaking process.

Ambitions and Contradictions of the U.S. Domestic and International Neoliberal Strategy

Within the overall dynamics of capitalism, neoliberalism is no exception. From its beginning, the ambitious neoliberal strategy, in both its class and international components, was undermined by important internal contradictions. There should be no surprise that a major crisis occurred. The present section considers separately the three major strands of these contradictions:

1. *The dizzy dynamics of the quest for high income.* Neoliberalism is a social order aimed at the generation of income for the upper income brackets, not investment in production nor, even less, social progress. In countries of the center, domestic capital accumulation was sacrificed in favor of income distribution benefiting the upper classes. Notably, U.S. neoliberalism meant a de-territorialization (transfer outside of a territory) of production to the benefit of a number of economies of the periphery. The original bet was that the countries of the center would gradually transform themselves into services economies, still concentrating a number of activities where knowledge, education, and research

are crucial, and supplying the world with financial services. The so-called intellectual property would, of course, be protected. Above all, these economies were supposed to become financial centers—Margaret Thatcher's dream that eventually became a nightmare. The risk, in this first respect, was that the new challengers would seek not only efficiency in manufacturing basic commodities but also the access to high technology, research, and innovation and, possibly, financial services, to such a point that the economies of the center would gradually lose ground to these ambitious challengers.

The same quest for income was the engine of financialization, nationally and internationally, in the overall context of deregulation proper to the neoliberal endeavor. A specific component of the rise of financial mechanisms, securitization and what is known as "structured finance" in general, mushroomed in the fertile soil of the large household debt in the United States. (A large fraction of these instruments was sold to foreign investors.) To this, one must add the tremendous expansion of the most daring procedures in derivative markets and a variety of risky financial operations such as carry trade around the globe.

Neoliberalism saw the construction of a fragile and unwieldy financial structure in the United States and in the rest of the world, based on very questionable practices. This process underwent a sharp acceleration after 2000. It went to such a point that the outstanding incomes and profitability levels claimed in the financial sector during those years became more dependent, each year, on the accumulation of dubious assets and precarious capital gains. This tendency can be described as a "propensity to the production of fictitious surplus." The crisis adjusted the mirage to reality.

2. *The impaired capability to govern the macroeconomy.* The free mobility of capital internationally impairs or prohibits macro policies in a given country. In the absence of global regulation and policy, or given their low efficiency, the unchecked progress of financialization and globalization posed a threat to the ability of major capitalist countries to control financial mechanisms and their macroeconomy.

Prior to the contemporary crisis, this threat had only hurt countries of the periphery joining the neoliberal international "community" (sometimes under extreme configurations, as in Argentina in the 1990s). Conditions changed gradually. Financial globalization forged ahead, and the masses of global capital available for investment in any part of the world exploded. The U.S. economy demonstrated the risks inherent in neoliberal globalization in advance of Europe.

Although the two types of developments above—quest for high income and impaired macro governance—were typical of the major capitalist countries in general, the financial-global hegemony of the United States—neoliberalism under U.S. hegemony—allowed the United States to push the neoliberal strategy to degrees beyond what other large countries of the center could accomplish. The United States revealed to the world the inner contradictions of the neoliberal endeavor.

3. *Forging ahead at the cost of a trajectory of declining accumulation and perilous cumulative disequilibria.* Another source of contradiction is the macro trajectory unique to the U.S. economy, which allowed the United States to move ahead of the other major capitalist countries. Exempt from the requirement of balancing their external trade as a result of their global hegemony, including the role of the dollar as international currency, the United States pushed the process of internationalization of commodity production to unprecedented levels. There were two aspects to these mechanisms. On the one hand, accumulation rates in the U.S. domestic economy followed a downward trend. On the other hand, the rise of consumption demand resulted in the upward trends of imports and growing trade deficits. A consequence of these tendencies is that the normal use of productive capacity and the corresponding levels of growth rates in the United States had to be maintained at the cost of a strong stimulation of domestic demand. This stimulus was based on the surging indebtedness of households, which fueled the corresponding boom in residential investment. This result was only achieved at the cost of perilous and risky financial innovations. The overall shift toward financialization and globalization (given their interconnectedness) provided all the necessary prerequisites for the dramatic growth of households' debt, with the collaboration of financial institutions and governments in the rest of the world.

The effect of this macro trajectory could have been merely the gradual erosion of the hegemony of the United States worldwide. But the occurrence of a major crisis was probable, even if the form in which it would manifest was difficult to predict. A first possible such scenario was that the neoliberal class strategy would be derailed by a financial crisis within major capitalist countries, notably the United States, leading to a contraction of output. A second option was a recession that would destabilize the fragile financial structure and would be, then, transformed into a major crisis. A third scenario was a major crisis in the periphery that would destabilize countries of the center. Finally, a fourth option was a crisis of the dollar. The first crisis scenario prevailed, but this was difficult to foretell and there is still a large uncertainty concerning possible forthcoming developments.

That the crisis was transmitted to the world from the United States as a result of the combination of extreme financialization, impaired ability to control the macroeconomy, and cumulative disequilibria does not offset the risks specifically inherent in the dependency of the U.S. economy on foreign financing. As of the end of 2009, the threat of a sudden or gradual crisis of the dollar represents a potential major development that would thoroughly transform the features of the contemporary crisis. The occurrence of such a currency crisis would precipitate the course of history, both concerning the new social order to be implemented and U.S. hegemony. Thus, not only would the crisis be longer than expected but also more spectacular.

Success or Failure?

Although there were differences, the neoliberal class strategy prevailed in all countries, and worked to the benefit of a privileged minority. It was so within advanced capitalist countries, countries of the periphery whose upper classes inserted their country into the neoliberal international division of labor, even in China. The problem, in this latter country, was not the restoration of the power of a capitalist class, but the formation of such a class. The development of a powerful capitalist sector was encouraged under a strong state leadership, as part of a bold development strategy, alongside a still powerful public sector. Although the proper global aspect of this class strategy, as in "neoliberal globalization" or "imperialism at the age of neoliberalism," is common to all advanced capitalist countries, the United States is unique because it is the hegemonic power.

Judged by its own class objectives, neoliberalism was an unquestionable success prior to the present crisis. There were important social resistances in the countries of the center, for example, to maintain a degree of welfare protection. There was also resistance around the world as in Latin America, a reaction to the devastation caused by neoliberalism.

This did not change, however, the fact that everywhere the income and wealth of the wealthiest segments of the population increased tremendously.

In sharp contrast with this success story, the deep character of the contemporary crisis, its global extension, its likely duration, and the measures taken during its treatment suggest a final failure of the neoliberal class strategy. The last chapters of this book converge toward such a conclusion. The construction of a new social order required by the resolution of the above sets of contradictions (both the unsustainable fragile financial structure and the trajectory of the U.S. economy) is not compatible with the class ambitions proper to neoliberalism under U.S. hegemony. Most likely, U.S. capitalism is entering into a fourth social order whose nature remains to be discussed.

U.S. Upper Classes and the U.S. Economy: Divorce and Reconciliation

The crisis will not offset in a few years the potential of the United States to dominate internationally, given, notably, its gigantic military apparatus. But new dynamics have been initiated. Indicators show the rapid decline of the U.S. economy in comparison to the rest of the world. The Chinese and Indian economies are simultaneously large and progressing, but similar, though less dramatic, trends are also manifest in other regions of the world. Not only is production in the U.S. domestic economy involved, but also the deployment of U.S. capital around the globe, and the dominance of the transnational corporations of the country. If a dramatic adjustment is not performed rapidly and efficiently, the leading position of the United States among the major international powers will diminish even more rapidly than suggested by ongoing trends.

There is a sharp contrast between the comparative decline of the U.S. domestic economy and the unquestionable success of the strategy of the upper classes. These classes increased and restored their own power and income, at least up to the crisis. In the pursuit of neoliberal class objectives, whether profits are realized in the United States or anywhere in the rest of the world is irrelevant, provided that the countries where investments have been made remain politically reliable. That the trajectory of the U.S. economy be increasingly dependent on foreign financing is also of little import. The same is true of the rising debt of the government and households, understood as increasing sources of financial income instead of perilous domestic developments. In the United States, this divergence reached such dramatic proportions that it is possible to refer to a "divorce" between the upper classes and the domestic economy of their own country.

What is really new in this pattern of events is not the disconnection itself. Many countries in the periphery are or have been ruled by upper classes or fractions of classes that are not committed to the progress of their own countries. Instead, the behavior of such elites is often determined by the desire to collaborate with imperialist countries of the center and increase their personal wealth (notably abroad). The consequences for local economies and societies are devastating. Nationalism or patriotism, on the part of the upper classes, is crucial to the advance of national economies. What was new since the 1980s is that neoliberal strategies meant a divorce in the center of the neoliberal world, similar to that observed in too many less advanced countries.

Symmetrical nationalist trends were established in a number of countries of the periphery, like China, seizing the opportunity—given other advantages (such as a cheap and a disciplined labor force, natural resources, and so on)—and, finally, threatening the domination of the center. The comparison with the powerful capitalist accumulation in China is, actually, very telling. It shows that what is described here as a *divorce* is not a general property of capitalist dynamics, not even neoliberalism in general. Considering the relationship between Chinese capitalist classes and the Chinese domestic economy in contemporary capitalism, the relationship is still one of *honeymoon.*

Underlying these mechanisms is a process of maturation, the fact of reaching a given stage in a given context. In the case of China, from the viewpoint of local capitalists or capitalists of the Chinese Diaspora, the national territory and population work as "attractors." Clearly, this class strategy cannot be separated from a deployment around the globe, as in investment abroad, but the objectives are still largely directed to national development. This international deployment is, to a large extent, motivated by specific targets such as the control of natural resources or the insertion of domestic financial institutions within global financial networks, not by the quest for outstanding profitability levels in comparison to profit rates as they can be obtained on national territory. That in the longer run, Chinese capitalist classes, or more generally upper classes, might move along paths similar to those of U.S. upper classes does not alter the basic features of the contemporary period.

In the case of the United States, the divergence between the neoliberal class strategy and the domestic economic trajectory was temporarily hidden by the "long boom" of the second half of the 1990s. (With the benefit of hindsight, the first crisis after 2000, the recession, and the fall of the stock market, which marked the end of this boom, can be interpreted as a rehearsal, foreshadowing the collapse that came at the end of the decade.) The 1990s will be remembered as the heyday of the neoliberal endeavor, and the following years as the decade in which neoliberalism went astray. Thus, the favorable episode of the 1990s created only the impression of a coincidence between the interests of the upper classes and the domestic economy.

From the viewpoint of the U.S. society and economy, a reconciliation is urgently needed. It will require a dramatic and, most likely, time-consuming adjustment, the transition of a new social order. If the class objectives and methods of neoliberalism are maintained, even assuming a degree of financial regulation susceptible of ensuring a degree of financial stability, the decline of U.S. hegemony will be rapid, probably too sharp to be tolerated by the U.S. upper classes.

New Social and Global Orders: The National Factor and the Option of a Neomanagerial Capitalism

A fundamental hypothesis concerning coming decades is that the correction of the trends underlying the comparative decline of the U.S. economy is not compatible with neoliberal strategies. A corporate governance directed toward capital income and stock-market performances is at odds with strong domestic accumulation rates. The same is true of free trade and the free movements of capital internationally. Both the rise of imports from countries with low labor costs and direct investment abroad place an unbearable pressure on the domestic economy. A financial sector aiming at the creation of outstanding high income for its owners and managers cannot be in the service of nonfinancial accumulation. In addition, such a financial sector tends to over expand financial mechanisms that threaten the stability of the economy. The alternative can be clearly set out: (1) a priority given to the pursuit of neoliberal objectives and the continuing decline of the United States as the leading country worldwide, or (2) a transition to a new social order, beyond neoliberalism, what the previous section described as a much needed "reconciliation" between the upper classes and the domestic economy:

1. *Neomanagerial capitalism.* All of the above requirements point to the establishment of a new period of managerial leadership, uncommitted to neoliberal objectives. The main aspects of this leadership could be (1) management aiming not at stock market and capital income, but at domestic investment; (2) limitations placed on free trade and the free mobility of capital; and (3) a financial sector in the service of the nonfinancial economy and adequately regulated. These are basic conditions needed for the strengthening of the U.S. economy on U.S. territory, the correction of U.S. disequilibria, and the stabilization of financial mechanisms.

A consequence of the contradiction between neoliberal objectives and the preservation of the domestic economy is that the determination to maintain the comparative international position of the country could become a crucial factor in the shift toward a new social compromise in the United States, as suggested in the first bifurcation in Diagram 1.4. The role of nonfinancial and government managers would be increased.

It is not obvious that such an adjustment will be undertaken. If it prevails over the narrow and short-term interests of the upper classes, it is also not clear that it will be established successfully. The correction of the trajectory of the U.S. economy will be far more demanding than is typically thought. The conflict between the maintenance of the purchasing powers of the great mass of wage earners (a condition for social peace), the preservation of profit rates, the expansion of transnational corporations, and the re-territorialization of production will be sharp.

2. *To the Left or to the Right?* The upper classes imposed the new rules of neoliberalism on the popular classes that thoroughly worked in favor of a

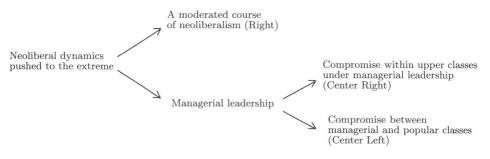

Diagram 1.4

minority. The crisis demonstrates the true nature of this endeavor and its unsustainable character, in particular under the forms that prevailed after 2000. The question that must be posed is, therefore: Would the popular classes allow the upper classes to define a new neoliberal trajectory, with limited adjustment, or to strike a new class compromise still at the top—two alternative social arrangements from which the popular classes would be excluded? A comparison with the Great Depression shows how the previous crisis of financial hegemony led to the establishment of a social compromise to the Left.

In contemporary capitalism, there is, however, no equivalent to the strong worker movement of the first decades of the twentieth century. As of 2009, in the United States, the election of Barack Obama raised the opportunity for such a social adjustment, timidly evocative of the New Deal. But the initiative does not appear to be on the side of the popular classes. Neither a return to a social democratic compromise nor a more radical transformation seems to be on the agenda.

If the national factor prevails over the continuation of a moderated course of neoliberalism, it seems rather unlikely that it will lead to a new social compromise to the Left as during the postwar compromise. As of the end of 2009—abstracting from the potential effects of a further expansion of the crisis (in its real, financial, and monetary components)—the contemporary crisis appears to be paving the way for a social compromise among the upper classes, still to the Right, but in a configuration distinct from neoliberalism. This is what is suggested in the second bifurcation in Diagram 1.4.

NEOMANA-
GERIAL
CAPITALISM

The class foundations of such a new social order would, as in neoliberalism, be a compromise between the upper classes, capitalists and managers, but under managerial leadership, with a degree of containment of capitalist interests, and without the welfare features of the postwar decades. This power configuration could be denoted as a "neomanagerial capitalism."

The exact content of the new power configuration would depend on the degree of the internal strife among the segments of the upper classes and the pressure exerted by the popular classes. Such a scenario opens a rather large spectrum of possible political orientations (abstracting from a far-Right alternative):

a. Concerning income flows in favor of the upper classes, it is important to emphasize that a strong determination to bolster U.S. preeminence worldwide would require significant limitations of both managerial and capitalist incomes. The new compromise would, however, still be among the upper classes, to the Right. A shift would occur within the comparative interests of these classes.

b. It is hard to imagine that such a far-reaching transformation would be accomplished without significant support from the popular classes. A degree of concession to the popular classes might be necessary. Consequently, a political orientation to the Center Right could be expected.

3. *Diversification in the rest of the world.* Such a new strategy of strengthening of the U.S. domestic economy would have important consequences for countries of the periphery profoundly engaged in the neoliberal international division of labor. But, in the long run, such trends open opportunities toward the establishment of national development models as was the case after the Great Depression (as in import-substitution industrialization in Latin America), the much needed alternative to neoliberal globalization.

Independent of the path followed by the United States, the situation will differ significantly around the globe. An increased diversity will be observed in the establishment of new social orders more or less to the Right or to the Left. Europe is not committed to international hegemony as is the United States, and the European Union is politically unable to pursue such an ambitious strategy. Europe might—paradoxically, given its history—become the traditional neoliberal stronghold in the coming decades.

It is still unclear whether social democratic trends in a few countries of Latin America will open new avenues to social progress. The crucial factor will be the impact of the contemporary crisis on China. Either, having successfully superseded the consequences of the crisis, China will experience strengthened neoliberal trends as if nothing had happened, or the experience of the crisis, in China itself or in the rest of the world, will work in favor of a "third way" along the contemporary pattern of the mixed economy that prevails in China.

Even if new social arrangements are successfully established in the United States, it is hard to imagine that U.S. hegemony will be preserved. There will be no clear substitute to an impaired U.S. dominance, and a multipolar configuration, around regional leaders, will gradually prevail in the coming decades. A bipolar world, Atlantic and Asian, is a possible outcome. Abstracting from rising international confrontation if conflicting interests cannot be superseded, the optimistic scenario is that new international hierarchies will be expressed within international institutions to which the task of global governance would be slowly transferred. This new environment would be favorable to the international diversification of social orders around the globe. This would mean a sharp break with the logic of neoliberal globalization, with a potential for developing countries depending, as in the case of the popular classes concerning domestic social orders, on what these countries would be able to impose.

The stakes are high.

2

Anatomy of a Crisis

The mechanics of the financial expansion and innovation after 2000, and the technical aspects of the macro trajectory of the U.S. economy are far afield from the discussion of periodization and social and international hierarchies found in the previous chapter. The explanation of the crisis of neoliberalism lies, however, at the intersection of these two categories of issues. One of the aims of the present study is to bridge the gap between technical mechanisms and historical interpretations.

In the investigations of the mechanisms that led to the crisis, the time frame often begins after the 2001 recession, when the most extreme components of financial innovation were implemented. But financial innovation can also be addressed in a historical perspective, since it was a general feature of neoliberalism from its origins. The same diversity of time frames is also implied in the analysis of macro mechanisms. Neoliberal trends over almost three decades were important factors of the crisis but, in this investigation, it is also necessary to keep track of shorter-term business-cycle fluctuations in the sense of the succession of the phases of recession and recovery.

The following sections have two main objectives. They restate the overall framework of analysis of the contemporary crisis in more technical terms than in the previous chapter, and summarize the main steps of the crisis, from the subprime crash to the Great Contraction.

A Fragile Structure and an Unsustainable Macro Trajectory

There is no synthetic technical explanation of the crisis. It was not the effect of deficient profit rates. It was also not the consequence of a lack of demand, the expression of the insufficient purchasing power of wages. If an overarching explanation must be sought, it lies in the objectives of neoliberalism, the tools used in their pursuit, and the contradictions inherent in these aims and methods. Since the present crisis is the crisis of neoliberalism, there is no surprise that the investigation must focus on this social order. Neoliberalism cannot be separated, however, from the hegemony of the United States worldwide, notably with respect to financial institutions and financial mechanisms.

From this first set of determinants to the occurrence of the crisis, two chains of mechanisms were at work, as illustrated in Diagram 2.1. They can be considered direct expressions of the contradictions of neoliberalism under U.S. hegemony (Chapter 1). They are, on the one hand, the unbound quest for high income, in combination with the associated achievements concerning financialization and globalization and, on the other hand, the unsustainable macro trajectory of the U.S. economy, exempt from the constraints placed on other capitalist countries of the center.

The separation between neoliberalism, globalization, and financialization in the diagram might seem surprising. These aspects of contemporary capitalism are considered here as three interrelated but distinct sets of phenomena (Box 2.1).

1. *The quest for high income, financialization, and globalization.* The first factor in the upper part of the diagram (**arrows A and B**) is the "quest for high income." High income refers here to **profits, capital gains**, and the high wages of the upper income brackets. (As used in the present study, "wages" include wages, salaries, exercised stock options, bonuses,

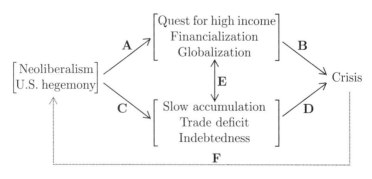

Diagram 2.1

Box 2.1
Neoliberalism, Globalization, and Financialization

Considering both the domestic and international aspects of neoliberalism—free-market economics, free trade, and the free mobility of capital—neoliberalism is actually what the word says, that is, a new liberalism. In the present study, the notion is, however, understood as a social order in which a new discipline was imposed on labor and new managerial criteria and policies established (with significant differences among countries and the various components of management). The so-called "free market" is an instrument in service of this objective.

Globalization is one of the notions that the analysts of contemporary capitalism are more inclined to use rather than neoliberalism. Although the process of globalization harks back to the early, even preliminary, stages of capitalism, commercial and financial international barriers were further alleviated during the last decades of the twentieth century. The economy of the twenty-first century is, more than ever, a global economy. Neoliberalism gave specific features to globalization (as in the phrase "neoliberal globalization") but neoliberalism is more than a phase of globalization.

The notion of "financialization" is fraught with the same ambiguities. Like globalization, it refers to mechanisms as old as capitalism and even to earlier precapitalist market economies, but one crucial aspect of the neoliberal decades is certainly the culmination of financial mechanisms reaching unprecedented levels of sophistication and expansion. In the present study, "financialization" always denotes, on the one hand, the expansion of financial institutions and mechanisms (and the corresponding masses of assets and debt), taking account of innovative procedures and, on the other hand, the imposition of managerial criteria such as the creation of value for the shareholder. The comparative size and profit rate of the financial sector is involved. The same is true of the expansion of the financial component of management within financial institutions and within nonfinancial corporations, as well as the spectacular rise of the income paid to financial managers.

Given the role conferred on financial interests in contemporary capitalism, the term "financialization" is also used in a broader sense in the literature, encompassing most of the features of neoliberalism. There is a lot of meaning in the assertion that neoliberalism is a "financialized capitalism," sometimes denoted on such grounds as "financial or finance capital(ism)." But this feature is not really new. The phrase "Finance capital" was coined by

(continued)

(continued)

Hilferding at the beginning of the twentieth century.[1] "Finance-led capitalism" would be closer to the perspective here, provided that a proper definition of "Finance" is given.

---

1. R. Hilferding, *Finance Capital: A Study of the Latest Phase of Capitalist Development* (1910; London: Routledge and Kegan Paul, 1981).

and pensions.) This quest was pushed beyond sustainable limits, to the production of a fictitious surplus, a pretext for the payment of real incomes.

Financialization and globalization were tools in the obtainment of high incomes. In sharp contrast with the limitations placed on financial mechanisms after World War II, neoliberalism had a strong stimulatory impact on the expansion of financial mechanisms. Crucial to the analysis of the crisis is the fact that financial mechanisms entered into a phase of even more dramatic expansion after 2000. This explosion was the combined effect of the growth of already existing mechanisms and of the introduction of innovative procedures. Free trade, the free movement of capital around the globe (investment abroad), and the globalization of financial and monetary mechanisms are the pillars of neoliberal globalization. These trends toward globalization were as threatening as financialization. Overall, financialization and globalization meant the construction of a fragile and unwieldy financial structure. An additional combined effect of these mechanisms was the impaired stabilizing potential of macro policies. In a world of free trade and free capital mobility, it is difficult to control interest rates, loans, and exchange rates.

2. *The macro trajectory of the U.S. economy.* The lower part of the diagram emphasizes the role played by the almost three-decade-long macro trajectory of the U.S. economy under neoliberalism (arrows C and D). Three basic aspects can be distinguished: (1) the low and declining accumulation rates, (2) the trade deficit, and (3) the growing dependency on financing from the rest of the world and domestic indebtedness. The two latter sets of determinants are often jointly referred to as "global imbalance," a euphemism for "the disequilibria of the U.S. economy." Clearly, the U.S. trade deficit is the other facet of the surpluses of trade observed in other

countries. But the present study pins the responsibility of these trends on the United States in the context of neoliberal globalization.

Deficient accumulation rates are a basic component of the trajectory of the U.S. economy, but these trends are not, alone, the cause of the crisis. Conversely, the rise of consumption, notably on the part of the upper income brackets, is at the center of the mechanisms that led to the crisis. Thus, the crisis must not be interpreted as the outcome of overaccumulation or underconsumption, but rather overconsumption, paralleling under-accumulation. In the United States, the opening of trade frontiers stimulated imports far more than exports, with a rising trend of trade deficits.

The two sets of tendencies, in the upper and lower parts of the diagram, respectively, already indicate intrinsically unsustainable developments. The causes of the crisis can, thus, be described in terms of "excess." Too much financialization meant a fragile financial structure, and too much globalization, an uncontrollable world economy. The gradual accumulation of debt on the part of U.S. households could not be continued without limit. At some point, a halt had to be placed on the dependence on foreign financing. It is, however, important to understand the relationship between the various categories of determinants as symbolically expressed in arrow E. The upward trend of the debt of households (in the lower part of the diagram) was certainly an outcome of the greedy pursuit of profit by financial institutions and deficient regulation (in the upper part of the diagram). The joint increases of the trade deficit and foreign financing (lower part of the diagram) were a consequence of an open world economy (upper part), given the international hegemony of the United States, which allowed for the growth of deficits without too severely impacting the stability of the dollar.

At the center of the crisis there was, however, an even more specific relationship in which all of the above are interconnected. The growth of the domestic debt (that of government, to the mid-1990s, and, increasingly, that of households) was the outcome of a macro policy intending to maintain decent growth rates and normal capacity utilization rates in an open economy. Three categories of mechanisms combined their effects:

1. The expansion of the demand of well-off households, an effect of neoliberal trends, was at the origin of a sharp *rise in consumption*. Given the opening of trade frontiers, a growing fraction of the demand for consumption goods was imported. Thus, to a large extent, these consumption

trends did not benefit U.S. domestic producers, but fed the rise of imports (well above the capability to export of the country, a property that accounts for the rising trade deficit).

2. Demand faced by domestic producers was chronically deficient and required the stimulation of consumption by a *bold credit policy*. As stated above, a growing fraction of this stimulation benefited foreign producers. (In this sense, the image of the U.S. economy as the engine of the growth of the world economy appears relevant.)

3. For various reasons—the absence of constraint to balance foreign trade, financial innovation loosening credit requirements, the explosion of derivative markets (credit default swaps [CDSs] and interest rate contracts), and so on—*the expansion of the debt of households was not constrained,* and took on cumulative proportions.

The explosion of mortgage-related markets in the United States and their subsequent collapse must be understood in this context. They were not an autonomous unfortunate side effect of financialization but, simultaneously, a component of the tremendous expansion of financial mechanisms (notably after 2000) and a necessary ingredient in the continuation of the macro trajectory of the U.S. economy (the combined effects of the upper and lower strands of determinants in the diagram). The housing crisis and the corresponding collapse of the pyramid of financial institutions acted like a seismic wave that destabilized an otherwise fragile financial-global structure. It was the trigger, not the cause of the crisis.

There is, obviously, a feedback effect of the crisis over the conditions that made it possible (arrow F). Neoliberalism and U.S. hegemony are both implicated, as the last section of Chapter 1 contends.

The Sequence of Events

The chain of events since the beginning of the crisis in August 2007 must be understood as the culmination of the latest phase of neoliberalism, with a history of almost thirty years when the crisis occurred. Prior to the crisis, neoliberalism passed through three successive phases that, more or less rigorously, coincided with the three decades, the 1980s, 1990s, and after 2000:

1. The first phase in the establishment of neoliberalism, a decade from 1980 to 1991, was difficult. This phase was marked by three recessions,

with negative growth rates in 1980, 1982, and 1991. Simultaneously, those years were ones of financial turmoil, with the crisis of banks and savings and loan associations.

2. The recovery from the 1991 recession, which introduced the second phase, was slow, but growth rates stabilized at high levels during the second half of the 1990s. Underlying this restoration was the wave of investment in information technologies. This period was also one of large direct investment abroad on the part of U.S. investors, and, reciprocally, foreign direct investment in the United States. During this favorable decade, neoliberal options were considered a new panacea, in particular when compared to Europe (ignoring recurrent crises in Asia and Latin America). In the wake of the boom of information technologies and the accompanying stock-market bubble during the second half of the 1990s, the U.S. economy entered the 2001 recession.

[margin note: WAVE OF INVESTMENT IN INFO. TECHNOLOGIES]

[margin note: 2001 RECESSION]

3. The following chain of events, after 2000, can be interpreted as an introduction to the crisis. The recovery from the 2001 recession was obtained only at the cost of the rise of residential investment, a boom of the housing sector, while productive investment remained low. The overall macroeconomy stabilized at moderate growth rates. Simultaneously, after a period of steady growth since the beginning of neoliberalism, the debt of households, the trade deficit, and the financing of the U.S. economy by the rest of the world soared. This period was also marked by the explosion of financial mechanisms. For example, the gross market value of derivative contracts was multiplied by 2.6 between the ends of 2001 and 2005. The period also witnessed a sharp increase in the instruments linked to mortgages, such as securitization and insurance against defaults. The Federal Reserve was aware of these trends, but the rise of the Federal Funds rate after the recovery from the 2001 recession did not succeed in checking the expansion of credit while regulation was not on the agenda.

Five stages can, then, be distinguished:

1. The early symptoms of a severe disruption were revealed at the transition between 2005 and 2006, with the first steps of the fall of building permits, home sales, and home prices. This is also when the wave of defaults started (at first affecting subprime loans with adjustable rates). Banks began to depreciate the loans in their accounts, and the riskiest mortgage-backed securities (MBSs) were devalued. During the first six months of 2007, a number of financial institutions directly related to mortgages were shaken.

2. August 2007 marked the beginning of the financial crisis proper. It was originally a liquidity crisis. The housing downturn deepened (with the further fall of permits, prices, etc.), and the crisis of MBSs led to a situation of great uncertainty in which securities could no longer be valued. With the disruption of the interbank market, the Federal Reserve stepped in to ease the situation, originally resorting to the traditional mechanism of open-market purchases at diminished interest rates. At the end of 2007, it became clear that open-market operations were no match for the severity of the crisis. The Federal Reserve created new instruments in which increasingly questionable securities were accepted as collateral. A certain relaxation prevailed, but it proved short-lived. Subprime mortgage loans were obviously only one component in a much broader set of determinants by which the true nature of neoliberalism became suddenly apparent.

3. The collapse of many financial instruments destabilized the overall financial structure. At the beginning of 2008, the increase of the losses incurred by financial institutions became manifest, with the beginning of an epidemic of bankruptcies. In March, Bear Stearns failed and the first manifestations of the weakness of Fannie Mae and Freddie Mac were revealed. From the beginning of 2008, the deteriorating situation of the financial sector degenerated into a crisis of the supply of credit to households and nonfinancial corporations, known as a "credit crunch."

4. The fourth quarter of 2008 marked a major break, with a new and sharp deepening of the crisis and an atmosphere of panic. Lehman Brothers, Washington Mutual Bank, and other financial giants failed. Others, such as AIG, Merrill Lynch, and Citigroup were saved at the last moment, but their stock price fell by more than 90 percent. Monetary policy was ineffective. The credit crunch took on increasing proportions. The contraction of output spread around the globe. Instability was observed on exchange markets and stock prices fell dramatically.

In this context, the Federal Reserve and the Treasury scaled up their activities, working as a substitute for private institutions. Active intervention was initiated to stimulate new loans to finance the purchase of goods and services. Capital financing (the purchase of shares of ailing corporations) supplemented credit financing (by loans). The Federal Reserve and the Treasury guaranteed (as insurers) dubious assets. Foreign currency swaps were organized to help foreign central banks lacking reserves (the Federal Reserve acting as a central bank for the global economy).

5. At the end of 2008, the Great Contraction began. The major component in the overall treatment of the crisis became the government deficit, with the corresponding rise of the government debt, and increased financing by the rest of the world and the Federal Reserve.

The Great Contraction—A Crisis of the Dollar

By 2009, the contraction in output had become the main development, reminiscent of the Great Depression. Between July 2007 and June 2009, the capacity utilization rate in manufacturing in the United States fell from 79.4 to 65.1 percent. But the decline was even larger in other countries. In the United States, the production of steel diminished by 56 percent between August 2008 and April 2009. U.S. imports of goods and services decreased 33 percent between August 2008 and May 2009. There was a major feedback effect from this fall in output on the respective situations of the financial sector, nonfinancial corporations, and households. The percentage of U.S. Treasury securities in GDP rose from 35 percent at the beginning of August 2007 to more than 54 percent at the end of 2009. The debt of governments and countries around the globe soared. As of late 2009, it is impossible to know how deep the contraction will be. Forecasts have recurrently been adjusted downward. A floor has, possibly, been reached. The capacity utilization rate in the United States in December 2009 was still 68.4 percent, that is, barely above the low point reached in June. (At the trough of the Great Depression, output had fallen by about 25 percent.)

How deep will the Great Contraction be? How long will it last? Much will depend on the urgently needed stimulation of economic activity. The key factors are the actual volume of this support, its content, the rapidity of its implementation, and the ability to address problems globally instead of country by country. In the United States, the government itself or central institutions closely related to the government stepped in to act as a substitute for the private sector. At least three aspects must be stressed: (1) large government deficits tend to compensate for the deficient demand emanating from the private sectors, in the context of the credit crunch; (2) securitization is performed by the federal agencies and the government-sponsored enterprises (GSEs), now owned by the government, while the action of private-label issuers is terminated; and (3) MBSs are bought by the Federal Reserve instead of private investors.

★!   Given the dependency of the U.S. economy on foreign financing and, in particular, the dramatic increase of the government deficit, a sudden fall in the dollar is a possible development. The nature and extension of the crisis would be altered. Even a moderate decline of the dollar would tend to export the crisis to the rest of the world, in particular to Europe. Arab countries are said to have initiated negotiations with China, Russia, and France, seeking new arrangements to avoid the dependency on the dollar in fixing the price of oil, using a bundle of currencies (and gold) as a substitute. Such a crisis would basically threaten the continuation of U.S. hegemony.

The Second Reign of Finance:
Classes and Financial Institutions

Much in the previous chapters anticipates the major findings in this book. The actual course of analysis begins, however, with the present part.

The book traces the contemporary crisis to the mechanisms inherent in neoliberalism and its specific features in the United States. Although the term "neoliberalism" is broadly used, there is no general agreement concerning the content of the notion, and it is sometimes considered a misnomer. A preliminary definition is needed.

The objective of Part II and those that follow is to gradually introduce neoliberalism as a class phenomenon and to provide some of the empirical details that support this interpretation. Chapter 3 discusses the restoration of the income of the upper income brackets independently of the source of the income. Chapter 4 is more specifically devoted to the rise of capital income (interest, dividends, and capital gains) during the neoliberal decades. Only Part III (Chapters 5 and 6) considers neoliberalism as a class phenomenon in the tripolar class configuration of the capitalist, managerial, and popular classes introduced in Chapter 1.[1]

3

The Benefit of Upper Income Brackets

Income statistics do not provide straightforward information on class patterns and their changing configurations and powers. One must be content with categories such as income brackets and a loose notion of "upper classes." But the historical transformation of income distribution is quite revealing of underlying social changes. This is the viewpoint in the present chapter.

The Concentration of Income at the Top

Interestingly, the sequence of the three social orders that jointly constitute modern capitalism is manifest in the historical profile of income distribution in the United States. The growing income and, more generally, social inequalities during the neoliberal decades, both within each country and globally, have been frequently discussed. Data gathered from income statements by Thomas Piketty and Emmanuel Saez strikingly illustrate these historical trends of distribution.[1] (Data from income statements are biased, but what is reported to the Internal Revenue Service [IRS] certainly does not overestimate higher income, and this is what matters most in the present investigation given the profiles observed.)

Figure 3.1 provides a first view of the historical profile of income hierarchies. It shows the share of total income received by households pertaining to the 1 percent upper income bracket. (In 2007, this means almost 1.5 million households, whose reported income annually was larger than $398,909.) Prior to World War II, this privileged group received 18 percent (yearly average 1913–1939) of total U.S. household income. Beginning with World War I, throughout the Great Depression and World War II, the

Figure 3.1 Share of total income received by the 1 percent higher income bracket: U.S. households (percent, yearly). Capital gains are included in the measure of income.

percentage fell gradually. It is noteworthy that no recovery took place to the end of the 1970s. (Other indicators[2] show that the comparative wealth of these upper strata was considerably diminished during the 1970s, a decade of depressed stock markets, very low or negative real interest rates, and limited distribution of dividends.) The size of the later recovery is spectacular, as the percentage rose from a minimum of 9 percent in the mid-1970s to prewar levels. One can surmise that this profile actually underestimates the amplitude of the recovery as a result of tax evasion (as in tax havens) on the part of the high income brackets, but the extent of this undervaluation is unknown.

The profile of purchasing powers (income deflated by the Consumer Price Index) relates a similar story. Figure 3.2 shows the yearly average purchasing power of households within the top 1 percent income fractile and for the remainder of households (the remaining 99 percent). The real income of the top 1 percent is measured on the right axis and that of the bottom 99 percent on the left axis, both in thousands of 2007 dollars. The unit on the right axis is twenty times larger than the unit on the left axis.

Before World War II, the ratio of twenty was maintained as shown by the superposition of the two lines. During the war, the purchasing power of the 99 percent (——) began to rise dramatically, reaching, in the 1970s, almost 3.3 times its average prewar level. Then, an almost horizontal trend

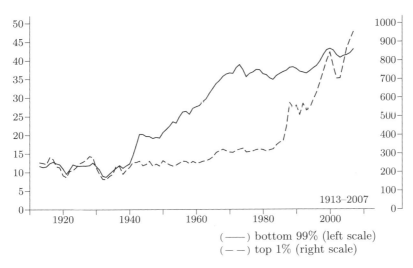

Figure 3.2 Real income of two income fractiles: U.S. households (thousands of 2007 dollars, yearly). Left axis: real income of the bottom 99 percent of households. Right axis: real income of the top 1 percent. The scale on the right axis is twenty times larger than on the left axis.

is apparent up to 2007. This profile provides a striking illustration of the specific features of the intermediate period, the first decades following World War II. One can attribute the first years of stagnation in the 1970s to a possible depressing effect of the structural crisis on incomes during the decade, but no new trend upward was established under neoliberalism. The second variable (— —) shows the purchasing power of the 1 percent upper income bracket. A symmetrical pattern prevails, almost stagnating to the early 1980s and then surging upward, also a multiplication by a factor of 3.6 after 2000 with respect to prewar levels (even more in 2007). It would be hard to be clearer. The variation of income hierarchies matches the sequence of the three phases in Chapter 1, with radically diverging effects for distinct income brackets.

This concentration of income and wealth at the top is not specific to the United States. During neoliberalism, financial wealth grew tremendously worldwide. Table 3.1 uses the notion of the high net worth individual (HNWI) of the World Wealth Reports of Capgemini–Merrill Lynch, that is, persons whose wealth (excluding the primary residence and subtracting debt) is above $1 million, a population of more than 10 million families worldwide. Between 1996 and 2007, the number of such individuals

Table 3.1 High net worth individuals worldwide (millions of individuals and trillions of dollars)

Year	Number of Persons	Financial Wealth	Year	Number of Persons	Financial Wealth
1996	4.5	16.6	2002	7.3	26.7
1997	5.2	19.1	2003	7.7	28.5
1998	5.9	21.6	2004	8.2	30.7
1999	7.0	25.5	2005	8.7	33.4
2000	7.0	27.0	2006	9.5	37.2
2001	7.1	26.2	2007	10.1	40.7

increased at a yearly average rate of 7.6 percent, and their total wealth grew at a yearly average of 8.5 percent (while the gross world product [GWP] increased at an average rate of 5.5 percent), indicating very substantial returns and capital gains. In 2007, the total wealth of HNWIs reached $41 trillion. (See Table 7.1 for a comparison with other figures in 2006.)

The High Wages of the Upper Income Brackets and Profits

Neoliberalism considerably transformed the overall patterns of income distribution, though, in the United States, not in the traditional sense of the respective shares of profits and wages in total income. (The term "wages" refers to total labor compensation, that is, the cost of labor for employers.)

Figure 3.3 shows (——) the share of wages in the domestic income of the U.S. corporate sector, that is, nonfinancial and financial corporations jointly considered. (In the analysis of the distribution of income, it is convenient to abstract from the noncorporate and the government sectors where, for distinct reasons, the division between wages and profits is problematic, and whose dynamics are the expressions of specific mechanisms.) With respect to levels, a first observation is that the share of wages fluctuated around 72 percent of total income, the remaining 28 percent corresponding to the sum of taxes and profits. With respect to trends, one observes that, after a period of limited growth of the wage share up to 1970, a plateau was reached. (This variable and the two others undergo fluctuations that tend to follow the ups and downs of the business cycle.) This constant percentage is rather specific to the U.S. economy, while, in a number of countries, the wage share decreased under neoliberalism, a factor in the restoration of profit rates at the beginning of the 1980s.[3]

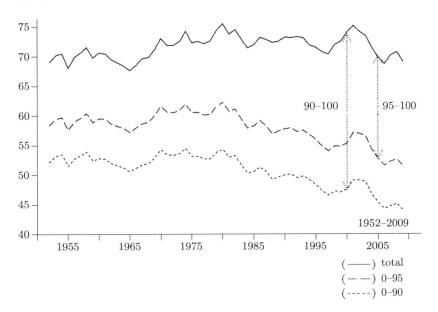

Figure 3.3 Shares of wages in total income: U.S. corporate sector (percent, yearly). Since data concerning the wages of income fractiles are not available within national accounting frameworks, the series (— — and -----) draw from the statistics used in Figure 5.1, obviously an approximation.

This finding apparently contradicts the view that neoliberalism was a period of increasing exploitation of labor. The deteriorating labor conditions, the stagnating purchasing power of the great mass of wage earners, and the cheapening of consumer goods resulting from the imports from countries with low labor costs are well known, and all support the intuitive assessment of a rising profit share.

The contradiction is only apparent. It is not possible to consider the share of wages as an accurate proxy for the division between the incomes of upper classes and popular classes, given the importance of the high wages of the upper income brackets. The second variable (— —) in Figure 3.3 shows the share in total income of the wages of the 95 percent of wage earners with lower wages (the 0–95 income fractile), that is, excluding the top 5 percent of wage earners when ranked by wage levels. (The annual wage of households at the boundary between the two fractiles was $143,000 in 2007.) Correspondingly, the distance between the two lines accounts for the share of total income going to the 95–100 fractile as wages (18 percent in 2009). The figure shows that, excluding the wages of the upper wage fractiles of households, a significant downward trend prevails during the neoliberal decades (between 1980 and 2009), a loss of 10.8 percentage points of total income, from 62.2 and 51.5 for the fractile 0–95.

There are no simple theoretical foundations on which the determination of a lower boundary for "high wages" at the top of income hierarchies can be established. A purely empirical category is used here. The observation of the declining trend of the share of wages other than the upper segment of the wage pyramid is, however, not subject to the choice of an accurately defined percentage. Similar trends are observed when the dividing line is set at 10 percent (-----). This observation demonstrates that the 90–95 fractile did not benefit from the concentration of income at the top typical of neoliberalism.[4]

Thus, a central element in the analysis of income distribution in the United States is the large share of total wages going to high wage brackets and their considerable impact on the profile of income distribution when total wages are considered. The rise of these wages hides the diminished percentage going to the great mass of wage earners, and accounts for the constant share of wages in total income.

Taxes account for an important fraction of the nonwage income. The remainder can be denoted as "profits." (The share of profits in this definition is obviously smaller than in measures in which all nonwage income is defined as profits.) Figure 3.4 shows such a measure of the share of profits (——), defined as 100 percent minus the percentage corresponding to the share of, jointly, wages and taxes. (Since the wage share in Figure 3.3 is about constant, the slight upward trend of this variable is the effect of the decrease in the share of taxes in total income.) For the last two decades in the figure, 12 percent of total income goes to profits (16 percent to taxes).

The second variable (— —) in Figure 3.4 measures the profits retained by corporations. The downward trend is impressive, from an average level of about 6.3 percent during the two first postwar decades to 3.5 percent during the neoliberal decades. The distance between the two lines accounts for the flow of profits paid out as capital income, the sum of interest and dividends. This capital income increased during the neoliberal decades. Thus, the figure illustrates the rising distribution of profits as capital income—interest and dividends, the second channel, besides high wages at the top, by which the income of the upper income brackets was

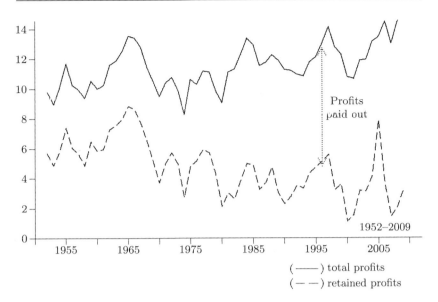

Figure 3.4 Shares of total after-tax profits and retained profits in total income: U.S. corporate sector (percent, yearly). Total profits are profits after all taxes and prior to the payment of interest and dividends.

increased. This inflexion of income distribution is a major feature of neoliberalism.

Figure 3.5 summarizes these observations. The main variable (———) is the share in total income of the sum of the two other variables, the wages (— —) of the 95–100 fractile and the profits paid out as interest and dividends (-----). A set of interesting observations follows. First, taking the two first decades 1952–1971 and the two last decades 1990–2009 as references, the share in total income of the sum of the two components rose from 15.5 percent to 25.8 percent. Second, high wages account for more than half of this total increase. Third, the profiles over time of the two components are, to some extent, distinct. While the share of high wages increased steadily from the 1970s onward, the share of profits paid out rose with a step upward with the formation of neoliberalism in the early 1980s. (Interest and dividends are unquestionably capital income but they, obviously, do not entirely go to the upper income brackets.)

In sum, the restoration of the income of the upper income brackets in neoliberalism was the combined effect of a downward trend in the shares of total income of both the great mass of wages and the profits retained by

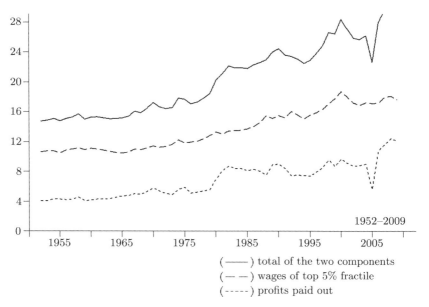

Figure 3.5 Shares of high wages and capital income in total income: U.S. corporate sector (percent, yearly).

enterprises, paralleling the joint increase in the share of high wages and the share of profits paid out as capital income. This is the empirical expression of the assertion that neoliberalism worked to the benefit of the upper income brackets.

The Instruments of a Discipline

Among the instruments that allowed for the restoration of upper incomes, it is important to distinguish between domestic components, that is, practices inherent in each particular economy, and the global aspect of neoliberalism. This dual character is what makes the joint reference to the two elements in the phrase "neoliberal globalization" really necessary. But there are important overlaps between the two categories of mechanisms.

A first basic aspect is the imposition of more demanding profitability criteria. The tools are the increased pressure on workers, improved organization in general, exports of capital, and the corresponding flows of profits from the affiliates abroad of transnational corporations. In each country, neoliberalism is based on a new discipline imposed on workers. The main aspects are the stagnation of purchasing powers (as in Figure 3.2 for the United States), the gradual dismantling of social protection, the more demanding labor conditions, and the so-called "flexible" labor market, that is, the freedom to hire and fire. Management also had to adapt to the new objectives. The difference between workers and managers is, however, that, in the stick-and-carrot metaphor, workers are on the stick side and upper management on the carrot side. Actually, management, in particular its upper layers, increased gradually its capability to set apart an increasing fraction of the surplus generated within enterprises to their benefit under the form of high wages in the broad sense used here.

Concerning management, besides the inducement to seek high profitability levels, one finds the subjection of private managers to a corporate governance aimed at the maximizing of stock value and the distribution of dividends. But there is also a policy component to these new rules, in which government officials and representatives are involved. Its main aspects are monetary policies intending to curb inflationary pressures instead of stimulating growth and employment, the privatization of social protection, the partial substitution of pension funds for pay-as-you-go public systems, and deregulation.

The two pillars of the international aspect of neoliberalism are free trade and the free international mobility of capital. The imposition of free trade was the outcome of a long and gradual process since World War II. Neoliberalism imposed the "open model" around the world, with the collaboration of local elites. Capital controls were gradually dismantled, beginning with the United States during the 1970s. From the 1990s onward, the flows of direct investment abroad (DIA) increased dramatically, an expression of the growth of transnational corporations. Obviously, there are important links between these various components, domestic and international. Investment abroad allowed corporations to seek high returns in countries of the periphery. Globalization placed the workers of advanced capitalist countries in a situation of competition with workers of the periphery. The imports of cheap consumption goods from countries where labor costs are particularly low decreased the nominal wages necessary to buy a given basket of goods within advanced countries. They, thus contributed to the restoration of profit rates, given the constancy (or decline) of the purchasing power of the bulk of wage earners.

Quite relevant to the analysis of the contemporary crisis are monetary and financial mechanisms. First, the rising debt of government and households was a source of large flows of interest. Second, financial deregulation and innovation allowed for the explosion of the activity and income of the financial sector. The procedures tending to the obtainment of high returns were pushed to the extreme, as well as the payment of dividends and very high wages. These practices reached the point of what the book denotes as "fictitiousness" (Chapter 9). The collaboration of officials and representatives was crucial in all of these fields.

4

The Apotheosis of Capital

The analysis in the previous chapter hinges around a statistical notion of "upper income brackets." Two components of such incomes are involved, high wages at the top of income hierarchies and capital income. The present chapter focuses on capital income, that is, the specifically capitalist aspect of social relations. Approached from this viewpoint, the social framework is familiar. It opposes capitalist classes and a class of workers broadly defined as wage earners. Part of the investigation in the remainder of this book can be conducted on such grounds. Neoliberalism is, thus, understood as the expression of the restoration of the power and income of capitalist classes.

The present chapter first considers the profitability of the entire corporate sector, then the sources of capital income (interest and dividends, and gains in the stock market). The more technical discussion of the comparative profit rates of nonfinancial and financial corporations can be found at the end of the chapter.[1]

Finance: Capitalist Classes in Neoliberalism

The notions of Finance and financial hegemony, as used in this study, refer to the upper segments of the capitalist classes and financial institutions. As is well known, there is a strong hierarchy within capitalist classes from the owners of small or medium enterprises to the holders of large portfolios of shares of transnational corporations. There is a process of concentration of capital historically, but new firms are still created and the traditional hierarchy between larger and smaller business is still there in contemporary capitalism. Small business is often subject to the domination of both large nonfinancial and financial corporations, and many aspects of this preeminence relate to financial mechanisms (not all, for example, the dependency and control resulting from outsourcing). Already during the first financial hegemony, the overall social dynamics, economics, and politics were dominated by the upper fraction of the capitalist classes.[2] These large owners were the main actors in the establishment of neoliberalism.

Financial institutions were built gradually. Around the banks and insurances of the nineteenth century, the new framework of stock exchanges; mutual, pension, and hedge funds; private equity firms and family offices; agencies and government-sponsored enterprises (GSEs); central banks; international institutions such as the IMF and the World Bank; a wealth of new instruments; and so on, gradually developed. The functions of these institutions were diversified and multiplied during the twentieth century. They play a central role within neoliberalism, be they private enterprises, government institutions, such as central banks, or international institutions.

The power of individual capitalists would remain quite limited in the absence of financial institutions. States were the agents of deregulation and imposition of free trade and the free movements of capital internationally. But, besides states, financial institutions are the agents of neoliberalism. Central banks impose policies favorable to the stability of prices instead of full employment, intending to increase capital income. Huge masses of capital are handled by asset managers (including the capital of pension funds) imposing neoliberal norms to nonfinancial corporations. More restricted financial institutions concentrate the cutting edge of financial operations to which the upper fractions of the capitalist classes have access.

The notion of financial hegemony refers to all of these practices. The upper fractions of the capitalist classes and their financial institutions, that is, Finance, imposed in neoliberalism new performances concerning their power and income.

One can note parenthetically that the joint consideration of the capitalist classes and financial institutions harks back to Marx's analysis. Marx had already written in volume 3 of *Capital*[3] that banks, the financial institutions of the nineteenth century, not only defined a specific financial industry among others, but acted as the "administrators" of interest-bearing capital (Box 4.1). This is what defines Finance, the joint consideration of capitalist classes and the (institutional) administrators of capital.

Box 4.1
Finance in Marx and Hilferding

The new trends of capitalism since the 1980s are sometimes described as a domination of "financial" or "finance capital"—as a sector in the economy, with its own capitalists—over "industrial capital" (to which commercial capital could be aggregated). This approach neither corresponds to that developed by Hilferding, one century ago, nor to the framework underlying the analysis in the present study.

Financial institutions are instruments in the hand of the capitalist classes as a whole in the domination they exercise over the entire economy. More specifically, financial corporations are simultaneously *a sector engaged in a specific category of operations,* what Marx denoted as "money-dealing capital"[1] and, also in Marx's formulation, *the administrators* of "interest-bearing capital" (a misleading terminology referring to loans, debt securities, and stock shares, preferably "financing capital").[2] The two types of mechanisms—industrial sector and administrator—reached unprecedented levels of development under neoliberalism. One can think, for example, of currency exchange, in the first case, and asset management, in the second case. Because of this second element, the administration of financing capital, it is not possible to simply view the relationship between nonfinancial and financial corporations in terms of competition. A hierarchical aspect is involved.

---

1. As opposed to "commodity-dealing." K. Marx, *Capital,* vol. 3 (1894; New York: Vintage Books, 1981), 431.
2. G. Duménil and D. Lévy, "Les trois champs de la théorie des relations financières de Marx. Le capital financier d'Hilferding et Lénine," in Séminaire d'Études Marxistes, *La Finance Capitaliste* (Paris: Presses Universitaires de France, 2006).

Profit Rates during the Neoliberal Decades

Although financial income is also based on interest flows from households and governments, central to the analysis of the capability of capital to generate financial income is the profitability of capital.

The investigation of the decline of profit rates to the structural crisis of the 1970s, and the ensuing new trend upward, occupies a central position in earlier investigation by the authors.[4] The calculations in Figure 4.1 update this earlier research. The figure shows a profit rate (——) denoted as *à la Marx,* that is, in which profits are total income minus labor compensation,

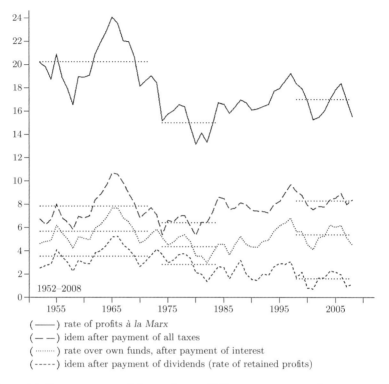

Figure 4.1 Four measures of the profit rate: U.S. corporate sector (percent, yearly). It would also be possible to calculate a profit rate over own funds, after the payment of all taxes but prior to the payment of interest. Such a rate for nonfinancial corporations is shown in Figure 10.4 where it is used to illustrate the impact of capital income in the determination of the rate of retained earnings. It is not, however, an appropriate variable to assess profitability trends. If the profit rate is measured on own funds, interest must logically be subtracted from profits.

and the stock of capital, in the denominator, is limited to fixed capital.[5] The unit is the corporate sector.

Dotted lines in the figure suggest successive levels for three periods, 1952–1971, 1974–1983, and 1998–2007, referred to as "the 1950s and 1960s," "the 1970s," and "the precrisis decade" for simplicity. The three values are 20.2 percent, 15.0 percent, and 17.0 percent, respectively. Thus, the profit rate in this measure recovered from the 1970s to the precrisis decade (a *recovery ratio* of 17.0/15.0, that is, 1.13), but the value prevailing during the first two decades was not restored (a *restoration ratio* of 17.0/20.2, that is, 0.84).

Both the labor cost and technology are involved in the analysis of profitability trends in this first definition. Using the well-known relation *Profit rate = share of profits * productivity of capital,* one can assess the respective contributions of the share of profits and the productivity of capital (the ratio of the price of output to the price of fixed capital). One finds that the two variables contributed almost to the same extent to the partial restoration between the first two postwar decades and the precrisis decade (0.84 = 0.93 * 0.91). (Chapter 3 already points to an upward trend in the share of wages before 1970, followed by a horizontal plateau from the 1970s to the precrisis decade) Both the import of cheap commodities and new information technologies certainly played a role in the restoration of the profit rate from the 1970s.

It is not possible to straightforwardly derive consequences of such trends on the profit rate susceptible of impacting the behavior of corporations and their capability to invest and generate capital income flows. Between a profit rate *à la Marx* and as "felt" by enterprises, the difference is large. The consideration of taxes dramatically modifies the levels and trends of profit rates. In the second variable (— —) in Figure 4.1, total taxes (taxes on production and profit taxes) have been subtracted. In this second measure, the restoration of the profit rate in the precrisis decade, when compared to the first decades after World War II, was more substantial than in the previous measure, although these movements are dwarfed in the figure because of the large vertical scale imposed by the pretax rate. The average profit rate (— —) for the period 1952–1971 was 7.8 percent; it declined to 6.4 percent during the 1970s; and reached 8.3 percent during the precrisis decade, a recovery ratio of 1.29 and a restoration ratio of 1.06. It is important to understand that this effect is due not only to diminishing corporate taxes within neoliberalism, but to the high levels of taxation immediately after World War II and their subsequent alleviation.[6]

In the third measure (· · · · ·), enterprises' own funds (that is, assets minus liabilities) are substituted for the net stock of fixed capital[7] (jointly with other minor changes) and, correspondingly, profits are determined subtracting the taxes and the interest payment. In this measure, the restoration ratio is almost 1.0.

The fourth measure (-----) accounts for the profit rate further subtracting dividends paid out from profits. It is the "rate of retained profits (that echoes the share of retained profits in Figure 3.4). While the three previous measures reveal a significant recovery of profit rates from the structural crisis of the 1970s to the precrisis decade, this last measure shows a continuous downward trend during the three periods. In other words, the rate of retained profit was even smaller during the precrisis decade than during the 1970s. Finally, the restoration ratio is 0.46!

To sum up, a slight upward trend of the corporate profit rate *à la Marx* was established within neoliberalism from the low levels of the structural crisis of the 1970s but rates remained inferior to those prevailing prior to this crisis decade. A return to the values prevailing during the 1950s and 1960s (or even a rise) is observed when profits are measured after tax, but as a result of the rise of dividends paid out by corporations, the rate of retained profit diminished consistently.

Interest Rates: The 1979 Coup

In the history of capitalism, as during World War I, episodes of inflation were at the origin of major transfers of wealth from lenders to borrowers. They had a dramatic impact on financial institutions and the wealth of holders of securities. From this historical experience results the aversion of the upper classes toward inflation.

When major capitalist countries entered into the structural crisis of the 1970s, a decade of declining profitability in all measures above, the growth rate of the GDP was more or less maintained within countries of the center. This was the effect of stimulative macro policies, and of the tolerance to inflation. Cumulative inflation was at the origin of such a large income transfer at the expense of lenders and to the benefit of the nonfinancial sector (and other borrowers such as a fraction of households and government). These policy trends were suddenly interrupted, with spectacular consequences on capital income flows. At the end of 1979, the Federal Reserve suddenly increased interest rates in the "1979 coup."

As shown in Figure 4.2, these developments are reflected in the profile of long-term and short-term real interest rates (interest rates minus the rate of inflation) for the business sector. In the 1960s and 1970s, both rates fluctuated around a plateau of about 2.1 percent (yearly average of long-term business, AAA) before falling to negative values during the crisis. Then the coup appears dramatically. A new, neoliberal, plateau was main-

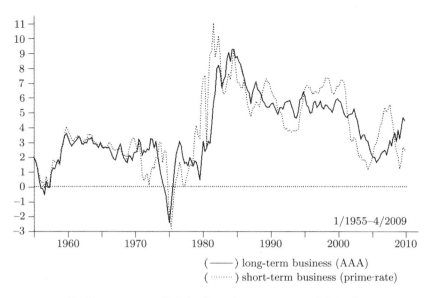

(————) long-term business (AAA)

(············) short-term business (prime-rate)

Figure 4.2 Real interest rates: U.S. business (percent, quarterly). Real rates are nominal rates minus the inflation rate.

Long-term U.S. government securities and mortgage rates are very similar to the long-term rate paid by enterprises shown in this figure. From the early 1990s onward, the nominal short-term prime rate is equal to the Federal Funds rate plus three percentage points.

tained during the second half of the 1980s and the 1990s at 5.9 percent still for long-term rates.

The about-face in the direction of a new strategy—following the earlier monetarist attempt at abandoning feedback policies—was dramatic. In the wake of the 1974–1975 recession, the Carter administration was still seeking the cooperation of the major capitalist countries to stimulate the economy worldwide. At the end of the year, Paul Volcker, appointed chairman of the Federal Reserve in August 1979, precipitated the hike of interest rates to unprecedented levels, causing a major financial crisis within the United States and European countries, the crisis of the third-world debt in 1982, and the more severe recession in the United States since World War II. In 1980, the Depository Institutions Deregulation and Monetary Control Act allowed for the elimination of previous regulatory frameworks (Chapter 9) and, simultaneously, increased the power of the Federal Reserve.

VOLCKER
SHOCK

The coup opened a period of relative macro stability and limited inflation, after 1983, typical of neoliberalism up to the 2001 recession, interrupted by a single recession in 1991.

The figure also illustrates the decline of real interest rates after 2000.
Complex mechanisms are involved (Box 14.2).

Distributing Dividends and Buying Back Stock

A second source of capital income is the payment of dividends by corporations. Figure 4.3 shows the shares of after-tax profits paid out as dividends by nonfinancial and financial corporations, respectively. In both
instances, prior to 1980, these shares fluctuated around 51 percent (yearly
average during the 1960s and 1970s, for nonfinancial corporations) and
then around 74 percent during the first two neoliberal decades (for the
same sector).[8] This sudden increase echoes the new corporate governance
to the benefit of shareholders. During the first decades of the postwar
period a much larger fraction of profits was conserved by nonfinancial
corporations with the purpose of productive investment. Paying out dividends and investing are combined decisions, and the new corporate governance worked in favor of dividend flows. Thus, within neoliberalism,

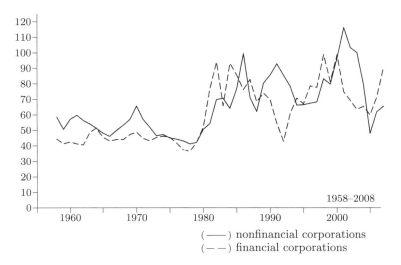

(——) nonfinancial corporations
(— —) financial corporations

Figure 4.3 Share of dividends in after-tax profits: U.S. nonfinancial and financial
corporations (percent, yearly). Dividends are dividends paid out. Dividends
received are added to after-tax profits.

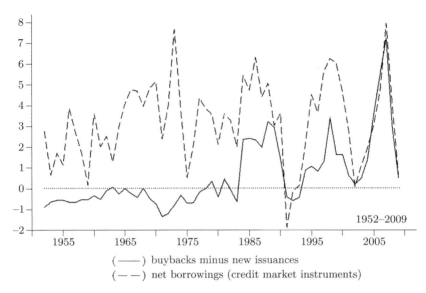

Figure 4.4 Buybacks minus new issuances of stock shares and net borrowings: U.S. nonfinancial corporations (percentage of the net stock of fixed capital, yearly). A positive value of the variable (———) indicates that buybacks are larger than new issuances.

profits are lavishly distributed, adding to the burden of increased interest rates, the two trends limiting the ability of nonfinancial corporations to invest.

Such distributions of profits are in line with neoliberal ideology. Once profits have been distributed to individuals or institutions, the new resources are supposedly available for an optimal allocation of capital among industries and enterprises where the best opportunities are opened. The problem with this line of argument is that, looking at U.S. nonfinancial corporations, profits paid out do not return to corporations, and accumulation is low.[9] This is a crucial feature of the neoliberal decades, a major factor in the determination of the long-term trajectory of the U.S. economy (Chapter 10).

To these observations, one can add the buybacks of stock shares by nonfinancial corporations intending to stimulate their stock-market indices. (This phenomenon is typical of nonfinancial corporations, not financial corporations.) Figure 4.4 shows the purchase of stock shares minus the issuance of new shares (———). The purchase of shares is basically the buyback of their own shares by corporations.[10] The variable is a percentage of the net stock of fixed capital. One can observe its rise during the neoliberal decades, with three bouts between 1984 and 1990, around 1998, and since 2004, a puzzling development. These practices point to an explicit strategy of "disaccumulation," with dramatic consequences for the growth of the U.S. economy, as will become clearer.

The second variable (— —) in Figure 4.4 shows the net borrowings (borrowing minus lending) of nonfinancial corporations. One can observe how the two variables move in tandem during the neoliberal decades, in particular after 2004. Within neoliberalism, these borrowings increasingly financed buybacks.

Skyrocketing Stock Prices

The imposition of new criteria made the stock market a central axis around which production and financial activity revolve. Figure 4.5 shows a stock-market index, deflated by the price of the GDP. Stock prices were dramatically depressed during the structural crisis of the 1970s.

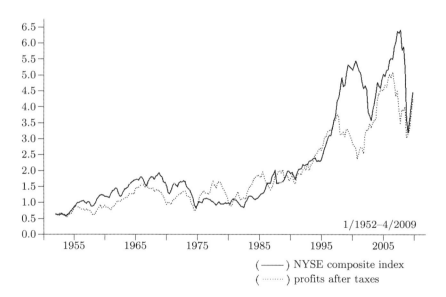

(——) NYSE composite index
(········) profits after taxes

Figure 4.5 New York Stock Exchange composite index and the profits of U.S. corporations (first quarter of 1980=1, quarterly). Both variables have been deflated by the GDP deflator.

But taking the first quarter of 1980 as 1, the New York Stock Exchange (NYSE) index peaked at 5.45 in the third quarter of 2000, prior to the crash in 2000–2001 (down to 3.58 in the first quarter of 2003). It is worth emphasizing that these outstanding performances are not limited to the U.S. economy. Similar trends prevailed in the major capitalist countries, as in Europe, with the exception of Japan whose late entry into neoliberalism and the subsequent crisis conferred specific features on indices.

The major episodes of the U.S. macroeconomy are apparent in these profiles:[11] (1) the booming economy of the 1960s; (2) the entrance into the crisis of the 1970s at the beginning of the decade (a division by a factor of 2, from 1.68 in the fourth quarter of 1972 to 0.84 in the fourth quarter of 1974); (3) the end of this crisis in the early 1980s (despite the crisis of banks and savings and loan associations); (4) the bubble during the boom of information technologies; (5) the crash in 2000–2001 and the recovery; and (6) the crisis from mid-2007 onward.

Such trends must not be interpreted as the mere expression of speculative behaviors. This is shown in the second variable (·······) in Figure 4.5, the after-tax corporate profits of the sector. Both variables evolve in tandem. When the two variables diverge significantly, as at the end of the 1990s or after 2005, one can speak of "bubbles."

Pumping Surplus

To economists familiar with a Marxian perspective, the notion of capital income harks back to Marx's surplus value, that is, to the sphere of production. The rise of interest rates during the first two decades of neoliberalism and the growing indebtedness of households and the government gave a particular importance to the appropriation of income from agents other than the workers of enterprises by way of an interest payment, as an alternative channel.[12] In Marx's terminology, the loans to households and the government refer to fictitious capital (Box 4.2).

During the first decades after World War II, the flows of interest paid by households rose consistently but moderately, to reach 4.4 percent of GDP in 1979.[13] With neoliberalism, a plateau was reached at about 5.7 percent of GDP. Interest paid by the government grew to 3.6 percent at the beginning of the 1990s, and declined to 1.9 percent in 2007. Thus, in 2007, interest paid by households and the government amounted to a total of about 8.1

Box 4.2
Fictitious Capital

Marx defines "capital" as value in a process of self-enlargement.[1] This definition simultaneously refers to the theory of surplus value (that accounts for "enlargement") and the theory of the circuit of capital passing through its three forms: money capital, commodity capital, and productive capital (that accounts for the "process" of capital).

Capital that does not match Marx's definition is said to be "fictitious."[2] Typical of fictitious capital are loans to the government. An interest is paid by the government, a genuine income for the lender but not a straightforward form of surplus value (as interest, dividends, or rents paid by enterprises). The money lent does not finance the circuit of capital but expenses and, on this account, is not capital according to Marx's definition. The same can be said of loans to households financing the purchase of homes or consumption goods. The holding of stock shares issued by nonfinancial corporations marks the ownership of a fraction of capital as "value in a process of self-enlargement" (in the assets of enterprises). Marx also points, however, to a "fictitious" capital since the shares have a price of their own on stock markets.

---

1. K. Marx, *Capital,* vol. 1 (1867; New York: Vintage Books, 1977), chap. 4; G. Duménil and D. Foley, "Marx's Analysis of Capitalist Production," in S. N. Durlauf and L. B. Blume, eds., *The New Palgrave: A Dictionary of Economics* (London and Basingstoke: Macmillan, 2008).

2. K. Marx, *Capital,* vol. 3 (1894; New York: Vintage Books, 1981), chap. 25; G. Duménil and D. Lévy, "Les trois champs de la théorie des relations financières de Marx. Le capital financier d'Hilferding et Lénine," in Séminaire d'Études Marxistes, *La finance capitaliste* (Paris: Presses Universitaires de France, 2006).

---

percent of GDP. This total is larger than the profits of U.S. nonfinancial enterprises prior to the payment of interest and taxes on corporate profits (thus, still included in these profits) that reached 7.6 percent of GDP in 2007.

Comparative Profit Rates

The investigation of the comparative profit rates of nonfinancial and financial corporations is uneasy and less reliable due to the difficulty of measurement. Concerning financial corporations, the appropriate mea-

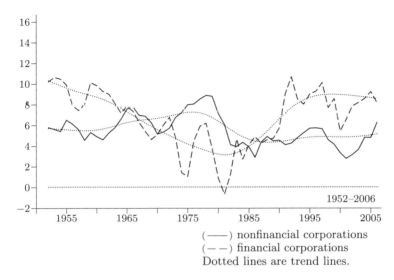

(——) nonfinancial corporations
(— —) financial corporations
Dotted lines are trend lines.

Figure 4.6 Profit rates: U.S. financial and nonfinancial corporations (percent, yearly). In this measure of profit rates, profits are determined after paying interest and taxes. A correction is made of the devaluation of financial assets and liabilities by inflation (or the devaluation of the net debt). Capital gains are considered. (Due to the large fluctuation observed, this latter component has been smoothed out.)

sure of capital is enterprises' own funds (as the stock of fixed capital is obviously inadequate). Profits must be determined by taking account of the net (received minus paid) flows of interest, prior to the payment of dividends to shareholders while dividends received are part of profits. It is important to consider capital gains in the stock market, and the devaluation of loans and debts by inflation. (Financial corporations hold debt susceptible of being devalued by rising prices if interest rates are constant.) Such profit rates on enterprises' own funds are known as rate of return on equity (ROE). Obviously, inasmuch as possible, the same definitions must be used for nonfinancial corporations to allow for the comparison.

Figure 4.6 shows measures of profit rates for nonfinancial and financial (—— and — —, respectively) corporations in this definition. Trend lines (·······) emphasize underlying tendencies abstracting from short-term deviations.

During inflation years (mostly the 1970s), a large transfer of income occurred from financial to nonfinancial corporations, as well as from

Box 4.3
A Reconciliation of the Measures of Profit Rates
in Figures 4.6 and 4.1

The definitions of profit rates in Figure 4.6 and in the third measure in Figure 4.1 (·······) are similar since, in both instances, interest payments are subtracted and capital is measured as own funds. The levels are about the same but the profiles observed are significantly distinct. A first reason is the consideration of capital gains in Figure 4.6. A second reason is the correction for the impact of inflation. This effect increases significantly the profit rate of the nonfinancial sector and diminishes the profit rate of the financial sector during the 1970s. In both cases, the interest payment encroached on the recovery of the profit rate, but in Figure 4.1 (·······) this encroachment was not sufficient to offset the recovery of the profit rate of nonfinancial corporations. On the contrary, Figure 4.6 manifests the fact that the end of inflation put a halt on the devaluation of debt. The profit rate of the nonfinancial sector taking account of this devaluation remained comparatively low. One can equivalently contend that the increase in the "real interest rate" offsets the restoration of the profit rate manifest in other similar measures in which the devaluation of debt by inflation is not considered.

noncorporate lenders. Thus, the profit rate of the financial sector plunged, while that of nonfinancial corporations was not only maintained but increased despite the decline of the profit rate *à la Marx* for the entire sector (Figure 4.1). Later in the 1980s, the situation of financial corporations was not immediately restored and low profit rates prevailed in this segment of corporations during the severe financial crisis at the end of the 1980s. The level reached was similar to that of nonfinancial corporations despite a large interest payment in favor of the financial sector.[14] During the neoliberal decades, the earlier hierarchy in favor of the nonfinancial sector was inverted. The profit rate of nonfinancial corporations fluctuated around an almost horizontal trend, while the profit rate of financial corporations increased. In addition to interest, financial corporations benefited from new profit flows linked to financial innovation and capital gains in the stock market.

It is also possible to determine the profit rate of the two sectors considered jointly. The result is not very different from the variable for the nonfinancial sector since the financial sector is much smaller than the nonfinancial sector. During the 1950s and 1960s, the own funds of financial corporations amounted to 12.6 percent of those of nonfinancial corporations, and 24.3 percent after 2000. (Box 4.3 compares the measures in Figures 4.6 and 4.1.)

To sum up, according to these data, a new hierarchy of profit rates was established between financial and nonfinancial corporations during the 1990s to the benefit of financial corporations while the profit rates of the nonfinancial sector remained stagnant. In this measure (the most sophisticated in this chapter) taking account of the effects of inflation, the recovery ratio for all corporations, financial and nonfinancial, was 0.76 and the restoration ratio was 0.82.

The Record Profitability Levels of the Financial Sector

The profitability levels reached by financial corporations, as in Figure 4.6, might be judged high. One must remember that neoliberal standards placed the ROEs of corporations as high as 15 percent (in enterprises' accounts). Even the declared ROE of insured banks, certainly not the more speculative of the profession and subject to the oversight of the Federal

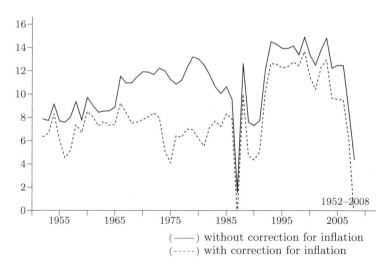

(———) without correction for inflation
(- - - - -) with correction for inflation

Figure 4.7 Annualized quarterly rate of return on equity: U.S. insured banks (percent, yearly). "Insured banks" refer to the main segment of depository institutions whose deposits are insured by the FDIC.

Deposit Insurance Corporation (FDIC), was close to this level during about ten years, at least up to 2003, and still 12 percent on the eve of the crisis.[15]

The ROE of the sector is shown in Figure 4.7 (——). One can observe that these elevated returns are concentrated between the recovery from the financial crisis of the late 1980s and the beginning of the contemporary crisis. The decrease of interest rates after 2000 and also the contraction of noninterest income encroached on the profitability of the sector, but the ROE was preserved thanks to a drastic contraction of noninterest expenses. (One can also note the decline and strong disturbance during the financial crisis and the recession around 1990.)

In the second variable (-----) in Figure 4.7, a correction is made for inflation. As could be expected, the ROE is significantly diminished between 1964 and 1985. Both the levels thus determined and the chronological profile are rather close to those observed for the financial sector in Figure 4.6, given the differences in units of analysis (a financial sector and the bank component of depository institutions) and sources (national and firm accountings).

Despite the difficulty of measurement, one can conclude that there was an explosion of the profit rates of financial corporations after the recovery from the financial crisis at the transition between the 1980s and 1990s.

A Tripolar Class Configuration: Breaking Wage-Earning Homogeneity

The approach in the previous part is based on either the broad notion of "upper classes" or the traditional class divide between capitalist owners and wage earners. Chapter 4 examines the bias neoliberalism imparted to income distribution in favor of capital income. The growing importance of high wages to the benefit of a privileged minority in contemporary capitalism reveals, however, the limits of this emphasis on capital income. The analysis of the upper income brackets in the United States and the historical profile of the income they receive show that the high and very high wages—including all forms of additional remunerations, such as bonuses and exercised stock options—are a major channel in the appropriation of a social surplus, to be considered jointly with capital income (interest, dividends, rents, and capital gains). Correspondingly, the changing situation of households pertaining to the high wage brackets is an important component in the succession of the various phases of modern capitalism. The analysis of the historical trends of income distribution confirms the importance of this component of social dynamics. (Moving to Part IX, where scenarios for the coming decades are discussed, the limits of the traditional dual pattern separating capitalists and wage earners become even more obvious.)

The perspective in Chapter 5 is historical-empirical, while Chapter 6 lays the foundations of a theoretical framework.

71

5

The Managerial and Popular Classes

Beginning with the observation that the distinction between capital income and wages does not account for the complexity of social relations in contemporary capitalism, the present chapter establishes the framework of a tripolar class configuration in which capitalist, managerial, and popular classes are distinguished. A special emphasis is placed on managerial classes, their functions, and their changing role along the phases of modern capitalism.

Wages within the High Income Brackets

The important role of wages in the formation of high income is clearly apparent in the data and increasingly so. This observation basically questions the treatment of wages as a homogeneous whole on, at least, two accounts. First, a large fraction of the income of the wealthiest segments of the population is made of wages. Second, the historical profile of variation of these wages is distinct from the trends prevailing for the wages of the rest of the population. These differences match the social features proper to each period of modern capitalism. Notably, the specific role played by managers in each social order and their changing relationship to the capitalist or popular classes is a crucial factor affecting these patterns of income distribution.

The first observation—the importance of wages in the high or very high income brackets—is the simplest to document. Table 5.1 shows the share of wages in the total income of various income fractiles for the high income brackets. Two periods are distinguished: (1) two postwar decades (1950–1969) prior to the crisis of the 1970s, and (2) neoliberalism (1980–2007). A

Table 5.1 Share of wages in the income of various income fractiles:
U.S. households (percent)

	90–95	95–99	99–99.5	99.5–99.9	99.9–100
1950–1969	87.4	71.8	48.3	41.5	29.3
1980–2007	89.8	82.0	70.7	64.3	48.8

The complement to 100 percent corresponds to entrepreneurial income and capital income, that is, interest, dividends, and rents. For the top 1 percent, as in Figures 3.1 and 5.1, the percentages are 40.7 percent and 60.5 percent, respectively.

preliminary observation is that these figures confirm standard insights. As expected, the share of wages is smaller for the higher income brackets during both periods. (The comparison between the two lines is discussed further below.) Wages still account for almost 90 percent of the income of the 90–95 fractile, and the percentage falls for higher incomes. A more surprising finding is the high percentage of wages within the high income brackets. After 1980 they account for about 50 percent of the income of the 99.9–100 fractile, that is, one household out of 1,000 when ranked by increasing order of income. (In 2007, this tiny group's annual family income was larger than $2,053,000.)

Historical trends are also telling. It is worth returning here to the historical profile of income distribution, but from the viewpoint of wages only. In Figure 5.1, the first variable (——) refers to the same group of households as in Figure 3.1, the top 1 percent in total income distribution (the fractile 99–100). But, while the variable in Figure 3.1 is the share of total income received by this upper 1 percent, the variable in Figure 5.1 is the share of total wages received by the group. One can observe (1) a downward trend (meaning a reduction of inequality) during World War II, from 8.4 percent (average 1927–1939) to 6.2 percent (average 1946–1949); (2) a slight decline to the late 1960s; and (3) a rise to 11.4 percent (average 2000–2007). (The first steps of this latter upward trend occurred during the 1970s.) Thus, while the percentage of *total income* accruing to the 1 percent jumped from 10.0 percent to 23.5 percent between 1980 and 2007 (Figure 3.1), its share within *only wages* rose from 6.4 percent to 12.4 percent. In both instances, figures were multiplied by about 2. This new observation confirms the diagnosis above. Besides capital income, the high wages of the upper income brackets were an important instrument in the concentration of income at the top of the pyramid during the neoliberal decades, not only capital income.

Figure 5.1 Shares of total wages received by two income fractiles: U.S. households (percent, yearly).

One advantage of the variable shown in Figure 5.1, where only wages are considered, over the one shown in Table 5.1, is that the former is not subject to the uncertainty surrounding the reporting of capital income by the very high income brackets. Although wages received in foreign countries may be underreported to some extent, the same observation as in Table 5.1 stands out in Figure 5.1, without question. Within neoliberalism, wages became a major channel in the formation of high or even very high incomes. Actually, wages were the main channel by which the restoration of the share of the 1 percent top income bracket in total income, as in Figure 3.1, was achieved.

The second variable (-----) in Figure 5.1 provides the same information for the 95–99 fractile. (Jointly, the two fractiles correspond to the top 5 percent, denoted as "high income brackets" in the previous chapters.) A similar decline is observed during World War II, but a moderate upward trend is apparent after the war and was maintained throughout the neoliberal decades. This slightly faster rise contrasts both with the growth of the great mass of wages and the stagnation of capital income during the first decades following World War II. Wages for the 95–99 fractile were the first beneficiaries of the new trends during the first postwar decades, after the reduction of inequalities during the war, and this observation matches the managerial features of the period. But it is also interesting to note that neoliberalism did not affect (neither accelerated nor slowed down) the steady concentration of wages in favor of this group, and this observation testifies simultaneously to the relationship between capitalist classes and the broad group of managers (when the 95–99 fractile is considered), and to the specific features of wages at the summit of wage hierarchies (in the 99–100 fractile).

Returning here to Table 5.1, a comparison between the two lines in the table reveals that the percentage of wages in total income rose during the neoliberal decades for all upper-income fractiles, instead of diminishing as could have been expected from the rise of capital income typical of neoliberalism. The rise was the most dramatic for the tiny upper fractile 99.9–100.

These trends demonstrate that the high wages received by the upper income brackets increased even more rapidly than capital income, as stated above.[1] Their historical dynamics are quite distinct from that of the rest of wage earners, as apparent during the first postwar decades and neoliberalism. Overall, both capital income and high wages at the top benefited from neoliberal trends in tremendous proportions. The interpretation here is that the profile of high wages mirrors the changing social position of the managerial classes and, symmetrically, their relationship to either the popular or capitalist classes.

It is the purpose of the following sections to interpret these changing patterns. This requires a closer examination of the functions of managers, and their changing location and role within social relations.

The Functional Figures of Managers

The main field of activity of managers, since the managerial revolution, is the organization of corporations. Thus, managers can be classified into various categories. One can typically distinguish between the technical, more strictly organizational, and commercial segments of management, on the one hand, and the financial spheres, on the other hand. But management is not limited to private corporations. From the early twentieth century, the methods of private management were rapidly exported to cities[2] and, gradually, to government services in general. The New Deal and the postwar decades saw a considerable development of the role of officials in government institutions (as during the 1930s, the war economy, and in the policies, notably macro policies, and social programs of the 1960s). Thus, to the managers of corporations, one must add the officials in administration within the managerial classes.

The objectives of managers depend on the social order in which management is performed. After World War II, management basically aimed at growth (within corporations and in the definition of policies) and technical change. In neoliberalism, the main target became the stock market and capital income. Consequently, a reciprocal relationship exists between the prevalence of one specific power configuration and the preeminence of one or the other component of management. The historical juncture of the New Deal conferred a degree of preeminence on government officials. It inflected the advance of management in this particular direction. The postwar compromise stimulated managerial capabilities in all respects, but with a particular emphasis on technology and organization. Neoliberalism biased managerial trends in favor of the financial component of management.

Managers should not be seen as merely passive agents in the determination of the course of history. Government officials played an active role in the conduct of the New Deal and the consolidation of the new social compromise after World War II. In neoliberalism, the managerial classes, in particular their upper fractions, actively participated in the formation of the new social trends, expecting high remunerations and with the goal of entering into the realm of active ownership. In fact, the imposition of neoliberalism would have been impossible, had not the new alliance been struck within the upper layers of the social pyramid between ownership and management.

Management at the Helm: The Three Facets of the Postwar Compromise

There is a clear problem of vocabulary in reference to the society of the first post-World War II decades. No generally accepted term has been found. The book uses the phrases "postwar," "social democratic," or "Keynesian compromise," but "managerial capitalism" or, in some countries, "mixed economies" would also be appropriate. Although this social arrangement prevailed in most major capitalist countries, the exact configurations and degrees were variegated, geographically and chronologically. Methods differed among countries and changed significantly over time.

The tripolar class perspective allows for a class interpretation of the features proper to postwar capitalism. The cornerstone of this social order was a compromise between the popular classes (of production and clerical workers), on the one hand, and the classes of managers, including officials, on the other hand, under the stimulative pressure of the popular movement. While the popular classes were the engine of the transformation, managers and officials were the linchpins of the new social order.

It is important to understand that three social actors are involved in the postwar compromise, which command three distinct viewpoints. First, there is a proper *social* (or welfare) component, and here the popular classes are center stage. Second, there is a *managerial* aspect to these dynamics. These decades were unquestionably those of managerial capitalism, within the private sector and with a strong involvement of officers in government institutions. A third aspect is the *containment of capitalist interests,* and this is where the situation of the capitalist classes must be considered.

1. *The social component (popular classes).* The notion of a postwar social compromise implies the alteration of the situation of the popular classes. This capitalism appears retrospectively as an economy and, more generally, as a society whose violence had been moderated, in sharp contrast to the first financial hegemony and neoliberalism. So the alternative denomination of "tempered capitalism" can also be used. The compromise with the popular classes was manifest in the progress of purchasing powers, policies aiming at full employment, welfare protection, education, health, retirement, and so on. The capitalism of the first postwar decades is often presented in this manner, with a strong Rooseveltian flavor in the United States, an implicit reference to the Popular Front in France, or to William Beveridge's England.

2. *Managerial autonomy (managers).* Concerning the situation of management, there are, actually, not many alternatives. The two observations, that workers were not in power and that the power of capitalist owners was contained, imply the enhanced role and autonomy conferred on the managerial classes. Overall, workers were not in power, the capitalist classes were contained, and organization was in the hand of managers. This autonomy grew on the foundations laid by the historical trends of the managerial revolution and found an opportunity to express its intrinsic potential within the political and economic circumstances of the New Deal, the war economy, and the postwar compromise. The intermediate period that stretches between the two financial hegemonies provides a unique history of such a social order in the United States.

Corporations were managed with concerns, such as investment and technical change, significantly distinct from the creation of "value for shareholders." Managers enjoyed relative freedom to act vis-à-vis owners, with a considerable share of the profits retained within corporations for the purpose of investment. In some countries, large sectors of the economy were under the control of governments as a result of nationalization. To this, one can add a financial sector in the service of the nonfinancial economy, and placed under the control of managers. This managerial autonomy was also manifest within the state apparatus of the postwar decades. A specific organizational role was conferred on officials. Policies devised by officials were often targeted to growth and employment.

Keynesian macro policies define a major aspect of this policy component. The notion that the macroeconomy must be controlled by central institutions—through fiscal and monetary policies, and with specific targets in terms of employment and prices—straightforwardly points to managerial practices. Information must be collected and decisions made. Results must be assessed. That these tasks are performed by officials within central institutions, instead of by managers within private corporations, broadens rather than offsets the managerial features of these mechanisms.

This managerial aspect is usually not clearly articulated by the actors or analysts of such *actual* middle ways (as opposed to *alleged* middle ways in neoliberalism), which tend to perceive this course of events in terms of moderation of the violence inherent in capitalism. An important exception is the reference, in the United States, to managerial capitalism at its climax during the 1960s and 1970s (Box 5.1).

3. *The containment of capitalist interests (capitalists).* Each of the features above testifies to the situation of the capitalist classes. The weak concern toward stock-market performances in the management of corporations is a clear example. The existence of a financial sector in the service of accumulation in the nonfinancial sector provides another striking expression of the demise of the capitalist classes. These classes partly lost control of the financial sector, a crucial instrument of their hegemony (that is, their power and income) as in Finance.

Concerning the containment of capitalist interests, the situation differed considerably among countries. In France, for example, where a strong public (in the sense of "state owned") sector had been established after World War II, including important segments of the financial sector,

Box 5.1
Managerial Capitalism

Much confusion surrounds the notion of "managerial capitalism." The diffi-culty arises from the combination of two types of determinants.

On the one hand, in modern capitalism, the delegation of organizational tasks to managerial and clerical personnel, and the ensuing advance in organi-zational efficiency, provided the foundation of the historical trends that led to the definition of managerial capitalism after World War II. There is no question-ing that, within contemporary capitalism, these managerial features and trends are still present. Corporations are managed, and more than ever within the new framework proper to neoliberal globalization, as in transnational corpora-tions. This requires more personnel, skills, and technology than ever before.

On the other hand, managerial capitalism proper points to a specific pe-riod in history, the first postwar decades, in which the historical advance of management combined its effects with the social compromise between man-agers and the popular classes of clerical personnel and production workers. From the Great Depression to the structural crisis of the 1970s, to various degrees depending on the country, this social order meant a larger autonomy of managerial personnel and officials vis-à-vis the owners of capital (with corresponding corporate governance and policies). Neoliberalism put an end to this autonomy because it implied a containment of capitalist interests and established a new compromise at the top of the social hierarchies, favoring financial managers in comparison to other segments. But neoliberalism did not stop the advance of management.

(continued)

this containment was stronger than in the United States. In Japan, na-tional development was straightforwardly in the hands of public and pri-vate managers, with a large degree of cooperation. The situation was again distinct in Latin America, in the context of import-substitution industri-alization (Box 23.1), which conferred a specific role on the "national" capi-talist classes.

In the three respects above, capitalism during these decades was less a capitalism than during the first financial hegemony or neoliberalism. In a sense, labor power was less a commodity as any other good in the economy. In the United States, emblematic of the beginning of this new period was the Employment Act of 1946 making full employment a duty of the govern-ment. The dynamics of accumulation were in the hands of managers. Many

(continued)

As a result of this coincidence between underlying economic determinants (growing managerial capabilities) and power configurations (the social compromise under managerial leadership), the managerial features of the postwar decades became rather conspicuous. The potential threat for the capitalists inherent in the managerial revolution—an object of concern in its early steps during the first decades of the century—finally materialized. During the postwar decades, precisely what some segments of the capitalist classes had feared happened, that is, a capitalism freed from financial hegemony and placed under managerial leadership. This legibility of managerial relations (the rise and autonomy of management) after World War II explains why the theory of managerial capitalism culminated during the 1960s and 1970s, as in the works of Alfred Chandler and Kenneth Galbraith.[1] The establishment of neoliberalism and the failure of the configuration of bureaucratic managerialism (the dominance of managerial classes in the absence of capitalist classes), as in Sovietism, discredited radical managerial experiments to the benefit of the dynamics of "markets," a euphemism for the violence of uncurbed capitalism.

---

1. A. D. Chandler, *The Visible Hand: The Managerial Revolution in American Business* (Cambridge, Mass.: Harvard University Press, 1977); J. K. Galbraith, *The New Industrial State* (New York: New American Library, 1967).

exceptions to the so-called market mechanisms had been implemented (which neoliberalism strove to offset). But the postwar society, if it was less a capitalism than during the first financial hegemony, was, however, a class society, where exploitation was based on the extraction of a surplus to the benefit of the upper classes. The two channels were capital income and upper wages, given the hierarchies and trends described earlier.

It is important to understand the relationships between the three components above. The two first aspects—the welfare features of the compromise and managerial autonomy—are structurally *independent,* meaning that one can exist independently of the other. It is true that, under specific historical circumstances, the establishment of managerial autonomy may be conditioned by the support of the popular classes, and that this condition may require a number of improvements to the benefit of the popular classes. But managerial autonomy could prevail within circumstances in which no particular favorable situation is made to the popular classes. In Nazism, a crucial role was conferred on officials in a social arrangement to the extreme Right. Conversely, the third component—the containment of capitalist interests—is typically a *consequence* of the two components above. The progress of the purchasing power of the popular classes and social protection encroaches on capital income, and managerial autonomy limits the power of the capitalist classes. In the postwar compromise, both aspects were combined.

Class Struggle in the Establishment of Managerial Autonomy

The engine of such historical transformations is class struggle. The Great Depression deeply shook the foundations of capitalism questioning its survival. Pessimism was everywhere among the tenants of capitalism.[3] In this context, what determined the exact contents of the New Deal and postwar compromise in the United States was the intense social strife, with the rise of the traditional worker movement and the emergence of allegedly socialist or communist countries, as they called themselves. These trends were manifest in the multiplication of civil wars (as in Spain, Greece, China, etc.). Such struggles on the part of the popular classes combined their effects with the tensions among the capitalist and managerial classes, weakening the compromise at the top. This happened within a broad spectrum of distinct configurations, for example, in the New Deal. But intense class struggle also meant possible extreme reactions on the part of the capitalist classes, as in fascism. In the United States, there is a debate to determine whether President Roosevelt saved the country from communism or fascism! The answer is obviously both. The two objectives, the moderation of capitalism to make it viable and the compromise with the popular classes to make it tolerable, converged.

In the United States, the implementation of the postwar power configuration was achieved by a mix of compromise and repression vis-à-vis all liberals (as in McCarthyism) and, obviously, vis-à-vis the most radical components as in the communist parties (nationally and internationally). In Charles de Gaulle's France, after World War II, a similar result was obtained by an ephemeral alliance with the Communist Party, set aside soon after. Everywhere, Keynesianism provided a framework for compromise, combining private initiative ("markets") with macro policy. Social democracy, in the strict sense, was typical of Northern Europe. The United Kingdom or France can be seen as intermediate cases with important public sectors, social protection, and development and employment policies. In the United States there was no nationalization as in Europe, but state entities were created or their functions broadened (agencies, GSEs) and both corporate management and policies (low real interest rates, policies targeted to industrial development, etc.) expressed the features of the postwar compromise, in combination with financial regulation and strong state intervention concerning social protection, research, and education. Financial repression was, however, less acute than in other countries.[4] As stated earlier, the case of Japan was at the extreme, with a tight collaboration between private managers and officials, a financial sector radically in the service of the production economy, and a minor role played by the capitalist classes.

As revealed after World War II, the new trends of technical change and the new levels of profit rates considerably contributed to the establishment of the compromise and its continuation during several decades. Probably no such favorable trends ever lifted the constraints usually weighing on distribution during earlier periods in the history of capitalism, at least certainly during the history of modern capitalism. (This is apparent in Figures 4.1 and 21.1.) The high levels of profit rates made compatible: (1) the preservation of the rates of retained profits within corporations; (2) the rise of corporate taxes and government receipts; and (3) the progress of the purchasing power of wage earners. This meant conditions favorable to accumulation, a big and active government (including in the conduct of wars), and the improvement of the situation of the great masses of wage earners.

Thus, highly favorable economic conditions converged with political circumstances in the determination of the features of postwar decades. Would the postwar compromise have prevailed in the absence of such underlying favorable circumstances? Such conditions were so crucial to the social order that the compromise did not survive the reversal of these technical-organizational trends and the ensuing fall of profit rates during the 1970s. This reversal created circumstances favorable to the victorious struggle of the capitalist classes and, more generally, of the upper classes under capitalist leadership. In this confrontation, a crucial factor was the lack of consistency of the social forces underlying the postwar compromise, a political weakness that paved the way to the imposition of neoliberalism.

Managerial Classes in Neoliberalism—The Bias
toward Financial Management

Neoliberalism did not stop the advance of management. Its first effect was to subject management to the class objectives of capitalists, but there was no respite in the advance of managerial functions. Large transnational corporations are huge managerial structures and the number of government employees continued to increase during neoliberalism.

This subjection was gradually extended along the successive phases of neoliberalism. More research would be necessary, but one can surmise that, during the 1980s, the disciplinary aspect of the new relationship between the capitalist and the managerial classes was dominant. Managers were told to "govern," as in corporate governance, to the benefit of owners. As the nature of this relationship was gradually altered to a more benevolent or enthusiastic collaboration (with probably significantly distinct degrees depending on the positions in the hierarchy and income levels), the difference between financial managers and the rest of the group was gradually established, as reflected in the hierarchies of income distribution. The 1990s marked a transition and, after 2000, financial managers had become a pillar of Finance.

Thus, neoliberalism biased managerial trends in favor of financial management. Managers are extensively active in financial mechanisms (maximizing shareholders' value, operations on derivative markets, conduct of mergers and acquisitions, and so on). Asset managers and traders are "scientific" financial managers, with a broad use of mathematics. The hierarchy between the technical and financial segments of management was profoundly altered. This is manifest in the fascination exerted by financial operations in the choice of careers and the large compensations offered.

At the top of managerial hierarchies, managers are involved in the dynamics of neoliberal corporate governance to such degrees that the financial facet of management tends to overwhelmingly dominate. Financial operations, notably mergers and acquisitions, play a preeminent role to the detriment of technical-organizational achievements. These latter functions are delegated to lower levels of the hierarchy and subject to the pressure of financial criteria. Top management is metamorphosed into financial management.

Financial management in neoliberalism gained so much importance that a quite specific relationship was established between the financial managers of both financial and nonfinancial corporations, and the capitalist classes. The rise of financial management meant the penetration of upper management into the core, most intimate mechanisms in which ownership is expressed. A tight collaboration is implied, but one can also contend that, in neoliberalism, capitalist owners are in a position of increasing dependency vis-à-vis the expertise of managers, in particular financial managers.

The Neoliberal Compromise—Hybridization at the Top

Concerning incomes and wealth, managerial classes benefited from neoliberal trends in two main respects, high wages and the accumulation of portfolios of financial assets. While the purchasing power of the bulk of wage earners was stagnating, upper wages increased sharply during the neoliberal decades, entailing a consumption boom and the accumulation of financial wealth on the part of high wage brackets. This convergence provided the economic foundations of the *neoliberal compromise* as opposed to the *social democratic compromise* of the postwar years. (This process is more advanced in the United States than in a number of European countries,[5] although it is also under way there.) This partnership in the new configuration of class power and income relations accounts for the use of the loose notion of upper classes in the previous chapters.

At the top of managerial hierarchies, more than an alliance occurred. Additional research would be necessary to make a more concrete analysis of these new social trends, but income patterns suggest that a process of "hybridization" or merger is under way. It is important to understand the bilateral features of this social arrangement. In these high spheres, contemporary capitalism combines capitalists who earn wages and wage earners who participate in capital income and ownership (Box 5.2). It is not only that very high wage brackets hold large portfolios of financial assets, but also that still basically capitalist families draw important income flows from corporations by the participation of some of their members in these hierarchies. The boundary between high-ranking managers and the capitalist classes is blurred.

One can surmise that this merger process was particularly strong within financial institutions. The managers of these institutions benefit from very high wages, and financial institutions are a favorite location where the holders of large portfolios of financial wealth can find a place within upper

---

Box 5.2
First- and Second-Tier Capitalism

Besides the joint objectives of the managerial and capitalist classes in neoliberalism, there is a second facet to the tight relationship between managers and capitalists. Managers also participate in the ownership of capital.

It has always been possible to distinguish within the capitalist classes, upper and lower segments, but specific to neoliberalism, at least in the United States, is the establishment of a "two-tier" pattern of capital ownership.[1] Within the institutions of "second-tier capitalism" (the lower category), a significant fraction of the population, as holder of securities (directly or within various types of funds) participates in the condition of capitalist owners, but this involvement does not basically determine their social position. To the contrary, first-tier capitalism refers to the proper capitalist classes, whose financial wealth significantly exceeds the requirements of consumption or retirement. All capital is not in pension or mutual funds.

The managerial class is not homogeneous in this respect. The lower fractions of managers, willing or not, accumulate capital for their retirement or other large expenses in various funds. The main purpose of this accumulation is to shift across time the benefits of an income whose original form was a wage, that is, storing income for the future rather than accumulating wealth. The situation is significantly different in the upper segments of management. This is where power is concentrated, and where the relationship with the upper fractions of the capitalist classes is the closest. This situation is, obviously, reflected in the levels of income and related to the notion of hybridization. The upper fractions of management enjoy significant access to ownership.

---

1. A framework introduced in G. Duménil and D. Lévy, "Neoliberal Income Trends: Wealth, Class and Ownership in the USA," *New Left Review* 30 (2004): 105–133.

---

managerial circles. This is so in the advisory boards of corporations or the management of private equity firms. Thus, financial managers are directly implied in the joint reference to the upper fractions of the capitalist classes and financial institutions, as in an extended concept of Finance that would include this social category.

Returning to the data earlier in this chapter, it is certainly not coincidental that the historical pattern of evolution of the highest wages, as in

Figure 5.1, is identical to the one observed in Figure 3.1 for the total income of the same group (while the profile of the fraction of total income accruing to the 95–99 fractile is quite distinct). A similar relationship is apparent in Figure 3.5. More research would, however, be necessary to determine which fractions are involved and through which mechanisms.

The sociopolitical consequences of such social arrangements are obvious. Hybridization at the top means convergence of objectives beyond the distinction between traditional capitalist income channels or wages in the broad definition used here. The relationship between the lower fractions of management and capitalist owners remains of a distinct nature but, overall, the alliance between the managerial and the capitalist classes was substituted for the previous alliance between the managerial and the popular classes. More than a temporary alliance is involved.

The State and Officials versus Markets and the Capitalists

Besides corporate managers, state officials are also an important component of the managerial classes. In given historical circumstances, this specific class position became a key factor within social dynamics. As already stated, it was so, for example, during the New Deal, a period of disruption of the earlier power configuration destabilized by the crisis, and intense class confrontation.

Under specific circumstances, the relationship of officials to other social groups, such as the capitalist classes, may manifest a degree of autonomy. But this shift of power in their favor is also one particular expression of the broader enhanced autonomy of the managerial classes in general, and of the containment of capitalist powers and interests. Such crisis circumstances are, however, transitional. In the case of the New Deal, the compromise was adjusted after the war, restoring the more normal relationship between social structures and government institutions. In the postwar compromise, government officials went on, however, playing a central role. This autonomy was one expression of the more general postwar managerial leadership.

Symmetrically, it is often contended that neoliberalism meant a setback of *states* in favor of *markets,* and the power of the capitalist classes is, correspondingly, interpreted in reference to market mechanisms. There would be a lot to say with respect to the fact that a society and economy in which managers enjoy a large autonomy can also be a market economy. Abstracting from such theoretical refinements, the main point here is that the characterization of the postwar and neoliberal decades in reference to states and markets, respectively, is at odds with the perspective in the present study where the state is always understood in the context of class relationships.

There is no denying the fact that, in neoliberalism, much emphasis is placed on "free-market" mechanisms, but in all countries, states acted in favor of the establishment of the new social order,[6] a condition to the imposition of neoliberalism. The tenants of neoliberalism oppose excessive state intervention whenever governments place limits on the freedom of business, protect the rights of workers, impose taxes on high incomes, and so on. Neoliberalism rejected the state of the social democratic compromise, not the state in general. Neoliberal states—as emanations and instruments of prevailing hegemonies and compromises at the top of social hierarchies—deliberately negotiated the agreements concerning free trade and the free mobility of capital that limited their own policy capability. This was, in particular, the case in Europe, with the formation of the European Union, but also in the United States (Chapter 14). The creation of the new context of neoliberal globalization was part of the deliberate objectives of the states, which mirror those of the classes they represent.

When the entrance into neoliberal globalization took the form of a transition between Sovietism (a model basically reproduced within the great majority or all so-called socialist countries) and capitalism, as in Russia, China, or Vietnam, the role of governments was and remained central in a process that can be denoted as "primitive accumulation of capital." Thus, these societies, to distinct degrees, share some of the objectives of neoliberalism, though not all of its methods. The involvement of states in such endeavors is stronger than within standard neoliberal countries, and expressed in specifically authoritarian configurations. The mix is complex, a combination of economic liberalization and state intervention, a course that the contemporary crisis will likely alter.

Overall, the role of the states is central in the establishment and preservation of class societies, making use of their legal potential and resorting to straightforward violence, during neoliberalism as before, but not less under neoliberalism. States are the central institutions in which the class hierarchies and compromises of each social order are defined. Depending on the political features of power configurations, more or less space is allowed for the expression of the tensions among the components of the compromise, but the states are always the institutions in which such compromises are defined and the instruments that ensure their prevalence.

6

A Theoretical Framework

The analysis in the previous chapter takes the tripolar class pattern as given. No attempt is made at laying the theoretical foundations of this approach. The purpose of the first section below is to establish such foundations in a framework of Marxist inspiration, adjusted to the features of modern capitalism. It elaborates on the distinction between ownership and management, separates between the capitalist and managerial classes, and introduces the category of popular classes in which clerical personnel and production workers are jointly considered. The second section summarizes the overall typology of social orders, including the alternative potential combination without historical precedent introduced in Chapter 1. In this framework, a renewed meaning can be given to the traditional notion of political orientation to the Right or Left.

The Socialization of Production: Ownership and Management

Breaking the alleged homogeneous social position of wage earners within social relations raises difficult theoretical issues to which much research has been devoted. In the United States, the development of a salaried management and the new pattern at the top of social hierarchies were the source of a broad literature concerning managerial capitalism[1] (Box 5.1) and, beginning with the managerial revolution, of some concern on the part of capitalist owners.[2] The focus on the theory of managerial capitalism is specifically on managers. Managerial and clerical personnel, taken together, are, however, commonly described as the new middle classes. Despite the explicit reference to classes, this latter characterization is often used to blur the existence of class divides. Marxist scholars alternatively saw in managerial and clerical personnel a new petty bourgeoisie or components of a broad proletarian class.[3] The viewpoint here is at odds with this latter interpretation. The hierarchy of wages is not simply the expression of the compensation of distinct degrees of skillfulness in the execution of specific tasks within a homogeneous production process. Such high wages are the remuneration of management (in a broad sense including the central or local organizational tasks of officials) within a class configuration manifesting distinct positions vis-à-vis relations of production. As reflected in these earlier controversies, the problem is actually twofold. A first issue is how to interpret the emergence of intermediate social groups in between traditional capitalist and proletarian classes. A second issue is the separation between the managerial and clerical components.

The analysis below is conducted in five steps:

1. *Classes and incomes.* A central element in an interpretation of class patterns is the tight relationship between income channels and classes. Marx, in the last chapter of *Capital* as published by Friedrich Engels, defines classes in relation to the various categories of income.[4] These income channels are wages, profits, and ground rent. Contrary to the "vulgar economy," Marx considers the two latter components as forms of surplus value, and sees, in wages, the prices of the labor power of the workers from which this surplus value is extracted. The same approach must be applied to modern capitalism, but the new point is that the high wages of management must also be included among the forms of appropriation of a social surplus. This is all the more true as capitalism evolves because of the historical progress of management. The difficulty comes from the fact that such high wages are called "wages" like any other form of labor compensation. There is no distinct category of income, as in a terminology like *salaries* and *wages*.

It is, unfortunately, not possible, neither theoretically nor empirically, to separate between such high wages and the bulk of wages, or to provide reliable estimates concerning the possible size of the surplus appropriated by high wage brackets. Available data suggests, however, the importance of this mechanism. (A ballpark figure is suggested in Box 6.1.)

2. *Relations of production and classes.* Another basic reference in the analysis of class patterns is their tight relationship to relations of production. The channels by which a social surplus is appropriated and distributed as income match prevailing relations of production. Thus, new configurations of relations of production imply new class patterns, and reciprocally. The correspondence is so strict that it is sometimes denoted as a "homology."

> **Box 6.1**
> **Surplus Labor Compensation and Profits**
>
> The analysis of income trends in the United States fundamentally questions the notion of "labor compensation," or in Marx's terminology the price of "labor power," when applied to the upper wage brackets. Two perspectives can be adopted. First, "labor compensation" on top of the income pyramid can be interpreted as the price of the labor power of a category of workers whose labor is recognized as "complex labor." This view is coherent with the dual traditional perspective, which opposes capitalists, on the one hand, and workers, on the other. Second, an alternative approach, coherent with the tripolar configuration, is to consider the high price of such categories of labor as the "form" of a social surplus, along with the straightforward appropriation of surplus value, a form of "surplus labor compensation" garnered by the higher fractions of wage earners, above the wages of the great mass of wage earners.
>
> The theoretical implications of this analysis clearly lie beyond the limits of the present study. The ambition of what follows is only to draw attention to the importance of the amounts involved. Empirically, the difficulty is to provide an approximation of a "standard labor compensation." The same source of data as in Figures 3.1 and 5.1 is used here. The standard labor compensation is estimated as the average labor compensation of the 0–95 income fractile. For the average of the ten years, 1997–2006, this standard compensation
>
> *(continued)*

This analytical framework is traditionally applied to the distinction between various modes of production, for example, feudalism and capitalism. Relations of production refer to the position of various groups vis-à-vis the means of production (access to goods, constructions, natural resources, etc.), including the capability to command labor power. In feudalism, the lords could benefit from the product of the labor of serves through various mechanisms such as, on the part of serves, working on the land of the lord, giving over a fraction of the crop, or paying rent in money. In capitalism, the capitalist class owns the means of production and extracts a surplus value from workers forced to sell their labor power since they have no access to means of production measuring up to the requirements of competition in the period considered.

(continued)
amounted to 80 percent of the average labor compensation of all wage earners.[1] Applying this percentage to the private sector as in National Income and Product Accounts (NIPA) in 2007, this calculation estimates the total standard and surplus compensations at $5,307 billion and $1,060 billion, respectively.

The purpose of this exercise is to compare the $1,060 billion of surplus labor compensation to profits as of 2007. Profits distributed as dividends were $642 billion and retained profits were $333 billion. Thus, the surplus labor compensation appears 1.6 times larger than profits paid out as dividends and even slightly superior to total profits.

One can parenthetically stress that, independent of any of the above estimates, dividends amounted to 10 percent of labor compensation, standard and surplus jointly considered, for the entire private economy.

---

1. An inquiry by the Bureau of Labor Statistics (BLS) provides rather detailed information concerning wages in the U.S. economy (www.bls.gov/ncs/ect/home.htm). From the entire list of occupations, one can select four "basic" categories that account for more than 40 percent of total employment that could be judged typical of the category of labor behind a "standard labor compensation": (1) sales and retail occupations, (2) office and administrative support, (3) production occupation, and (4) transportation and material moving occupation. In 2007, the average yearly compensation for the four categories amounted to 82 percent of the average labor compensation for the entire economy, an estimate close to the one retained in the present calculation.

A closer examination of historical dynamics suggests the use of these same basic principles in the investigation of historical transformations within a given mode of production. Thus, a periodization—the distinction between various phases within a mode of production—is involved, more detailed than in the analysis of the broad succession of modes of production. Feudalism as well as capitalism went through such phases. Crucial to the analysis here is the interpretation of the three revolutions at the turn of the twentieth century that ushered in modern capitalism. Transformations of relations of production, class patterns, and income channels were all basic aspects of the establishment of modern capitalism.

3. *Ownership and control.* The main point concerning relations of production is that, prior to modern capitalism, it was possible to treat jointly the two basic facets of the ownership of the means of production known

as "ownership in the strict sense"—"ownership" for short—and "control," that is, management. The institutions in which ownership and control are expressed, as well as class patterns, underwent major transformations at the turn of the twentieth century.

The joint evolution of these two sets of developments is revealing of the nature of the transformations. They cannot be interpreted as any casual institutional change. Instead, they must be understood as smaller links in the long chain of the overall historical dynamics of which modes of production are the broader links. A direction in history is implied (Box 1.2), since the transformation of the institutions in which the ownership of the means of production is embedded is the product of the gradual sophistication of the social coordination of production. These trends are manifest in the growth of autonomous organizations (typically enterprises), nationally and internationally, the development of transportation and communication, and the supervision emanating from central institutions (private organizations, government, and international institutions). This is what Marx used to call the "socialization of production."

As a result of the separation between the two components of the ownership of the means of production—ownership supported by securities (stock shares and bonds) and the delegation of management to salaried employees under the supervision of shareholders[5]—the class of salaried managers grew in number and importance within private corporations at a distance from owners. The number of officials within central and local governments increased in parallel. Both components of management in this broad sense were surrounded by what has been denoted as "white collars," actually clerical personnel, in the strict sense, and other components such as maintenance or commercial personnel.

4. *The polarization between managers and clerical personnel.* As the delegation of management to a salaried personnel advanced, a sharp polarization occurred between the upper and lower strata, as in the phrase "managerial and clerical personnel." Among the salaried personnel in charge of conception, organization, trade, accounting, financing, and so on, the division of tasks was not merely *functional* but *hierarchical,* and this hierarchy still defines a basic feature of social relations in contemporary capitalism. Typical of this polarization is the concentration of initiative and direction at the top, and execution at the lower levels in the hierarchy, as between managers and clerical workers. The conditions in which clerical labor are accomplished are strictly defined from above. In a number of activities, the

work of clerical labor takes increasingly features proper to production labor. And these hierarchies are mirrored in those of wages.

5. *The transformation of production labor and the formation of the popular classes.* Symmetrically, production labor was also the object of major transformations. Sociologists point to the fact that the labor of production workers took, more and more, the forms of clerical labor, in particular in relation to the development of information technologies.[6] Although differences remain significant in many fields in contemporary capitalism, it appears gradually more adequate to refer to the popular classes,[7] considering jointly production workers and commercial-clerical workers. At least, this is a useful simplification.

Overall, for the traditional pattern of the new middle classes (managerial personnel and clerical personnel) between capitalists and production workers, it appears much more relevant to substitute the tripolar configuration that combines the capitalists, managerial classes, and popular classes as in <u>Diagram 1.1</u>. This framework has major advantages over the traditional capitalists-workers dual pattern. First, it acknowledges management as a new class relationship, a key to the understanding of contemporary capitalism. Second, it provides theoretical foundations to the loose categories of the upper classes or the upper income brackets, directly suggested by empirical observation, as in the previous chapters. "Upper classes" refers to both ownership and management, capitalists and managers, with significant overlap. Third, it lays the foundations for an analysis of the popular classes, and solves the problems posed by the observation of the numerical decline of production workers in the strict sense.

A Typology of Alternative Social Orders

The tripolar pattern of class relationships—capitalist classes / managerial classes / popular classes—provides a simple framework in which alternative social orders can be formally classified. Each of the three such orders proper to modern capitalism can be characterized by a form of unequal social alliance (a power configuration), under the leadership of one class. (The term "compromise" emphasizes the tensions still inherent in such social arrangements.) A fundamental criterion in such a typology of social orders is whether the prevailing class alliance is established upward in the direction of the upper classes or downward toward the popular classes. The first option is typical of the compromise between the capitalists and the managerial classes as in neoliberalism, and the second, of the postwar compromise between the managerial and the popular classes. In terms of the traditional distinction between the Right and the Left, the first configuration can be said "toward the Right" and the second, "toward the Left" (or to the Right or Left). This is a crucial distinction that provides class foundations to political orientations.

In this classification, it is possible to further separate between alternative cases depending on the leadership exerted by either one of the two groups participating in the alliance. Within the compromise to the Right, the capitalist classes may lead, as in neoliberalism, but a leadership of the managerial classes would also be possible. Within the compromise to the Left, the managerial classes may assume the leadership, but the symmetrical case of a popular leadership could also be contemplated. Thus, four configurations are defined in Table 6.1.

A major difference between the third and fourth configurations and the two first configurations is the absence of historical precedents in the United States, which renders their definition more problematic.

In the two first configurations, a direction is meant, as in the expressions "toward the Right" or "toward the Left." It is possible to be more specific,

Table 6.1 Alternative social orders

	Alliance between:	Under the leadership of:		
Toward the Right	Capitalists/ Managers	[1] Capitalists (neoliberalism)	[3] Managers (neomanagerial capitalism)	
Toward the Left	Managers/ Popular classes		[2] Managers (postwar compromise)	[4] Popular classes ("socialism")

[1] A compromise between the capitalist and the managerial classes, toward the Right, under the leadership of the capitalist classes, as in the first financial hegemony and neoliberalism.

[2] A compromise between the managerial and the popular classes, toward the Left, under the leadership of the managerial classes, as in the New Deal and postwar compromise.

[3] A compromise between the capitalist and the managerial classes, toward the Right, under the leadership of the managerial classes.

[4] A compromise between the managers and the popular classes, toward the Left, under the leadership of the popular classes.

and neoliberalism can be denoted as "Right" and the postwar compromise as "Center Left."

In the analysis of the third configuration [3]—a compromise to the Right under managerial leadership—a comparison with alternative configurations can be helpful:[8]

1. In the New Deal and postwar compromise [2], there were three main aspects. Managerial classes played a key role in corporate governance and policies; a new attitude, more favorable to labor, prevailed; significant limits were placed on the hegemony of the capitalist classes. The basic idea in the third configuration is to treat distinctly these various aspects. This new configuration would manifest the features proper to the leadership of the managerial classes without the alliance with labor, and a degree of containment of capitalist interests, though moderated to some extent, given that the compromise is between the upper classes. This social arrangement can be broadly characterized as (1) a managerial capitalism, but (2) without the social features of the postwar compromise. In the first respect, this power configuration could be denoted as a "neomanagerial capitalism."

2. Such a social order can also be defined in comparison to neoliberalism. In neoliberalism, the compromise is at the top of the social hierarchies under the leadership of the capitalist classes. Within the third configuration, the compromise is also established upward, but the leadership passes from the capitalist classes to the managerial segment of the upper classes. The new aspect is the alteration of the balance of power and income between the components of the upper classes along the dividing line ownership/management, with distinct objectives and methods. In the reference above to a neomanagerial capitalism, there is obviously a play on words with the denomination "neoliberalism." Neoliberalism was, to a large extent, a new liberalism, despite the crucial role played by the state in the establishment and functioning of this social order. The same is true of neomanagerial capitalism, a new managerial capitalism, although the absence of the welfare component of the postwar decades and the alliance among the upper classes alter significantly its social features.

Concerning the income pattern that might prevail within such a power configuration, two additional factors must be taken into account:

1. It is important to consider the consequences of what has been denoted above as "a process of hybridization at the top." The new managerial trends in this social arrangement would typically favor managerial income channels (high wages, always in the broad sense) in comparison to

traditional capitalist channels (dividends and interest), but the same individuals, to some extent, benefit from the two types of income flows.

2. A strong determination to correct the U.S. macro trajectory would require a form of containment of all high incomes. This necessity would reflect the amplitude of the adjustment to be realized on the part of all upper classes to straighten the trajectory of the U.S. economy.

The fourth option [4] in Table 6.1 is also without historical precedent, since the victory of alleged socialist revolutions in the past always led to the establishment of new class hierarchies. But radical alternatives can also be contemplated, in which a popular leadership would prevail. Such a project is typical of political orientations in parties at the left of what is called "the Left," or in the alter globalist movement. This is where the criticism of the specifically neoliberal features of capitalism and of capitalism per se can be found. Within such radical political orientations, one finds a broad spectrum of alternative social projects—a mix whose exact contents are difficult to define. Underlying the radical discourse that emphasizes the power of popular classes, one can detect political perspectives, located somewhere in between the second and fourth configurations above. Socialism is obviously in the minds of those most committed to radical social change. The discussion of such far-reaching social transformations lies, however, beyond the limits of the present study.[9]

IV

Financialization and Globalization: Lifting Barriers—Losing Control

Financialization and globalization jointly refer to deeply rooted historical tendencies in capitalism, and this property prohibits the straightforward fusion of the two notions within that of neoliberalism. Nonetheless, neoliberalism conferred specific features on the two sets of developments, and neoliberalism without neoliberal financialization and neoliberal globalization would be something else. Thus, the two sets of mechanisms are located directly downstream of neoliberalism in Diagram 2.1.

Chapters 7 and 8 successively address the transformations of the financial sector, and the real and financial components of globalization. The emphasis is on the decade preceding the crisis, a period of tremendous developments in these two respects. The objective is to provide basic information concerning a broad specter of phenomena relevant to the analysis of the contemporary crisis. Chapter 9 is devoted to the fragile structure that resulted from such trends.

The conclusion is straightforward. The stage was set for a major collapse, although the exact channel by which the disaster would come to the world remained undetermined.

7

A New Financial Sector

As could be expected, neoliberalism and neoliberal globalization deeply altered the structure and functioning of the financial sector. In many instances, this was specifically true after 2000. The present chapter does not purport to systematically account for these trends but to draw the attention to the dramatic expansion of financial mechanisms, and to locate in which institutions and through which instruments this was performed, as a preliminary to the analysis of the crisis.

The mere consideration of the masses of assets and debt provides a straightforward illustration of what the size of financial expansion is in neoliberalism. Table 7.1 compares a few figures as of the end of 2006, prior to the crisis.

The first section below provides a broad picture of the masses of assets held by all U.S. financial institutions.[1] The second section is devoted to the expansion of debt in the U.S. economy, in particular the debt of the financial sector. The remaining sections introduce three broad categories of mechanisms to which reference is made in the technical analysis of the financial component of the crisis: (1) conduits, structured investment vehicles, and asset-backed commercial paper; (2) leverage buyouts; and (3) derivatives contracts.

Financial Institutions

A straightforward approach to financialization is the consideration of the comparative masses of financial assets held by various categories of institutions and their transformation over time. Figure 7.1 shows such totals for the U.S. economy, as percentage of U.S. GDP. Institutions are classified

Table 7.1 How big is "big"? (as of 2006, trillions of dollars)

Total derivatives (notional) worldwide (11)	415
Global financial assets (7)	167
Gross world product (PPP dollars)^c (6)	77
Assets of the 1000 largest banks worldwide (10)	74
Assets under management worldwide (500 largest managers) (8)	64
Domestic market capitalization (all stock exchanges) (3)	52
Financial wealth of high-net worth individuals (4)	37
Total foreign assets of banks worldwide (11)	26.2
Financial assets directly held by U.S. households^a (1)	21.8
Assets of U.S. pension and mutual funds (1)	18.5
U.S. assets held by the rest of the world (1)	14.4
Total liabilities of U.S. households (1)	13.4
Tangible assets of U.S. nonfinancial corporations (1)	13.4
U.S. GDP (2)	13.2
Financial assets of U.S. commercial banks (1)	10.2
Gross market value of derivative contracts (11)	9.7
Total liabilities of U.S. federal government (1)	6.2
Financial wealth of billionaires (4)	3.5
Foreign exchange markets, daily turnover^b (11)	4.0
Assets of sovereign wealth funds (5)	3.0
GDP of Africa (PPP dollars)^c (6)	1.8
Assets under management by hedge funds (9)	1.7

Numbers in parentheses refer to sources in Appendix B.

a. Life insurance reserves, pension funds reserves, and equity in noncorporate business excluded.

b. Average April 2007.

c. Purchasing power parity (PPP) exchange rates are virtual exchange rates that would equalize price levels in the countries considered.

in four components.[2] With the exception of the Federal Reserve, the variables cover all U.S. financial institutions.

The first group (——) is the composite of commercial banking (investment and deposit banks) and insurance companies, plus savings institutions and credit unions. The figure reveals a steady and moderate rise of the variable from 107 percent of GDP in 1980 to 157 percent in 2009. The second variable (— —) describes the tremendous expansion of the assets of pension, mutual, and closed-end[3] funds during the first two neoliberal decades. In 1980, they amounted to 33 percent of GDP, they reached 149

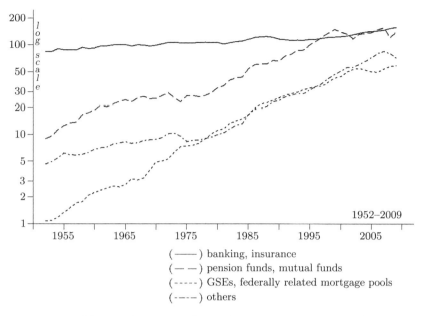

(———) banking, insurance
(— —) pension funds, mutual funds
(-----) GSEs, federally related mortgage pools
(- - - -) others

Figure 7.1 Total financial assets: U.S. financial institutions (percentage of GDP, yearly). The data cover all U.S. financial institutions, with the exception of the Federal Reserve.

percent in 1999, and peaked at 156 percent in 2007. The masses of capital involved are handled by asset managers, a major industry and actor within neoliberalism. The concentration of huge masses of capital in the funds controlled by asset managers allows for the exercise of the discipline of capital. The muscles of such institutions were multiplied during the neoliberal decades. The third sector (-----) is GSEs (notably, Fannie Mae and Freddie Mac, originally federal agencies) and Ginnie Mae, an agency also closely related to the crisis. Besides the steep upward trend, one can notice their quasi stagnation in relation to GDP after 2000. The last category of financial institutions (- - - -) is the group of newcomers, the really interesting new generation with respect to the crisis. Who are they? Not too surprisingly, the major component is the sector of private-label issuers of asset-backed securities (ABSs) (that is, issuers other than Ginnie Mae, Fannie Mae, and Freddie Mac), and security brokers and dealers.[4] Between 1980 and 1997, the group grew at about the same speed as funds and GSEs, but they went on growing during the latter years, up to 2007.

The rise of the last two sectors was at the origin of the rising debt of the financial sector, a major development to which the following section is devoted.

Growing Indebtedness

Rising indebtedness is a familiar factor in the analysis of the crisis. Much attention is devoted to the soaring debt of households, and not erroneously, but the growing indebtedness of the financial sector is also a major feature of the neoliberal decades.

Table 7.2 documents the rise of the debts of all U.S. sectors as a percentage of GDP. This growth remained moderate after World War II, from 126 percent in 1952 to 155 percent in 1980, and exploded during the neoliberal decades, up to 353 percent in 2008.

In 1952, the debt of the financial sector amounted to 3 percent of GDP and, in 1980, still to only 20 percent, to be compared to 119 percent in 2008. Table 7.2 also shows that, in 2008, the debt of the financial sector was larger than the debt of households, followed by the debt of the nonfinancial business sector. Thus, the indebtedness of the financial sector is a new and spectacular phenomenon, typical of the neoliberal decades. This dramatic increase was mostly the effect of the rise of the issuance of securities by the latter two sectors in Figure 7.1, notably private-label issuers of ABSs and GSEs, to finance the loans to households as in the procedures of securitization, in which loans or securities are financed by the issuance of new securities. Contrary to the above components, the bulk of the debt of households and the debt of government share the common property of

Table 7.2 Gross debt of U.S. sectors (end of year, percent of GDP)

	1952	1980	2008
Nonfinancial sectors	124	136	234
Households	25	48	96
Business	30	51	78
Government	68	37	60
Financial sector	3	20	119
Total	126	155	353

Debt: Credit market instruments.

directly financing a flow of demand in goods and services for consumption and investment purposes (the residential investment of households and equipment and infrastructure by the government).

Any agent may borrow and lend (in credit market instruments). Thus, both gross and net debts (debt minus assets, both in credit market instruments) are involved. Table 7.3 shows that, as could be expected, the financial sector is a net lender.[5] In 2008, its loans amount to the equivalent of 271 percent of GDP, and its borrowings to 119 percent (Table 7.2). Thus, the financial sector appears as a net lender for 152 percent, as in the last column of Table 7.3. Conversely, nonfinancial sectors are predominantly borrowers, with gross borrowings amounting to 234 percent of GDP in 2008, lendings to 42 percent and, thus, net borrowings reaching 192 percent of GDP.

The rise of borrowings in the financial sector is typically the fact of institutions distinct from banks, either truly autonomous entities such as the special-purpose vehicles of securitization of private-label issuers, where assets have been pooled when the entity was established, or GSEs and agencies. (Notions such as securitization and vehicle are defined in Box 7.1.) Huge masses of assets, loans or securities, are transferred to these entities and financed by the issuance of new securities. As is well known, the securitization by private-label issuers was a crucial factor in the occurrence of the crisis. (They are analyzed in Part VI.)

Independent of the exact procedures, the important finding here is the emergence of the financial sector as a major borrower during neoliberalism. The difference between the figures for 2008 and the 1950s is striking. In 2008, the gross borrowings of the financial sector represented 76 percent

Table 7.3 Net debt of U.S. sectors (end of year, percent of GDP)

	1952	1980	2008
Nonfinancial sectors	79	102	192
Households	-3	30	68
Business	19	40	67
Government	60	25	48
Financial sector	-82	-103	-152
Rest of the world	3	1	-40
Total	0	0	0

Net debt: Credit market instruments.

Box 7.1
Securitization and Asset-Backed Security Issuance

Originally, the term "securitization" was coined to refer to the transformation of loans (in the assets of financial corporations) into securities, a procedure allowing for the sale of these loans to investors by the originators of the loans. The securities, thus issued, are known as asset-backed securities (ABSs).

A number of loans are pooled into a special entity, a "vehicle" (a new entity, typically another corporation), and securities (bonds) are correspondingly issued and sold to investors. The loans are the "collateral" of the bonds. The money resulting from the sale of the bonds goes to the original holders of the loans.

Once the entity has been established, the amortization of the loans and the accompanying interest payment are transferred to the benefit of the holders of the securities issued. This is denoted as "pass-through." A specific feature of securitization, which justifies the denomination "asset-backed," is that the responsibility for the service of the new securities is neither on the originator nor on the vehicle that issued them. The holders of ABSs are con-

(continued)

---

of those of households and government considered jointly, and more than each separately!

Conduits, Structured Investment Vehicles, and Asset-Backed Commercial Paper

Commercial paper conduits and structured investment vehicles (SIVs) are (or "were," since they were much affected by the crisis) two major examples of off-balance-sheet entities (OBSEs) (Box 9.3). Their common aspect is the financing of long-term assets by shorter-term securities. They earn profits from the difference in yields between the typically short-term securities they issue, such as commercial paper and medium-term notes (MTNs), and the longer-term assets they purchase, typically the product of securitization. This is a potentially very profitable activity, but also highly leveraged and risky, and this explains why banks developed it off–balance sheet. It was at the origin of large borrowings on the part of the financial sector.

(continued)

sidered the "owners" of the loans. If a loss is incurred due to defaults on the debt, it is borne by the owners of the new securities, not by their originators, or by their issuers who acted as ephemeral intermediaries.

There are two facets to this mechanism: financing and risk transfer. On the one hand, securitization is a powerful mechanism that allows for the re financing of institutions, such as banks. The structure of the balance sheet of the originator is transformed, improving basic financial ratios. On the other hand, this procedure is a powerful lever to transfer the risks associated with the holding of certain categories of assets.

This instrument appeared so efficient that ABSs were issued in the same fashion on the basis of already existing securities (making the term "securitization" somewhat of a misnomer). ABSs are pooled in the same manner within new entities, and new securities are issued along the same procedure. Thus, ABSs may be based on securities, not only loans, including already existing ABSs!

Securitization is performed either by GSEs and the agency Ginnie Mae or by private-label ABS issuers.

Commercial paper conduits are large vehicles whose basic characteristic, as their name indicates, is the issuance of commercial paper that provides 100 percent of their financing, while the bulk of SIVs' funding comes from MTNs, supplemented by commercial paper. SIVs invest in longer-maturity corporate bonds and lower-rated structured credit products, such as traditional long-term assets, ABSs, and collateralized debt obligations (CDOs).[6] In 2007, the total balance sheet of U.S. conduits amounted to $1.4 trillion, and that of SIVs worldwide, to about $400 billion.[7]

The issuance of asset-backed commercial paper (ABCP), the main source of financing of conduits, provides a spectacular illustration of the financial explosion, specifically after 2000, in particular from 2005 onward. This is shown in Figure 7.2, where the first variable (——) is the stock of ABCP. At the end of 2004, ABCP outstanding amounted to $689 billion. In the second week of August 2007, this amount culminated at $1,226 billion and fell to $734 billion at the end of 2008 and to $416 billion in August 2009. The second variable (-----) accounts for the stock of commercial paper other than ABCP used by large corporations to ensure their liquidity.

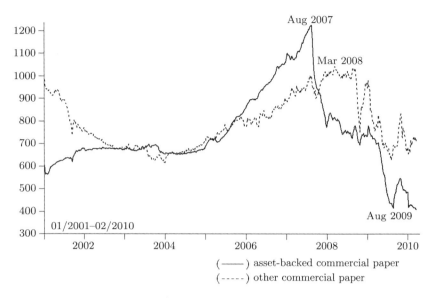

Figure 7.2 U.S. commercial paper outstanding (billions of dollars, weekly).

They were also part of the financial boom though to a lesser extent. They culminated in March 2008 (and fell in a later phase of the crisis, more an effect than a cause).

Leveraging and Leveraged Buyouts

How could financial corporations, prior to the crisis, claim returns of 15 percent or above? In the obtainment of such performances, the use of funds other than a corporation's own funds, financed by deposits and borrowings, played a crucial role. With exceptions, such as operations on derivative markets or sharp rises of stock prices, there is no financial operation whose original return reaches such levels. But when such activity is financed by other investments (typically bonds) content with lower returns, the profit rate on own funds may reach much higher levels. Leveraging must be understood as a "profitability multiplier," a traditional instrument in the functioning of capitalism. (Enterprises always borrowed funds at the cost of interest rates inferior to profit rates.) But leveraging may reach outstanding levels in the financial sector or in the financial operations of the nonfinancial sector.

Leveraged buyouts (LBOs) are one of the financial activities to which much attention has been paid. An enterprise is purchased, reorganized, possibly broken into various segments, and sold. Typically, a private equity firm (the sponsor) buys a company, financing the transaction by considerable borrowings, with the assets of the purchased firm used as collateral. The percentage of debt typically ranges between 50 percent and 80 percent of the overall financing but, in some instances, may be closer to 100 percent. (A special case is management buyouts, in which management is the sponsor.) The purpose of such endeavors is obvious. Very large returns are obtained if the buyout succeeds, that is, if the corporation purchased is sold at a high price after reorganization. But major failures are also part of the history of LBOs.

LBOs are another component typical of the wild financialization after 2000. This is clearly illustrated in Figure 7.3 that shows the rise of LBOs in the United States and Europe. Before 2003, the flow (——) of LBOs in the United States fluctuated around $12 billion (yearly average 1993–2003). In 2007, the maximum was reached at almost $380 billion, a multiplication by a factor larger than thirty. The figure also shows (-----) that a similar wave of LBOs was also observed in Europe, peaking at $290 billion in 2007.

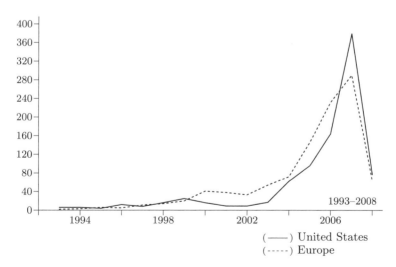

Figure 7.3 Flows of LBOs in the United States and Europe (billions of dollars, yearly).

Derivative Contracts

Last, but certainly not least, another major development is the rise of derivative markets, a juicy source of profits but also one of the riskiest fields of financial activity. Derivative markets are considered as the most explosive components of financial operations (Box 7.2), as confirmed by the final collapse of some of them during the crisis.

Derivatives are financial contracts in which a payment will occur to the benefit of one contractor at a certain future date depending on a predetermined event. The price of a share on a stock market, the price of a commodity, the exchange rate of a currency, the interest rate on a loan or its default are typical such events. Derivative contracts can be used as insurance, that is, a protection (hedging) against an unfavorable event, for example, a default on a loan or the rise of the price of a commodity that one of the parties wants to buy at a certain date. They can provide actual financial services but are also instruments of speculation. They are highly leveraged and a large degree of uncertainty is involved in derivatives and, in all these respects, they are considered highly risky (for example, insuring against defaults on securities that are not held).

The vast majority of such transactions occur over the counter (OTC), that is, as straightforward contracts between two participants without intermediary. Such transactions are unregulated. The remainder of transactions is performed within exchanges (in the United States, notably the Chicago Board of Trade, also in Europe, Korea, etc.) and subject to margin requirements, meaning that a deposit must be made to attest the commitment of one of the parties and limit the risks of the other.

Notional (or face) amounts outstanding are the nominal values used to calculate payments (for example, the value of a loan).[8] In most instances, the risks run by contractors are considerably lower, though still tremendously high. The gross market values provide a better (and quantitatively much smaller) estimate of risks incurred. The calculation of market values simulates, at a given date, that all contracts are settled according to ongoing market prices and risks. The amount, thus determined, is the average anticipated value payment, given the present assessment of risks.

Derivatives in general are not new,[9] but the total sums involved are huge and their notional value grew dramatically during the neoliberal decades. The global notional value of OTC derivatives reached amazing levels after 2005. The total worldwide soared from about $72 trillion in June 1998 to

Box 7.2
Time Bombs

The famous billionaire Warren Buffett made the following statement concerning derivatives in 2002:

> [Charlie and I] view derivatives as time bombs, both for the parties that deal in them and the economic system. . . . Before a contract is settled, the counter-parties record profits and losses—often huge in amounts—in their current earnings statements without so much as a penny changing hands. Those who trade derivatives are usually paid, in whole or part, on "earnings" calculated by mark-to-market accounting.[1]
>
> Another problem about derivatives is that they can exacerbate trouble that a corporation has run into for completely unrelated reasons. This pile-on effect occurs because many derivative contracts require that a company suffering a credit downgrade immediately supply collateral to counter-parties. Imagine then that a company is downgraded because of general adversity and that its derivatives instantly kick in with their requirement, imposing an unexpected and enormous demand for cash collateral on the company. The need to meet this demand can then throw the company into a liquidity crisis that may, in some cases, trigger still more downgrades. It all becomes a spiral that can lead to a corporate meltdown.[2]

---

1. "Mark-to-market" means that the values of assets are estimated at their present value on a market.
2. Berkshire Hathaway Report (Omaha, Neb.: Berkshire Hathaway, Inc., 2002), 13 and 14, www.berkshirehathaway.com/2002ar/2002ar.pdf.

$684 trillion in June 2008. The major component is interest rate contracts reaching $458 trillion in June 2008. Specifically relevant to the analysis of the contemporary crisis are credit default swaps (CDSs). CDSs were created in the mid-1990s and grew to $58 trillion. They are eight times smaller than interest rate contracts.

After 2000, not only OTC derivatives increased, but also derivatives traded within organized exchanges. The notional amount of such derivatives was about $2 trillion in 1990, $14 trillion in 2000, and culminated slightly below $100 trillion in 2007.

Concerning gross market values, total contracts worldwide reached $20 trillion in June 2008 ($32 trillion in December 2008), about thirty-five

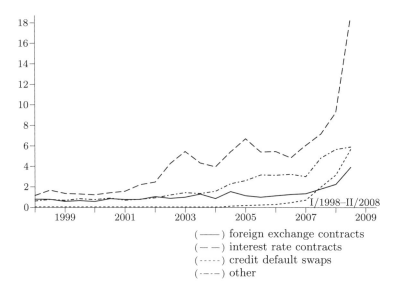

Figure 7.4 Gross market value of OTC derivatives contracts worldwide (trillions of dollars, semiannual).

times less than notional amounts, but "$20 trillion" means more than U.S. GDP. The main component is still interest rate contracts that amounted to slightly less than half of the total in June 2008. Figure 7.4 clearly illustrates the sharp rise of derivative contracts after 2002, when a first acceleration is observed. A new increase occurred at the end of the period. The outburst of CDSs is striking. Within the category "other," the growth is concentrated in commodity contracts, not equity-linked contracts.

The diagnosis is the same as for earlier instruments: (1) growth during the neoliberal decades, (2) explosion after 2000, and (3) a final hike at the end of the decade.

8

Free Trade and the Global
Financial Boom after 2000

The present chapter recalls and documents the main aspects of neoliberal globalization, the combination of tightly interconnected trends. Free trade, the free international mobility of capital, the globalization of financial institutions and mechanisms, and foreign exchange transactions are the four main components. The emphasis is on the sharp acceleration of globalization, real and financial, since the mid-1990s, in particular after 2000, one among the basic determinants of the contemporary crisis. The same acceleration is observed as in the previous chapter.

Inasmuch as possible the perspective here is that of the global economy. Due to the emphasis on the United States, the specific situation of the country in globalization, and the lack of coherent global data, the U.S. economy is used as a privileged example.

Foreign Trade and Direct Investment Abroad

A first feature of neoliberal globalization is the expansion of foreign trade. This was achieved gradually by bilateral agreements, negotiation within the General Agreement on Tariffs and Trade (GATT) after World War II,[1] within the WTO from 1995 onward, and by the establishment of zones of free trade as in Europe.

The difference between the first decades after World War II and neoliberalism is striking. The variable in Figure 8.1 is the share of exports of commodities (also imports since trade is balanced globally) within the GWP. Prior to the first oil shock, foreign trade amounted to slightly more than 10 percent of GWP. At this point the profile of the variable was affected by the sudden fluctuation of relative prices (notably, the rise in the

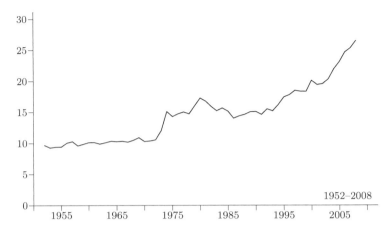

Figure 8.1 Foreign trade (exports) worldwide (percentage of GWP, yearly).

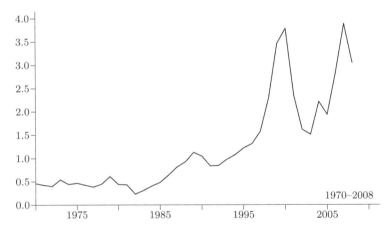

Figure 8.2 Flows of direct investment abroad worldwide (percentage of GWP, yearly).

price of oil). After this break, the upward trend of foreign trade prevailed gradually and remained moderate up to the mid-1990s. One can then observe a significant acceleration in two steps, the first step up to the first years after 2000, and after. A percentage of 26.5 was reached in 2008.

Although flows of DIA amount to a much lesser percentage of GWP than international trade, a similar profile is obtained in Figure 8.2, notably the sharp acceleration in the later years. Up to 1980, the percentage of the flows of DIA worldwide fluctuated around 0.5 percent of GWP. The steep neoliberal trend upward was then established, up to 3.9 percent in 2007. The perspective here is on historical trends, but it is impossible to abstract from the tremendous bulge of DIA during the second half of the 1990s, a movement that must be related to the boom in information technologies.

An important difference with imports and exports is that flows of DIA accumulate. This cumulative effect is spectacular. In 2007, the outstanding stock of DIA worldwide reached about 29 percent of GWP and 25 percent of global stock-market capitalization.[2]

The U.S. Economy in Globalization

The United States is a major player in global capitalism. The present section emphasizes two crucial aspects of globalization from the viewpoint of this country: (1) the international flows of capital income, and (2) the globalization of financing channels as in the purchase of newly issued U.S. securities.

The rise of direct investment and nondirect investment in foreign countries throughout the world manifests itself in a simultaneous increase of global income flows derived from such investment (corporate profits from

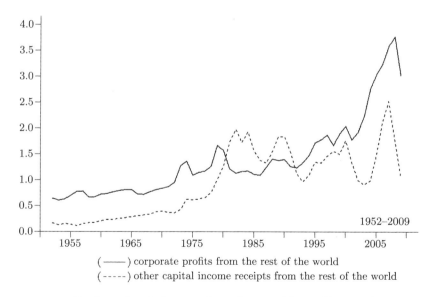

(——) corporate profits from the rest of the world
(-----) other capital income receipts from the rest of the world

Figure 8.3 Profits and capital income from the rest of the world: United States (percentage of U.S. GDP, yearly).

the rest of the world—with its two components, profits retained abroad within the affiliates of transnational corporations, and interest and dividends paid out by affiliates to the U.S. parent corporation—and other capital income). The first variable (——) in Figure 8.3 measures the flows of corporate profits from the rest of the world generated by U.S. DIA, as a percentage of U.S. GDP. One can observe that the variable actually increased more rapidly prior to neoliberalism than during the 1980s. New trends are, however, apparent from the 1990s onward. During this decade, the variable rose from 1.4 percent of GDP to 2.0 percent. The upward trend in the last phase, that is, after 2000, appears particularly steep (3.8 percent in 2008). The second variable (-----) accounts for other capital income from investment abroad (deposits, loans, and portfolio investment in securities). The break with the establishment of neoliberalism is, here, spectacular, an effect of the sharp increase in interest rates. On can observe at the end of the period the depressing effect of the 2001 recession and the

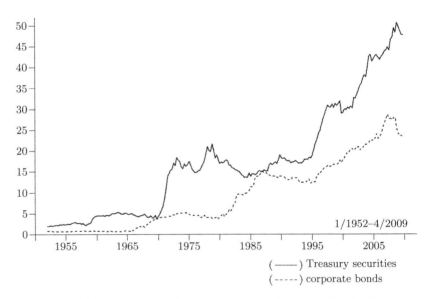

(——) Treasury securities
(-----) corporate bonds

Figure 8.4 U.S. Treasury securities or corporate bonds outstanding held by the rest of the world (percentage of total Treasury securities and total corporate bonds outstanding, quarterly). The steep upward trends during the latter decades mean rising flows of purchases by the rest of the world. For example, at the beginning of 1952, 2 percent of Treasury securities were held by the rest of the world; at the end of 1980, 17 percent; and at the end of 2009, 48 percent. For corporate bonds, the percentages are respectively: 0.8, 4.2, and 23.7.

ensuing steep rise, an expression of the acceleration of financial mechanisms during those years. (The country symmetrically pays financial income to the rest of the world as a result of its growing reliance on foreign financing.)

Obviously, the U.S. economy is not the unique actor in the appropriation of flows of profits and financial income from the rest the world. The United Kingdom stands much ahead of the United States in this respect (Box 8.1).

Box 8.1
Major Capitalist Countries in Financial Globalization

Figure 8.5 shows, for four countries, the flow of financial income from the rest of the world as a percentage of the GDP of the country. The position of the United Kingdom within global financial mechanisms is dramatically expressed in the amount of financial income received by this country. Between 1991 and 2000, the yearly average value of the variable was 3.5 percent in the United States, 5.3 percent in Germany, and 5.1 percent in France, but 13.0 percent in the United Kingdom.

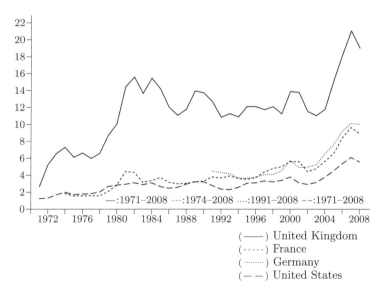

Figure 8.5 Flows of financial income from the rest of the world: four countries (percentage of the GDP of the country, yearly). The variable for the United States is the total of the two variables in Figure 8.3.

Concerning financing channels, the example of the U.S. economy is particularly revealing, given the external deficit of the country. Newly issued securities are sold and, finally, held by foreign investors. Figure 8.4 shows the percentage of U.S. Treasury securities and corporate bonds outstanding held by the rest of the world. The rise for Treasury securities (——) at the beginning of the 1970s mirrors the transformation of the reserve balances in dollars of central banks into Treasury securities. The figure clearly illustrates the steep upward trend beginning during the second half of the 1990s. Concerning the rise of the second variable (-----), the stock of securities emanating from the private sector, one can observe that 24 percent of such securities are held in the rest of the world, with again a steep upward trend since 1995.

Banking Worldwide

The expansion of trade and investment worldwide would have been impossible in the absence of the parallel development of banking activity and the globalization of financial mechanisms. Thus, another important indicator of financial globalization is the amount of foreign assets held by banks in the world.[3] These assets amounted to only 9 percent of GWP at the end of 1977 and reached 59 percent at the beginning of 2008. A sharp acceleration occurred during the last years, a development that must, obviously, be related to the last phase of financialization prior to the crisis.

It is possible to identify the total loans and securities due by all agents (government and private corporations) in various countries to banks established in other countries. Two observations follow:

1. International banking is predominantly a system of reciprocal relationships among the most developed countries. Considering yearly averages for the period 2000–2008, within the total external assets of reporting banks, 79 percent is held on developed countries. A second component, 12 percent, is held on offshore centers. Only 7 percent is held on developing countries.

2. A really dramatic development is the tremendous upward trend from 2004 onward, an expression of the expansion of financial mechanisms worldwide after 2000. Figure 8.6 shows the total loans and securities due to foreign banks by Brazil, Russia, India, and China, the four so-called BRIC countries and South Korea.

One can parenthetically notice that the figure illustrates the rise of loans and securities from the beginning of the 1980s—with a sharp accel-

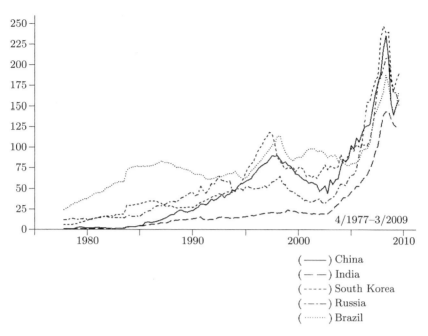

Figure 8.6 Debts to foreign banks: five countries of the periphery (billions of dollars, quarterly). The variable accounts for loans and securities held by banks (reporting to the BIS). The debt for Russia refers to the Soviet Union prior to the collapse.

eration in the second half of the 1990s for South Korea, Brazil, and China and, to a lesser extent, Russia—in all of the five countries with the exception of India. Obviously, this development must be related to the crises in some of these countries during the late 1990s. The trends were later reversed for South Korea, China, and Russia during a number of years.

These figures cannot be straightforwardly interpreted as the "external debts" of the countries, since nonbank agents also finance foreign countries. Data from the joint external debt hub[4] confirm, however, that the loans and securities in the assets of banks account for the bulk of the foreign debt of the countries considered. For example, considering Brazil, the external assets of reporting banks on the Brazilian economy amounted to 83 percent of the gross external position of the country in 2008 (excluding intercompany DIA). Thus, the variable in Figure 8.6 is a good indicator of the external debt of this country.

Tax Havens

The multiplication and expansion of tax havens can be clearly interpreted as a neoliberal accomplishment. One purpose of these centers is tax evasion, as sought by rich households and corporations. A second aspect is deregulation and privacy. This is where trusts, partnerships, family offices, OBSEs, and so on are located. Tax havens, in particular the Cayman Islands, are the territory of hedge funds, and the British Islands are a paradise for the wealth of individuals. This is also where banks established the most sophisticated institutions of structured finance, notably CDOs.

In the absence of statistics concerning the actual assets invested in tax havens, one interesting indicator is the activity of foreign banks in tax havens. Figure 8.7 shows the growth of the external assets of banks located in such centers (as percentages of GWP). Unfortunately, the situation prior to 1984 is not adequately described within Bank of International Settlements (BIS) data. For this reason, the variables in Figure 8.7 begin in the first quarter of 1984.

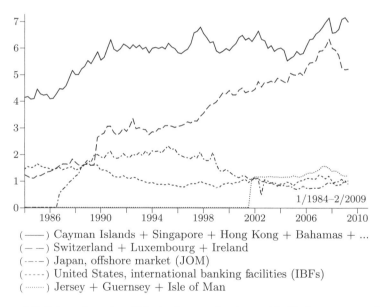

(——) Cayman Islands + Singapore + Hong Kong + Bahamas + ...
(− −) Switzerland + Luxembourg + Ireland
(−·−·) Japan, offshore market (JOM)
(-----) United States, international banking facilities (IBFs)
(·········) Jersey + Guernsey + Isle of Man

Figure 8.7 External assets within tax havens: banks worldwide (percentage of GWP, quarterly). Banks are classified depending on the tax haven in which they are established, not their nationality.

The giants are the well-known islands (——), such as the Cayman and the Bahamas, jointly with Hong Kong and Singapore. They grew tremendously during the second half of the 1980s and at the beginning of the 1990s. Then comes the group of the three European countries (——), Switzerland, Luxembourg, and Ireland, whose external assets are after 2000 about the same size as those of the above. It is interesting to stress the sharp growth of these first two groups since about 2004, clearly related to the wave of financial expansion prior to the crisis. The Japan offshore markets (JOMs) (----) appeared in 1987, rose considerably, and gradually lost their comparative importance. The establishment of U.S. international banking facilities (IBFs) (-----) was allowed by a decision of the board of governors of the Federal Reserve at the end of 1981. Their comparative importance also diminished. The British Islands, Jersey, Guernsey, and the Isle of Man (·········) only appeared after 2000.

Asset Management

Table 8.1 shows the outstanding assets managed by asset managers worldwide, a total of more than $74 trillion in 2007, five times the U.S. GDP, about 37 percent of financial assets worldwide, more than twice their value in 1998.

All aspects of the social logics of neoliberalism are manifest here. First, the management of these assets represents a juicy source of profits. Fees amount to a minimum 0.5 percent of the assets of pension funds. The average mutual fund charges between 1.3 and 1.5 percent. Hedge funds and private equity firms charge 2 percent of assets and retain 20 percent of capital gains. In 2006, the global fees amounted to a minimum of $400 billion (to be compared to $462 billion for the total corporate domestic pre-tax profit of the U.S. financial sector). Second, these assets are also powerful instruments in the hands of the financial sector, by which the new discipline is imposed on the workers and managers of nonfinancial corporations, by the pending threat of disinvestment whenever returns do not measure up to going standards.

Table 8.2 shows a measure of the total assets of hedge funds worldwide. Despite the considerable role they played during the contemporary crisis, these assets are small in comparison to those of asset managers, but the total amount was multiplied by a factor of nearly twenty in twelve years, and these funds hold the lion's share in specific categories of transactions.

Table 8.1 Global fund management of conventional assets (assets under
management, trillions of dollars)

Year	Assets	Year	Assets
1998	33.4	2003	45.1
1999	40.1	2004	49.0
2000	37.7	2005	53.8
2001	38.2	2006	65.2
2002	36.0	2007	74.3

Table 8.2 Global hedge-fund assets (trillions of dollars)

Year	Assets	Year	Assets
1996	0.13	2002	0.59
1997	0.21	2003	0.79
1998	0.22	2004	1.00
1999	0.32	2005	1.40
2000	0.41	2006	1.75
2001	0.56	2007	2.25

More specifically, in 2006, hedge funds managed $1.75 trillion as com-
pared to $65 trillion for conventional funds worldwide (pension, mutual,
and insurance funds), or $74 trillion for the assets of the 1,000 largest
banks in the world. They managed 25 percent of high-yield debt, 60 percent of credit derivatives, 45 percent of "distressed debt" and emerging
market bonds, and 32 percent of leveraged loans.[5]

Carry Trade

It is hard to exactly assess the amplitude and effects of capital flows worldwide. The crises of the 1990s and the years after 2000 in the periphery
drew attention to the capability of such flows to destabilize the macroeconomy of given comparatively smaller economies. The financial boom
that preceded the crisis and the crisis itself reveal the impact of such capital movements on stock-market indices and exchange rates among currency, even with respect to large countries. They testify to the importance

of such flows, another expression of neoliberal globalization and its culmination after 2000.

A key mechanism is currency carry trade, or "carry trade" for short. The phrase is used to refer to a specific category of financial operations in which money is borrowed in one country (whose money is called the "funding currency"), where interest rates are low, to finance an investment in another country (whose money is called the "target currency"), where high returns are expected. Obviously, the exchange rate between the two currencies involved in the transaction and its variations play an important role. Investors seek countries where the target currency is expected to appreciate vis-à-vis the funding currency. In a straightforward form of carry trade, money is borrowed in a country and then lent in another country, and the gain derives from the interest rate differential (or securities are bought and capital gains are expected).[6] But any type of investment is potentially involved.

After 2000, the Swiss franc and, even more, the yen are cited as funding currencies. The Australian dollar, the New Zealand dollar, the pound sterling, the Brazilian real, and the South African rand are considered typical target currencies. But it is also the case of the U.S. dollar.

There are no statistics available concerning carry trade, but estimates as high as a few trillion dollars a year are frequently cited. The effects of carry trade were clearly apparent during the financial boom prior to the crisis (Chapter 9) as well as during the crisis. The new phase in which the crisis entered in the last months of 2008 coincided with dramatic fluctuations of exchange rates, notably in favor of the yen, as investors, in particular hedge funds, unwound their carry trade, returning to funding currencies (Chapter 20).

Exchanging Currencies

Contrary to carry trade, difficult to measure, the astounding volumes of currency exchanges are frequently mentioned and well documented by the statistics of the BIS. In 2007, the daily turnover for spot exchanges was superior to $1 trillion. (Recall that the mass of financial assets worldwide is estimated at $167 trillion in 2006, Table 7.1.)

Since the data in Table 8.3 begin only in 1989, it is impossible to assess the effect of neoliberalism on the volume of exchange from its beginning. Nonetheless, between 1989 and 2007, the flows of foreign exchanges were

Table 8.3 Foreign exchange markets: Daily global turnovers (billions of dollars)

	1989	1992	1995	1998	2001	2004	2007
Spot transactions	350	394	494	568	386	621	1,005
Outright forwards	240	58	97	128	130	208	362
Foreign exchange swaps	—	324	546	734	656	944	1,714
Estimated gaps in reporting	0	43	53	61	28	107	129
Total turnover	590	820	1,190	1,490	1,200	1,880	3,210

In 1989, forwards and swaps cannot be separated.

multiplied by a factor of about 5.4, and forwards and swaps, by almost 9, unquestionably the leaders in the race toward the globalization of financial mechanisms. The profile of currency exchanges echoes the explosion of international financial mechanisms during the precrisis decade.

9

A Fragile and Unwieldy Structure

The analysis in the previous two chapters points to the tremendous expansion of financial and global mechanisms, sometimes in a very short period of time, and the dramatic consequences of neoliberalism and neoliberal globalization in their most advanced configuration. All barriers—regulations and frontiers among countries—were lifted. The wild dynamics of a world of free trade and free international movements of capital upset the basic economic mechanisms. Macro policies lost their stabilizing potential. The latter bout of expansion after 2000 marked the ultimate phase in the construction of a highly fragile and unwieldy structure.

The Unchecked Quest for High Income

The root of the expansion of financial mechanisms and globalization during the neoliberal decades is the quest for high profits and, more generally, high income. (This is what arrow A expresses in Diagram 2.1.) Notably, the financial expansion in the precrisis decade was led by the most advanced segments of the upper classes and the cutting edge of financial institutions. Capitalist owners, top managers, and financial managers were jointly involved within financial corporations, nonfinancial corporations, and private equity firms. This quest was pushed to the extreme.

Judged according to its own objectives, this endeavor was highly successful, up to the crisis. There is no need to repeat here the demonstration in Parts II and III. The income of the upper income brackets increased dramatically during the neoliberal decades. The rise of profits and stock values of financial corporations fed skyrocketing gains. There is no way of assessing the degrees reached within the restricted world of hedge funds

---

Box 9.1
Excess Savings and Financialization

Among Left economists, an interpretation makes excess savings the "cause" of financialization, either the savings of households or those of nonfinancial corporations.

Concerning households, reference is made to the concentration of income within the upper-income brackets, the large savings of these social categories allegedly feeding and stimulating financial mechanisms. The hypothesis points to savings in search of the investment opportunities that the nonfinancial sector is unable to provide.[1]

A difficulty with this interpretation is that the rate of savings of these social groups actually diminished during neoliberalism.[2] There was, actually, nothing like income in search of investment opportunity that nonfinancial corporations would no longer provide, but rich households borrowing to spend more. Concerning nonfinancial corporations, financialization is interpreted as the "consequence" of the divergence between the restoration of their profits and their stagnating investment rate. Again financialization is seen as the manifestation of excess savings. The difficulty with this interpretation is the same as above. Considering the economy globally, profits paid out as interest and dividends by corporations finance consumption and residential investment, as the saving rate of the entire country is negative.

(continued)

---

and private equity firms, except listening to the hedge fund managers' boastful speeches concerning their high returns.

Between the observation of outcomes and an interpretation that traces financialization and globalization to the quest for high income, there is, however, some distance. Central to the overall class interpretation of neoliberalism here is the contention that what neoliberalism did to the benefit of a minority is what this minority—in its enterprises, governments, international institutions, and so on—strived to achieve. Such performances would have been impossible if regulation, notably financial regulation, and limitations on international trade and the movements of capital had not been suppressed. The crisis retrospectively demonstrates that the logic was stretched beyond reason, a fact on which most analysts now agree, with the exception of die-hard worshippers of the free-market ideology.

(continued)

None of the new features of the dramatic wave of expansion of financial mechanisms after 2000—derivatives, conduits and SIVs, carry trade, and LBOs—manifested the availability of extra savings in desperate search of investment opportunities. To the contrary, they were the expression of the quest for high income. They were frequently highly leveraged, manifesting the dramatic extension of financing beyond the potential opened by the flow of savings.

---

1. This is the interpretation given in the volume published by the French alter-globalist association, Attac: "The increasing mass of profits that are not invested was, mostly, distributed as financial income, and this is where the source of the process of financialization can be located. The gap between the profit rate and the investment rate is a good indicator of the degrees reached by financialization." From J. M. Harribey and D. Plihon, *Sortir de la crise globale: Vers un monde solidaire et écologique* (Paris: La Découverte, 2009). Despite diverging assumptions concerning the trend of the profit rate, there is a relationship between this interpretation and that developed by Immanuel Wallerstein and Giovanni Arrighi in which a phase of comparatively strong accumulation (Phase A of a long wave) leads to a situation of overaccumulation, whose effect is a declining profit rate. Capitalist classes, then, attempt to compensate for these unfavorable trends by investment in financial mechanisms, the root of financialization. One can consult the summary given in G. Arrighi's last book, *Adam Smith in Beijing: Lineages of the Twenty-first Century* (London: Verso, 2009), chap. 3.

2. D. Maki and M. Palumbo, "Disentangling the Wealth Effect: A Cohort Analysis of Household Savings in the 1990s" (Working paper, Washington, D.C.: Federal Reserve, 2001).

To sum up, the objective was the quest of high income; the agents were financial managers; financialization, including financial innovation and jointly with globalization, was a major instrument; and the consequence was the fragile financial structure. There are, obviously, other interpretations. For example, an explanation of financialization points to excess savings (Box 9.1).

Fictitious Gains and Real Income Flows

The history of neoliberalism at its climax is one of subtle transition between reaching and trespassing limits, what could be denoted as the "dialectics of performance and fictitiousness." Were the profits of the financial sector real profits? On what grounds were the tremendous gains of the upper wage brackets in the sector based? Boundaries are difficult to draw.

Box 9.2
UBS

The Swiss bank UBS[1] is a leading global investment banking and securities firm, with total assets of $1.9 trillion in 2007, and one of the largest wealth managers in the world, managing $1.2 trillion of assets.

To the end of 2006, it was hard to imagine a healthier situation. According to the Basel Accords, Tier 1 capital must cover 4 percent of a bank's risk-weighted assets (Box 9.4). At UBS, the ratio was about 12 percent. In 2005, the ROE reached 25 percent and still 23.9 percent in 2006. The stock price was booming (Figure 17.2).

Strangely enough, the situation was suddenly reversed in 2007 with a ROE of −11.7 percent, and −54.4 percent in 2008. This means that the own funds of UBS lost two-thirds of their value in two years! The stock price diminished by 78 percent between its maximum value and the end of 2008. To prevent a total collapse, in October 2008 the Swiss National Bank (SNB) accepted the transfer of $60 billion of "illiquid" securities (an amount later reduced to $39 billion) into a fund at the SNB, created to this end. In this total, $16 billion is explicitly designated as from U.S. origin, but there is a large category of "others" that covers European and U.S. assets.

The income account of UBS is quite telling of the volumes and profile of "surplus labor compensation" (Box 6.1). Table 9.1 shows labor compensation

(continued)

The analysis of the financial sector in the United States suggests, however, the formation of a strong bias toward fictitiousness, at least from the second half of the 1990s, with a dramatic expansion after 2000.

The measures of the profit rates within the financial sector in Chapter 4 (Figures 4.6 and 4.7) provide striking images of the euphoria prevailing within the financial sector, prior to the crisis. The first variable (——) in Figure 4.7 is straightforwardly based on the accounts of insured banks. One can repeat here that up to 2007, the ROE of the sector was close to 12 percent, almost 15 percent, the standard value for the precrisis decade, before falling sharply. In 2006, the Swiss giant UBS declared a ROE of 23.9 percent, in no way exceptional and, suddenly, tremendous losses (Box 9.2).

How was it possible? A crucial aspect was the increasing recourse on the part of major financial institutions to procedures of externalization—off-balance sheet, often off-shore (Box 9.3)—aiming at the dissimulation of either losses or gains and tending to the falsification of accounts.

(continued)

(with a rough estimate of the division between salaries and bonuses) and profits (taxes on profits, dividends, and retained profits) between 2006 and 2008:

Table 9.1 UBS. Incomes (billions of dollars)

	2006	2007	2008
Salaries	9.5	10.7	10.7
Bonuses[a]	10.0	10.0	1.5
Net profit	12.0	−4.7	−19.1

a. Discretionary variable compensation payments.

One can broadly impute all bonuses and an undetermined fraction of salaries to surplus labor compensation that appears larger than profits (before taxes) for 2006. One can also notice that, while profits fell to negative levels in 2007, bonuses remained unscathed. They were only reduced (though still positive) in 2008 when a tremendous loss was registered.

---

1. "UBS" refers to the corporation resulting from the fusion of Union des Banques Suisses and Société de Banques Suisses in 1998.

Another well-known factor of the fictitious character of balance sheets was mark-to-market accounting. In the accounts of corporations, securities were recorded at their ongoing market price, thus simulating that they were sold. If there is no such market, as in the case of CDOs, mark-to-model or other indices were used as substitutes. (Within traditional accounting procedures, securities were cautiously estimated at the price at which they had been purchased, with potential provision for devaluation if necessary, but no anticipation on gains.) The crisis demonstrated that potential losses were dramatically underestimated. Marked-to-market in the accounts of corporations, the rising price of shares fed the profits of financial corporations, in turn stimulating the overvaluation of stock-market indices. With mark-to-market accounting procedures, the market invaded into corporations, nurturing the overestimation of profits and inflating their net worth. Involved here are dynamics similar to a self-fulfilling prophecy, up to the burst of the bubble and the collapse of the

Box 9.3
"Externalization"

During the neoliberal decades, huge masses of assets were transferred to special securitization vehicles where the responsibility of the originator was severed and risks sold, notably to foreigners. In the case of conduits and SIVs, the link with a parent corporation (the "sponsor") was somehow maintained under rather obscure conditions. Assets could appear or not within the reports of sponsors. The relationship between the sponsor and the entity is complex, and practices are tricky. While international financial reporting standards stipulate that firms must disclose their relationships to OBSEs, even if they own less than half of the assets, the information can be provided in a footnote of the firm's report.[1] Such transfers of asset off-balance sheets allowed corporations to increase leverage well beyond accepted ratios.[2]

The procedure introduced in Chapter 7 consisting of originating (that is, issuing) loans to then systematically selling off these loans by securitization, expanded so rapidly that it was described as the originate-to-distribute model.[3] Originators tend to maintain volumes without much concern for the quality of the loans, selling loans judged as comparatively risky.

---

1. International Monetary Fund, *Global Financial Stability Report: Market Developments and Issues* (Washington, D.C.: IMF, April 2008), 69, note 12.

2. R. Wayman, "Off-Balance-Sheet Entities: The Good, the Bad, and the Ugly" (Edmonton, Alberta: Investopedia, 2009), www.investopedia.com/articles/analyst/022002.asp.

3. Governor F. S. Mishkin's speech at the U.S. Monetary Policy Forum (New York, February 29, 2008).

---

system. Rating agencies proved unable to do the work for which their services were bought. The apparent good shape of corporations confirmed their optimistic forecasts.

To this, one can add that the wave of acquisitions, as during the second half of the 1990s, led to the inclusion in the accounts of corporations of the excess of the price at which firms were purchased over their accounting value, a difference known as "goodwill," with also a large potential for devaluation.

The other side of the coin is that such *fictitious* gains nourished the income flows paid out by financial corporations as wages to upper management or dividends, *real* drains on the own funds of corporations. One can return here to the estimate of a surplus labor compensation as in Box 6.1. One specific feature of the financial sector is the concentration of very high wages. Considering this sector instead of the entire private economy, the result is significantly different from that in Box 6.1, and even more spectacular. Applying that methodology to the sector, one obtains $2,606 billion for the total of surplus labor compensation and dividends in the financial sector, for the five years 2003–2007, to be compared to only $668 billion of retained profits. (Box 9.2 provides estimates for UBS.) All was not fictitious in the profits of financial corporations, but these figures, actually, compare to those of losses as assessed by international institutions, or the sums made available to financial institutions by the Federal Reserve (Chapters 15 and 18).

The consequences of these practices were at the measure of the tremendous values involved. Table 7.1 points to masses of financial assets worldwide of $167 trillion or the total assets of the 1,000 largest banks of $74 trillion. An overvaluation of assets by 10 percent means fictitious gains of, respectively, $17 and $7 trillion! Such figures may be judged exaggerated but the order of magnitude is similar to what was lost on the NYSE. (The total capitalization peaked at $22 trillion and fell to $8.5 trillion in March 2009.)

There is obviously a reciprocal link between the overvaluation of profits and the flows of high income paid out. First, the overvaluation of gains fed distribution. Second, the distribution of stock options directly induced CEOs and high managers to inflate profits and postpone the acknowledgment of losses. The addition of misinformation and fraud created even worse damage. The case of Enron is quite telling. It can be described as a combination of mark-to-market accounting, and dissimulation of potential losses and actual levels of indebtedness. One can also mention here the scandal around Bernard Madoff. Considering the financial sector as a whole, the problem is, however, not fraud in the legal sense of the term, but a form of collective blindness and euphoria from which resulted a tremendous overestimation of profits and gains that led to the payment of huge flows of high income, actually a puncture on corporations' own funds.

Deregulation

The above practices would have been impossible within a regulated financial economy. But while such highly risky procedures were developing, the overall trend was toward deregulation. The inspiration and the objectives were clearly the same. They combined their effects.

Already during the 1970s, neoliberal ideas were advancing considerably. From the Bretton Woods agreements in 1944 to the establishment of the euromarkets in the 1960s, the crisis of the dollar in the early 1970s (that led to the inconvertibility of the dollar in gold and the floatation of exchange rates), and the 1979 coup, the history of international monetary and financial mechanisms never ran smoothly. After much confusion at the beginning of the 1970s, the real move toward deregulation was initiated. The United States removed its capital controls in 1974, the United Kingdom in 1979, and Japan during the 1980s.[1] In 1992, the Maastricht Treaty established the free mobility of capital within the European Union and vis-à-vis the rest of the world.[2] In the 1990s, capital movements had recovered a degree of freedom similar to that enjoyed during the 1920s.

At the beginning of the 1980s, two important pieces of legislation, the Depository Institutions Deregulation and Monetary Control Act of 1980 and the Garn–St. Germain Act of 1982, marked the entrance into neoliberalism proper. The two acts aimed at the extension of competition among depository institutions, notably savings and loan associations. One particular objective of the former—quite distinct from deregulation—was, however, to increase the control of the Federal Reserve on depository institutions in the fight against inflation. The distinction between member banks and nonmember banks was eliminated and the Federal Reserve extended its control and support to all depository institutions.

The first wave of deregulation was an important factor in the crisis of banking and thrift institutions in the late 1980s and early 1990s, well ahead of the contemporary crisis. The Depository Institutions Deregulation and Monetary Control Act eliminated interest rate ceilings on depository accounts (on which checks can be written), and authorized the creation of new types of accounts, such as NOW accounts. Credit unions and savings and loan associations were allowed to offer checking deposits. (Federal insurance on deposits was increased from $40,000 to $100,000.) The ability of some institutions to grant mortgages or consumer loans was increased. Subprime loans became easier as a result of the elimination of usury controls, allowing originators to charge higher interest rates on borrowers with higher credit risks. The Garn–St. Germain Act of 1982 further extended the deregulation of savings and loan associations. Limits on the loan-to-value ratio were lifted, and savings and loan associations were allowed to differentiate their loans in the directions of consumer and commercial loans.

These measures led to the bankruptcy of numerous financial institutions in a major financial crisis at the end of the 1980s and beginning of the 1990s. More than half of the thrift institutions disappeared in the collapse of the housing market around 1990. The crisis of banks was severe. Between 1985 and 1992, 1,373 banks disappeared.

About a decade later, in 1999, the Glass-Steagall Act was repealed. The easing of the regulatory framework of the act had already been discussed by the board of the Federal Reserve in 1987, but had been opposed by Paul Volcker. In 1987, Alan Greenspan became chairman of the board and, between 1989 and 1998, a continuous series of decisions paved the way to the repeal of the Glass-Steagall Act, including, in 1996, the decision allowing bank holding companies to own investment banks. The merger of the insurer Traveler Group with Citicorp to form Citigroup (or Citi), in April 1998, led to the passage of the Gramm-Leach-Bliley Financial Services Modernization Act, allowing the joint operation of investment banking, commercial banking, and insurance services.

A similar story can be told concerning derivative markets originally regulated by the Commodity Futures Trading Commission Act of 1936. Further restrictions had been imposed during the 1970s and early 1980s. The Commodity Futures Trading Commission Act of 1974 had considerably extended the definition of "commodity" to include practically any assets, including financial instruments, but could be interpreted as prohibiting the trading of futures outside of exchanges. The Shad-Johnson jurisdictional accord of 1982 had banned single-stock futures. These restrictions were, however, lifted, at least partially, in 1992 by the Futures Trading Practices Act and the Commodity Futures Modernization Act of 2000. (The ban of the Shad-Johnson accord was cited as a factor in the bankruptcies of Enron and Lehman Brothers.) The deregulation of credit default swaps also occurred in this new context favorable to deregulation.

There was obviously no international substitute for national regulation. Neither the IMF nor the WB performs such tasks. In an overall environment of deregulation, the self-disciplinary rules defined by the Basel Accords of

> **Box 9.4**
> **The Basel Accords**
>
> The so-called Basel Accords refer to two sets of agreements, signed in Basel, Switzerland, in 1988 and 2004 (Basel I and Basel II, respectively).[1] The accords define minimum ratios of banks own funds to assets, as a form of self-discipline. Basel II was intended to correct the defects of Basel I. The participants are the countries of the G-10 (France, Germany, Italy, Japan, Luxembourg, the Netherlands, Sweden, Switzerland, the United Kingdom, the United States) and Spain. The central banks of the participants are in charge of the enforcement of the rules in their own countries.
>
> The capital of banks is divided into two fractions: Tier 1 and Tier 2 capitals. Tier 1 capital is made of reserves and stock. Provisions for losses and certain categories of debts form Tier 2 capital. The total of Tier 1 and Tier 2 capital must represent a minimum of 8 percent of the total of weighted loans (a minimum of 4 percent for Tier 1 capital). The weights are defined according to risk.
>
> In Basel I, there were four categories of assets, weighted at 0 percent, 20 percent, 50 percent, or 100 percent. For example, sovereign debt in domestic currency belonged to the first category (0 percent), and residential mortgage to the third (50 percent). Several important criticisms were addressed toward
>
> *(continued)*

1988 and 2004 under the aegis of the BIS were unable to counteract the effects of deregulatory trends (Box 9.4).

Policy in Globalization: Lessons from Bretton Woods

Besides the factors—the unbound quest for high income, real-income flows based on fictitious surpluses, biased managerial trends, and deregulation—addressed above, the tendencies inherent in neoliberal globalization had a strong destabilizing impact on macroeconomic stability.

The monetary policy of the central bank, possibly supplemented by fiscal policy when required, is a crucial component of the control of the macroeconomy. It was so prior to as well as during the neoliberal decades. The function of monetary policy is to adjust credit levels according to the situation of the macroeconomy, upward as well as downward. The macroeconomy (output and prices) would go astray in the absence of such policies. (A number of basic principles are recalled in Box 14.1.)

(continued)

these procedures. Securitization allowed banks to sell the less risky loans while holding the riskiest (as in the junior tranches of CDOs yielding high returns), since the rules did not distinguish between risks within a given category of assets (for example, all mortgages were considered jointly). For a category of borrowers, short-term debt was in the category weighted at 20 percent and long-term debt at 100 percent. Banks were, thus, encouraged to favor short-term loans. To correct for such defects, Basel II weighs loans according to their rating, for example, 0 percent for loans rated AAA and 150 percent for loans rated below B–. These ratings can be defined by rating agencies, set internally by the bank (using its own models), or a combination of the two.

According to the basic ratios, the situation of banks could be judged sane prior to the crisis. Considering FDIC-insured banks, their ratio of own funds to total (unweighted) assets rose from 8.4 to 10.2 percent between 1989 and 2007.[2]

---

1. A helpful summary can be found in B. Balin, "Basel I, Basel II, and Emerging Markets: A Nontechnical Analysis" (Washington, D.C.: The John Hopkins University, School of Advanced International Studies, 2008).

2. Federal Deposit Insurance Corporation, Quarterly Banking Profile (Washington, D.C.: FDIC, 2008).

In the discussion of such mechanisms, it is useful to return to the context of the Bretton Woods agreements at the end of World War II. Neoliberal globalization lifted the limits placed by the agreements on the international movements of capital, which had been considered basic requirements for the conduct of macro policies.

The agreements were executed in the wake of the shock of the Great Depression with the explicit objective of establishing the foundations of a stable international economy. A central concern at the end of the war was to avoid the repetition of a contraction of output and international trade, similar to what had occurred during the 1930s. Besides a tighter cooperation between countries internationally, the agreements contemplated the easier provision of credit in strong currencies to countries facing a disequilibrium in their current account. But the access to financing was not considered sufficient. Simultaneously, the capacity of each country to conduct policies of macro stimulation had to be ensured, and this is the relevant issue here. Three aspects must be distinguished:

1. The fact that capitals tend to flow from one place to another responding to interest rate differentials or other incentives (including the anticipation of the ups and downs of exchange rates) and that these movements prohibit independent national macro policies was well known. For this reason, the implementation of strict limits on capital mobility was considered a necessary ingredient in the Bretton Woods system, at least in Keynes's mind. The risks inherent in the free international mobility of capital were clearly stated by Keynes in one of his interventions in the House of Lords in May 1944, where he discussed the Bretton Woods agreements. Keynes linked the "power to control the domestic rate of interest so as to secure cheap money" to capital controls: "Not merely as a feature of the transition, but as a permanent arrangement, the plan accords to every member government the explicit right to control all capital movements. What used to be a heresy is now endorsed as orthodox."[3]

After heavy amendment, the Bretton Woods agreements acknowledged the principle of controls, which were later never fully accepted by the United States. Practically, this recognition of controls in the agreements and the necessities of the period resulted in a complex structure of permanent or temporary, statutory or fiscal, measures, up to the move toward liberalization in the 1970s and 1980s described earlier.[4]

2. Besides the destabilizing potential of international capital flows, free trade added to the difficulties met in the conduct of macro policies. In an open economy the stimulation of domestic demand by credit is partially exported to the rest of the world since a fraction of demand is imported. There are two ways of correcting for this mechanism. One is exceptions made on free trade and the other is the manipulation of exchange rates. For these reasons, Keynes was also in favor of strict limitations to free trade: "Defense of free trade theory is, I submit, the result of pure intellectual error, due to a complete misunderstanding of the theory of equilibrium in international trade."[5]

3. Although exchange rates were fixed in the Bretton Woods system, the various currencies were often adjusted (typically devaluing with respect to the dollar), another prerequisite to the conduct of autonomous macro policies.

It is obvious that the mechanisms governing the contemporary global economy are at odds with Keynes's recommendations and the original goals of Bretton Woods. In particular, financial mechanisms worldwide reached outstanding proportions and are responsible for huge flows of capital throughout the globe resulting in dramatic variations of exchange and interest rates. This property has important consequences that limit the potential of effective monetary policy.

At a more structural level of analysis, exchange rates are an important variable susceptible of impacting the disequilibrium of external trade or can be used as a tool in active development policies, as was the case within import-substitution industrialization in Latin America in the wake of the Great Depression and is still the case in China since the reforms. Although China was able to maintain the exchange rate of the yuan at a low level, pegged to the dollar, many countries in the periphery lost their ability to influence their exchange rates, and sometimes lost all forms of control as in dollarization.

During the 1990s and after 2000, the macroeconomies of many countries of the periphery were deeply affected by dangerous capital movements. Figure 8.6 shows the foreign assets of banks for a set of countries of the periphery. The impact of massive capital flows during the 1980s and 1990s is all too well known, but these movements are dwarfed by the tremendous rise of the mass of loans and securities during the precrisis decade.

Fundamentals in the Financial-Global Storm

It is easy to illustrate the devastating potential of financial globalization. The present section successively considers interest rates, and exchange rate and stock-market indices. The main contention is that the explosion of capital movements after 2000 thoroughly upset the basic mechanisms, disrupting the course of fundamental economic variables. To hell with Keynes.

1. *Long-term interest rates.* A first effect of financial globalization was the convergence of long-term interest rates around the globe, the deprivation of any potential of adjustment to domestic circumstances. (Impacting short-term interest rates, central banks expect an effect on the long-term rates prevailing in their own countries.)

Figure 9.1 shows long-term interest rates on government bonds in France, Italy, the United Kingdom, the United States, and Japan, corrected for inflation rates in each country. A clear break can be observed in 2000, as a tighter gravitation is observed. (In France and Italy, two countries of the euro area, the common currency certainly played an important role.) There is apparently no more space for the national dynamic of long-term

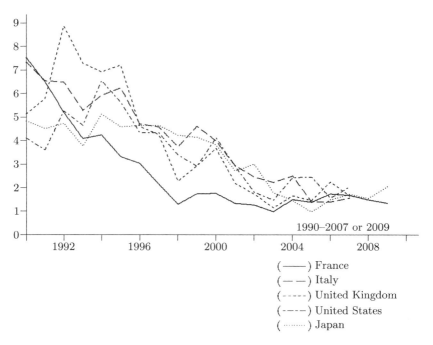

Figure 9.1 Real interest rates on long-term government bonds (percent, yearly): five countries.

interest rates matching macroeconomic conditions (growth, inflation, etc.) within particular countries. A similar process is also apparent when nominal rates are considered, with the exception of Japan, a maverick, where interest rates are continuously lower than in other countries. (The short-term interest rates of central banks are shown in Figure 20.6.)

One can, parenthetically, notice that the precrisis decade is also the period during which the new downward trend of long-term real interest rates in the United States (as in Figure 4.2) was established (Box 14.2).

2. *Exchange rates and stock-market indices.* The huge financial flows after 2000 and the crisis drew the attention to strange new developments. A first aspect was the tight relationship between rates of exchange and stock-market indices within a number of countries. To this, one must add the observation of the coincidence between periods of joint rise or decline of the two variables in various countries. This is another manifestation of the huge proportions taken by international capital flows—besides the con-

vergence of interest rates above—also foreshadowing the forthcoming financial storm worldwide.

Figure 9.2 illustrates the case of Europe. The variables are the exchange rate of the euro vis-à-vis the yen and the Euronext 100. (The Euronext is made of the Paris, Amsterdam, Brussels, and Lisbon exchanges.) Nine months are considered, from January to September 2007. The two variables closely followed one another during the rise as well as during the contraction. The relationship is not always so strong but such very high correlations are apparent for a significant number of distinct countries and at the same time. (Chapter 20 provides similar observations for 2008.)

A very likely interpretation is that important masses of capital cross exchange borders, flowing to Europe when the expectations concerning the Euronext are favorable, simultaneously stimulating the index and pushing the euro upward, and conversely when expectations are poor.

The case of Brazil is similar to that of Europe, with a major fluctuation and a high correlation between the exchange rate of the real against the yen and the Ibovespa (the main index of the Brazilian exchange) during the same period. (As expected, the analysis of foreign portfolio investment toward Brazil reveals exceptionally large flows and sharp fluctuations in 2007 when the correlation prevails.) From the low point in March and the

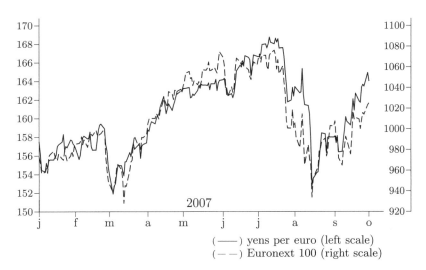

Figure 9.2 Exchange rate and stock-market index: yens per euro, and the Euronext 100 index (January to October 2007, daily).

high point in early July, gains on exchange rates amounted to 11 percent in Europe and 21 percent in Brazil, and gains in the price of stocks amounted to 14 percent in Europe and 37 percent in Brazil. Despite such differences, the correlation is very strong in both countries. The same relationship is observed for the United States (between the exchange rate of the dollar against the yen and the Dow Jones industrial index).

A comparison with other currencies shows that the yen unquestionably plays a central role. This observation suggests that, besides the fact that Japan widely invests in the rest of the world, carry trade is at the origin of these movements (Chapter 8). Investors of any nationality (including Japan) borrow from Japanese banks, taking advantage of the low interest rates, and invest in other countries. In numerous countries and during given periods, this practice had a major impact on exchange rates and stock-market indices.

Such practices account for an extreme form of disruption of basic economic mechanisms. The dramatic fluctuation of exchange rates after 2000 retrospectively emphasizes its impact. One example is the variation of the Australian dollar during those years. Between the end of 2001 and mid-2008, the exchange rate of this currency against the U.S. dollar doubled. Between July and October 2008, it was divided by 1.6. Analysts agree that these changes were the effects of huge flows of carry trade. Part of the fluctuation of the exchange rate of the dollar is, thus, imputed to carry trade.[6]

The differences in inflation rates among countries and balances of trade are assumed to be reflected in the movement of exchange rates; stock indices are supposed to mirror the performances of corporations. In a world in which exchange rates and stock-market indices are subject to broad fluctuations strongly influenced if not determined by international capital movements, one may wonder what role is left to domestic fundamentals. Even if these flows are not permanent, the destabilizing potential of the international movements of capital is clearly very strong.

To sum up, the analysis in the present section points to the uniformization of long-term interest rates and the perturbation of exchange rates and stock-market indices as consequences of the free movements of capital internationally. They share a common disruptive potential concerning the capability of individual countries to conduct stabilizing macro policies. Chapters 14 and 20 show that these mechanisms played an important role in the contemporary crisis.

V

Neoliberal Trends:
The U.S. Macro Trajectory

It would be hard to overstate the importance of the financial-global roots of the crisis of neoliberalism as in the previous part. The stage was set for a major disruption, although it was obviously difficult to tell when and through which mechanism. As suggested in Diagram 2.1, a second strand of determinants, the threats inherent in the trajectory of the U.S. economy, acted in combination with the above.

The present part formally replicates the line of argument in Part IV. While the link (arrow A) was established between neoliberalism, on the one hand, and globalization, financialization, and the quest for high income, on the other hand, the present part focuses on the relationship between neoliberalism under U.S. hegemony and the macro trajectory of the U.S. economy (arrow C). The problems posed to the macro trajectory of the U.S. economy follow from the basic features of neoliberalism under U.S. hegemony. They are consequences, not incidental difficulties. The rise of domestic indebtedness and the wave of financing from the rest of the world are both involved. They are the other facet of the declining trend of accumulation and the rising consumption of households in the overall context of neoliberal globalization.

The most interesting issue is how the two categories of determinants, financial and macroeconomic, converged during the years 2000–2009. Once the two sets of determinants have been separately introduced, the relationship between them can be investigated (arrow E). This convergence determined the timing and the modality of the collapse.

10

Declining Accumulation and Growing Disequilibria

There are five components to the unsustainable macro trajectory of the U.S. economy: (1) an increasing deficit of the balances of trade or current account;[1] (2) the corresponding financing of the U.S. economy by the rest of the world; (3) the rise of the demand emanating from households; (4) the growing indebtedness of households; and (5) the declining trend of domestic investment. (Government demand and indebtedness have potentially the same effects as demand and indebtedness emanating from households, but they were not the main aspects after 2000.) U.S. hegemony worldwide was a crucial factor in the maintenance of the first two trends, the external disequilibria, during several decades.

Among the potential effects of the trajectory of the U.S. economy, one must distinguish long-term and shorter-term possible impacts. In the long run, the trajectory meant a de-territorialization of commodity production with important side effects concerning the technical and, more generally, scientific leadership of the country. It also meant a gradual penetration of foreign capital within national capital spheres, also a threat posed on U.S. hegemony. The emphasis in the present part is, however, on shorter-term impacts, as in the growing macro imbalance that may lead to a crisis, and actually did in combination with other determinants.

In the years after 2000, the trajectory could already be judged unsustainable. The most threatening developments were the rising domestic indebtedness and the reliance on foreign financing. In the second half of the decade, the fragile financial structure was destabilized by the seismic wave triggered by the collapse of financial instruments related to the debt of households. The destabilizing potential of the reliance on foreign financing remains a major threat, constantly pending on the exchange rate of the dollar and, consequently, on the U.S. and world economies. It did not materialize to date.[2]

A Growing Dependency from the Rest of the World

The first development questioning the continuation of the macro trajectory of the U.S. economy is the growing trade or current account deficits of the country, and the corresponding increasing reliance on financing from the rest of the world, the two first disequilibria above.

As shown in Figure 10.1, the trade deficit of the United States rose from about zero in the mid-1970s to a peak of 6 percent of GDP at the end of 2005. The formation of this deficit was gradual, with an ephemeral reprieve around 1990, an effect of the simultaneous recovery of exports (in the context of a diminished exchange rate of the dollar) and stagnation of imports during the 1991 recession. The figure emphasizes, in particular, the dramatic rise of deficits since 1992.

U.S. agents make financial investments (foreign direct investment, loans, portfolio investment, and deposits) in other countries and, reciprocally, foreigners make similar investments in U.S. assets. Figure 10.2 shows the amazing divergence between the stock of foreign assets held by the

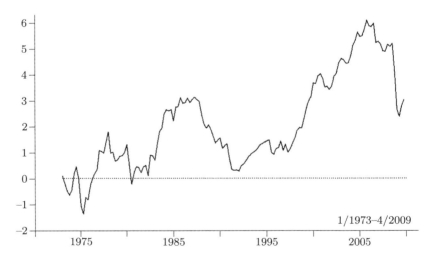

Figure 10.1 Trade deficit: U.S. economy (percentage of GDP, quarterly). The variable is imports of goods and services minus exports (both of goods and services).

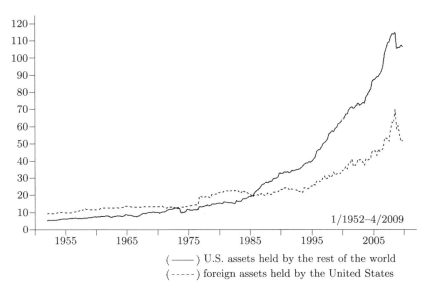

Figure 10.2 Foreign assets held by the United States and U.S. assets held by the rest of the world (percentage of U.S. GDP, quarterly). "Assets" refers to all financial assets, that is, deposits in other countries, trade credit and loans, portfolio investment, and direct investment abroad.

United States and U.S. assets held by foreigners (the net foreign-asset position of the United States being measured by the distance between the two lines). The simultaneous growth of the two variables is certainly an effect of the underlying trends of financial globalization that prevailed during those years, but, in the case of the United States, this movement appears highly biased in favor of the rest of the world as foreigners hold gradually many more U.S. assets than U.S. agents own foreign assets. The divergence began in the mid-1980s, and the gap continued to widen during the subsequent decades. In the fourth quarter of 2009, the last observation in the figure, U.S. assets held by foreigners reached $15.4 trillion, that is, twice the foreign assets held by U.S. individuals or institutions, 107 percent and 52 percent, respectively, of U.S. GDP.

Contrary to what is often believed, three-quarters of the investments of the rest of the world in the United States (as of 2007) go to the private sector (Table 10.1). Within the remaining quarter, a significant share goes to agency and GSE securities (whose status is ambiguous, private to a large extent prior to their bailout), and only slightly more than 15 percent to

Table 10.1 The components of U.S. liabilities toward the rest of the world (end of 2007, percent of total liabilities)

Treasury (and municipal) securities	15.5
Agency and GSE securities	9.8
Private economy	75.1
Foreign direct investment	15.1
Corporate equities	17.5
Corporate bonds and loans to U.S. corporate business	18.6
Other (securities RP, deposits, etc.)	23.8
Total U.S. liabilities	100.0
Total U.S. liabilities ($ trillion)	16.1

governments, including municipal securities. Overall, the destination of the investments from the rest of the world is mostly the private U.S. economy, although the crisis is considerably altering these proportions.[3]

Rising Consumption

The third trend is the rise in the consumption of households, as shown in Figure 10.3 (——). The constant share of wages in total income (Figure 3.3) did not result in an equally constant share of consumption but in a rising proportion. Prior to neoliberalism, the percentage of this variable in GDP remained about constant, around a plateau of 62 percent (yearly average 1952–1980). Then a steady upward trend prevailed up to a plateau of 70 percent since 2001. Such a shift of 8 percentage points in about twenty years represents a major historical transformation of the course of macro variables, a figure without precedent. This boom of consumption must be interpreted as one of the economic foundations of the neoliberal compromise between the capitalist classes and the upper fractions of wage earners, thus participating in the benefits of the new social order for the minority.

The second variable (— —) in Figure 10.3 shows the consumption of U.S. households in a broad definition, including residential investment.[4] When the perspective is that of total demand, it is this variable that must be considered. The trend is the same, though the fluctuation in this total is larger than for consumption in the strict sense, because of the large successive upward and downward movements of residential investment. The

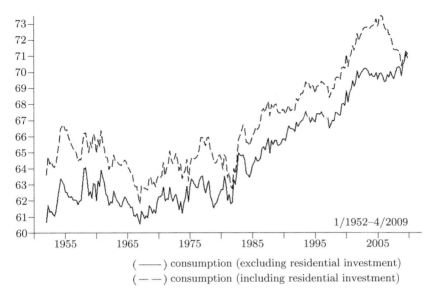

(——) consumption (excluding residential investment)

(— —) consumption (including residential investment)

Figure 10.3 Demand: U.S. households (percentage of GDP, quarterly).

figure clearly describes the gradual decline of residential investment (measured by the distance between the two lines), beginning in 2006.

In this chapter and the following, the term "consumption," without further specification, is often used in the broad sense of the purchase of commodities and services by households and their residential investment. (Thus defined, the notion also differs from the total expenses of households that include other components such as interest payments.)

Another expression of these trends is the declining savings rate of households since 1980, to the contemporary crisis. Figure 10.4 shows two saving rates (in accord with the two variables in Figure 10.3): (1) the traditional definition, that is, disposable income minus consumption in the strict sense (——); and (2) disposable income minus total consumption (— —) (as in the definition of financial savings). Prior to neoliberalism, households used to save, in the first measure above, 9.3 percent of their disposable income (average 1965–1980). When residential investment is included within consumption, the variable displays an upward trend prior to neoliberalism to more than 8 percent in 1975. Then, the two percentages follow rather steady downward trends to less than 1.2 percent and –3.7 percent, respectively (third quarter of 2005). Considering the entire country, that is, adding enterprises and government to households, the savings

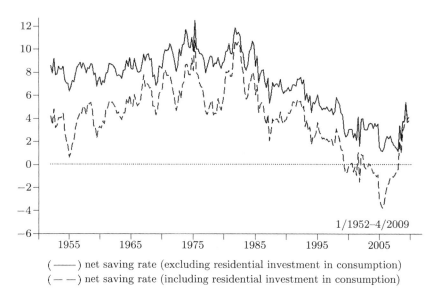

(——) net saving rate (excluding residential investment in consumption)
(– –) net saving rate (including residential investment in consumption)

Figure 10.4 Savings rate: U.S. households (percentage of GDP, quarterly). The savings of households are equal to their total disposable income minus consumption, or minus consumption and residential investment.

rate plunged to negative values, –3.0 percent of GDP (average 2004–2007).[5] The trends and fluctuations of saving rates manifest those of consumption. In particular, the final upward movement of saving rates (– –) mirrors the collapse of residential investment, beginning in 2006.

The increase in the percentage of households' consumption in GDP contrasts with the greater stability of the purchase of goods and services by the government,[6] whose tendency is about horizontal. Since the beginning of the contemporary crisis, an upward trend is apparent, as government demand begins to work as a substitute for the demand of households.

The rising consumption of households is a major development in the macroeconomics of the United States, not an ephemeral fluctuation. As in the case of the other trends discussed in this chapter, it is a structural feature of neoliberalism.

The Indebtedness of Households and Government

While the debt of the financial sector is linked to the expansion of financial mechanisms, the debts of households and government, considered jointly, directly feed demand flows, and their growth is related to neoliberal macroeconomic trends.

Figure 10.5 shows the total of the net debts (gross debt minus assets) in the market instruments[7] held by U.S. households and by the U.S. government, and the two components, as percentages of GDP. The profile of the total (——) is what is more relevant to the present analysis of the *formation of demand*, while the importance of the separation between the two components (households and government) affects the *sustainability* of these trends. From the viewpoint of outlets for enterprises, the demand may come from households or government, but the risks involved in the rising debt of either one of the two agents are not equivalent. The profile of the total debt is quite telling of the historical inflexion of trends in neoliberalism. The percentage fluctuated around a horizontal line from World War II to 1980, amounting to about 58 percent of GDP (average 1952–1980). An upward trend was then established during the neoliberal decades, up to 121 percent of GDP (fourth quarter of 2009).

Interestingly, one can, thus, observe that after World War II, the decline of the government debt (-----) was exactly compensated by the rise of the

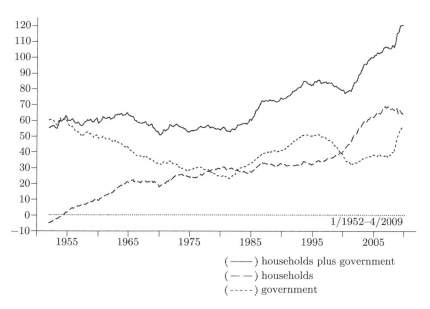

Figure 10.5 Net debts: U.S. households and government (percentage of GDP, quarterly).

debt of households (— —). The debt of government began a new hike with
the rise of interest rates at the beginning of the 1980s, later corrected by
the surplus of the budget during the long boom of the second half of the
1990s. This is precisely when the net debt of households began to soar,
pushing the total debt of the two agents toward its maximum. Finally, the
treatment of the crisis caused the rise of the government debt.

The variable most frequently discussed in relation to the financial crisis
is the gross debt of households. The upward trend of the gross debt of U.S.
households is clearly apparent in Figure 10.6, with the well-known sharp
acceleration after 2000. (Since households hold comparatively fewer credit
market instruments in comparison to their gross debt, and since the percentage of these credit market instruments in GDP remained about constant, the profiles of the gross and net debts of households in the two figures are similar.) The figure also demonstrates that the major component
in the growth of households' debt is mortgage debt. This observation
suggests an increase in residential investment larger than the growth of
consumption in the strict sense, but, as already stated, this is not what
happened.

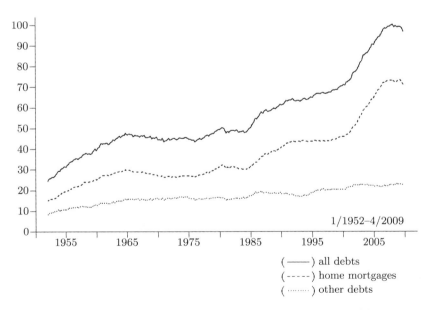

Figure 10.6 Gross debt: U.S. households (percentage of GDP, quarterly). In
Figures 10.5 and 10.6 assets and debts are credit market instruments.

The interpretation of this divergence is to be found in the peculiarities of credit mechanisms in the United States. As is well known, a fraction of mortgage loans is used to finance consumption expenditures, typically college tuition, home improvement, or health care. This can be done by home equity loans (HELs) and home equity lines of credit (HELOCs), a lump sum or a revolving line of credit, respectively, where the value of the home serves as collateral. Another procedure is cash-out refinancing, in which the existing mortgage is renewed for a larger amount (possibly taking advantage of the higher price of the home), with free cash available for other expenditures. Considering only cash-out volumes for all prime conventional loans, they amounted to about $26 billion in 2000 and reached $318 billion in 2006 (to fall to $17 billion in the fourth quarter of 2008).[8]

Income Brackets in Consumption and Debt

The rise of the share of consumption in GDP and the fall of the savings rate in the U.S. economy are major phenomena that could be judged paradoxical, given the dramatic distortion of the profile of distribution to the benefit of high incomes, the category of households that is often assumed to save more.

Various studies show that it is actually the wealthiest fraction of the population that increased its spending.[9] With respect to GDP, the expenses of high incomes added to total spending for two reasons. First, even assuming a constant savings rate, their consumption rose with the concentration of total income in their favor during the neoliberal decades. Second, their savings rate diminished dramatically. (The savings rate of the rest of the population was about maintained.) These consumption patterns are frequently imputed to a wealth effect reflecting the growth of stock-market indices.

The Downward Trend of Accumulation

Figure 10.7 shows the declining trend of domestic investment in fixed capital. The variable considered is a rate of accumulation (——), defined as the growth rate of the net stock of fixed capital of nonfinancial corporations. The horizontal line represents the average accumulation rate prior to neoliberalism.

In spite of the ephemeral recovery during the second half of the 1990s, the rates prevailing during the neoliberal decades appear consistently inferior to this earlier level, with a downward trend. After twenty-five years, the stock

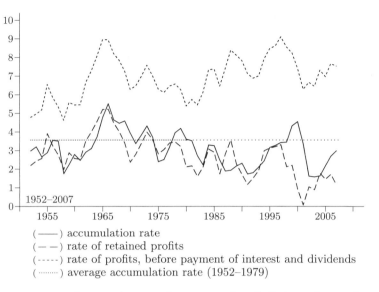

(——) accumulation rate
(− −) rate of retained profits
(-----) rate of profits, before payment of interest and dividends
(········) average accumulation rate (1952–1979)

Figure 10.7 Rate of accumulation and two rates of profit: U.S. nonfinancial corporations (percent, yearly). The rate of accumulation is the ratio of net investment to the net stock of capital, that is, the growth rate of the net stock of fixed capital.

of fixed capital is 32 percent lower than it would have been, had the earlier average rate been maintained. The growth rate of the U.S. economy was, somehow, preserved as a result of the growing productivity of capital in the sector of nonfinancial corporations and the dynamics proper to other sectors of the economy (financial corporations and noncorporate business). Nonetheless, for any given profile of the productivity of capital, 32 percent of fixed capital lost also means an equal loss in the productive capacity of nonfinancial corporations.

Corporate Governance and Investment Rates

In the two profit rates in Figure 10.7, profits are measured after taxes and the denominator is the own funds (or net worth) of corporations. The difference between the two variables concerns the payment of capital income: (1) a rate of profit before the payment of interest and dividends (-----); and (2) the rate of retained profits (— —), in which interest and dividends paid out are subtracted from profits (----- in Figure 4.1).

Figure 10.7 clearly demonstrates the tight relationship between the accumulation rate (——) and the rate of retained profits (— —), while the profit rate before the payment of interest and dividends remains significantly higher and displays a horizontal trend. This relationship indicates that corporations basically self-finance their investment. This ability depends on the rate at which they retain profits, that is, do not pay interest or distribute dividends. This relationship retrospectively justifies the emphasis placed in Part II on the rate of retained profits in the analysis of income distribution. Retained profits condition accumulation.

The tight relationship between retained earnings and investment is puzzling. It suggests that, considering the sector globally, nonfinancial corporations do not finance investment out of new borrowings. Underlying these mechanisms is the preservation of balance-sheet ratios in which tangible assets are about equal to the net worth of corporations. These proportions have been approximately maintained since the 1950s,[10] even prior to neoliberalism.[11] Nonfinancial corporations borrow but these borrowings are used for other purposes, for example, to buy back their own shares, as shown in Figure 4.4. One may wonder why nonfinancial corporations do not use the leverage inherent in the borrowings (at interest rates inferior to profit rates) in the conduct of real investment. This finding is all the more surprising in that leverage is a key element in the conduct of financial operations by financial institutions and might also be used by nonfinancial corporations to the same end. As contended in Chapter 4, neoliberalism, on the one hand, imposed a new corporate governance and, on the other hand, established new relationships and hierarchies between the nonfinancial sector and financial institutions. The observation made in the present section concerning the investment of nonfinancial corporations must be understood in this overall framework. The high levels of real interest rates up to 2000 (Figure 4.2) could be an explanatory factor.

The small deviations between the accumulation rate and the rate of retained profits can be imputed to the ups and downs of business-cycle fluctuations (the variations of the capacity utilization rate) inducing corporations to temporarily borrow or pay back these loans, to adjust their investment to such movements in the short run. The peak during the second half of the 1990s manifests the exceptional degree reached by this mechanism during the long boom of the second half of the 1990s, the expression of an ephemeral wave of borrowings (supplemented by a large flow of direct investment into the United States on the part of the rest of the world, with the same stimulative effect on investment).

The Macro Trajectory of a Hegemonic Power

The overall macroeconomics of neoliberalism are implied in the interpretation of this set of observations in the present chapter, but one must supplement this statement by the reference to U.S. dominance in contempo-

Box 10.1
Net Foreign Assets in Europe

As shown in Figure 10.8 the United States (——), the euro area (— —), and the United Kingdom (·······) all benefit from foreign financing. Concerning the euro area, the percentage remains, however, rather stable and low since 1995, around 4 percent of European GDP. The contrast is sharp with the United States, where the contribution of the financing from the rest of the world increased from 17 percent in 1995 to 56 percent in 2007 (as already evident in the difference between the two variables in Figure 10.2). Both the dimension of the phenomenon and the trend of the variable differ.

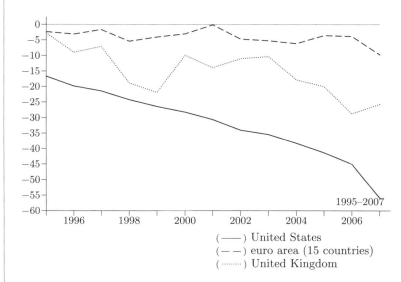

(——) United States
(— —) euro area (15 countries)
(·······) United Kingdom

Figure 10.8 Net foreign assets held by the United States, the euro area, and the United Kingdom (percentage of the GDP of each unit, yearly).

rary capitalism. The features of both neoliberalism and U.S. hegemony are involved. No such pattern could have been maintained in the absence of this privileged position. No such trends prevailed in Europe with the exception of the United Kingdom (Box 10.1), whose situation is as an intermediary between the United States and the euro area (given the prominent role of the City within global finance).

The key element in this respect, making the difference, is the absence of external constraint. The continuation of such a trajectory in the United States, despite the growing current-balance deficit of the country, would have been impossible had not foreigners accepted to invest the corresponding flows of dollars into U.S. enterprises, GSEs, and government. Obviously, the international recognition of the dollar as an unrivaled global currency is a crucial factor in this respect. The direction of causation between the trajectory of the U.S. economy and the international dominance of the country is certainly reciprocal, as the deficit of the U.S. current balance created an opportunity for foreign financial investment and the willingness to finance by the rest of the world allowed for the continuing rise of this deficit without pushing the dollar to the floor.

11

The Mechanics of Imbalance

The previous chapter emphasizes the prevalence of five major trends in the U.S. economy since the 1980s. They relate to (1) the balance of trade or current accounts, (2) foreign financing, (3) consumption, (4) the indebtedness of households and government, and (5) accumulation. Considered jointly, these trends define the trajectory of the U.S. economy.

The simultaneous prevalence of these trends is not coincidental. The present chapter introduces a framework in which they are analyzed as properties of a system of interdependent variables, the manifestations of the same underlying mechanisms.

A classification of countries is introduced, depending on their propensity to run deficits or surpluses. These distinct situations condition the capability of a country to ensure the normal utilization of its productive capacity and maintain decent growth rates. This framework allows for the investigation of the consequences of the gradual transformation of the U.S. economy with respect to both distribution and exposure to international competition as in a global world of free trade. These trends define two major gradual shifts characteristic of the neoliberal decades in the United States. An important finding is the diminishing efficiency of credit as a macro stabilizer in the country.

An Analytical Framework

The basic mechanisms involved in the analysis of the trajectory of the U.S. economy can be investigated in a framework in which only four agents interact. (A model is presented in Appendix A.) Households and government are considered jointly and their demand can be treated as consumption in the broad sense, despite the fact that the former invest in housing and the latter in infrastructures, buildings, and armaments. Thus, the term "investment" is used only in reference to enterprises, to refer to the purchase of the components of fixed capital, aimed at the enhancement of enterprises' productive capacity. (Investment is net of depreciation.) The four agents follow:

1. *Nonfinancial enterprises.* They produce investment goods, consumption goods, and services. They buy investment goods to themselves or import these goods. They receive flows of payments from consumption and exports. They pay incomes (wages, capital income, and taxes) to households and government, denoted as "consumers." These flows depend on the level of production (the value of the capacity utilization rate). Enterprises self-finance their investment; that is, they do not borrow to this purpose.

2. *The financial sector.* It makes loans to consumers and receives loans from the rest of the world. Abstraction is made of the corresponding income flows (such as interest). The flow of domestic credit is controlled by the monetary policy of the central bank.

3. *Consumers: households and government.* Consumers receive the incomes paid by nonfinancial enterprises (wages, capital income, and taxes). The purchasing power of households results from the income they receive and the new loans from the financial sector, but they can deposit a fraction of this purchasing power into the financial sector (more generally, make financial investment). Therefore, their demand is

$$\text{Consumption} = \text{Income} + \underbrace{\text{New loans} - \text{Deposits}}_{\text{Net borrowings} = -\text{Savings}}$$

Concerning financial operations, only the net flow of new loans (new loans minus deposits) is considered and denoted as "borrowings" or "savings." (Borrowings and savings are equal with opposite signs.)[1] Government receives taxes, may borrow, and consumes. Consumers buy consumption goods either produced by domestic enterprises or imported from the rest of the world.

4. *The rest of the world.* The rest of the world sells goods or services (the imports of the country) to consumers and enterprises, and buys goods and services from enterprises (the exports of the country). Depending on the comparative values of these two flows, the rest of the world borrows from

or lends to the financial sector. Whenever the rest of the world sells more than it buys, it automatically finances the economy of the country. This is not a simplifying assumption but the basic accounting identity between the balances of the *current account* and the *financial account* (abstracting from the *capital account,* about null).

The share of total income distributed to consumers, the share of demand that is imported (that is, not bought from domestic producers), and exports, measured as a fraction of productive capacity, are taken as given (structural parameters in the model of Appendix A). A fourth exogenous parameter is the flow of net new loans (or borrowings) provided by the financial sector whose value is controlled by the central bank in the conduct of its monetary policy. For each set of values of these parameters, one can determine the other variables.

Foreign Trade, Exchange Rates, and Deficits

In this framework, no mechanism accounts for the potential influence of exchange rates on the balance of trade. The empirical analysis of U.S. imports and exports reveals a small impact of the exchange rate of the dollar on the exports of the country, but no impact on imports. Notably, the lower value of the dollar (Figure 23.1) during about ten years, between 1988 and 1997, had a favorable effect on the capability of the U.S. economy to export while imports were steadily increasing. This movement is reflected in the profile of the deficit of foreign trade of the country, which was temporarily diminished, but the tendency was not offset (Figure 10.1).

Despite its limited revaluation during the period considered (by about 21 percent between July 2005 and July 2008), the yuan was consistently pegged to the dollar at a low value. This situation certainly had an impact on the upward trend of the U.S. trade deficit. It is important to consider, however, that, as of 2007, 69 percent of the trade deficit on goods of the U.S. economy originated from countries distinct from China. This is shown in Table 11.1, where the total U.S. deficit on goods is broken down for various regions of the world. The prevalence of deficits is notably observed vis-à-vis Europe and Japan, two regions of the world for which the U.S. deficit cannot be imputed to exchange rates systematically biased downward.

Table 11.1 U.S. balance of trade in goods (2007, percent of total)

Total, all countries	100
Europe	16
Canada	9
Latin America	13
China	31
Japan	10
Middle East	4
Africa	8
Others[1]	9

1. Other Asia and Pacific and other Western Hemisphere.

An abstraction is made here of the temporary impact of the exchange rate of the dollar on U.S. exports, since the emphasis is on longer tendencies, not on fluctuations around trends. Beyond such fluctuations, Figure 10.1 emphasizes the stubborn establishment of an upward trend of deficits, the expression of rising consumption in the context of a globalized economy.

Other observations in the present study show that exchange rates respond only slightly to foreign trade deficits and are strongly influenced by international financial flows. A striking empirical observation is the influence of carry trade, where exchange rates appear highly dependent on financial flows from funding currencies to target currencies, as in Chapter 8. This observation adds to the conclusion that, in contemporary capitalism, exchange rates do not serve as foreign trade stabilizers, if they ever did.

In 2005, Ben Bernanke discussed the origin of the U.S. trade deficit. He placed the responsibility on the policies of countries of the periphery that were shaken by the crisis of the 1990s, not on U.S. domestic factors (Box 11.1).

External Imbalance and the Twin Indebtedness

The three first trends—the balance of trade, foreign financing, and consumption—of the trajectory of the U.S. economy are tightly related. As recalled above, the relationship between the trade deficit and the rise of the financing by the rest of the world is an accounting identity. But the

---

Box 11.1
Bernanke's Global Savings Glut: "The U.S. Trade Balance Is the Tail of the Dog."

In a lecture in March 2005,[1] Ben Bernanke explained that the main factor of U.S. foreign trade deficits is to be found in excess global savings:

> I will argue that over the past decade a combination of diverse forces has created a significant increase in the global supply of saving—a global saving glut—which helps to explain both the increase in the U.S. current account deficit and the relatively low level of long-term real interest rates in the world today.

Following Bernanke, the cause of this phenomenon can be found in the development policies of countries of the periphery. These strategies are based on exports, which are not compensated by larger flows of imports (another possible symmetrical component of a development strategy). Why did these countries change their policies, and notably, why do they accumulate reserves?

> In my view, a key reason for the change in the current account positions of developing countries is the series of financial crises those countries experienced in the past decade or so.

An additional question is why such trends affected mostly the United States. The answer is the specific attractiveness of the countries to the eyes of foreign investors (from "saving" countries):

> Thus the rapid increase in the U.S. current account deficit between 1996 and 2000 was fueled to a significant extent both by increased global saving and the greater interest on the part of foreigners in investing in the United States.

(continued)

---

framework in this chapter also accounts for the link between the domestic debt, related to the growth of consumption, and the external debt, a second, less obvious, relationship.

Only in a closed economy are *domestic savings* equal to *domestic investment*. When the rest of the world contributes to the financing of the domestic economy, this foreign financing, sometimes denoted as "foreign savings," must be added to domestic savings. (Any of these components can be positive or negative.) The sum domestic savings (savings of

(continued)

The link with low interest rates is explicitly established (Box 14.2):

> From a narrow U.S. perspective, these low long-term rates are puzzling; from a global perspective, they may be less so.

A first observation is that Bernanke fails to recall that such strategies on the part of less-developed countries appear well in line with the objectives and methods of neoliberal globalization (in sharp contrast with import-substitution industrialization, Box 23.1). Neoliberal globalization implies free trade and the free mobility of capital, with alleged benefits and obvious risks. They require a tight management of currency reserves. Imputing the U.S. deficit to neoliberal globalization is certainly rather sensible, but Bernanke's speech aims at the responsibility of less-advanced countries, not neoliberalism per se.

At the center of global trade deficits, one finds the United States and China. The reference to the crises of the 1990s does not seem to match the conditions met in China. The concern of the Chinese authorities is not about the lack of currency reserves but rather the potential devaluation of these reserves that might follow from a crisis of the dollar. The Chinese development strategy is not the cautious behavior described in the lecture. Should China stimulate its economy, encouraging the massive import of capital goods from the United States with the effect of straightening the U.S. trade balance? Toward 20 percent growth?

---

1. Remarks by Governor Ben S. Bernanke at the Sandrige Lecture, Virginia Association of Economics, Richmond, Virginia, March 10, 2005, www.federalreserve.gov/boarddocs/speeches/2005/200503102/.

enterprises and consumers) *plus* foreign savings is equal to domestic investment:

$$\text{Investment} = \begin{pmatrix} \text{Savings of} \\ \text{enterprises} \end{pmatrix} + \begin{pmatrix} \text{Savings of} \\ \text{consumers} \end{pmatrix} + \begin{pmatrix} \text{Foreign} \\ \text{savings} \end{pmatrix}$$

A feature of the U.S. economy is, however, that investment in fixed capital is basically self-financed, that is, equal to the savings of enterprises. A consequence of the above relationship is, therefore, that the savings of consumers are equal (with opposite signs) to foreign savings; that is, the flow of borrowings by consumers is equal to the financing from the rest of the world:

$$\begin{pmatrix} \text{Savings of} \\ \text{consumers} \end{pmatrix} = -\begin{pmatrix} \text{Foreign} \\ \text{savings} \end{pmatrix} \quad \text{or} \quad \begin{pmatrix} \text{Borrowings} \\ \text{of consumers} \end{pmatrix} = \begin{pmatrix} \text{Foreign} \\ \text{financing} \end{pmatrix}$$

It is important to understand that these equations are the combined outcome of basic accounting relationships and the observation that enterprises' investment is self-financed.

This "twin indebtedness," domestic and international, is an important feature of the macro trajectory of the U.S. economy. The phrase is not fully appropriate because of the presence of stock shares (not loans or debt securities) in the financial investment of households and the rest of the world, but the central idea is there. (Loans and debt securities are, actually, the major components of foreign financing, Table 10.1.)

Figure 11.1 illustrates this relationship. (Debt is limited here to credit market instruments.) The first variable (——) is the net debt of households and government, considered jointly as in Figure 10.5. The second variable (— —) is the net debt of the country toward the rest of the world. One can observe the two plateaus prior to neoliberalism and the parallel upward trends during the neoliberal decades.

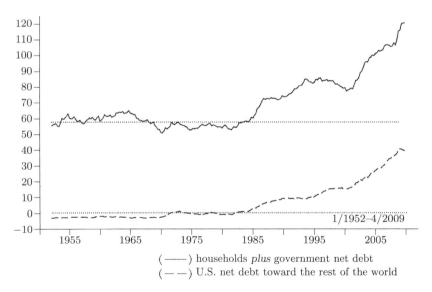

(——) households *plus* government net debt
(— —) U.S. net debt toward the rest of the world

Figure 11.1 Net debts: U.S. households and government considered jointly, and the U.S. economy toward the rest of the world (percentage of U.S. GDP, quarterly). The variables are debts in credit market instruments.

The twin indebtedness is a cousin of the famous "twin deficits" of the 1980s. In those years, the rising external financing was ascribed to the deficit of government. Figure 10.5 allows for the interpretation of this exclusive reference. Between the mid-1980s and the mid-1990s, the rise of total domestic indebtedness as a percentage of GDP could, actually, be imputed to the debt of government, therefore, also the corresponding rise of foreign financing. But government debt decreased during the long boom of the late 1990s and stabilized after the boom, while the debt of households began its hike with the same relationship to foreign financing.

A conclusion of this investigation is, therefore, that the trends typical of the trajectory of the U.S. economy can be reduced to only three. The first component is the upward trend of the share of consumption in total income. The second is "deficit and indebtedness." It jointly refers to the deficit of external trade and the twin debts. The third is the declining trend of accumulation.

Capacity Utilization versus Deficit and Indebtedness

In the present framework, larger loans to consumers positively impact their demand and, consequently, the use of productive capacity. The difficult point in the conduct of macro policies is, however, that these flows also tend to increase imports, thus, deficit and indebtedness (directly concerning domestic indebtedness and, indirectly, as an effect of the trade deficit concerning foreign financing). Symmetrically, a limit placed on loans in order to curb deficit and indebtedness negatively impacts the capacity utilization rate. Except by a fluke, it is impossible to reach simultaneously a normal capacity utilization rate and the equilibrium of the trade balance that commands the stabilization of the stock of foreign financing.

As a consequence, the central bank faces a trade-off in the exercise of monetary policy. A normal capacity utilization rate (and the stability of the general level of prices) is a central target as should also be the equilibrium of foreign trade and the stabilization of indebtedness, but decisions on loans impact the two variables in opposite directions. The difficulty is, thus, to manage a set of diverging variables manipulating a single lever (since exchange rates do not contribute to the correction of foreign trade disequilibria). Monetary policy can alternatively calm down or stimulate demand in the economy, with more or fewer effects influencing capacity utilization rates and inflation; a stimulative policy will increase the trade deficit with the corresponding consequence on debts.

The Propensity to Trade Deficit

Important differences may prevail among countries concerning international trade. This is what renders the trade-off between capacity utilization and the equilibrium of foreign trade more or less acute.

Countries can be classified according to the prevailing situation under the assumption of a normal capacity utilization rate. Under such circumstances, the prevalence of a deficit or surplus of trade is an important structural feature of an economy, which can be called its "propensity to run a deficit." (Appendix A gives a technical definition of this notion.) This deficit or surplus associated with the normal use of productive capacity depends on the values of the structural parameters. Two types of countries can be distinguished: (1) those with a propensity to run a surplus of trade, and (2) those with a propensity to run a deficit.

For a country with a propensity to run a surplus, there is no obstacle to the normal use of productive capacity. When this situation is reached, it is the amount of profits retained by enterprises that limits growth. The economy of the country finances the rest of the world since a surplus of trade prevails. Germany could be judged emblematic of this first configuration, up to the contemporary crisis. In the second instance, that of a propensity to run a deficit when productive capacity is used at a normal level, the constraints proper to the above trade-off prevail. Three cases must be distinguished:

1. *The economy is not constrained to balance its trade nor to stabilize domestic and foreign indebtedness.* The normal use of capacity can be ensured with a simultaneous trade deficit, in combination with domestic and external borrowings. This was the case of the U.S. economy during the neoliberal decades. (As already stated, this absence of external constraint was the expression of the willingness of foreigners to finance the external deficit of the country, avoiding a sharp devaluation of its currency, given the position of the dollar as international currency, used in foreign transactions and reserve money.)

2. *The economy is subject to the requirement to balance its trade and limit foreign financing, that is, an external constraint prevails.* In this case, the consequences of the trade-off are directly felt. The utilization of productive

capacity must be limited to a lower value, with detrimental consequences on growth. This is somehow the case in France or in other European economies. This situation is manifest in the prevalence of a stubborn lack of demand. Enterprises slow down their investment but a normal use of capacity cannot prevail.

3. *The economy is subject to a constraint on its domestic debt.* As above, a normal utilization of productive capacity cannot be reached. As far as households' debt is concerned, the crisis created such a situation in the U.S. economy. The U.S. government must step in to borrow and spend. Which is what it does.

To sum up, returning to U.S. neoliberal trends, one can contend that the specific features of the trajectory of the U.S. economy originated in a policy that intended to maintain normal use of its productive capacity, despite the high propensity of the country to import more than export, and given the tolerance by the rest of the world.

The Distributional and Free-Trade Shifts

The analysis in the previous sections remains static, in the sense that parameters concerning distribution and foreign trade are given. This perspective accounts for degrees of deficit and indebtedness, but not upward trends.

The present section addresses the transformation of the above mechanisms during the neoliberal decades (more specifically, the variation of the three structural parameters, the share of total income distributed to consumers, the share of demand that is imported, and exports, measured as a fraction of productive capacity). The progress of neoliberal corporate governance (that determined high wages at the top, dividend flows, interest rates, etc.) and neoliberal policy trends, on the one hand, and globalization, the advance in the opening of the country to foreign trade (that determined the propensity to import or export), on the other hand, are all involved.

Two basic gradual transformations must be considered:

1. *The distributional shift.* The figures in Part II amply document the more generous payment of high wages in the broad sense, the distribution of dividends, and the large burden of net interest on enterprises, denoted here as the components of the "distributional shift." (The flows of profits lost by enterprises as capital income are apparent in Figure 10.7.) This

transformation can also be considered from the viewpoint of households, where it is expressed in the rise of capital income and high wages at the top. The distributional shift enhanced the purchasing power of households on the part of those receiving high wages and capital income and, finally, increased the total purchasing power of households considered globally.

Table 11.2 compares two periods: (1) the 1970s, the last decade prior to neoliberalism; and (2) the neoliberal years (1980–2008). The figures show that personal income gained 3.3 percentage points of GDP. This transformation was the combined effect of a diminished share of wages (–1.4 percent) despite the increase of upper wages, and a large increase in the share of capital income (+4.4 percent). (In addition, proprietors' income lost 0.4 percent.)

This movement was reflected in the rise of the disposable income of persons in comparison to other income categories, as in Table 11.3. The gain amounted to 2.7 percentage points of GDP. The table also shows that the revenue of governments (federal, state, and local) rose by 1.5 percent, to be added to the 2.7 percent above. Thus, the total gain reached 4.2 percent of GDP. Simultaneously, profits retained by nonfinancial corporations lost 1.6 percent of GDP on the 2.7 percent that they used to retain and invest prior to neoliberalism. The impact on investment was spectacular.

2. *The free-trade shift.* Chapter 8 shows how the establishment of neoliberalism meant the generalization of free trade, the growth of foreign trade, that is, the rising tendency to purchase goods from foreign countries and to export. Involved here is the rising trend toward foreign trade, not an increasing propensity to deficit.

Table 11.2 Breakdown of personal income: U.S. economy (percent of GDP)

	Average 1970s	Average 1980–2008	Variation
Personal income	80.6	83.9	3.3
Compensation of employees	58.5	57.1	–1.4
Proprietors' income	7.5	7.0	–0.4
Rental income of persons	1.5	1.5	–0.0
Personal income receipts on assets	9.6	14.0	4.4
Personal interest income	7.4	10.7	3.2
Personal dividend income	2.2	3.4	1.2
Transfer receipts minus social insurance	3.5	4.2	0.7

Table 11.3 Shares of incomes: U.S. households, governments, and nonfinancial corporations (percent of GDP)

	Average 1970s	Average 1980–2008	Variation
Disposable personal income	70.9	73.6	2.7
Current receipts of governments	27.9	29.3	1.5
Undistributed profits (without adj.) of nonfinancial corporations	2.7	1.1	–1.6

Shifts and Trends

The two neoliberal shifts account in a straightforward manner for the five major trends that compose the macro trajectory of the U.S. economy. (In the model in Appendix A the two shifts are expressed in the rise of two structural parameters, λ and α, and their impact on the equilibrium values of the variables can be determined.) The distributional shift determined the gradual decline of the rate of accumulation (Figure 10.7). The free-trade shift impacted the division of consumers' demand between domestic and foreign producers and the ability to export. This latter movement caused a declining share of the purchases to domestic firms, not offset by rising exports in total demand, which, in turn, rendered necessary the provision of loans in rising proportions in order to maintain a normal use of the existing productive capacity in the U.S. economy. Such trends implied simultaneously a rising share of imports and an increasing trade deficit, as exports did not follow suit (Figure 10.1). This rising deficit entailed the hike of the masses of financing from the rest of the world (Figure 10.2). The policy targeted to the maintenance of the capacity utilization rate required a rising indebtedness of households (Figure 10.6) and, simultaneously, their rising consumption (Figure 10.3) and declining savings rate (Figure 10.4). The shifts account for the rise of the share of consumption in GDP.

One can observe here how the two neoliberal shifts increased the trade-off between the utilization of productive capacity and deficit and indebtedness. To obtain a normal use of productive capacity, a proportionally larger increase of consumer debt was required.

The Diminishing Efficiency of Credit as Macro Stabilizer

Free trade accounts for a well-known limitation of macro policies. In an open economy, the stimulation of output by credit is impaired by the propensity of the economy to import or export. (New loans also stimulate the macroeconomies of the countries from which goods are imported.) The free-trade shift accounts for the increasing difficulties met in the conduct of macro policies. It is, thus possible to refer to a diminishing efficiency of credit in the stimulation of the domestic macroeconomy.

Since the financing by the rest of the world is the other facet of domestic indebtedness, this diminishing efficiency of credit in the stimulation of the domestic macroeconomy accounts for the simultaneous rise of the twin debts. The determination to maintain the utilization of productive capacities in domestic industry and to stimulate growth rates required an aggressive credit policy, gradually more demanding due to the free-trade shift, and pushing ahead the domestic and external debts.

The Convergence between the Two Strands of Determinants

The fragility of the overall financial-global structure and the unsustainable character of the trajectory of the U.S. economy are the two strands of determinants that led to the crisis, as in Diagram 2.1. One the one hand, the absence of constraint to the preservation of the equilibrium of the current account of the country allowed for the continuation of the quest for high income on the part of the upper classes via the daring advance of financialization and globalization. Simultaneously, only the expansion of financial mechanisms to the extreme made possible the rise of the debt of households, a basic condition for the continuation of the trajectory of the U.S. economy without which it would have come to a halt (the alternative being rising government debt).

Concerning the stability of the overall structure, both the rising financing from the rest of the world and the domestic debt, considered intrinsically, represented perilous developments. The threat most frequently cited in this respect is the possible consequences of U.S. deficits on the exchange rate of the dollar. Will foreigners go on lending to a country whose external debt grows consistently? Although the private sector is at the origin of the bulk of foreign financing to the U.S. economy, many commentators point to the debt of the government. Will China continue to buy U.S. Treasury securities? The trigger of the crisis was not, however, the collapse of the dollar. Neoliberalism under U.S. hegemony was destabilized by the seismic wave of the crisis of mortgage markets, signaling the weakness of the debt of households, a basic component of the trajectory of the U.S. economy. This is where the relationship between the two strands of determinants (arrow E in Diagram 2.1) is crucial. The weakness inherent in the debt of households can be imputed separately to each strand of determinants:

1. The rise of the debt of households can be approached as a component of the trends toward financialization and globalization proper to neoliberalism. It was motivated by the quest for high income, made possible by daring financial innovation, and pushed to the extreme by the financing capability of the rest of the world. Enough to destabilize an overall fragile financial structure.

2. This rising debt of households was a straightforward product of the trajectory of the U.S. economy and the two neoliberal shifts. Year after year, more credit was required by the continuation of this trajectory. More, up to the limit of sustainability. Again, enough for a major financial collapse.

The debt of households defines actually the intersection between the two strands of determinants, their convergence point. This convergence does not explain the crisis in itself. It defines the exact modality, that is, how the crisis came to the world.

VI

From the Housing Boom to the Financial Crisis: U.S. Macroeconomics after 2000

The contemporary crisis is the crisis of neoliberalism under U.S. hegemony. It is, therefore, in the inner dynamics of this social and international order that the original causes of the crisis must be sought, notably in the quest for high income (Part II). Parts IV and V focused, respectively, on each of the two strands of determinants originating from this same root: (1) neoliberal globalization and financialization; and (2) the unsustainable macro trajectory of the U.S. economy. As suggested in Diagram 2.1, both categories of factors converged to the determination of the crisis. The seismic wave of the collapse of mortgages destabilized a financial-global structure much broader than the mortgage markets, already in itself a perilous development.

The present part discusses the determinants of the tremendous levels of domestic indebtedness after 2000. There are always two facets to a wave of credit expansion. Two sets of questions must be posed: (1) Who is borrowing, and for what purpose? and (2) Who is lending, and through which instruments? As is well known, the wave of credits originated in a very specific sector, housing, and was consequently based on mortgages; there were also originators motivated by the usual quest for profits. Two conditions had to be met for this encounter: (1) lower requirements toward borrowers, and (2) guarantees concerning the risks incurred by lenders (at least, alleged guarantees). The gap was bridged by the massive entrance into subprime mortgages, the expansion of securitization, and insurance against defaults. Another truly puzzling aspect of these mechanisms is that financial authorities did not stop the rise of lendings, be it a problem of willingness or ability.

Chapter 12 shows how the housing boom allowed for the recovery of the macroeconomy in the wake of the collapse of the information technologies boom. Chapter 13 is devoted to the formation of the mortgage wave. Chapter 14 discusses the circumstances that impaired the efficacy of monetary policy.

12

The Second Reprieve: The Housing Boom and Crash

One of the central aspects of the trajectory of the U.S. economy is the declining investment rate of nonfinancial corporations, with obvious consequences on growth rates. This development was, however, temporarily hidden by the boom of investment in information technologies during the second half of the 1990s, which came suddenly to a halt in the 2001 recession. The recovery from this recession was achieved thanks to the housing boom, itself fueled by the explosion in households' indebtedness, notably its subprime component. The first symptoms of the housing crisis were observed as early as the beginning of 2006, when the decline of the wave of residential investment was initiated after its peak at the end of 2005. The financial crisis came less than two years later, after a failed attempt by the Federal Reserve to moderate the expansion of loans.

U.S. Macroeconomics in the 1990s and after 2000

As a preliminary to the analysis of the housing boom, one must enter into some of the details of the macroeconomics of the United States. Figure 12.1 shows the growth rate of U.S. GDP. One can easily recognize the recessions in the early 1980s, when neoliberalism was imposed, and in 1991. Relevant to the present analysis are the long boom of the second half of the 1990s, the 2001 recession, the subsequent slack recovery, and the entrance into the Great Contraction as of 2008.

Although the growth rate of U.S. GDP did not turn negative in the variable in the figure,[1] the 2001 recession was rather severe. A plunge of growth rates into a six-quarter-long contraction (Phase I in the figure) occurred, followed by a nine-quarter-long recovery (Phase II). It was the first recession

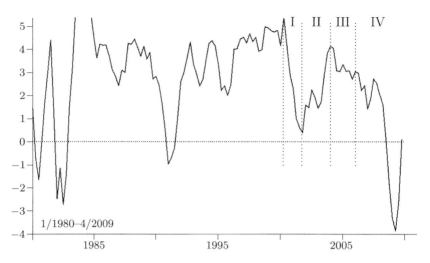

Figure 12.1 Annual growth rate of GDP: U.S. economy (percent, quarterly). The variable is the growth rate of real GDP in one quarter with respect to the same quarter of the previous year. Vertical dotted lines mark (I) the second quarter of 2000, (II) the fourth quarter of 2001, (III) the first quarter of 2004, and (IV) the second quarter of 2006.

since the early 1990s. The nine years between 1992 and 2000 were a period of steady growth, in particular during the long boom of the second half of the 1990s. The recovery was followed by a short plateau, actually tilted downward (Phase III). The downturn of housing markets at the beginning of 2006 marked the entrance into a new phase (Phase IV) and the economy slid toward what could originally be understood as a new recession, actually the first steps of the contraction.

Concerning enterprises' investment, since 1980, the downward trend of the accumulation of fixed capital (the first variable [——] in Figure 10.7) in U.S. nonfinancial corporations was interrupted by only one significant upward fluctuation of investment during the boom of the second half of the 1990s. The profile of investment during this boom—a five-year-long boom ending with the collapse into the 2001 recession—is that of a classical business cycle of major amplitude, the temporary relaxation of a downward trend. But the aesthetics of the cycle hide the interaction of the more complex mechanisms that underlie the U.S. macro trajectory.

The First Reprieve: The Boom of Information Technologies

Figure 12.2 allows for a closer examination of the dynamics of investment underlying business-cycle fluctuations.

The upward trend of investment in information technologies (-----) was not affected by the 1991 recession, went on ballooning during the 1990s, and culminated in 2000. It is this component of investment that gave to the long boom its truly dramatic character. This rise sustained the macroeconomy during a number of years, finally peaked in the fourth quarter of 2000, and came to an end. The profile of equipment and structures (········), the remainder of nonresidential investment, is quite distinct,

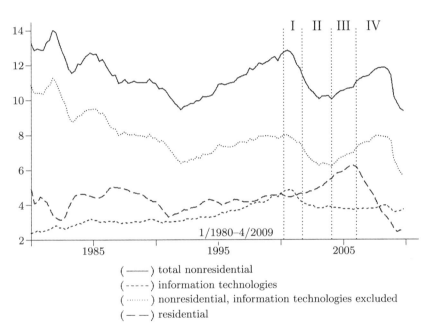

(———) total nonresidential
(-----) information technologies
(········) nonresidential, information technologies excluded
(— —) residential

Figure 12.2 Investment rates: U.S. economy (percentage of GDP, quarterly). The figure breaks down total investment into nonresidential (———) and residential investment (— —). The two other variables (----- and ········) are the components of nonresidential investment that add up to the total of this investment.

There are three differences in the measure of nonresidential investment here (———) in comparison to the variable in Figure 10.7: (1) Investment, in Figure 10.7, is net of depreciation instead of gross here. (2) The denominator is the stock of fixed capital instead of GDP. (3) The unit of analysis is nonfinancial corporations instead of the private economy.

trended downward. It accompanied the long boom though in a less spectacular manner.

There was, indeed, a financial bubble paralleling the boom of investment in information technologies. A major divergence is observed between the stock-market index and profits in Figure 4.5.[2] The temporary divergence between the third quarter of 1997 and the first quarter of 2003 is clearly apparent in the figure. Its amplitude is large. Between the peak of profits in the third quarter of 1997 and the peak of the stock market exactly three years later, the stock price rose 30 percent, while profits declined 24 percent!

The 2001 Recession and Residential Investment

The various components of final demand—residential and nonresidential investments (Figure 12.2), the consumption of households (the first variable [——] in Figure 10.3), and government purchases of goods and services—played distinct roles in the fluctuations of growth rates around the 2001 recession.

The four phases introduced in Figure 12.1 must be distinguished:

1. Beginning with Phase I, the decline of the components of nonresidential investment, in particular the collapse of investment in information technologies, was the main factor of the recession. Residential investment or government purchases played no role in the downturn, while the consumption of households went on growing.

2. During Phase II, nonresidential investment was clearly not the engine of the recovery. The first component, investment in information technologies, went on declining, and the remainder of nonresidential investment did not recover. The share of households' consumption in GDP was stagnating, though at a very high level. The housing boom and government expenditures in goods and services were the two main factors of the recovery. Residential investment, which had not been affected by the contraction of output, grew dramatically at the beginning of Phase II, gaining 1.7 percentage points of GDP. The contribution of government expenditures was more modest. It gained 0.4 of a percentage point during Phase II. (One can observe, parenthetically, that military expenses contributed to 60 percent of this rise.)

There was, actually, a form of substitution within the final demand of households. From the beginning of 1997 to the end of Phase I, the consumption, in the strict sense, of households rose rapidly, before stagnating in relation to GDP. Exactly when this break occurred, residential investment rose sharply.

3. Turning to Phase III, when the new growth rates prevailed after the recovery, and nonresidential investment resumed its growth, the main development was the culmination of residential investment at a very high level, while other variables went on their way. There was only a short, stable plateau of growth rates around 2005, rather ephemeral and at a comparatively low level.

4. Residential investment was destabilized at the beginning of Phase IV, slightly ahead of the rise of defaults and delinquencies in 2006, followed by the financial crisis of 2007 and the subsequent contraction of output in 2008.

As strikingly illustrated in Figure 12.2, residential investment was the crucial component of demand throughout Phases I and II. It worked as a "second reprieve," after the collapse of the boom of information technology. There was no decline of residential investment during the recession and this component of demand kept increasing steadily as the economy went out of the recession. It was the engine of this recovery toward a new fragile plateau of growth rates, as the housing boom reached its maximum.

The Mortgage Wave

If the engine of the recovery from the 2001 recession was the wave of residential investment, this surge was only made possible by the wave of mortgage loans, whose value outstanding gained more than 15 percentage points of GDP only over Phases I and II. This rise of household debt was, in turn, made possible by the outburst of low-quality mortgages, a perilous development, as is well known.

Figure 12.3 shows the quarterly flows of mortgages. New loans, excluding refinancings, are denoted as "purchases." One can observe the steady growth of mortgage origination for this component (——), culminating in 2005. (The series is not de-seasonalized but a trend line is shown.) Prior to 2004, the profile of refinancings fluctuated more, with a peak in 2003 (during the decline of interest rates in Phase II). These large flows materialized in rising stocks of loans. The stock of mortgage loans outstanding (Figure 10.6) grew from 47 percent of GDP before the 2001 recession, at the beginning of Phase I, to 61 percent at the end of Phase II, and culminated at 73 percent at of the beginning of 2007.

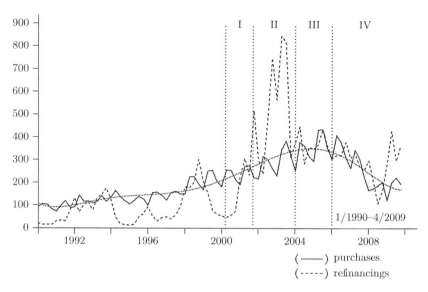

Figure 12.3 Mortgage origination: U.S. households, quarterly flows (billions of dollars). Dotted lines are trend lines.

The financial sector originating the loans issued huge masses of MBSs to support its activity. (Standard bonds are also a source of financing but less important than MBSs, see Table 13.2.) Figure 12.4 shows the profiles of the issuance of U.S. corporate bonds for financial (——) and nonfinancial (— —) corporations. The wave of issuance of bonds by the financial sector peaked at 8.0 percent of GDP during Phase III. The contrast is sharp with issuances of bonds by the nonfinancial sector. They reached a first maximum value in 2001, declined to very low levels during Phase III, and finally returned to a higher value. (The movement of this latter variable echoes the profile of borrowings in credit market instruments and buybacks on the part of nonfinancial corporations after 2004 in Figure 4.4.)

Dubious Loans?

Although the notion of a subprime crisis points to the rising indebtedness of households pertaining to the lower income brackets, most loans were contracted by high income brackets. Indebtedness is not typical of the poorer fractions of households.

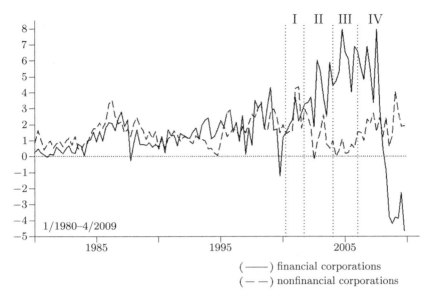

Figure 12.4 Issuance of corporate bonds: U.S. financial and nonfinancial corporations (percentage of GDP, quarterly).

Figure 12.5 shows the proportion of U.S. households with mortgage loans by income quintile. Two years are considered, 1984 and 2007. It clearly demonstrates that, in both years, the proportion of households with loans is positively correlated with income levels, from between 13 and 17 percent for the first quintile to between 72 and 75 percent for the upper quintile. A second observation is that neoliberalism, including after 2000, did not substantially modify this pattern. There was no rise in the indebtedness of the poorest segments of households in terms of number of mortgages. The largest increase appears typical of the middle classes, for which the distance between the two variables is larger, reaching 10 percent for the third and fourth quintiles.

This observation is confirmed by the consideration of the charges (principal and interest) that the payment of the debt represents as a percentage of the income of the group. Overall, higher income brackets pay a larger percentage of their after-tax income (an average of about 10 percent during the 1990s and after 2000[3]). The rising burden of indebtedness is apparent for the three quintiles 20–40, 40–60, and 60–80, whose payments rose consistently since the early 1990s.

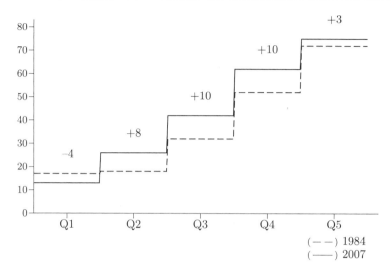

Figure 12.5 Proportion of U.S. households with a mortgage loan in various income brackets in 1984 and 2007 (percent). The horizontal axis shows the income of households by quintile from the lowest to the highest quintile.

A major feature of this increasing indebtedness is, however, that it meant the inclusion within the mass of mortgage borrowers of households that did not comply with traditional requirements, often families already facing difficulties in their payments (probably the lower segments of the middle classes, such as the 20–40 and 40–60 quintiles). These loans are known as "subprime loans," now famous worldwide.[4]

What is a subprime loan? Mortgages are generally defined in reference to *conforming* or *agency* mortgages as guaranteed by the Federal Housing Administration (FHA), Fannie Mae, and Freddie Mac (Chapter 13). Subprime borrowers are described by a number of specific events: (1) one- or two-month delinquency during the last one or two years; (2) judgment, foreclosure, repossession, or charge-off in the previous two years (Figure 16.1 caption); (3) low credit score (FICO);[5] (4) amortization and interest/income ratio larger than 50 percent; and so on. "Subprime" is actually the lowest category in a hierarchy of problematic loans such as Jumbo, Alt-A, and subprime. "Jumbo" refers to large loans, often corresponding to so-called luxury residencies, a riskier market; and "Alt-A," short for Alternative A-paper, is riskier than A-paper (another name for "prime") but less risky than subprime. Many of these loans were adjustable rate mortgages (ARMs), with a pending risk in the event of a rise of interest rates.

Risky loans ballooned in the mid-2000s, beginning in 2004. As shown in the left part of Table 12.1 (Origination), subprime and Alt-A loans accounted for about 12 percent of total origination in 2001, 11 percent in 2003 and, then, rose to 40 percent in 2006, a late but dramatic hike. (The right part of the table is used in Chapter 13.)

Issuers resorted to various procedures to entice borrowers into indebtedness, even more perilous than ARMs. One of them was "interest-only" mortgages, in which borrowers are allowed to pay only interest, usually during five or ten years. Even more daring was "negative amortization" or "deferred interest," in which payments can be inferior to interest, the difference being added to the debt.

The Hike of Home Prices

The comparative easy access to borrowing fueled the rise of home prices. The S&P/Case-Schiller home price index is shown in Figure 12.6, deflated by the GDP deflator, for the average of the country and within three large cities. Between the first quarter of 1996 and the first quarter of 2006, the index rose at a yearly average rate of 6.7 percent above the GDP deflator.

The increase of prices added, in turn, to the expansion of loans for three reasons. First, more expensive homes require more borrowings. Second, the new higher values of homes given as collateral allowed for new borrowings when refinancings were performed. This is the procedure known as "cash-out" in which borrowers receive additional cash. Third, lenders see in the increasing values of homes a guarantee in case of default. At least, lenders and borrowers were not expecting a decline of prices.

The 2005–2006 Housing Downturn

As shown in Figure 12.7, the number of housing permits culminated in September 2005 at 2,263,000 units and fell abruptly, reaching 1,381,000 in July 2007 and slightly less than 500,000 in April 2009.

The sales of existing homes underwent a similar movement (Table 12.2), culminating at 7,075,000 units in 2005, before declining to 5,652,000 in 2007, and to less than 5 million in 2008. An even stronger decline is observed for new homes. Simultaneously, the stock of unsold homes began its

Table 12.1 Mortgage origination and issuance of ABSs: U.S. economy (2001–2006, billions of dollars)

	Origination					Issuance of ABSs	
	Total	Subprime	Alt-A	Subprime + Alt-A		Subprime + Alt-A	
							Percent/
					Percent/Total		Origination
	$	$	$	$		$	
	(a)	(b)	(c)	(d) = (b) + (c)	(e) = (d)/(a)	(f)	(g) = (f)/(d)
2001	2,113	190	60	250	12	99	39
2002	2,773	231	68	299	11	176	59
2003	3,765	335	85	420	11	269	64
2004	2,600	540	200	740	28	521	70
2005	2,755	625	380	1,005	36	797	79
2006	2,520	600	400	1,000	40	814	81

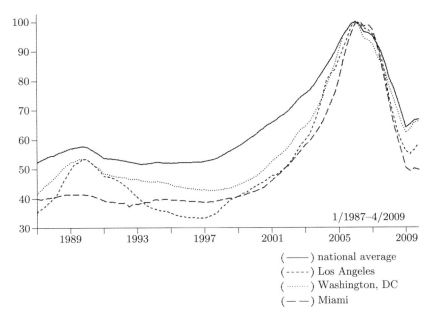

Figure 12.6 Home-price indices deflated by the GDP deflator (maximum of the series =100, quarterly). The four indices culminated either in the first or second quarter of 2006.

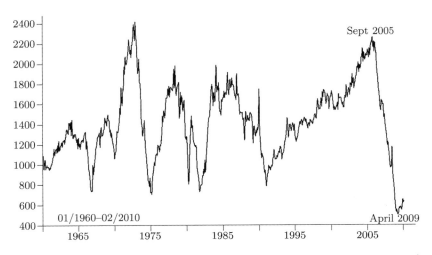

Figure 12.7 New privately owned housing units authorized by building permits: United States (thousands, annualized monthly data).

Table 12.2 Home sales: U.S. households

	Sales of single-family homes (thousands of units)		Variation since 2005 (percent)	
	Existing homes	New homes	Existing homes	New homes
2004	6,723	1,200	—	—
2005	7,075	1,285	0.0	0.0
2006	6,478	1,051	−8.4	−18.2
2007	5,652	776	−20.1	−39.6
2008	4,912	482	−30.6	−62.5
2009	5,150	372	−27.2	−71.1
2010[1]	5,197	387	−26.5	−69.9

1. Forecast as of May 2010.

hike from slightly more than 2.8 million to 4.6 million between the end of 2005 and July 2008 (or from 4.5 to 10.9 months of sales).[6]

This was, in no way, the first disruption of housing markets in the United States but it was the largest. The earlier most dramatic episode since 1960 was the crisis in 1973 (Figure 12.7). A specific aspect of the housing crisis after 2005 is that it came in the wake of a long period of steady growth from 1991 onward. Contrary to the 1973 crisis, it occurred in a context of stability of the GDP deflator.

The collapse of home prices was part of the overall housing downturn. After the maximum reached at the beginning of 2006, a sharp decline of home prices was observed (Figure 12.6).

13

Feeding the Mortgage Wave

The mortgage wave after 2000 and its subprime component made the housing boom possible, but the rise of loans would have been itself impossible in the absence of the support from securitization and the insurance against defaults, two crucial financial devices. Both categories of mechanisms simultaneously expanded tremendously and underwent significant transformations during the decade. The traditional activity of Ginnie Mae and GSEs (Fannie Mae and Freddie Mac) in the issuance of MBSs, was supplemented by the new generation of private-label issuers. The business of insuring against credit defaults spurred the activity of the new boiling derivative market of CDSs.

These developments were crucial to the expansion of the mortgage wave. They were also basic components of what Chapter 9 denotes as a "fragile and unwieldy structure." Obviously, such instruments did not develop simply because they were necessary to the continuation of the U.S. trajectory! Origination, securitization, and insurance are all profitable businesses.

U.S. Agency Securitization: A Historical Perspective

The contemporary procedures of securitization are only the latter episode of a long history, whose origins must be traced to the treatment of the Great Depression, during the New Deal and the war. The thorough transformation of these mechanisms, originally under strict government control, to the expansion of private-label issuers was an important factor in the contemporary crisis.

In 1934, Congress passed the National Housing Act intending to restore the conditions prevailing in the housing market and to prevent future collapses. The act created the FHA, in charge of providing lenders with protection against losses. The Federal National Mortgage Association (Fannie Mae) was established in 1938, at the request of President Roosevelt. It was a government agency buying the mortgage loans of banks, thus providing them with fresh cash and multiplying their potential activity. Fannie Mae was originally financed by the issuance of plain bonds sold to investors, with the guarantee of the federal government. It only purchased loans insured by the FHA.

In the 1960s, a reform process was initiated with the purpose of alleviating the involvement of the federal government in the support of the mortgage activity of banks and to remove the activity of Fannie Mae from the federal budget. In 1968, Fannie Mae's capital was opened to investors, becoming a GSE, a stockholder-owned corporation. Simultaneously, the administration created a new agency, the Government National Mortgage Association (Ginnie Mae), prolonging the government's commitment in Fannie Mae concerning specific programs (such as the housing of veterans).

Two important changes occurred in 1970. First, Ginnie Mae developed a new procedure, securitization, issuing MBSs. Second, a new major piece was added, with the creation of the Federal Home Loan Mortgage Corporation (Freddie Mac). Its status was similar to that of Fannie Mae, with the special purpose of securitizing mortgage loans (other than those handled by Ginnie Mae), joined in this activity by Fannie Mae.

There is some ambiguity concerning the legal status of these institutions and their activity. Ginnie Mae is thoroughly controlled and guaranteed by the government and known as a federal agency. To September 2008, Fannie Mae and Freddie Mac were privately owned corporations, with stock shares in the stock market but subject to specific regulation. They are both classified as GSEs. Their situation, again, changed in 2008.

Abstracting from the crisis conditions prevailing since September 2008, Fannie Mae and Freddie Mac, the largest institutions, simultaneously issue standard securities (or plain bonds, that is, not the result of securitization) and are at the origin of the mortgage pools issuing MBSs. A few other GSEs, such as the Federal Home Loan Banks (FHLBs) or the Federal Agricultural Mortgage Corporation, are also active in the refinancing of mortgage originators, though they are much less important.

Figure 13.1 describes the progress of the overall activity of these institutions (and a few, much smaller, others) since the 1950s. The first variable

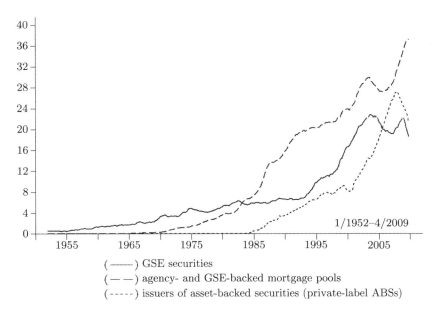

(——) GSE securities
(— —) agency- and GSE-backed mortgage pools
(-----) issuers of asset-backed securities (private-label ABSs)

Figure 13.1 Securities outstanding: securities other than MBSs issued by GSEs, MBSs issued by Ginnie Mae and GSEs, and ABSs issued by private-label issuers (percentage of GDP, quarterly).

(——) is the total stock of standard securities issued, as a percentage of GDP. One can notice the accelerated growth of this total from 1993 onward to 2003, when these institutions were the objects of serious attacks. The percentage peaked at about 23 percent of GDP. The second variable (— —) shows the MBSs outstanding issued by Ginnie Mae and the GSEs. In 1983, this stock became larger than the amount of standard securities, rising tremendously. It culminated at 30 percent of GDP in 2003. The total liabilities (standard securities and MBSs) of these institutions reached 53 percent of GDP in 2003 (to be compared, for example, to 136 percent for all assets of U.S. banks and insurance or, equivalently, 132 percent for the financial assets of mutual and pension funds, Figure 7.1).

New legislation (notably the Community Reinvestment Act [CRA] of 1977) induced Fannie Mae and Freddie Mac to change the conditions at which they were supporting mortgage origination, with the purpose of making borrowings affordable to a larger number of people. The objective was to end the discrimination against low- and moderate-income neighborhoods, in particular black communities. Other pieces of legislation, such as the Federal Housing Enterprises Financial Safety and Soundness Act of 1992 required that Fannie Mae and Freddie Mac devote a percentage of their lending to support such loans. These programs gradually developed to the 2000s and were probably responsible for part of the ensuing losses in the crisis. In July 2008, Fannie Mae and Freddie Mac were placed under the conservatorship of the Federal Housing Finance Agency (FHFA) and their role increased (Figure 13.1 [— —]) and will likely keep increasing in the coming years.

Private-Label ABS Issuers

Beginning in the mid-1980s, securitization developed in the United States on the part of financial corporations distinct from Fannie Mae, Freddie Mac, and Ginnie Mae. The phrases "private-label ABSs" and "non-agency ABSs" are alternatively used to refer to ABSs thus issued.

The outburst of securitization by private-label ABS issuers is illustrated in Figure 13.1, where the third variable (-----) accounts for the total of ABS securities thus issued. After 2000, they continued to grow at an accelerated pace, up to the end of 2007, that is, to the very beginning of the crisis. At this date, they amounted to 27 percent of GDP and 87 percent of the stock of MBSs of Ginnie Mae and GSEs (53 percent of the total of the MBSs and plain securities of the two institutions).

The securitization of mortgage loans is the major component of the overall issuance of ABSs by private-label issuers. This is shown in Table 13.1. (Table 13.1 displays yearly flows, instead of total amounts outstanding in Figure 13.1.) In 2006, within the $1.69 trillion of the total issuance of private-label ABSs in the United States, mortgages and home-equity loans amounted to $1.32 trillion (including $0.16 trillion of subprime loans). All the components (public MBSs, subprime, HELs, and commercial mortgage-backed securities [CMBSs]) increased steadily from 2000 onward. One can notice, in particular, the very high value and large growth rate of home-equity loans. They reached $0.38 trillion in 2006, that is, ten times more than in 2001.

Year after year, the vast majority of subprime and Alt-A loans were securitized. This is shown in Table 12.1, where the two right columns (Issuance of ABSs,) display the total amounts securitized for the total of the two categories of loans. In 2001, already 39 percent of subprime and Alt-A loans were securitized, but in 2006 the percentage reached 81 percent!

Table 13.1 Private-label securitization: U.S. yearly issuance (billions of dollars)

	2000	2001	2002	2003	2004	2005	2006	2007
Mortgages and HELs		315	438	627	860	1,243	1,321	908
Public MBSs	66	143	214	297	329	540	566	436
Subprime mortgages		61	78	104	171	175	161	205
HELs		37	95	139	261	354	380	32
Commercial MBSs	49	74	52	86	99	174	214	236
Other		234	241	262	258	346	366	357
Credit cards		70	73	67	51	67	75	93
Auto loans (prime)		48	56	52	41	56	52	38
Other ABSs		117	111	142	166	224	240	226
Total	390	549	679	888	1,118	1,589	1,687	1,266

HELs: Home equity loans.
Public MBSs: MBSs registered at the Securities and Exchange Commission (SEC).

The issuance of ABSs was a significant source of profits. Considering only U.S. FDIC-insured banks, net securitization income accounted for about 12 percent of the noninterest income in 2006.[1] They were also a very efficient mechanism intending to protect originators from pending defaults.

Prior to the crisis, ABSs were a major component of total bonds outstanding. This is shown in Table 13.2, which gives a synthetic view of the total bonds outstanding in the U.S. economy at the end of 2007. For four sectors, it distinguishes between the stocks of plain bonds and ABSs. Within a total of $24.50 trillion, ABSs amount to $8.35 trillion, that is, about one-third.

The Late Outburst of Collateralized Debt Obligations

Like ABSs in general, CDOs, issued by a specific category of vehicles, played a central role in the financial crisis and are now rather well known, although the technicalities of CDOs are somewhat tricky (Box 13.1).

Table 13.2 Total bonds outstanding: U.S. economy (end of 2007, trillions of dollars)

Sectors	Plain bonds	ABSs	Total
NONFINANCIAL SECTORS			
Government	Treasury securities / Municipal securities 7.29		7.29
Nonfinancial corporations	Corporate bonds 3.56		3.56
FINANCIAL SECTORS			
Ginnie Mae, GSEs	Debt securities 2.91	Agency- and GSE-backed mortgage pools 4.46	7.37
Others	Corporate bonds 2.39	ABS issuers 3.89	6.28
TOTAL	16.14	8.35	24.50

Why such sophisticated devices? For various basic regulatory reasons, the securities issued by ABS issuers are typically sold to banks, insurance companies, and mutual and pension funds, which would not engage into investments in lowly rated securities, in particular when the counterpart includes a significant fraction of subprime loans. This is where CDOs stepped onto the stage. Prior to the crisis, when subprime loans were accumulating, CDOs worked as transformers of pools of dubious assets into upper-grade investments, since investors holding senior tranches were assumed to run practically no default risk. Thus, huge piles of lowly rated non-prime loans or junk bonds were metamorphosed into quasi-AAA investment products. Simultaneously, the risk was concentrated within junior tranches, bought by investors attracted by higher yields, typically hedge funds. By this magic, huge baskets of dubious loans were sold around the globe.

Box 13.1
Securitization: A Variety of Instruments

This box supplements the first definition of securitization in Box 7.1. A variety of ABSs exists according to (1) the peculiarities of the entity (a "vehicle") in which the securities (bonds) are issued, and (2) the nature of the assets used as collateral. An important category is mortgage-backed securities (MBSs), either commercial mortgage-backed securities (CMBSs) or residential mortgage-backed securities (RMBSs).

The bonds issued can be classified hierarchically into various subcategories, denoted as "tranches" (French for "slices"). When the cash flow (interest and amortization paid on loans or securities) reaches the vehicle, the upper ("senior") tranches are paid first, and so on, gradually, down to the lower, "junior" tranches. Obviously, interest rates are lower for seniors than for juniors.

It is useful to know that the terminology is not uniform among the various sources providing data concerning these instruments. When a new category is introduced, the previous generic term is often used to refer to a category of "others." Thus, ABSs may refer to all types of asset-backed securities or to specific subsets. The same convention is used here, whenever meanings are obvious.

An important category of such securities is CDOs. The bonds issued are divided into tranches. The collateral assets can be either loans or securities, possibly already ABSs.[1] In the first case, the bonds are called collateralized loan obligations (CLOs).

---

1. Collateralized bond obligations are specialized in junk bonds; the assets of ABS CDOs are ABSs; those of CDO squared are CDOs, and so on.

The Explosion of the Issuance of ABSs after 2000

Although the role of the United States was central, the rise of private-label securitization after 2000 was a global phenomenon. The figures in Table 13.3 are yearly issuances, worldwide and in the United States, between 2000 and 2008, distinguishing between CDOs and other ABSs.

A first straightforward observation is the sharp rise in global ABS issuance. In 2006, prior to the crisis, the total issuance of ABSs (CDOs, MBSs, and other ABSs) amounted to $2.65 trillion to be compared to $0.56 trillion in 2000, a multiplication by a factor of almost five in six years. Concerning

Table 13.3 Private-label securitization: Issuance worldwide (billions of dollars)

	2000	2001	2002	2003	2004	2005	2006	2007	2008
ABSs: Worldwide	488	687	825	1,108	1,358	1,938	2,200	1,845	1,192
ABSs: U.S.	390	549	679	888	1,118	1,589	1,687	1,273	188
ABSs: Non-U.S.	98	138	146	220	240	349	512	571	1,004
CDOs: Worldwide	79	80	88	83	128	241	445	421	156
Total	566	767	913	1,190	1,486	2,179	2,645	2,266	1,348

"ABSs" refers to ABSs other than CDOs.

the last years, one can notice that, in the United States, the growth rate of the issuance of ABSs began to decline in 2006 (a growth rate of 6 percent compared to an increase of 42 percent between 2004 and 2005), while issuance was expanding rapidly in the rest of the world, though from a much lower level. Figure 13.2 shows (——) the profile of the issuance of U.S. non-agency MBSs (monthly issuance), a dramatic illustration of the explosion of these mechanisms after 2000, which echoes the trends introduced in Chapter 7.

The profile of the issuance of CDOs worldwide is quite specific and telling. Figure 13.2 (— —) shows its tremendous late rise, from the beginning of 2005 to the crisis. Concerning issuances both in the United States and worldwide, Figure 13.2 confirms that CDOs contributed to the protracted expansion of securitization in the latter years, just prior to the crisis, when the decline of residential investment was already under way and subprime mortgages were accumulating.

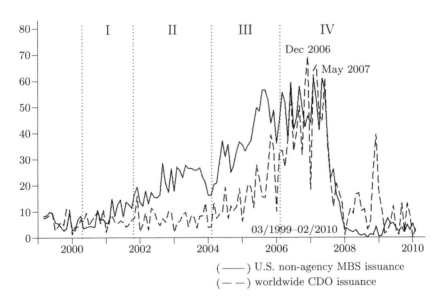

(——) U.S. non-agency MBS issuance
(— —) worldwide CDO issuance

Figure 13.2 Issuances of U.S. private-label (non-agency) MBSs and total CDOs worldwide (billions of dollars, monthly). Monthly data are used instead of yearly data as in Table 12.3.

Credit Default Swaps

The insurance against credit defaults by private corporations has grown as a major activity, paralleling the rise of risky loans and securitization. The main instruments of credit default insurance are credit default swaps. Although the market for CDSs is in no way the largest component of derivative markets, their volume and growth are fascinating. While, at the end of 2004, the total debt insured (the notional value of CDSs) amounted to $640 billion, this total reached $58 trillion (almost 100 times more) at the end of 2007, another striking illustration of the outburst of financial mechanisms during those years.[2] (Figure 7.4 shows the total outstanding of the gross market value of OTC CDSs.)

The insurance of debt is or was, prior to the crisis, performed by specialized institutions (such as Ambac and Municipal Bond Investor Assurance [MBIA]), known as "monoline insurers," whose main activity is CDSs, insurance companies (such as American International Group [AIG]), banks, and hedge funds. CDSs were originally contracts between insurers and the holders of debts (loans or securities), but they became important instruments on OTC derivative markets, where CDSs are traded, that is, sold, purchased, and resold. CDSs are a prominent speculative instrument. They are frequently contracted for debts that are not held, by agents expecting that the value of the security insured will diminish (allowing its purchase at a lower price and, in case of default, benefiting of a protection at the favorable price contracted earlier). A consequence is that the total notional value of CDSs outstanding is much larger than the underlying debt insured.

In this respect, it is interesting to compare the above $58 trillion, the notional value of CDSs in 2007, to the total debt outstanding of all U.S. nonfinancial sectors, that is, households, government, and nonfinancial business. This total reached $31.7 trillion in 2007. The two figures clearly illustrate the excesses to which the dynamics of free (financial) markets may lead.

14

Losing Control of the Helm in Times of Storm

Financial authorities did not passively observe the housing boom, the mortgage wave, and the explosion of financial mechanisms. But, given the propensity to deregulate, monetary policy was the unique instrument in the late attempt at checking the rise of household debt and the financial craze (Box 14.1). This policy was manifest in the gradual increase of the Federal Funds rate as soon as the recovery from the 2001 recession was obtained. The attempt failed.

It is also important to understand that there was no panacea in a monetary policy susceptible of impacting long-term rates to solve the problems of the period. Had the Federal Reserve more promptly stopped the rise of mortgages, the crisis would have come earlier, though its amplitude could have been reduced. There was no elegant way out. But the Federal Reserve lost control of the helm in times of financial storm, a quite unfortunate development and an object of complaint on the part of then-Chairman Alan Greenspan.

The Failure of Monetary Policy

Three categories of problems combined their effects to impair the efficacy of monetary policy. A central aspect of macro dynamics during the period is involved, the effect of the diminished efficiency of credit as macro stabilizer introduced in Chapter 11. The rising indebtedness of households became a necessary support of U.S. macroeconomic activity. Chapter 11 ascribed this phenomenon to the features of the trajectory of the U.S. economy (the distributional and free-trade shifts). Government debt would have been an alternative to household indebtedness, but it was not on the agenda.

Box 14.1
Monetary Policy

Monetary policy refers to a set of mechanisms by which the central bank, motivated by various objectives, modifies the conditions to which loans are granted to economic agents and, thus, impacts the levels of demand (consumption and investment) and production in the economy. ("Monetary policy" is somewhat of a misnomer for "credit policy.") The targets of monetary policy are the stabilization of the macroeconomy (limiting overheatings and recessions, and fighting unemployment) and the control of inflation. Within neoliberalism a priority is given to price stability.[1]

The basic instrument is the interest rate charged by the central bank on its loans to financial institutions. In the United States, the Federal Reserve adjusts a "target rate" and transactions are finally performed at what is known as the Federal Funds rate. The manipulation of this rate alters the ability of banks to lend to the agents that are at the origin of production and demand.

The difference between short- and long-term interest rates is important. In the United States, the impact of the Federal Reserve's policies on the short-term interest rates that banks charge to borrowers is immediate[2] and intrinsically impacts the decisions made by economic agents (typically, enterprises in search of liquidities). A crucial lever of monetary policy is, however, the

(continued)

A second problem was the overall context of deregulation and the rise of private-label issuers. If securitization had remained the monopoly of agencies or GSEs, as during the first postwar decades, it would have been much easier to control these mechanisms, provided that the willingness to do so existed. The consequences of these problems were multiplied by a third difficulty, the impaired capability of the Federal Reserve to impact long-term interest rates in the prevailing context of financial innovation and globalization. The Federal Reserve, very untimely though not coincidentally, lost a considerable fraction of its power to impact long-term interest rates, and the move toward stricter monetary policy failed.

The following sections enter into some of the details of these mechanisms.

(continued)

ability to indirectly influence long-term interest rates, notably those charged on mortgage loans, the main channel by which monetary policy affects final demand (with effects on both residential investment and consumption in the strict sense).

There are two basic conditions to the efficacy of monetary policy. First, there must be a demand for loans in the economy. Under usual conditions, this requirement is fulfilled. If the eagerness to borrow is temporarily too weak or slow, government must step in as "a borrower of last resort," as in fiscal policy. A rather "healthy" credit system is a second requirement. In the conduct of monetary policy, the credit system works as a "transmission belt," since the central bank finances financial institutions, notably banks, in turn lending to economic agents at the origin of demand flows. Consequently, a banking crisis may render monetary policy ineffective, as was the case in the early 1930s or in the contemporary crisis. When the transmission belt is broken or slack, credits contract in what is called a "credit crunch."

---

1. Another function of the central bank (possibly supplemented by other institutions) is controlling the activity of the financial sector.

2. Since late 1992, short-term interest rates on bank loans to business (prime rates) are equal to the Federal Funds rate plus three percentage points.

Monetary Policy after 2000

In the analysis of the Federal Reserve's policy, it is helpful to return to the periodization as in Chapter 12, based on the ups and downs of the growth rate of GDP. The variations of the Federal Funds rate, as in Figure 14.1, follow rather tightly the sequence of the four phases:

1. *Cutting interest rates (Phase I).* It was clearly difficult for the Federal Reserve to stop the decline of the growth rate, although nominal short-term and long-term interest rates were low in comparison to the previous two decades. The dramatic action of the Federal Reserve, cutting its rates, is well known and clearly evident in Figure 14.1. The small increase at the end of the 1990s was suddenly reversed.

2. *Maintaining low-interest rates (Phase II).* The Federal Funds rate was maintained at a low value, with a one-year plateau between June 2003 and June 2004 at 1 percent nominally. After correcting for inflation, negative

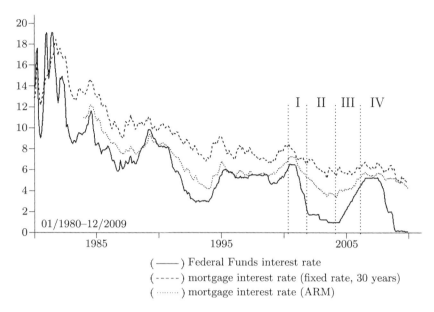

Figure 14.1 Interest rates: U.S. economy (nominal rates in percent, monthly).

rates prevailed during almost three years. Thus, an exceptionally strong stimulation was realized. During these first two phases, other short-term interest rates (······ in Figure 4.2) diminished in tandem, as well as the rates on ARMs (······ in Figure 14.1).

3. *Increasing interest rates (Phase III).* During this period, growth rates stabilized and the Federal Funds rate was gradually increased from 1 percent to 5.25 percent, in seventeen steps upward of 0.25 percent each, between June 2004 and June 2006. The problem was the very limited rise of rates on fixed-rate mortgages and the simultaneous hike of mortgage loans.

4. *Maintaining and, then, sharply diminishing interest rates (Phase IV).* Beginning in the first quarter of 2006, as the first symptoms of the incoming crisis became manifest, the Federal Reserve continued its policy of high-interest rates. In the third and fourth quarters of 2007, the Federal Funds rate was, finally, cut as a result of the disruption of the interbank credit market, signaling the outburst of the financial crisis at the beginning of August (from 5.25 to 4.75 percent during the third quarter of 2007 and to 4.25 during the following quarter). Then the Federal Funds rate declined to about zero.

The Diminished Ability to Impact Long-Term Rates

After 2000, the potential effect of monetary policy on the general level of activity was impaired by a diminished ability on the part of the Federal Reserve to influence long-term interest rates. This misadventure of monetary policy was first manifest during the attempt at checking the contraction of output during Phases I and II but, to an even larger degree, in the later attempt at checking the growing indebtedness when the recovery prevailed in Phase III.

This is apparent in Figure 14.1 concerning fixed-rate mortgages. Prior to Phase I, the rates moved in tandem. During Phases I and II, the Federal Funds rate was dramatically diminished with a very small impact on the rates of fixed-rate mortgages (-----). One can also notice that the small decline of these rates at the beginning of Phase I, actually occurred prior to the reduction of the Federal Funds rate, and that no impact of the Federal Funds rate is apparent during Phases III and IV concerning fixed-rate mortgages.

The situation concerning ARMs was substantially different. There was an impact of the Federal Funds rate on the cost of these loans. The interest rates on ARMs (········) moved much more in parallel to the Federal Funds rate. This rising cost of ARMs was, however, not sufficient to put a halt on the overall upward trend of mortgages. From January 2003 to March 2005, the percentage of ARMs in the total origination of mortgage loans grew from 20 percent to a maximum of 46 percent but, in September 2007, it had declined to 9 percent.[1] The peak was reached during the period in which the Federal Reserve was increasing its rates. There was actually a shift toward fixed-rate mortgages that undercut the potential effect of the policy of the Federal Reserve.

To a large extent, the Federal Reserve lost control of long-term interest rates and, thus, of credit flows (Box 14.2). Figure 10.6 confirms that the debt of households went on growing steadily independent of the action of the Federal Reserve.

The Responsibility of the Financial-Global Boom

In the traditional framework governing mortgage lending after World War II, the ability of credit originators to grant new loans was highly dependent on the support of agency securitization and the levels of the Federal

---

Box 14.2
The Strange Dynamics of Interest Rates during the Years 2000–2009

Several observations in the earlier and present chapters point to the puzzling dynamics of interest rates in the United States and the rest of the world during the precrisis decade. Figure 4.2 emphasizes the sudden rise of long-term interest rates at the end of the 1970s, the "1979 coup," and the latter decline after 2000. Figure 9.1 shows the gradual convergence of real long-term interest rates in various countries. The present chapter stresses the difficulty met in the conduct of monetary policy—the impaired capability of the Federal Reserve to control long-term interest rates. One can surmise that these various mechanisms are related—an object of complaint on the part of Alan Greenspan.

Greenspan's explanation for the decline of real interest rates after 2000 is the excess of savings worldwide, basically the same argument as the one Ben Bernanke advanced in 2005 (Box 11.1). Even if China is not explicitly mentioned, the country is in all minds. Strangely enough, no reference is made to Japan, a country that apparently contributed strongly to carry trade, the yen being a favorite funding currency, given the low levels of interest rates in the

(continued)

Funds rate. With neoliberalism, private-label securitization—not subject to the same regulatory framework and benefiting from the new performances attached to CDOs (the ability to transform non-prime loans or junk bonds into AAA bonds and to sell them)—allowed credit originators to refinance their activity as much as needed. Lenders were gradually less constrained by a possible shortage of liquidities as a result of tighter monetary policies. In addition, securities pooled in vehicles were sold at the long-term rates prevailing in the rest of the world independent of the Federal Reserve's policies. There were apparently no limits to these mechanisms.

The difficulty to sell the new securities issued could have placed limits on the fresh autonomy of the financial sector vis-à-vis the Federal Reserve but, given U.S. external deficits, the rest of the world received large flows of dollars and was in search of financial investment. This large availability of funds further added to the impaired capability of the Federal Reserve to impact long-term interest rates and credit flows.

It is difficult to determine exactly what percentage of ABSs was purchased by foreigners. Figure 14.2 shows the rising percentage of all bonds (ABSs or standard bonds) newly issued in the United States (as in Figure

(continued)

country. In this particular case, it is not "excess savings" that created these circumstances, but rather the depressed juncture in the country and the explosion of the globalization of financial mechanisms. More research would be necessary to determine whether these financial-global mechanisms (capital movements) are actually the cause of the convergence of interest rates as in Figure 9.1. If it were so, this mechanism might account for the new downward trend of real long-term rates as the outcome of tendencies prevailing around the world (be they the result of saving behaviors or the practices of banks), thus "imported" to the United States.

As shown in Figure 4.2 for the United States, short-term interest rates tend to fluctuate around long-term rates, with sometimes significant periods of deviation. This relationship is important concerning the effectiveness of monetary policy, since central banks directly impact short-term rates and, only indirectly, long-term interest rates. Pushed to the extreme the new global circumstances would lead to an inverse relationship between the dynamics of short- and long-term rates, the central bank having to adapt its short-term rates to the movements of long-term rates imposed from outside.

12.4), purchased by the rest of the world. An upward trend is apparent since the early 1990s, with a sharp acceleration after 2002, and the percentage reached 84 percent in the second quarter of 2007, just prior to the crisis. But this is for all bonds. A ballpark figure for the proportion of purchases of the products of U.S. securitization by the rest of the world is about half.

The consequences of financial globalization on the efficacy of monetary policy were large (in line with the analysis in Chapter 9). Refinancing by the issuance of ABSs was all too easy, with a large demand from the rest of the world. Beginning around 1998, interest rates in major capitalist countries converged (Figure 9.1), testifying to the globalization of financial mechanisms. Whatever the exact mechanisms, these observations point to the diminishing dependency of national financial institutions on the policies of their own central banks.

Alan Greenspan's Awareness and Diagnosis

Alan Greenspan was well aware of the new autonomous behavior of long-term rates. He was, in particular, concerned by the fact that these rates did

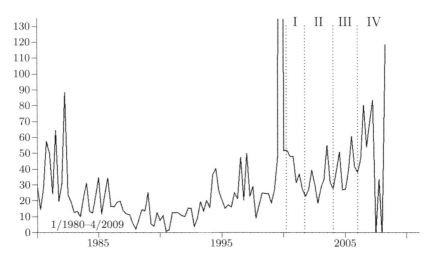

Figure 14.2 Share of the issuance of U.S. bonds purchased by the rest of the world (percentage of the total issuance, quarterly). In the fourth quarter of 1999, the percentage reached 597 percent. This observation has been deleted as well as the observations from the third quarter of 2008 onward because of negative or very small total issuances.

not respond as expected to the increase of the Federal Funds rate in the wake of the recovery from the 2001 recession, when his policy manifested a determination to curb the credit boom. In July 2005, that is, about in the middle of Phase III, when the Federal Reserve had already increased its rates during one year without any significant impact on long-term rates, Greenspan mentioned this puzzling development in testimony to the Committee on Financial Services of the House of Representatives: "The drop in long-term rates is especially surprising given the increase in the Federal Funds rate over the same period. Such a pattern is clearly without precedent in our experience."[2]

Greenspan enters into some of the details of the sequence of events, notably how markets originally reacted in a standard fashion given the increase in the Federal Funds rate, and how, in two instances, this policy seemed to produce the expected result but finally failed. He is conscious of the impact of globalization but confesses that he has no well-established explanation of the global downward trend of interest rates. First, his interpretation points to the favorable long-term expectations of markets, a self-eulogistic and unconvincing line of argument. Second, he refers to the equilibrium between world savings and investment on a market whose balance is ensured by the flexibility of a specific price, long-term interest rates, a line of argument in the pure neoclassical-neoliberal vein. The so-called savings of foreigners provided a large supply of credit worldwide, depressing long-term interest rates, in spite of Greenspan's own efforts. This line of argument directly echoes Ben Bernanke's global savings glut, as in Box 11.1.

The other tool in the hands of the Federal Reserve was reregulation but ongoing trends were in favor of deregulation (Chapter 9). Despite Greenspan's die-hard commitment to free-market economics, the final outcome of this pure interest-rate policy on the part of the Federal Reserve was not the expected soft landing but the outburst of the subprime crisis.[3] In the crisis, Greenspan acknowledged that he was actually wrong: "I made a mistake in presuming that the self-interest of organizations, specifically banks, is such that they were best capable of protecting shareholders and equity in the firms."[4]

A surprising late vindication of Keynes's analysis.

Financial Crisis: Storm in the Center— Global Capitalism Shaken

Part VI showed how the rise of residential investment led the U.S. macro-economy out of the 2001 recession, how mortgages were supported by securitization and insurance against defaults, and how the Federal Reserve, committed to deregulation, lost its capability to control long-term interest rates and moderate the expansion of loans.

Part VII moves one step further. It shows how the fall of the mortgage wave destabilized the fragile financial-global structure. Its main object is, however, the crisis proper, that is, the ensuing collapse of the financial sector and the subsequent contraction of activity in the United States and around the globe.

15

A Stepwise Process

The outburst of the crisis is officially dated to the disruption of the interbank market in August 2007. The importance of this date in the overall dynamics of the crisis is obvious, but it was neither the beginning nor the end of what was originally denoted as the "subprime crisis." The Federal Reserve Bank of Chicago (the Chicago Fed) letter of August 2007 states: "We believe that the subprime mortgage problems are not likely to spill over to the rest of the mortgage market or the broader economy."[1] But they did.

The period covered here includes this initial event but is much longer. It goes from the last stage of the housing boom and the ensuing downturn— between the end of 2005 and the beginning of 2006—to the end of 2009. The last months of 2008 stand out as a crucial episode, when the global character of the financial crisis became clearly evident and the contraction of output began within most countries.

The purpose of this chapter is introductory. It summarizes the overall chain of events. "Financial sector" is meant here as a "private" sector, as opposed to the Federal Reserve and the Treasury, both considered central institutions. But to these two institutions, one must add federal agencies and the GSEs, specifically Fannie Mae and Freddie Mac, under government control in the period considered. (The phrase "federal agencies" is used here and in the following chapters to refer to Fannie Mae, Freddie Mac, and Ginnie Mae.)

Identifying Broad Periods

The chronology of the crisis, as considered here, begins when the growth rate of the U.S. GDP was destabilized after the short plateau maintained in the wake of the 2001 recession, that is, at the entrance into Phase IV in the periodization of Chapter 12. The crisis developed gradually in a stepwise fashion. From the beginning of Phase IV four broad phases are further distinguished:

A. *The turning point on housing markets: defaults and the crisis of MBS-related markets (January 2006–August 2007).* The beginning of the fall of building permits, home sales, and home prices, at the transition between 2005 and 2006, marked the entrance into Phase A. The wave of defaults developed simultaneously. Under such circumstances, banks were forced to depreciate some of their assets, and the devaluation of the riskiest segments of MBSs began. The first impacts were felt within a number of institutions acting on mortgage markets.

B. *The crisis of the financial sector in the United States (August 2007 to September 2008).* The entrance into Phase B coincided with the liquidity crisis on the interbank market that forced the Federal Reserve to intervene. This disruption was the consequence of the underlying turmoil on MBS-related markets. From August 2007 to September 2008, U.S. financial institutions were under stress, confronting severe liquidity problems and incurring gradually larger losses, with an increasing risk of failure. The rest of the world was also affected but the crisis basically remained a U.S. phenomenon.

During Phases A and B, it is possible to trace the effects of the housing crisis and its subprime components, a lasting seismic wave. The propagation was felt during almost two years.

C. *Panicking: the global crisis and the contraction of output (September 2008 to February 2009).* From September 2008 onward, the financial crisis became much more severe in the United States, with the multiplication of failures at the beginning of the period, and spread to the entire globe. The beginning of the contraction of output, marking the entrance into Phase C, was sudden and violent. The growth rates of major economies began to decline into the Great Contraction. This is the period in which the first steps of the rise of U.S. government deficits and the corresponding increase of U.S. Treasury securities were observed.

D. *A low plateau (February 2009–).* Beginning in February 2009, the macroeconomy began to stabilize at the low level reached, given a very large deficit of government spending, and a slight improvement was observed. The total support from the Federal Reserve to the financial sector remained high. As of late 2009, these loans returned to the levels typical of the end of Phase B, but the Federal Reserve engaged massively in the purchase of agency MBSs, and the total support to the economy was maintained. Thus, new trends became apparent in the composition of the total support to the economy on the part of the Federal Reserve.

Entering into Some of the Details

A more detailed analysis allows for the identification of distinct subperiods within Phases A and B.

A1. *Defaults.* The wave of defaults on mortgage loans became apparent around the beginning of 2006 (simultaneous to the downturn in housing markets). To the end of 2006, there were no clear consequences of the incoming financial turmoil on financial institutions.

A2. *MBSs under strain.* In December 2006, the first signs of the devaluation of MBSs were revealed, affecting the riskiest securities. But the consequences were felt only by the institutions that specialized in subprime loans. A number of originators were already filing for bankruptcy protection, a first expression of the epidemic of failures and bailouts during the subsequent periods.

With the entrance into Phase B, the crisis acquired a general character and provoked important dysfunctions within the U.S. financial sector. From August 9, 2007, onward, the history of the crisis in Phases B to D is well mirrored in the progress of its treatment by the Federal Reserve as in Figure 15.1. The figure distinguishes between the loans given by the Federal Reserve to private financial institutions and the securities held (Treasury and federal agency securities), jointly denoted as "credits," as in the balance sheet of the Federal Reserve.

The support provided by the Federal Reserve increased tremendously. The first variable in Figure 15.1 is total credits (——). Comparing its average value during Phase A to the high plateau reached in November 2008, December 2008, and January 2009 (in Phase C), this support was multiplied by a factor of 2.9 (a factor of 2.5, when the comparison is made with the average value in Phase D). No significant relaxation is apparent to the end of 2009.

Three periods can be distinguished within phase B:

B1. *Lost confidence and the entrance into the liquidity crisis.* In addition to the crisis of CDO and MBS markets already under way, this is when the difficulties of ABCP markets became manifest. The disruption of the interbank market led to the diminution of the Federal Funds rate, the first in

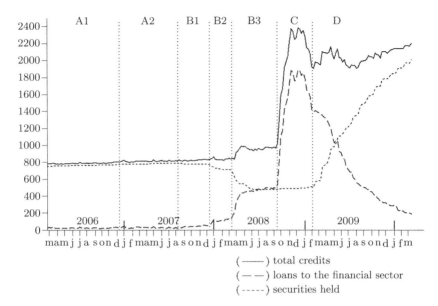

Figure 15.1 Total credits by the Federal Reserve (billions of dollars, weekly). Credits are the sum of loans and securities. Average figures of loans to the financial sector for the periods:

A1 March 2006–December 2006, $27 billion.
A2 December 2006–August 2007, $30 billion.
B1 August 2007–December 2007, $45 billion.
B2 December 2007–March 2008, $109 billion.
B3 March 2008–September 2008, $433 billion.
 C September 2008–January 2009, $1,540 billion.
 D March 17, 2010, $181 billion.

a long series of further cuts. Throughout the period, the Federal Reserve gradually increased its loans to alleviate the liquidity crisis, which had become the central feature of the period. Not coincidentally, it is during this period that the stock market initiated its decline from its maximum value in October 2007.

B2. *The broadening of the support from the Federal Reserve, an ephemeral relaxation, and the first signs of the credit crunch.* With the deepening and generalization of the crisis, the Federal Reserve suddenly increased and diversified its support in December 2007. This development ushered in a period of relaxation. During the first months of 2008, there was a general sense that enough had been done to solve what could still be seen as a liquidity crisis. Time was allegedly ripe for recovery. But symptoms of a new deterioration were accumulating. New loans to the nonfinancial corporate sector peaked in the third quarter of 2007 and contracted sharply, joining the fall of mortgages to households. This new development marked the beginning of the crisis of the supply of credit, the credit crunch, beyond the collapse of the mortgage markets.

B3. *Bailouts, bankruptcies, and the furthering of the credit crunch.* The relaxation was short-lived. The true nature of the crisis was gradually revealed. It was actually a deep crisis of financial institutions, caused by tremendous losses, not only a liquidity crisis that the Federal Reserve could have easily cured. Bear Stearns filed for bankruptcy, and this event symbolically marked the transition between Phases B2 and B3. A second, even larger, increase in the supply of credit to the economy by the Federal Reserve appeared necessary in March 2008, at the beginning of the period, introducing to a lasting higher plateau of credits. During the summer of 2008, at the end of the period, the difficulties of Fannie Mae and Freddie Mac were publicized. Commercial banks further cut their supply of loans to enterprises and households, an important step forward in the progress of the crisis and a new transformation of its nature with the entrance of the nonresidential real economy into the overall dynamics of the crisis. After its peak in the second quarter of 2008, nonresidential investment began to decline.

C. *The implosion of the financial sector and the first steps of the Great Contraction.* September and October 2008 were a period of panic, marked by a chain of bankruptcies. The entire financial system was apparently imploding. Output and trade began to contract around the globe. The global economy seemed out of control. During this new phase, the Federal Reserve was a priori determined to implement any intervention that could avoid the total collapse of the financial sector and slow down the contraction of output, but with little impact.

Figure 15.1 illustrates the tremendous increase of the credits (— —) provided by the Federal Reserve in September 2008, leaping from $1 trillion at the end of Phase B to almost $2.4 trillion during December 2008. Despite a Federal Funds rate close to zero, new loans to the nonfinancial economy fell dramatically and banks began to accumulate reserves at the Federal Reserve.

From September 2008 onward, the collapse of the macroeconomy was rapid. Concerning policies, a new emphasis was placed on the direct stimulation of demand (the purchase of goods and services). One instrument was the encouragement of the provision of loans to households, but with little effect. The main instrument still in the hands of policy makers was the deficit of the government.

D. *Consolidating a fragile floor.* While the total of the support to the economy (——) was maintained throughout Phase D, a major change in the composition of this support occurred. The two other variables in Figure 15.1 break down total credits into the loans to the financial sector (— —) and securities held (-----). (These securities are issued by the Treasury or by federal agencies—bonds directly issued or the products of securitization within the pools of these institutions.) During the period of reduction of loans, the holding of agency securities by the Federal Reserve increased dramatically.

After February 2009, a stabilization of the macroeconomy is apparent, notably in the movements of the capacity utilization rate within the manufacturing sector, retail sales, and international trade. Nothing proves that this stabilization or slight improvement will be consolidated. In 2009, the deficit of the government reached 12 percent of GDP. The Federal Funds rate remains extremely low. A new development is the direction of the support of the Federal Reserve toward the purchase of agency securities, either the bonds directly issued or the products of securitization within the pools of these institutions. Given the sizes of the government deficits and the volumes of the credits provided by the Federal Reserve, the situation testifies to more of a reprieve at still dramatically low levels than a situation of recovery. And the rising government debt poses a considerable threat to the stability of the dollar.

16

The Seismic Wave

The crisis began in the housing sector and spread sequentially from mort-gages to the entire financial sector, with the crucial intermediate link of securitization and MBSs. As could be expected from the tremendous expansion of financial mechanisms after 2001, a number of instruments among the most daring, such as CDOs, were devalued. In August 2007, an important step forward was accomplished that revealed underlying trends. Other instruments such as SIVs, the holders of important portfolios of ABSs, were also hurt and sometimes destroyed. For the remainder of the financial sector directly engaged in such operations or holding the prod-ucts of securitization, the main blow was originally less the size of losses than the disruption of financial mechanisms, a liquidity crisis, manifest-ing a generalized lack of confidence. All components of the financial sec-tor were affected: mortgage companies, deposit institutions, investment banks, insurance companies, hedge funds, and so on. The Federal Reserve gradually scaled up its loans to financial institutions. This is the subject of the present chapter, which traces the crisis from the wave of defaults to the disruption of the U.S. interbank market.

Defaults

The crisis began as a wave of defaults, that is, delinquencies on the part of borrowers. Delinquency may lead to charge-off and foreclosure on the part of lenders, as defined in the caption of Figure 16.1. The figure shows that delinquencies (——) on residential loans began to rise in the first months of 2010 at the beginning of Phase IV, marking the entrance into Phase A. The mere chronology indicates that the rise of delinquencies was

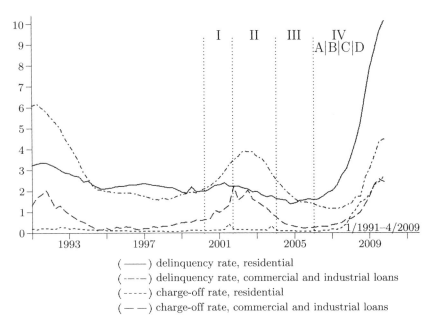

Figure 16.1 Delinquencies and charge-offs on residential loans, and commercial and industrial loans: U.S. commercial banks (percentage of loans outstanding, quarterly). The variables are quarterly annualized rates.

Quoting the Federal Reserve: "Delinquent loans and leases are those past due thirty days or more." "Charge-offs are the value of loans and leases *(net of recoveries)* removed from the books and charged against loss reserves." Foreclosure refers to the procedure to which the lender resorts: "the legal proceedings initiated by a creditor to repossess the collateral for a loan that is in default."

As shown in the figure, Phase IV is now divided into the four subphases, denoted as A, B, C, and D (Chapter 15).

not an effect of the 2001 recession but a consequence of the housing boom that allowed for the recovery from this recession.[1] The charge-off rate (-----) is greatly inferior to the delinquency rate (——). During the 1991 and 2001 recessions, the charge-off rate had hardly been affected. The final rise of charge-offs in Phase IV paralleled the growth of delinquencies. This increase, much larger than preceding rises, was not anticipated, and this lack of anticipation led to the overvaluation of all MBSs.

The housing boom was truly exceptional in size (Figure 12.2), as was the expansion of mortgage loans. It is, consequently, not surprising that it was also followed by exceptional defaults and charge-offs.

Figure 16.1 also shows the same variables for commercial and industrial loans (delinquencies ---- and charge-offs — —). The cyclical component is, here, noteworthy, the two variables peaking during recessions, and the contrast is sharp with delinquencies on residential investment. One can also notice the final rise of charge-offs for this category of loans as usually observed when the economy contracts. This movement cumulated its effects with those of residential investment.

The consequences of the rises of delinquencies and charge-offs were severe. Since April 2008, the number of monthly new foreclosure filings (sometimes several for a single home) remained above 250,000, after a period of steady growth from a monthly average of about 70,000 in 2005. The total figure for 2008 is 3 million, for 126 million housing units.[2]

As could be expected, the proportions of foreclosures were highly dependent on the types of loans, fixed-rate mortgages or ARMs, and prime or subprime loans. For example, in the third quarter of 2008, the percentages of foreclosure starts (on total loans of the category outstanding) were (1) 0.34 percent for prime fixed rates, (2) 1.77 percent for prime ARMs, (3) 2.23 percent for subprime fixed rates, and (4) 6.47 percent for subprime ARMs. In the fourth quarter of 2008, 48 percent of subprime ARMs were at least one payment past due.[3]

A source, based on 80 percent of all mortgages, indicates that 7.5 million mortgages, that is, 18 percent of properties with a mortgage loan, were in a negative equity position at the end of September 2008 (meaning that the prices of homes were inferior to loans, as an effect of the fall in prices). An additional 2.1 million mortgages were close to it.[4] As of the end of 2009, the situation was even worse, since prices went on declining (Figure 12.6).

Several developments accounted for the wave of defaults on mortgages during Phase IV. A basic factor was the mere relaxation of the conditions to which loans were granted that fed the expansion of loans (Chapter 13). In a period of stable or increasing home prices, borrowers facing difficulties can sell their homes and pay their debt. In a period of crisis they cannot, or only at prices that do not allow for the payment (negative equity). Another factor was the successive fall and rise of the Federal Funds rate. Once the economy had recovered from the 2001 recession, the Federal Reserve gradually increased its rates (Figure 14.1). As shown in Chapter 14, the rates on fixed-rate mortgages rose to a small extent, and rates on ARMs increased more. Between March 2004 and July 2006, they rose 1.3 percentage points for the former, and 2.4 percentage points for the latter.

(The rates on ARMs had been diminished during the contraction of activity in 2001, a move that had stimulated the rise of this category of loans.)

MBS-Related Markets at Pain

The rise of private-label MBSs and CDOs, two instruments directly related to the mortgage wave, are typical of the dramatic expansion of financial mechanisms that paralleled the housing boom after 2000 (Figure 13.2). The reversal came about one year after the housing downturn, marking the entrance into Phase A2. The transmission belt between housing markets and the disruption of these MBS and CDO markets was the wave of defaults.

Although the volumes of CDOs are large, the majority are negotiated OTC and there is, consequently, no market on which their price can be easily observed. Prices are derived from the market where the CDSs insuring the bonds are exchanged. A company, Markit,[5] produces indices since the first semester of 2006, known as the ABX.HE. These indices are used as estimates of the value of various tranches issued during a given semester.

Figure 16.2 shows two of Markit's indices. The initial step in the devaluation of BBB tranches (——) is clearly evident in the figure, at the end of 2006, as indicated by the first vertical line. This development, the first impact of defaults on a financial instrument, marked the entrance into Phase A2. This downward step introduced a plateau. In April 2007, rating agencies downgraded a large number of ABSs collateralized by subprime mortgages, in particular CDOs. In June and July 2007, at the end of Phase A2, a further depreciation was observed, down to 50 percent of the original value of BBB tranches. (Until this point nothing had happened concerning AAA tranches, ― ―.)

The beginning of the devaluation of BBB tranches at the end of 2006 was only an early symptom of the incoming crisis of MBS-related markets whose actual outburst came about eight months later (the financial crisis acknowledged as such). A set of major events signaled this entrance into Phase B in August 2007:

1. A further downgrading by rating agencies with a new devaluation of BBB tranches and the first devaluation of AAA tranches (― ―).

2. Not coincidentally, July 2007 is also the month in which the issuance of CDOs and private-label MBSs began their dramatic contraction (Figure 13.2). In May 2007, the issuance of U.S. private-label MBSs culminated at $61 billion and, in July, it had already been reduced to $37 billion and $7 billion

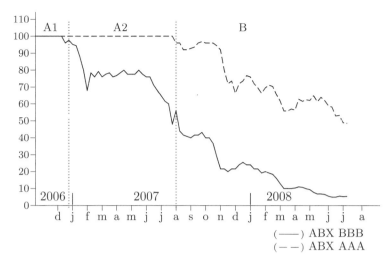

Figure 16.2 Indices of BBB and AAA tranches (percentage of their original value when issued, weekly). Series are generated that measure the average value of a bundle of securities sharing two common features: the semester of issuance and the rating of the tranche (Box 13.1). For example, considering the issuance during the first semester of 2006 (the basis of the first indices built by Markit), estimates are defined for tranches originally rated AAA, AA, BBB, and so on (from senior tranches to junior tranches) issued during this semester.

in December. The same figure shows that, in a similar manner, CDOs worldwide peaked in December 2006 at $69 billion (with three other peaks above $60 billion in February, March, and June 2007) and fell to $35 billion in July and $14 billion in December. The devaluation of AAA tranches, foreshadowing likely other devaluations in the near future, caused a growing uncertainty regarding the overall valuation of structured credit products.

As the wave of depreciation progressed, a growing number of subprime mortgage originators, often mortgage companies or small specialized institutions whose situation was fragile, were under stress. Their bankers withdrew their funding and they became unable to refinance on secondary mortgage markets. They stopped issuing and selling MBSs. They were the first victims of the liquidity crisis, in particular within the subprime component of mortgage markets.

The contamination to the rest of the financial sector was rapid. Hedge funds and the investment funds of large U.S. and foreign institutions were hit. For example, on August 9, 2007, BNP Paribas announced that it could not fairly value the underlying assets in three funds as a result of exposure to U.S. subprime mortgage lending markets.

The Crises of ABCPs, Conduits, and SIVs

Another instrument, also directly related to securitization, is asset-backed commercial paper (ABCP). It shares with CDOs its late explosion from 2005 onward and the ensuing collapse, with a devastating effect on conduits and SIVs. The amount outstanding peaked in August 2007 (Figure 7.2). ABCP was directly hurt by the crisis of August 2007 with a continuing decline during two years (a minimum in August 2009).

As explained in Chapter 7, SIVs and commercial paper conduits issue short-term securities, such as ABCP, as a counterpart for the holding of risky long-term securities such as MBSs. Rating agencies publicizing the devaluation of their assets, SIVs, and commercial paper conduits were unable to renew (roll over) or extend their short-term financing (as notes were paid back while new issuance was blocked). This development is typical of a liquidity crisis. A number of institutions became rapidly insolvent due to accumulated losses. (One can mention, for example, the default of the SIV Cheyne Finance in October 2007, sponsored by Cheyne Capital Management, sold at a price corresponding to 44 percent of the original values of securities, a figure that matches the index in Figure 16.2.)

SIVs and commercial paper conduits are actually OBSEs sponsored by banks or other financial institutions. There were three alternative outcomes. A number of banks (such as Citigroup, HSBC, Rabobank, and Société Générale) came to the rescue of their SIVs and returned them to their balance sheet to avoid downgrading or default. Others (such as Standard Chartered Banks) abandoned them. Victoria Ceres Capital Partners LLC filed for bankruptcy in the spring of 2008. In some instances, both the SIV and its sponsor went bankrupt. (In February 2008, the U.K. bank Northern Rock—the sponsor of Granite, its subsidiary SIV—was nationalized by the U.K. government.)

A Reciprocal Lack of Confidence

The crisis on MBS-related markets was at the origin of the turmoil on the interbank market. It was, actually, the result of the accumulation of bad news concerning these markets and their effects on the situation of banks.

The chronology of events introduced in Chapter 15 strikingly matches the developments on the interbank market. Figure 16.3 shows the London Interbank Offered Rate, LIBOR, at which banks can borrow from one another (more precisely, the three-month U.S. dollar LIBOR) and the Federal Funds rate. One can observe the comparative rise of the LIBOR on August 9, 2007, manifesting the initial tension on the interbank market. The spread (the difference between the two variables) remained large throughout Phase B1 (and the beginning of Phase B2), manifesting the permanence of such tensions. In January 2008, as the spread was reduced to zero during most of Phase B2, the single period of relaxation, it seemed that the Federal Reserve had remedied the crisis. In March 2008, the situation again deteriorated with a new rise of the spread. That was nothing, however, in comparison to the entrance into Phase C, when the spread jumped to unprecedented levels (paralleling the surge in the overall support by the Federal Reserve). In each case, the rise of the spread was linked to new bankruptcies or threats of bankruptcies (as of Bear Stearns, Lehman Brothers, AIG, etc.).

In August 2007, all banks were not to the floor. The tensions observed on the interbank market were the manifestations of the lost reciprocal confidence between financial actors, a crucial aspect of the crisis from its early

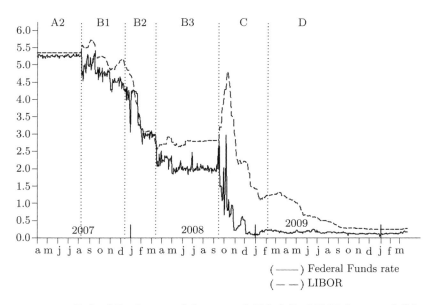

Figure 16.3 Federal Funds rate and three-month U.S. dollar LIBOR (percent, daily).

steps. Rather, independent of the actual losses incurred, it became difficult to borrow, including to simply maintain the stock of financing at its previous levels. The Federal Reserve, using standard procedures, was able to remedy two major alerts, during the transitions of Phase A2-B1 and B2-B3. The third crisis led, however, to the final collapse of the interbank market. In Phase C, the Federal Reserve had fully replaced private banks in the provision of liquidity. Instead of borrowing on the interbank market when they needed it, banks accumulated large reserves within the Federal Reserve, given the support from this latter institution (as discussed in more detail in Chapter 18, Figure 18.2).

The phrase "credit crunch" is generally limited to references to the contraction of loans financing expenditures in goods and services. The above developments can be described as a credit crunch in the supply of credit within the financial sector itself.

The Financial Structure Shaken

The financial crisis gained in extension and severity between August 2007 and September 2008 (Phase B). Its nature was profoundly altered. The new development was that, besides the proper "liquidity component" of the crisis, financial institutions incurred major losses. The devaluation of the net worth of corporations was reflected in the declining prices of their shares, the punch line being sometimes bankruptcy. Another major feature of the period was the massive intervention of central institutions.

The dimension of the devastation was suddenly revealed under the pressure of events. This came after years of blindness, underestimation of risks, overvaluation of assets and, in a number of cases, deliberate dissimulation of losses. Tremendous ROEs were claimed to the last moment and large flows of income distributed.

Global Losses on U.S. Credit-Related Debt

It is difficult to assess the dimension of losses incurred by financial institutions. A broad diversity of debt must be considered, in the United States and in the rest of the world, on U.S. debt or globally, and so on. A key interrogation is whether losses were sufficient to destabilize financial institutions and lead them to bankruptcy. The answer is obviously positive, as the deepening of the crisis amply demonstrated. Financial institutions lost or are programmed to lose the equivalent of several years of accumulated profits, a development that dramatically encroached on their net worth.

The October 2008 report of the IMF provided estimates under the heading "near-term global losses on U.S. credit-related debt." Each word is important. "Near-term" refers to the consideration of past and incoming losses.

In other words, the IMF estimated the losses of financial institutions at the date of the preparation of the report, but these losses had not yet necessarily materialized. "Credit-related debt" refers to both loans and securities. The mentions of "U.S. debt" and "global losses" indicate that only debt originating in the United States is considered while the losses may be supported within other countries. Losses are determined "marked to market," that is, based on current market prices. The estimates illustrate the contamination effect of the residential investment crisis to investors worldwide.

Table 17.1 shows a selection among the IMF figures. It separates loans and securities. The instruments are classified within three categories: (1) credits directly related to mortgages to households (loans, MBSs, etc.); (2) credits to the financial and nonfinancial corporate sectors; and (3) others (CMBSs, consumer credit, CLOs, etc.). (The corporate sector includes nonfinancial corporations, traditional financial corporations, and conduits, SIVs, or other OBSEs.)

Total losses are estimated at $1,405 billion, with about one-third for loans and two-thirds for securities. More than half of this total can be straightforwardly imputed to residential debt, but it is impossible to estimate precisely the value of losses incurred as an indirect effect of losses on residential debt, though this amount is certainly large. Corporations, destabilized by such direct losses or unable to renew their financing because of the collapse of the corresponding markets (for example, the consequences of the crisis on ABCP markets), were unable to pay their own debt. The report does not indicate whether these corporations are part of the financial or nonfinancial sectors, but one can surmise that most of the losses were the consequence of the failure of financial institutions.

Table 17.1 Losses on U.S. credit-related assets (billions of dollars, estimates by the IMF)

	Loans	Securities	Total (Oct. 2008)	Total (Apr. 2008)
Total	425	980	1,405	945
Residential debt	170	580	750	565
Corporate debt	120	210	330	90
Others	135	190	325	290

Obviously, these figures are only rough estimates, but they point to a devastation. They can be compared to the profits of the U.S. financial sector as defined in NIPA. More was lost than the total after-tax profits of the sector in five years. Between 2003 and 2007, total profits amounted to $1,367 billion (of which $688 billion were retained), a period of record profits.

It is also interesting to relate the estimates as of October 2008 to those in the previous report of April 2008. The comparison reveals an increase by almost 50 percent in six months. Most of the rise came from corporate debt. In October, the losses on corporate debt amounted to $330 billion, to be compared to $90 billion in April.

Although the definitions used are distinct, the Bank of England provided converging estimates. In its report of October 2008, figures are put forward that emphasize the appalling amount of losses for three regions of the world. (These figures are examined in more detail in Chapter 20, which is devoted to the global crisis.) Only securities are considered (not loans) and the losses are classified by the nationality of the investors who purchased them (independent of the country of issuance). Thus, considering only securities, estimated losses are set as high as $1.58 trillion, only for the United States, and U.S. $2.8 trillion for the three regions, with the following commentary that reveals the potential of the crisis: "Total mark-to-market losses across the three currency areas have risen to around U.S. $2.8 trillion. This is equivalent to around 85 percent of bank's precrisis Tier 1 capital[1] globally of U.S. $3.4 trillion, though only some of these market value losses are directly borne by banks."[2]

Real Incomes versus Fictitious Surplus

In the estimates of losses, one fraction certainly refers to the occurrence of new defaults on mortgages, but another fraction can be imputed to the adjustment of the mark-to-market (or mark-to-model) value of assets whose probability of devaluation had been consistently rising from the beginning of the crisis. A clear example is CDOs, from the origin assets whose valuation was questionable but that were only lately downgraded by rating agencies. (Box 7.2 stresses the risks of mark-to-market accounting procedures, a source of overestimation of the value of assets.)

The meaning of the observations above is that the outstanding surpluses garnered during the years preceding the crisis were, to a large extent, fictitious, as contended in Chapter 9. Conversely, the outstanding flows of high wages at the top of the wage pyramid and the dividends paid to shareholders were quite real. When accounts were adjusted to reality, the cost of these real drains on fictitious surpluses was dramatically revealed in the sudden meltdown of corporations' own funds.

Using the methodology of the surplus labor compensation in comparison to profits in Box 6.1, but applied here to the financial sector instead of the entire private economy, one finds even more spectacular results. In 2006, the surplus labor compensation for the financial sector amounted to 117 percent of standard labor compensation instead of 20 percent for the entire economy, an effect of the concentration of high wages to management in the financial sector. It reached more than 2.5 times profits paid out as dividends, and also twice and a half retained profits (1.3 times total profits). All of these figures are well above those for the nonfinancial economy. Extending the comparison to the five years 2003–2007, still for the financial sector, one obtains the estimate put forward in Chapter 9.[3] The figures are $2,606 billion for the total of the surplus labor compensation and dividends, to be compared to the losses of $1,405 billion as estimated by the IMF or the $1,577 billion estimated by the Bank of England.[4]

Going Bankrupt

The wave of bankruptcies of financial institutions and bailouts stresses the proportions taken by the crisis around September-October 2008, the entrance into Phase C. More technically, one can refer here to the dramatic surge of the spread between the LIBOR and the Federal Funds rate (Figure 16.3) that testifies to the rising distrust among banks.

A number of financial institutions, whose activity is directly related to mortgage origination, securitization, or insurance, such as monoline insurers or hedge funds, had already been eliminated during the earlier phases of the crisis. Considering only the depository institutions insured by the FDIC, the number of failures or assistance transactions rose gradually. This number reached three during the twelve months of 2007, four during the first six months of 2008, twenty-six during the second six months of 2008, fifty-three during the first six months of 2009, and ninety-five during the second six months of 2009. The major development within the transition to Phase C was, however, the fall or bailout of some among the largest and most prestigious financial institutions in the United States

---

Box 17.1
The Fall of the Giants: The Rearrangement of the Financial Sector (United States)

Between June and October 2008, major U.S. financial institutions suffered or fell:

June 2008. Lehman Brothers and Morgan Stanley declare large losses.

July 2008. The control of IndyMac Bank is transferred to the FDIC, and Henry Paulson announces the support of Fannie Mae and Freddie Mac by the U.S. government.

September 2008:
— Lehman Brothers files for bankruptcy.
— Bank of America buys Merrill Lynch.
— The Federal Reserve refinances AIG.
— Goldman Sachs and Morgan Stanley choose to become insured
  U.S.-chartered bank holding companies to benefit from the guarantees
  offered to such institutions.
— Nomura Holdings takes hold of the activity of Lehman Brothers in
  Asia and Europe.
— Berkshire Hathaway invests in Goldman Sachs.
— Washington Mutual Bank closes, and its assets are transferred to
  JPMorgan Chase.

October 2008:
— Warren Buffett's Wells Fargo buys Wachovia.
— Mitsubishi UFJ Financial Group allies with Morgan Stanley.

---

and the world. The list is impressive: AIG, Lehman Brothers, Morgan Stanley, Fannie Mae and Freddie Mac, Merrill Lynch, Citigroup, and so on (Box 17.1).

Losses Seen from Wall Street

As could be expected stock-market indices reacted rapidly to the financial crisis, notably at the transition between Phases B and C. These turbulences are apparent in the fall of the indices of the NYSE for all sectors, notably for financial corporations.

Figure 17.1 shows market capitalizations for two sectors, financial and nonfinancial corporations. (The profiles of capitalizations and of indices are practically identical, but capitalizations allow for breakdowns and estimates of the potential losses due to the fall of indices.) The capitalization of the nonfinancial sector is about three times larger than that of the financial sector. The variables in the figure are the distances in percentage points between the values of market capitalization on each day and these values when capitalizations peaked, on June 4 (——) and July 13 (-----) 2007, respectively. For example, minus 10 percent for the financial sector means that the market capitalization of this sector became 10 percent lower than it was on June 4, 2007.

Despite recurrent ups and downs, the figure reveals a rather steady decline from mid-2007 to March 2009, with a larger fall for the financial sector. There was a sharp acceleration at the beginning of Phase C. Between the dates of their maximum values and the minimum reached, the capital-

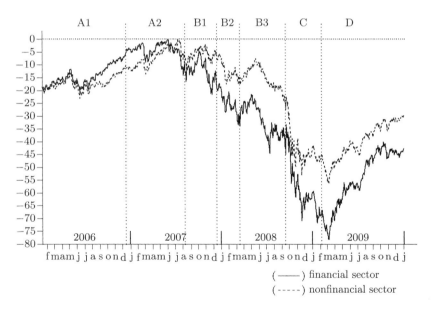

Figure 17.1 NYSE: Distances of market capitalizations from their maximum values (percent, daily). The maximum values of the two series were reached, respectively, in June 4 (——) and July 13 (-----), 2007. The capitalization of the nonfinancial sector refers to the capitalization of all sectors underlying the composite index minus the capitalization of the financial sector.

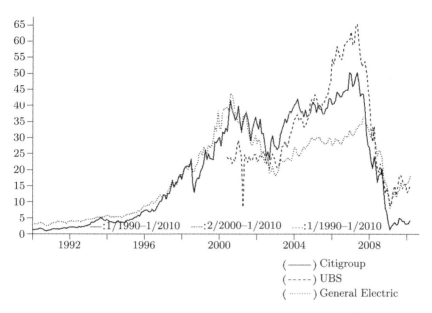

Figure 17.2 Stock prices: Citigroup, UBS, and General Electric (dollars, daily).

izations had lost 56 percent for the nonfinancial sector (a loss of $9.3 trillion), and 78 percent for the financial sector (a loss of $4.4 trillion). These figures dwarf the losses estimated by the IMF or the Bank of England. The figure also illustrates the partial recovery at the end of the period that testifies to the feeling on the part of investors that the worst of the crisis belongs to the past.

Figure 17.2 shows the stock prices of Citigroup, UBS, and General Electric. The profiles observed illustrate the dramatic devaluations of the stock prices of some among the largest corporations (after a period of tremendous expansion).

The State to the Rescue of the Financial Sector

Despite the deeply rooted faith in free-market economics and the so-called discipline of the markets, the crisis initiated a chain of interventions from central institutions. There is nothing surprising in this sharp reversal away from the basic tenets of the neoliberal creed. Neoliberalism is not about principles or ideology but a social order aiming at the power and income of the upper classes. Ideology is a political instrument. Considered from this angle, there was no change in objectives. In neoliberalism, the state (taken here in a broad sense to include the central bank) always worked in favor of the upper classes. The treatment of the crisis is no exception, only circumstances and, consequently, instruments differ. That a deep and lasting structural crisis might usher in a new social order, the expression of distinct class hierarchies and compromises, is another issue.

The present chapter is devoted to the measures taken to support the financial sector. A degree of complexity is created by the variety of instruments, such as the supply of credit to the financial sector, the participation in the capital of ailing corporations, or regulation. (Fiscal policy is discussed in Chapter 19.) In addition, there is a chronological aspect in the chain of measures, matching the major phases of the crisis. Besides August 2007, when the Federal Reserve first stepped in to soothe the liquidity strain, the present chapter emphasizes the turning point during the last quarter of 2008, marking the entrance into Phase C.

A Broad Variety of Devices

At least seven categories of mechanisms can be distinguished, alternatively or jointly, that intend to (1) solve liquidity problems and avoid bankruptcies, and (2) directly support new lending to households (to stimulate their demand) or to enterprises (to encourage their activity). This latter type of intervention lies at the boundary between the mechanisms considered in the present chapter and the following. Overall, the Federal Reserve, the Treasury, and the federal agencies were forced to gradually perform tasks that the financial sector could no longer assume.

Beginning with the first category of measures:

1. The outright purchase of bad debt is a straightforward option.

2. A set of measures is targeted to the provision of new loans to financial institutions. Such loans are granted by the Federal Reserve or federal agencies (possibly with the indirect support of the Treasury).

3. Another form of support is the purchase by the Treasury of stock shares newly issued by financial institutions, called "equity financing." This procedure is sometimes denoted as "nationalization," in particular if the participation in the capital of the corporation is large. The Treasury must finance these purchases and this necessity increases its own borrowings.

4. To the above, one can add measures affecting the structure of the financial sector, such as help linked to acquisitions, the transformation of the legal status of a corporation, and new regulation.

Turning to the second category:

5. Specific types of borrowing facilities are opened to financial corporations when they provide new loans to households or nonfinancial enterprises. There, the concern is not only to bolster ailing institutions but to stimulate loans to the economy, that is, to counteract the credit crunch. In the same vein, one can mention the provision of guarantees concerning ABSs backing new loans.

6. Also contributing to the stimulation of demand is the direct support of the expenses of households. This can be performed by giving subsidies or cutting taxes.

7. An important device, during Phase D, was the straightforward substitution of central institutions for private mechanisms, as federal agencies ensure the continuation of securitization and the Federal Reserve bought large amounts of MBSs.

Prior to August 2007 (Phase A): The Lack of Awareness

Each of the small steps made prior to August 2007 testifies to a degree of concerns but also to a general lack of real awareness concerning the magnitude of the process under way since the beginning of 2006.

Prior to August 9, 2007, or immediately thereafter, a few limited actions were undertaken in relation to the issuance of mortgage loans and, in particular, their subprime component.[1] In April 2007, that is, a few months after the beginning of Phase A2, when the first manifestations of the routs of structured finance were already apparent, financial institutions were encouraged by federal financial regulating agencies (federal regulators or the federal bank, thrift, and credit union regulatory agencies) to work with market borrowers who were unable to make their payments. In May, information was made available to consumers on what are known as "nontraditional mortgages," and a pilot project to improve the supervision of subprime mortgage lenders was defined. In June a "final statement" was established. On August 14, a few days after the outburst of the crisis on the interbank market, these agencies issued "illustrations" (explanations and a chart of possible risks) on such loans.

August 2007–September 2008 (Phase B): Mostly Liquidities

During the first year of the open financial crisis (the entire Phase B), the major support to the financial sector came from the Federal Reserve, cutting its interest rates and establishing less restrictive procedures for lendings to alleviate what was originally a liquidity crisis. These two forms of interventions are illustrated in Figures 16.3 and 18.1.

Figure 16.3 shows the Federal Funds rate and the LIBOR. At the beginning of Phase B1, the downward adjustment of the target Federal Funds rate came promptly, but remained originally limited (from 5.25 to 4.75 percent on September 18, 2007). This decision came in response to the tensions on the interbank market, apparent in the spread between the two rates, but this move did not measure up to the size of the liquidity crisis. The Federal Funds rate was repeatedly diminished as the crisis deepened, first moderately to 4.25 percent at the end of Phase B1, and more dramatically, to 3 percent, at the end of January 2008. This decline had a tranquilizing effect and the spread between the two rates returned to zero. A new decrease occurred in March 2008, an important date in the deepening of

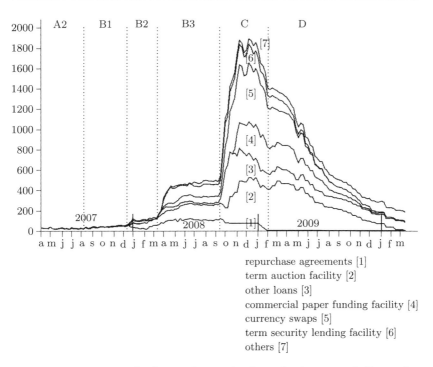

repurchase agreements [1]
term auction facility [2]
other loans [3]
commercial paper funding facility [4]
currency swaps [5]
term security lending facility [6]
others [7]

Figure 18.1 Support to the financial sector by the Federal Reserve (billions of dollars). The variable for the total is the same as in Figures 15.1 (— —) and 20.7 (— —).

the crisis (with the first major bankruptcy at Bear Stearns). During the six months of Phase B3 (March to September 2008), the target Federal Funds rate remained about constant around 2.25 percent and then 2 percent, and the LIBOR fluctuated around 2.8 percent. In September, the apparition of a large spread signaled that the earlier tensions had not been relaxed despite the low levels of the Federal Funds rate. This marked the entrance into Phase C.

Figure 18.1 shows the total loans from the Federal Reserve to the financial sector, broken down into seven components. Beginning in Phase B, the main developments were as follows:

1. *Traditional instruments (Phase B1).* In August 2007, the Federal Reserve used repurchase agreements, the standard mechanism of monetary policy. Loans rose from $19 to $46 billion, an additional contribution of $27 billion. Important restrictions were, however, limiting the operations

---

Box 18.1
The New Instruments of the Federal Reserve (Facilities)

The notion of facility refers to a channel by which the Federal Reserve issues loans to the financial sector. The enhancement of the lending capability of the Federal Reserve was typical of the first year of the crisis, including the break at the end of the first quarter of 2008, up to the plunge of the financial sector in September.

- Prior to September 2008 (Phases B1, B2, and B3).

To increase its support to the financial sector beyond the traditional open market and discount window, the Federal Reserve introduced three new instruments:

1. *The Term Auction Facility (TAF) in December 2007.* With term-auction credits, the Federal Reserve accepted from depository institutions a broader set of collaterals, those usually reserved for the discount window. Auctions became more frequent and were made for longer periods of time (biweekly auctions and for 28 days).

2. *The Term Securities Lending Facility (TSLF) in March 2008.* The main difference between the TSLF and the TAF is that the Federal Reserve provided Treasury securities instead of cash. The instrument was strengthened in September 2008.

(continued)

---

of the Federal Reserve due to the prevailing conditions on the types of securities accepted as collateral and the terms of the loans. For this reason, the first massive support came from federal agencies, notably the FHLBs, a creation of the New Deal. The advances (secured loans) to banks by these institutions increased from $640 billion at the end of June 2007 to $824 billion at the end of the third quarter of 2007, that is, a contribution amounting to $184 billion that dwarfed the above $27 billion from the Federal Reserve.

2. *New instruments (Phase B2).* These restrictions to the action of the Federal Reserve were gradually lifted. In December 2007, a first significant increase occurred in the support by the Federal Reserve, with a transformation in its composition. A new instrument was introduced, the Term Auction Facility (TAF), meaning the acceptance of a broader set of collateral (Box 18.1). The stock of repurchase agreements diminished in February 2008, but the total loans outstanding more than doubled, from $56 to $129 billion throughout Phase B2. Considering the respective averages

(continued)

3. *The Primary Dealer Credit Facility (PDCF) in March 2008.* The PDCF is similar to the TSLF, with the broadening of open-market operations to investment-grade corporate securities, municipal securities, MBSs, and ABSs for which a price is available. A specific aspect of the PDCF is that the Federal Reserve finances directly its primary dealers.[1] The set of eligible collaterals was broadened in September 2008.

- After September 2008 (Phase C).

4. *The ABCP MMMF Liquidity Facility (AMLF) in September 2008; the Commercial Paper Funding Facility (CPFF) in October 2008; and the Money Market Investor Funding Facility (MMIFF) in October 2008.* These new facilities aimed at improving the liquidity in short-term debt markets. In comparison to earlier facilities, the measures were more specific, targeted to commercial paper, conduits, SIVs, and money market mutual funds (MMMFs).[2]

5. *The Term Asset-Backed Securities Loan Facility (TALF) in November 2008.* The TALF authorized loans by the Federal Reserve, backed by eligible ABSs, with the protection of the Treasury.

---

1. As of February 2009, the sixteen large banks and broker dealers that act as intermediaries in open-market operations between the Federal Reserve and depository institutions.

2. Mutual funds investing in money market instruments.

of Phases B1 and B2, the total value of loans by the Federal Reserve was multiplied by a factor of 2.4, introducing the period of relaxation when the spread between the LIBOR and the Federal Funds rate was reduced to practically zero.

3. *Awareness (Phase B3).* The atmosphere in March 2008 suddenly deteriorated with the failure of Bear Stearns. Mid-March, Alan Greenspan and Lyle Gramley[2] declared that the ongoing financial crisis could be judged as the most wrenching since World War II. Martin Feldstein[3] declared that the country was in recession. Exactly at the same time, the Federal Reserve issued a nonrecourse loan[4] of $29 billion to cover part of the losses of Bear Stearns's investment in MBSs and other dubious investments, while the company was purchased. JPMorgan Chase made an original offer at $2 (finally raised to $10) a share, while a share of the corporation had reached $169 one year earlier. Ben Bernanke testified that the default of Bear Stearns could have "severe consequences" and lead to a major crisis.

In March and April 2008, total loans suddenly rose to a new plateau, actually a slightly upward-trended slope from about $400 billion to $500 billion (Figure 18.1). Both traditional open-market operations (repurchase agreements) and TAF increased dramatically, while two new instruments were introduced: (1) the Term Security Lending Facility (TSLF), and (2) the Primary Dealer Credit Facility (PDCF). The TSLF is explicitly represented in Figure 18.1. One can observe its comparative importance during Phase B3. The PDCF is part of "Other loans" in the figure. Its size remained limited.

At the end of July 2008, Congress passed the Housing and Economic Recovery Act, offering a $300 billion guarantee from the FHA for mortgage refinancing to the benefit of half a million home owners. This measure failed, as very few households used the opportunity.

The levels and composition of the support provided by the Federal Reserve remained surprisingly stable throughout Phase B3, that is, to the beginning of September 2008. The same was true of interest rates, as if a new stabilization had been achieved.

Overall, as of the beginning of September 2008 (at the end of Phase B3), the situation was one of very large stocks of loans to financial sectors and a low Federal Funds rate. The composition of the assets of the Federal Reserve had been thoroughly altered. The spread between the Federal Funds rate and the LIBOR was larger than in Phase B1 (Figure 16.3), the first phase of the financial crisis proper, the proof that confidence had not been restored among large banks.

Late 2008 (Phase C): Desperate Bolstering and Gradual Substitution

In September 2008, the world discovered that the deepening of the financial crisis avoided in March was now under way. In addition, it became clear that the contraction of activity would be severe and that the crisis had now taken global proportions. Thus, the entrance into Phase C marked the beginning of an all-out and rather disorderly effort at bolstering financial institutions, either by the provision of additional loans or the entrance into the capital of corporations. But, with the deepening of the crisis, central institutions came to act gradually more as substitutes for failing financial corporations in the provision of loans to the economy or in the insurance of these loans.

A broad diversity of measures was taken:

1. *More lending from the Federal Reserve.* The entrance into Phase C coincided with a dramatic rise in the loans by the Federal Reserve to the financial sector (Figure 18.1). This meant, in particular, a further extension of eligible collateral and the introduction of new devices (such as the Money Market Investor Funding Facility [MMIFF], the Commercial Paper Funding Facility [CPFF], and the Term Asset-Backed Securities Loan Facility [TALF]). The figure clearly illustrates the dilatation of "Other loans" and the TAF. In November 2008, the TALF authorized the Federal Reserve Bank of New York to make up to $200 billion of loans with one-year maturity, secured by eligible ABSs. The Treasury Department guaranteed $20 billion of credit protection to the Federal Reserve. The TALF provides an interesting illustration of the gradual substitution of central institutions for private corporations. The Federal Reserve took standard ABSs as collateral as a private corporation would do, and the Treasury provided the accompanying insurance like a private insurer, selling CDSs.

2. *The support from the Treasury.* A dramatic innovation was the Supplementary Financing Program of the Treasury Department in September 2008, to be dealt with in the section that follows devoted to the Federal Reserve.

3. *Bolstering a set of ailing corporations—the bailout of Fannie Mae and Freddie Mac.* The first involvement of the Federal Reserve in the bailout of a particular corporation occurred in March 2008, prior to Phase C, when JPMorgan Chase bought Bear Stearns. The main development was, however, the rescue of Fannie Mae and Freddie Mac, two financial giants (Chapter 13). As of the end of 2007, their total on-balance-sheet liabilities amounted to $1.61 trillion and the MBSs in their mortgage pools, to $3.50 trillion. The first straightforward alert concerning their survival came mid-July 2008, when Henry Paulson, President Bush's Treasury secretary, announced the government's commitment to back the two institutions if necessary in the wake of the revelation of the losses, which provoked the dramatic devaluation of their shares on the stock market. At the end of July, the Housing and Economic Recovery Act (Box 18.2) placed these institutions under the conservatorship of the Federal Housing Finance Agency (FHFA). This meant an actual takeover.

In mid-September, the Federal Reserve bailed out the insurer AIG, hurt by major losses on CDSs. The corporation having shown that it was unable to obtain the necessary financing from commercial banks, the Federal Reserve issued an $85 billion loan and, as a counterpart, the U.S. government

---

Box 18.2
Legislative Action (Acts)

Two acts were passed for the restoration of financial conditions. The main fields were loan insurance, the support of GSEs, and the purchase of bad debt:

1. *The Housing and Economic Recovery Act in July 2008.* The objective was the expansion of insurance on mortgage refinancing. In addition, the Federal Housing Finance Agency (FHFA) was created to be in charge of, among other functions, the conservatorship of Fannie Mae and Freddie Mac.

2. *The Emergency Economic Stabilization Act in September-October 2008 (the "Paulson plan").* The act was originally targeted to the purchase of illiquid debt but was actually used to purchase the shares of corporations (equity financing). It also raised the ceiling on deposits insured by the FDIC to $250,000.

---

took an almost 80 percent stake in the equity of AIG. In November 2008, this loan was supplemented by an additional contribution on the part of the Federal Reserve Bank of New York. As of the beginning of 2009, the support reached the record amount of $173 billion.

4. *Supporting troubled loans.* Another form of intervention is the provision of guarantees to problematic loans and the purchase of illiquid loans. They share the common property that a central institution commits its own responsibility in case of problems and to the extent of the losses (unknown when the decision is made). This purchase of bad debt was directly inspired by the treatment of the Great Depression in 1933. The so-called Paulson plan of September 2008 was originally calibrated to $700 billion. An amended version, the Emergency Economic Stabilization Act, was finally adopted at the beginning of October 2008. The law authorized the Treasury to immediately use $250 billion under the Troubled Asset Relief Program, but the plan was redirected to capital financing, the direct entrance into the capital of corporations.

In January 2009, the Federal Reserve announced that it would begin the operations allowed under the MBS Purchase Program (decided mid-November 2008) to buy MBSs from Fannie Mae, Freddie Mac, and Ginnie Mae, as well as consumer-related debt. At the beginning of 2010, the total amount of MBSs in the accounts of the Federal Reserve became larger than $1 trillion.

5. *Guarantees to MMMFs.* At the end of September 2008, the Treasury decided to guarantee the price of the shares of MMMFs, under certain conditions as usual. This measure is known as the Temporary Guarantee Program for Money Market Funds. It was extended during the following months.

6. *Capital financing: the Treasury enters into the capital of corporations.* The Paulson plan was actually redirected to the purchase of corporate shares.[5] The first such operations, under the Capital Purchase Program, occurred at the end of October 2008 with the refinancing of nine major banks or other financial institutions. As of the end of 2008, the largest such bailout was Citigroup for $25 billion supplemented, at the end of December, by another $20 billion in a specific program, the Targeted Investment Program. The Capital Purchase Program reached more than $200 billion in more than 500 banks.

7. *Insuring the deposits of banks.* Besides the major investment banks that went bankrupt, a number of major deposit institutions (banks and savings and loan associations) also failed. The largest bankruptcy was Washington Mutual Bank in September 2008. The liquidation was conducted by the FDIC. Another example is IndyMac, a large savings and loan association. Such failures could have caused a rush on banks and savings and loan associations. The Emergency Economic Stabilization Act increased the ceiling on deposits insured by the FDIC to $250,000 to prevent such rushes.

8. *Reorganizing and regulating.* Simultaneously, in addition to the above measures, a few steps were made in the direction of reorganization and regulation. The Housing and Economic Recovery Act of 2008 created the FHFA, in charge of supervising the fourteen GSEs (including Fannie Mae and Freddie Mac) and the twelve FHLBs. A broad set of regulations was discussed. The process will be time-consuming given the global implications of such measures.

After February 2009 (Phase D): The Decline of Loans to Financial Institutions and the Rise of the Holding of Federal Agency Securities

February 2009, marked the entrance into a new phase: Phase D. A first feature was the decline of the previous categories of loans to financial institutions. This is clearly evident in Figure 18.1. The figure reveals the decline of all the components of the loans to financial institutions. Figure 16.3 shows that another feature of the period was the diminution of the LIBOR, at extremely low levels, with a corresponding reduction of the spread with the Federal Funds rate.

As will be shown in the following section, these new trends testify to a redirection of the support of the Federal Reserve to the economy to the benefit of federal agencies.

The Federal Reserve in the Storm

The analysis in the previous sections emphasizes the masses of loans supplied by the Federal Reserve to the financial sector and the various instruments used at distinct stages of the crisis. Another way of approaching the action of the Federal Reserve is to consider the trends apparent in the main components of its balance sheet.

Figure 18.2 shows a set of major accounts of the Federal Reserve's balance sheet. Total loans to the U.S. financial sector (——), and Treasury and federal agency securities (-----) held (the two components of total credits

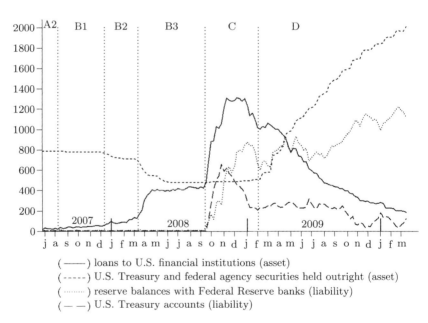

(——) loans to U.S. financial institutions (asset)
(-----) U.S. Treasury and federal agency securities held outright (asset)
(⋯⋯) reserve balances with Federal Reserve banks (liability)
(— —) U.S. Treasury accounts (liability)

Figure 18.2 Assets and liabilities of the Federal Reserve (billions of dollars, weekly).

excluding currency swaps as in Figure 15.1) remain the two basic variables. A first observation is that these two variables moved in opposite directions during the entire Phase B. While total loans to U.S. financial institutions were rising, the holding of securities was declining, notably at the beginning of Phase B3. Financial institutions were borrowing from the Federal Reserve, using the various available instruments as in the previous sections, and the corresponding injection of funds into the economy was compensated by a symmetrical sale of securities by the Federal Reserve to the financial sector, actually Treasury securities (not federal agency securities). The loans feed the reserve balances of financial institutions, while the sale of securities to the same institutions pumps on these reserves, whatever the exact mechanism. This procedure is sometimes denoted as "sterilization." Thus, during Phase B3, bank reserves (·······) remained stable at a very low level, as is usually the case.

The situation changed radically with the entrance into Phase C in September 2008, when the crisis dramatically deepened. The following measures were taken:

1. The Federal Reserve suddenly scaled up its loans from the average of $433 billion during Phase B3 to a plateau at $1,779 billion in November 2008, December 2008, and January 2009.

2. Financial institutions began to accumulate excess reserves for similar amounts. This is expressed in Figure 18.2 in the rise of the third variable (·······).

3. The Treasury, in a joint program with the Federal Reserve, stepped in, in an attempt to reabsorb the corresponding liquidity as the Federal Reserve had done during Phase B3. This was performed in the Supplementary Financing Program of September 2008. The Treasury issued securities to be purchased by financial institutions, and the proceeds were deposited into an account of the Treasury in the books of the Federal Reserve. It is the Treasury accounts, also shown in Figure 18.2 (— —). This move did not stop the rise of the reserve balances of financial institutions, which went on growing. (Simultaneously, the holding of Treasury and federal agency securities by the Federal Reserve remained about constant.)

As a result of these new developments, the total balance sheet of the Federal Reserve strongly increased.

The concern about the holding of excess reserves by financial institutions is that such behavior might impair the capability to conduct monetary policy (whose instrument is the control of reserves by an appropriate monitoring of interest rates). Anyhow, under ongoing circumstances, notably very low interest rates, one can have serious doubts concerning the effectiveness of monetary policy. In October 2008, the Federal Reserve began to pay interest on reserves, a move that, allegedly, strengthened its control.[6]

New trends were established with the entrance into Phase D. Figure 18.2 reveals: (1) the decline of loans to U.S. financial institutions (——); (2) the symmetrical rise of U.S. Treasury and federal agency securities (-----); (3) a slight upward trend of reserve balances (········); and (4) the stabilization of the U.S. Treasury account (— —). Two major developments must be stressed:

1. Financial institutions, in the context created by the dislocation of the interbank market and overall large uncertainty, are eager to hold very large reserves at the Federal Reserve. This behavior is encouraged by the payment of interest on these reserves.

2. Phase D testifies to a transformation in the support of the economy by the Federal Reserve. Figure 18.3 breaks down the total securities held (----- in Figure 18.2, —— in Figure 18.3) into three components: (1) Trea-

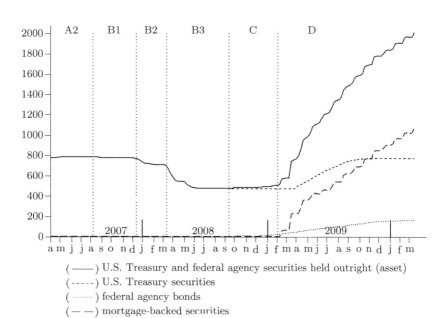

(——) U.S. Treasury and federal agency securities held outright (asset)
(-----) U.S. Treasury securities
(········) federal agency bonds
(— —) mortgage-backed securities

Figure 18.3 Total and the three components of securities held by the Federal Reserve (billions of dollars, weekly).

sury securities (-----); (2) federal agency securities (·······); and (3) MBSs, also issued by federal agencies in their mortgage pools (— —). A first observation is that the Federal Reserve initiated a return to the holding of Treasury securities to levels similar to those prevailing prior to the crisis. Second, while Treasury securities were the exclusive, or nearly so, component of securities to the end of Phase C, the entrance into Phase D saw the rise of federal agency securities, predominantly MBSs. This was the major substitute for the loans to the financial sector. This latter development must be linked to the observation that, since the beginning of 2008, securitization by private-label issuers fell to practically zero, while securitization by federal agencies boomed (Figure 13.1).

A new important trend is, thus, apparent. On the one hand, securitization is in the hand of federal agencies (now owned by the U.S. government) and, on the other hand, it is supported by the Federal Reserve, acting as "buyer of last resort" of the bonds issued, in place of financial institutions, households, and the rest of the world.

Figure 18.4 summarizes the overall support given by the Federal Reserve to the national and international economy. The variables are the net liabilities (liabilities minus assets) of three agents to the Federal Reserve, including foreigners, and their total amount. In these metrics, it appears that the Federal Reserve scaled up its total support (——) during Phases B3, C, and D, with an apparent trend toward precrisis levels in Phase D. The net loans to foreigners,(----), as in currency swaps, were large during Phase C, with a gradual reabsorption during Phase D. As stated earlier, the main development is, however, the substitution between the net loans to U.S. financial institutions (— —) and the holding of U.S. Treasury and federal agency securities (-----). At the end of the period, the reserves of financial institutions are dramatically larger than the loans supplied to the sector by the Federal Reserve. But the support of the economy by the purchase of MBSs displays an upward trend, with no sign of relaxation to the last observation in March 2010.

Out of the Financial Crisis?

The observation of the downward trend of the loans granted by the Federal Reserve to financial institutions can be interpreted as supporting the conclusion of a termination of the financial crisis. A more detailed analysis questions this interpretation.

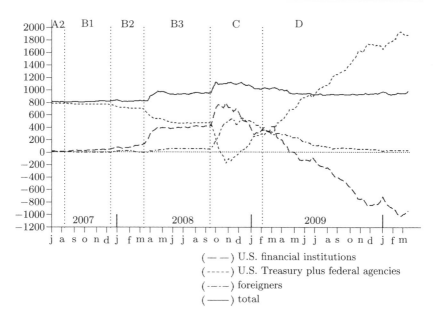

Figure 18.4 Net assets of the Federal Reserve: U.S. financial institutions, U.S. Treasury and federal agencies, and foreigners (billions of dollars, weekly). In the figure, the variable "U.S. financial institutions" denotes the total loans granted by the Federal Reserve minus the reserve balances of the financial institutions. (Both variables are shown in Figure 18.2.)

   "U.S. Treasury plus federal agencies" refers to the securities of the U.S. Treasury and federal agencies minus the accounts of the Treasury at the Federal Reserve (also the difference between the two variables shown in Figure 18.2). The variable "foreigners" measures currency swaps minus foreign official accounts at the Federal Reserve. The total is the sum of the three components.

   First, the propensity of financial institutions to accumulate reserves at the Federal Reserve testifies to the continuing disruption of the interbank market, a sign of the lack of confidence. Second, a substitution occurred among the components of the support of the Federal Reserve to the economy, rather than a contraction. Thus, crucial traditional segments of the functioning of the U.S. financial system are still not ensured by the so-called markets, that is, private institutions: (1) Mortgages (the main component of loans to households) are financed by securitization on the part of federal agencies, while the action of private-label issuers resulted in negative flows (instead of issuance); and (2) Households and the rest of the world diminished their purchases of such securities, and the Federal Reserve had to step in as a substitute. This action of the Federal Reserve is manifest not only in high amounts but in upward trends.

There are two ways of interpreting such developments and assessing their implications for coming years. Either the situation is not stabilized yet and a return to earlier mechanisms—in a possibly newly regulated framework—can be expected in the coming years, or a new configuration will prevail, in which the Federal Reserve would play an increased role. Such choices can be made only under the pressure of events.

19

The Great Contraction

As of the end of 2009, the diagnosis concerning the overall amplitude of the downturn of the GDP, which began in the last months of 2008, is straightforward. It will be large, a Great Contraction. The first manifestations of these exceptional proportions are already evident. A recession could, in any case, be expected after the housing boom, but the financial crisis conferred a dramatic character on this downturn. The size of the contraction is at the image of the collapse of credits to households and nonfinancial corporations, the credit crunch proper and, reciprocally, the decline of output adds fuel to the financial fire.

The support of the financial sector (credit and capital financing) tended to indirectly bolster the real economy. In the absence of such policies, things would certainly have been worse, but the intervention of central institutions did not stop the credit crunch and the downturn. The new development since the entrance into Phase C is that the decline of output aroused policies in which central institutions directly act as substitutes for the private financial sector. These policies aim at the stimulation of demand (the purchase of goods and services) and the support of the mortgage markets. Under such crisis circumstances, the government must, simultaneously, act as *consumer* (including investment) and *borrower* of last resort.

2005–2007: The Protracted Credit Boom

It is useful to return here to the boom of credit mechanisms that preceded the crisis. The U.S. economy recovered from the 2001 recession, in the wake of the collapse of the boom of information technologies, thanks to the expansion of the housing sector (Chapter 12), itself supported by the wave of mortgages and securitization (Chapter 13). The housing boom could not last forever, and it came to an end at the transition between 2005 and 2006. From the beginning of 2006 to the end of Phase B (a period of almost three years), the demand from households was, more or less, maintained, and the growth of GDP continued in spite of the downturn in housing markets.

Underlying this continuation of demand flow was the ability of the financial sector to supply loans to the economy. Figure 19.1 shows the flow of new loans to households and nonfinancial corporations as percentages of GDP. It reveals a general upward trend since the beginning of the period, despite significant fluctuations during overheatings and recessions and a more spectacular decline around 1991.

In 2006 and 2007, loans to households (in particular, mortgages) remained surprisingly elevated, despite the housing crisis. During the fourth quarter of 2007, the percentage in GDP of new loans to households was still larger than during the long boom of the second half of the 1990s (5.6 percent in comparison to 4.9 percent for the average of 1995–2001). Loans

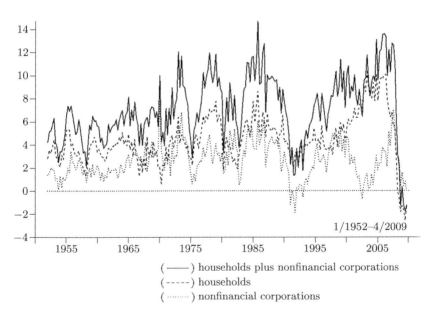

(———) households plus nonfinancial corporations
(- - - - -) households
(··········) nonfinancial corporations

Figure 19.1 New loans to households and nonfinancial corporations: U.S. economy (percentage of GDP, Quarterly).

to nonfinancial corporations went on increasing during 2007, with again percentages larger than during the long boom, actually the highest values since 1952 (abstracting from the detached peak in the second quarter of 1970). In 2007, the slight decrease of loans to households was compensated by the rise of loans to enterprises. Considering jointly households and nonfinancial corporations the average flow of new loans for the period 2005–2007 reached 11.9 percent, an exceptionally high level. But the situation changed dramatically in the following years.

The Credit Crunch

There is no surprise in the discovery that the outburst and deepening of the contemporary financial crisis ended up in a contraction of loans much beyond the usual decline during recessions. One can return here to the observation of the decline of loans at the end of the 1980s and beginning of the 1990s. It was the effect of the crisis of banks and savings and loan associations, causing a crisis in the supply of credit, a credit crunch. A credit crunch is, again, a central component of the contemporary crisis. Its effect will be much larger than the previous. From the high level in 2007 to an unprecedented negative value at the end of the period, 14 points of GDP were lost.

The series in Figure 19.1 describe the first steps of this new development. From the first quarter of 2008, loans began to strongly contract. With the entrance into Phase C in September 2008, monetary policy became ineffective, a development that manifested itself in the deepening of the credit crunch, with the flow of loans reaching negative levels since the fourth quarter of the year.

There is an obvious link between the transformations of the balance sheet of the Federal Reserve (Chapter 18) and the credit crunch. All along 2008, the Federal Reserve dramatically increased its loans to banks (Figure 15.1), but this support failed to stop the collapse of credits to the economy. After September 2008, nothing was able to put an end to the contraction of loans. Banks were accumulating reserves at the Federal Reserve, without effects on their loans. What could have been a slowdown of the macroeconomy was transformed into a major collapse. The only effective tool is, then, government spending.

This new development marked the culmination of a longer-term trend toward the erosion of the efficacy of monetary policy. Chapter 14 shows how the movements of the Federal Funds rate were gradually less reflected in those of mortgage rates (fixed and adjustable rates) and, thus, impacted to a lesser extent the flow of mortgages. This was, in particular, the case during the last phase of the housing boom, up to the second quarter of 2006 when mortgage loans reached their maximum.

The Feedback Effect

In the previous section, the emphasis was placed on the effects of financial mechanisms on the macroeconomy, but there is, and there will be even more, a feedback effect of the contraction of output on financial mechanisms.

The reduction of demand to enterprises impacts their capability to pay their debts and the same is true of households confronting a reduction of hours worked or unemployment. Potential defaults add to the diminished supply of credit by financial institutions. The rise in the defaults on debts that are not directly related to mortgages, as defaults on commercial and industrial loans in Figure 16.1, is a telling indicator of the impact of the contraction of activity on defaults. There is, however, much more to come. The example of the Great Depression provides an appalling example of the potential spiraling dynamics of such mechanisms, as the banking sector fell from 1930 to 1933, and the macroeconomy plunged (Chapter 21).

LBOs provide a well-known illustration of the variety of forms in which this feedback effect can manifest itself (Box 19.1). They demonstrate how financial mechanisms may be sensitive to recessions with potential reciprocal damages on the real economy.

Entering a Recession

The first steps of the Great Contraction were observed in 2008. Figure 19.2 shows the capacity utilization rate in the U.S. manufacturing sector. After the recovery from the 2001 recession, the capacity utilization rate culminated in the third quarter of 2007 and began to decline, with a strong acceleration, from the second quarter of 2008 upward. (The fall was particularly sharp for durable goods as is usually the case.) The contraction of the growth rates of GDP began in this second quarter of 2008 (Figure 12.1).

The contraction of output in a recession is a cumulative movement downward in which the decisions made by enterprises, scaling down production,

Box 19.1
LBOs: A Pending Threat

An example of the feedback effect of the contraction of output on financial activity is LBOs. As of 2007, the flow of LBOs was dramatically larger than in the late 1990s (Figure 7.3), and there was a strong similarity between the lax procedures in non-prime mortgage markets and LBOs, notably due to the sharp rise of covenant-lite loans[1] in 2007.

Data reveal that the major ratios (for example, the debt/earnings ratio before interest, taxes, depreciation, and amortization [EBITDA]) of LBOs are highly dependent on the phases of the business cycle. The percentage of outstanding leveraged loans in default or bankruptcies culminates during recessions (10 percent in 2002).

These observations—inflated volumes, loose credit requirements, and exposition to the ups and downs of the macroeconomy—suggest that the contraction of output in which the United States is entering will be associated with a wave of failures of LBOs, more damaging than during the 2001 recession when volumes were inferior, thus adding to the contraction.[2]

---

1. Granted without many requirements.
2. See the pessimistic report by H. Meerkatt and H. Liechenstein, *Get Ready for the Private-Equity Shakeout* (Barcelona and Madrid, Spain: The Boston Consulting Group, IESE, University of Navarra, December 2008).

and by households, cutting their demand, combine their effects. Such behaviors are the expression of the situation enterprises and households must confront (diminished demand, reduction of hours worked or unemployment), increased by the anticipation of forthcoming developments.

Such chains of events are observed in any recession, but during the contraction of activity of 2008, a downward trend of stock prices was under way. Reference is sometimes made to a "negative wealth effect," meaning that the devaluation of portfolios of securities, notably concerning pensions or mutual funds, might impact negatively the purchases of households. (The fall of market capitalizations, as in Figure 17.1, caused a large devaluation of the assets of households in such funds, from $18.5 trillion in the third quarter of 2007 to $13.2 trillion in the first quarter of 2009.)

The truly exceptional character of the contraction of output is apparent in the unusually dramatic fall of some of the components of demand from

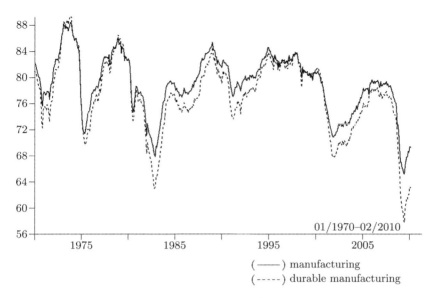

(———) manufacturing
(- - - - -) durable manufacturing

Figure 19.2 Capacity utilization rate: U.S. manufacturing sector (percent, monthly). Besides the entrance into the 2008 contraction of output, the figure illustrates some of the features of U.S. macroeconomics during the neoliberal decades for the manufacturing sector. Between 1985 and 2000, the capacity utilization rate fluctuated around a plateau of 81 percent, similar to the average of the earlier much less stable decade of the 1970s. The figure illustrates two important features of the precrisis decade: first, the 2001 recession was long (a slow recovery); and second, the recovery was partial, with comparatively low rates (79 percent, average 2006–2007).

households. Figure 19.3 shows the total of retail sales in the United States. No such movement is observed in the figure during the 2001 recession and nothing similar since World War II. Even more spectacular is the fall in the sales of motor vehicles (29 percent from the maximum in October 2007 to March 2009).

Demand Policy: Households and Nonfinancial Corporations

To the last months of 2008, the support of the economy was overwhelmingly of the nature of loans from the Federal Reserve to the financial sector to confront the liquidity crisis. This policy had no effect on the supply of loans to the economy, as banks began to accumulate reserves at the Federal

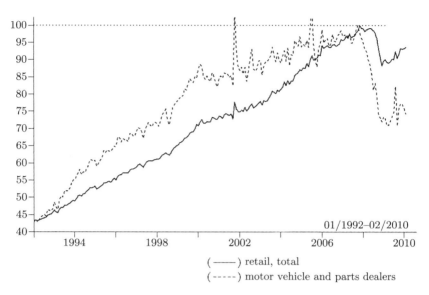

Figure 19.3 Total retail and motor vehicle sales: U.S. economy (constant dollars, monthly, normalized to 100 at the peaks of the variables).

Reserve during Phase C. With the credit crunch, the direct support of demand became a major concern.

Such support can be performed granting subsidies to households and cutting taxes, or guaranteeing loans. A number of such devices have already been considered in Chapter 18. Concerning taxes, the main measure taken by the Bush administration was the Economic Stimulus Act, in February 2008, at the beginning of the downturn. It introduced a stimulative package of $152 billion for 2008, mostly tax rebates, which delayed the contraction but did not alter the tendency. In mid-October 2008, the FDIC initiated its Temporary Liquidity Guarantee Program, offering guarantees to the newly issued unsecured debt of banks, thrifts, and a number of holding companies. In November 2008, a project known as the Loss Sharing Proposal to Promote Affordable Modifications was contemplated by the FDIC but set aside. The idea was to create affordable conditions for indebted households, by cutting interest rates, extending terms, and so on. In particular, a limitation of payments to a certain percentage of monthly income was considered. At the end of November 2008, the Federal Reserve created the TALF, supporting the issuance of new ABSs, based on student, auto, and credit card loans, as well as loans to small businesses.

To these measures, one can add the direct support of nonfinancial corporations as in the Automotive Industry Financing Program of the Paulson plan, in which $24.8 billion of additional capital were injected in December 2008 and January 2009 to the benefit of General Motors (GM) and Chrysler. The total amount peaked at $85 billion.

The main conclusion is, however, that these measures had very limited effects.

Demand Policy: Government

Under such dramatic circumstances, when the failure of credit policy is obvious, the stimulation of demand can come only from government spending, another lesson of Keynesian economics.

Figure 19.4 shows the balance of the government budget (federal, state, and local governments). There was originally little impact of the treatment of the crisis on government expenses. Up to the fourth quarter of 2007, the deficit of the budget was kept at rather moderate levels, that is, not larger than 3 percent of GDP. It finally reached almost 12 percent of GDP since the second quarter of 2009, a result of diminished receipts and increased expenditures.

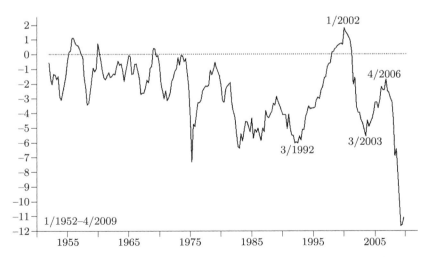

Figure 19.4 Balance of total receipts and expenditures: U.S. federal, state, and local governments (percentage of GDP, yearly).

To the second quarter of 2008, there was little impact of the crisis on the debt of the federal government. During the third and fourth quarters of 2008, the net debt rose, however, from 40 percent to 48 percent of GDP (Figure 10.5, -----). It was the effect of the Supplementary Financing Program of the Treasury Department, the Paulson plan, in September 2008, that added to the ongoing deficit. The policy changed with the arrival of the Obama administration. In February 2009, the new Congress passed the American Recovery and Reinvestment Act (ARRA), which combined tax cuts, welfare measures, and infrastructure programs. The net debt rose to 56 percent of GDP. The gross debt of the Treasury held by the public[1] increased by more than $2 trillion between the entrance into Phase C and the end of 2009, the beginning. (The issue of the growth of government debt in the United States is discussed in Chapter 23).

The crucial question must be raised: Who will lend to the government? Treasury securities, at least federal securities (as opposed to municipal), can be considered as offering little risk of default, only the risk of a devaluation of the dollar, and a growing share of the new securities issued by the government is purchased by the rest of the world (Figure 8.4). That this flow will be continued is doubtful, given the threat on the exchange rate of the dollar. The *deus ex machina* is the direct or indirect financing of the deficit by the Federal Reserve, that is, radical neoliberal apostasy. Many other countries will also resort to this device.

World Capitalism Unsettled

September 2008 marked not only the deepening of the crisis in the United States, but also the entrance of global capitalism into crisis. The financial crisis took on global proportions, with a dramatic impact on currencies. This broadened scope led to the implementation of a set of policies intending to bolster financial corporations worldwide, with a significant degree of cooperation among central banks. Nonetheless, growth rates plunged, arousing a second generation of such policies, whose main instrument is budget deficit.

This extension to major capitalist countries and countries in the periphery was the combined effect of three sets of developments: (1) the financial seismic wave coming from U.S. mortgage markets; (2) the fragile financial institutions proper to other countries; and (3) the advance of globalization.

Losses Worldwide

Chapter 17 stresses the amplitude of losses worldwide on U.S. credit-related debt (loans and securities) and of the losses on securities in three large regions of the world (the United States, the euro area, and the United Kingdom) as estimated by the IMF and the Bank of England.

As shown in Table 20.1, between April and October 2008, losses on securities about doubled in the three zones. As of October 2008, within the almost $2.8 trillion of losses put forward by the Bank of England, the euro area accounted for about $1 trillion (to be compared to $1.6 trillion in the United States). Up to September 2008, the threat of bankruptcy basically remained a U.S. phenomenon, with a dramatic expansion from September

Table 20.1 Losses on securities (billions of dollars, estimates by the Bank of England)

	United States	Euro area	United Kingdom	Three zones
April 2008	739	443	97	1,278
October 2008	1,577	1,010	189	2,776

onward, but the epidemic finally spread around the globe (Box 20.1). It began at the end of September, precisely in the wake of the U.S. bout.

Global Financial Turmoil

The global extension of the crisis is manifest in the simultaneous fall of stock prices. Figure 20.1 shows indices for five markets. They are the NYSE composite index, the Euronext 100, the Nikkei 225, the Brazilian Ibovespa, and the Korean Kospi. The indices have been set equal to 100, the day each index peaked.

The declines for the three major zones, the United States, Europe, and Japan, were similar from the beginning of the crisis to the beginning of 2008, although the NYSE composite index fell less, the Euronext more, and the Nikkei even more. From March to June 2008, a limited recovery occurred. The figure finally illustrates the simultaneous plunge to the end of 2008, in all countries, a fall between 32 and 47 percent in two months (between August 27 and October 27, 2008). Even more spectacular movements were observed in China. The index for the Shanghai stock exchange culminated twice, once in October 2007, then, at a lower level, in January 2008, after a multiplication by three in slightly less than one year. The ensuing fall to the end of 2008 completely offset this earlier rise.

The synchronism and the size of the falls observed in stock prices are all the more striking that, prior to September 2008, the various economies were affected to quite distinct degrees by the crisis. This observation suggests the preeminence of global financial mechanisms over strictly national determinants in the movement of stock prices, an expression of the extension of financial globalization. In the last observation in the figure, the NYSE is still 30 percent below its maximum. The recovery was more dramatic for the Brazilian and Korean indices.

Box 20.1
The Fall of the Giants (Rest of the World)

September 2008

— Fortis is refinanced by the governments of Belgium, the Netherlands, and Luxembourg.
— Hypo Real Estate (HRE) is saved by a loan from the German government.
— Dexia, weakened by its U.S. affiliate Financial Security Assurance (FSA), is saved by a joint participation of the French and Belgian governments.
— The U.K. government announces the nationalization of the mortgage bank Bradford & Bingley.
— The Icelandic government nationalizes Glitnir, acquiring 75 percent of its capital.
— The Italian bank UniCredit goes bankrupt.

October 2008

— Fortis is nationalized by the Dutch government, which makes a loan to Fortis Netherlands.
— BNP Paribas buys part of the activities of Fortis, with a contribution of the governments of Belgium and Luxembourg.
— The Dutch government refinances ING.
— HRE announces the failure of the earlier bailout. The German government adopts a new bailout of this institution.
— The government of Iceland nationalizes Landsbanki, the second largest bank in the country, and makes a loan to the largest bank in Iceland, Kaupthing, which it later nationalizes.
— The stock exchange of Reykjavik is temporarily closed.
— Gordon Brown decides on the partial nationalization of various U.K. banks and on a plan to save the Royal Bank of Scotland (RBS) and Halifax–Bank of Scotland (HBOS).
— RBS is finally nationalized.
— Ireland extends a guarantee to the deposits of five foreign banks.
— The Japanese insurer Yamato Life goes bankrupt.
— Mitsubishi UFJ enters into the capital of Morgan Stanley.

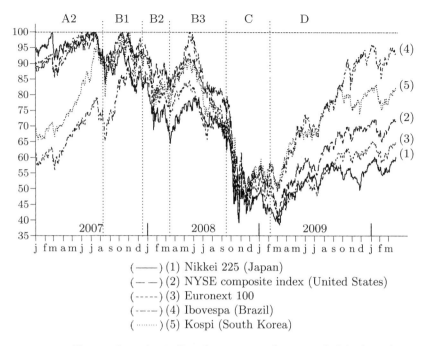

Figure 20.1 Five stock-market indices (maximum value = 100, daily). The indices are normalized to 100 the day they reached their maximum value: (1) Nikkei, July 9, 2007; (2) NYSE composite index, October 31, 2007; (3) Euronext 100, July 16, 2007; (4) Ibovespa, May 20, 2008; and (5) Kospi, October 31, 2007.

Another interesting development, tightly related to the above and also revealing of the globalization of the crisis, is the sudden disruption of exchange rates. Figure 20.2 shows the exchange rates against the yen of four currencies, the real, the euro, the U.S. dollar, and the pound sterling. A dramatic fall of all exchange rates against the yen occurred with the entrance into Phase C. Between the maximum values against the yen and the values at January 21, 2009, when the minimum is reached, the various currencies lost 49 percent for the real, 44 percent for the pound, 33 percent for the euro, and 21 percent for the dollar. Consequently, the rates of exchange between the various currencies were also dramatically affected. For example, the dollar gained 20 percent against the euro and 31 percent against the pound.

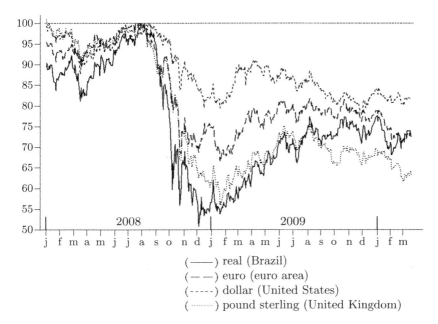

Figure 20.2 Exchange rates: Yens per unit of currency (maximum value = 100, daily).

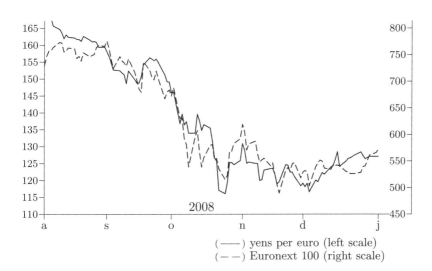

Figure 20.3 Exchange rate and stock-market index: Yens per euro and the Euronext 100 index (August to December 2008, daily).

Nominal Japanese short-term and long-term interest rates remained much lower than rates in other countries. The Japanese yen became a typical funding currency in the conduct of carry trade (Chapter 8). With the development of carry trade financed by loans in yens, episodes of very tight correlation prevailed between the rates of exchange of target currencies against the yen and stock-market indices in each country and among countries. As a result of the financial crisis, the run for liquidity, and the difficulty to renew loans, investors unwound their carry trade. Money went back to the funding country, Japan, causing massive sales of stock shares within target countries and flows of exchanges, with a high demand for yens and a large supply for all other target currencies. As shown in Figure 20.3, a relationship, symmetrical to the one observed in 2007 (Figure 9.2), where a supply of yens and a demand for other currencies were involved, prevailed during Phase C. As in Chapter 9, similar relationships are observed for Brazil and the United States.

Contamination, Fragility, and Financial Globalization

One interpretation of the global crisis ascribes the main responsibility of the devastation to the United States in a world subject to neoliberal globalization. Clearly, the country played a major role in the opening of trade and financial frontiers, allowing for the transmission of perturbations throughout the globe. It is also true that the original shock came from the United States. The mortgage wave originated in this country. This is where securitization and structured finance took tremendous proportions. A prominent factor was the sale of dubious assets to the rest of the world. Many non-U.S. financial corporations were the victims of important losses due to the purchase of U.S. securities. Each new bankruptcy or bailout testifies to this contamination effect.

There is no straightforward measure of the exact extension of this phenomenon, but an estimate of the amplitude of the purchases of financial securities by the rest of the world can be derived from related operations. One can estimate that a percentage not much different from 50 percent of the bonds issued by the U.S. financial sector during the precrisis decade was sold to the rest of the world (as stated in Chapter 14). In 2008, the rest of the world held about $3 trillion of corporate bonds issued by the U.S. financial sector.[1] The potential for a contamination throughout the globe was large.

It is also important to moderate this judgment concerning U.S. responsibility since the United States had no exclusivity in the bold financial developments of Chapter 9. One can think, in particular, of the United Kingdom and its City. Other European governments led their country into the
neoliberal endeavor, and their upper classes also benefited from these new
trends.

The Great Contraction and Its Treatment

While the financial crisis affected real economies with a significant delay,
the contraction of output in major capitalist countries came more or less
simultaneously with the decline in the United States (sometimes even anticipating the fall of the U.S. economy). The new development was the
parallel collapse of growth rates and international trade within the major
countries of the center and some countries of the periphery. There is nothing exceptional in the joint entrance into recession of a number of coun-

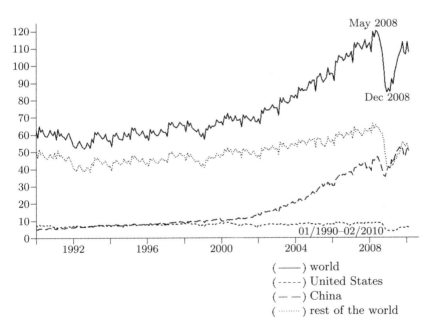

Figure 20.4 Production of steel: World economy and three regions (millions of
tons, monthly).

tries worldwide, but the global character taken by the financial crisis was a crucial factor. The entrance into Phase C marked the beginning of the Great Contraction worldwide.

Figure 20.4 shows the production of steel in various countries or regions of the world, an interesting indicator of underlying trends. Total global steel output (——) grew to May 2008, and then declined by 30 percent to the end of 2008. The collapse occurred simultaneously, though to different extents: 54 percent in the United States, 15 percent in China, and 37 percent in the rest of the world. (The figure also strikingly illustrates the low levels of production in the United States, the spectacular rise of output in China after 2000, and the rapid recovery in this country.)

The contraction of international trade began during the first semester of 2008. Figure 20.5 shows the exports of goods by four countries and the euro area. Japan and the euro area culminated at the beginning of 2008 and Korea, the United States, and China followed suit within a few months. Thus, in the United States, the decline of exports occurred practically si-

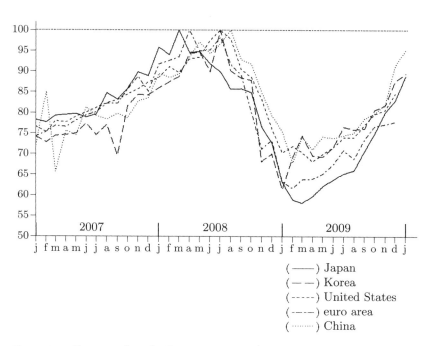

(——) Japan
(— —) Korea
(-----) United States
(----) euro area
(·······) China

Figure 20.5 Exports of goods: Four countries and Europe (maximum value = 100, monthly).

multaneously to the contraction of output. From the maximum to the minimum, the falls in the five zones ranged between 32 percent and almost 42 percent.

Policies in Europe and Japan

The first instrument to which the Federal Reserve resorted in the treatment of the crisis is the Federal Funds rate (Figure 16.3). The same was true of other central banks. Figure 20.6 shows the interest rates of the European Central Bank (ECB), the Bank of England, and the Bank of

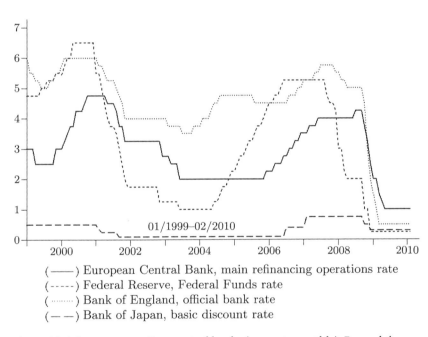

(——) European Central Bank, main refinancing operations rate
(-----) Federal Reserve, Federal Funds rate
(········) Bank of England, official bank rate
(— —) Bank of Japan, basic discount rate

Figure 20.6 Interest rates: Four central banks (percent, monthly). Beyond the fluctuations manifesting the more or less stimulative or repressive character of monetary policy along the phases of the business cycle, important differences in average levels are observed. From 1999 to 2008, the rate of the Central Bank of Japan remained to the floor, given the macroeconomic conditions prevailing in this country. The rates of the Bank of England appear specifically high. Contrary to what is often contended the interest rate of the ECB is not higher than the Federal Funds rate. The rate of the ECB fluctuates less than the Federal Funds rate and with a lag of between 5 to 18 months.

Japan, jointly with the Federal Funds rate for comparison. A preliminary observation is the difference in average levels. The contrast is sharp with the convergence of long-term interest rates noted in Chapter 9.

During the first phases of the crisis, one observes the resilience of the two European rates that remained at precrisis levels, contrary to the early decline of the Federal Funds rate. The globalization of the crisis, with the entrance into Phase C in September 2008, is manifest in the profile of European interest rates. The Bank of England and the ECB began to diminish their rates, respectively 3 and 13 months after the Federal Reserve did so. Thus, Figure 20.6 fully confirms the dynamics of the treatment of the crisis that coincided with its extension to the rest of the world.

The distinct chronologies of the crisis in the United States and the rest of the world are also reflected in the different profile of the masses of loans supplied by central banks. Figure 20.7 shows the total support to the financial sector in the United States and the euro area. While the loans to the financial sector in the U.S. economy rose gradually throughout Phase B, the contribution of the ECB was scaled up only at the entrance in Phase C. (The figure also shows that the financing by the ECB was structurally larger than in the United States, as explained in the caption of Figure 20.7.)

Within the action of the ECB, a significant fraction was the effect of the collaboration with the Federal Reserve pouring dollars into the world. The creation of the TAF (Chapter 18) was part of a coordinated set of actions with the Bank of Canada, the Bank of England, the ECB, and the Swiss National Bank, acting as intermediaries on their own territory. The Federal Reserve provided the dollars by way of currency swaps. Mid-December 2007, the ECB announced its first operations in dollars.

In December 2007 and January 2008, this injection of dollars by the ECB alone reached a total of $20 billion outstanding before declining to zero in February 2008. After having fully stopped its previous joint operations, the ECB initiated a new intervention on European markets on behalf of the Federal Reserve, an additional injection of TAF to a plateau of $50 billion to August 2008, but to these dates, these operations remained rather limited and are not apparent in Figure 20.7. The explosion of currency swaps occurred in September 2008, as manifest in Figure 18.1. The masses of swaps increased gradually to December 10, 2008, when the situation was tense, with the following telling declaration:

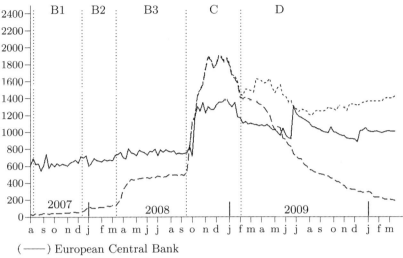

(——) European Central Bank
(— —) Federal Reserve: loans
(-----) Federal Reserve: loans plus federal agency securities and MBSs

Figure 20.7 Total credit to financial institutions (billions of dollars, weekly): The European Central Bank and the Federal Reserve. The variable (— —) for the Federal Reserve is the same as in Figure 15.1 (— —) or the total in Figure 18.1. Prior to the crisis the levels of the loans from the Federal Reserve appear strikingly low in comparison to the ECB. Standard open-market operations in the United States are of the nature of what is denoted as "fine tuning" in Europe. A specific feature of the U.S. financial system is the role played by GSEs in the support of lending by U.S. financial institutions.

Accordingly, sizes of the reciprocal currency arrangements (swap lines) between the Federal Reserve and the BOE [Bank of England], the ECB, and the SNB [Swiss National Bank] will be increased to accommodate *whatever quantity of U.S. dollar funding is demanded*. The Bank of Japan will be considering the introduction of similar measures.[2]

To this support of financial institutions worldwide, one must add the direct commitment of governments to bail out ailing corporations. The importance of this new form of intervention grew during the same period of time (Box 20.1).

The Shadow of the Great Depression: Difficult Transitions

If there is a precedent to the contemporary crisis, it is, unquestionably, the Great Depression. The two crises occurred at the ends of the first and second financial hegemonies. They are two "crises of financial hegemony."

The overall pattern of Diagram 2.1 could easily be adapted to the analysis of the Great Depression. For "Neoliberalism and U.S. hegemony," one should substitute "First financial hegemony." Inasmuch as financial expansion and innovation and the quest for high income are concerned, the upper part of the diagram would still be valid. The two crises came in the wake of decades of rapid expansion of financial mechanisms culminating, in both instances, in a final acceleration of hardly a decade. Despite the determination of monetary authorities to act since the beginning of the contemporary crisis, in sharp contrast to the more passive attitude observed between October 1929 and March 1933, the collapse of the financial sector and the contraction of activity remained unchecked for a considerable period of time in the two historical junctures. In the case of the Depression, financial mechanisms also combined their effects to nonfinancial determinants as in the lower part of the diagram (Chapter 21). The exact contents of the two sets of nonfinancial developments were, however, distinct, as discussed below.

The comparison between the interwar years and the contemporary crisis is also revealing of the treatment of the crisis and its likely consequences. This is the focus of Chapter 22, which is devoted to the New Deal. "A new New Deal" is, actually, what would be required in the United States and the world economy after 2000.

21

Eighty Years Later

Despite obvious differences in historical contexts, the common aspects between the first half of the twentieth century and contemporary capitalism are striking. Eighty years later, the same stubborn logic underlying the pursuit of profit and high income led capitalism along a new unsustainable historical path, where regulation and control were sacrificed on the altar of the unbounded freedom to act of a privileged minority. Similar dynamics led to comparable outcomes.

There is no general agreement concerning the interpretation of the Great Depression, a multifaceted phenomenon (Box 21.1). Alternative explanations are either excess or deficient competition, a structural lack of demand due to a bias in income distribution, a mistake in the conduct of policies, the consequences of the fall of stock prices on demand, and so on. This diversity of diagnoses is the expression of more basic divergences in the broader interpretation of the history of capitalism.

Profitability Trends

As in the Great Depression, the crisis of neoliberalism occurred during a period of restoration of the profit rate, not declining profitability trends.

In the third volume of *Capital*, Marx analyzed the propensity of capitalism to undergo phases of diminishing profit rates.[1] He contended that such phases lead to situations of slow accumulation, increased instability, and financial turmoil. Although Marx does not use the phrase, these situations can be denoted as "structural crises." This theoretical framework is highly relevant to the analysis of the history of modern capitalism.

Box 21.1
Interpreting the Great Depression

During the 1930s, interpretations ascribed the Depression either to the deficient degree of competition as in the work of Arthur Burns,[1] or to "cutthroat" competition. The most popular interpretation was, however, the lack of demand due to the deficient purchasing power of wage earners. This thesis was defended at the Brookings Institution during those years. In the words of Harold Moulton:

> Inadequate buying power among the masses of the people appears to be fundamentally responsible for the persistent failure to call forth our productive powers.[2]

This deficient purchasing power was in turn imputed to deficient competition responsible for the lack of flexibility of prices. The biased distribution of income in favor of profits, the high value of the profit rate, and the ensuing deficient purchasing power of wage earners still define a widely held interpretation of the Great Depression in the Left academy (as in the French Regulation School).[3] It is, again, put forward with respect to the contemporary crisis, also imputed to the deformation of the distribution of value added in favor of profits, a view that cannot be defended, neither theoretically nor empirically.

Milton Friedman and Anna Schwartz are certainly correct when they emphasize the importance of the banking crisis in their interpretation of the Great Depression.[4] The statement that the contraction of credit on the part of banks was due to an error in the conduct of monetary policy is, however, unconvincing. The overall framework of monetary policy was immature, given the severe character of the contraction and the preceding wave of financialization. A much more vigorous state intervention was required with no guarantee that it would have been sufficient to stop the Depression.

(continued)

Figure 21.1 shows the historical profile of the profit rate in the U.S. private economy since the Civil War. "Profits" refer here to the excess of income over labor compensation, a broad surplus of which a considerable fraction went to the government after World War II.[2] (Because of the large fluctuations of the profit rate, the effects of the ups and downs of the business cycle, it is important to identify the trends underlying these movements as suggested by the four dotted segments in the figure.)

(continued)

Another interpretation emphasizes the sharp rise of stock prices during the 1920s and their fall at the end of 1929. The "spending hypothesis" of Peter Temin (as opposed to the monetary interpretation of Friedman and Schwartz) points to an autonomous contraction of demand in construction and to the diminished spending by households following the fall of the stock market.[5] One can finally recall the interpretation by Charles Kindleberger that imputes the Depression to the lack of global governance. In the absence of an international institution susceptible to stabilizing the global economy, this function is conferred on a hegemonic power. The dual pattern during the 1930s when the United States and the United Kingdom (the dollar and the pound, respectively) shared this hegemony is judged perilous.[6]

1. A. R. Burns, *The Decline of Competition: A Study of the Evolution of the American Industry* (New York: McGraw-Hill, 1936).

2. H. G. Moulton, *Income and Economic Progress* (Washington, D.C.: Brookings Institution, 1935), 87. Moulton refers in 1935 to this view of the administration: "The theory underlying the wage-raising program of the National Recovery Administration was that an increase in money wages throughout industry would expand the purchasing power of the masses and thus call forth a larger volume of production which would automatically absorb unemployment" (ibid., 103). See also S. H. Slichter, *Towards Stability: The Problem of Economic Balance* (New York: Henry Holt, 1934), iv; and G. Duménil and D. Lévy, "Pre-Keynesian Themes at Brookings," in L. Pasinetti and B. Schefold, eds., *The Impact of Keynes on Economics in the 20th Century* (Aldershot, England: Edward Elgar, 1999), 182–201.

3. M. Aglietta, *A Theory of Capitalist Regulation* (London: New Left Books, 1979).

4. M. Friedman and A. Schwartz, *A Monetary History of the United States, 1867–1960* (Princeton, N.J.: Princeton University Press, 1963).

5. P. Temin, "Notes on the Causes of the Great Depression," in K. Brunner, ed., *The Great Depression Revisited* (Boston: Kluwer-Nijhoff, 1981), 108–124.

6. C. P. Kindleberger, *The World in Depression, 1929–1939* (Berkeley: University of California Press, 1973).

A sharp decline of the profit rate occurred in the late nineteenth century, introducing the depression of the 1890s and the three revolutions of the late nineteenth and early twentieth centuries (the corporate, financial, and managerial revolutions). The first symptoms of a recovery of the profit rate became rapidly apparent from the early twentieth century, initiating a new trend upward. Through two major perturbations (the Depression and World War II), this upward trend culminated during the 1960s. About eighty years after the first downward trend, a new such tendency prevailed,

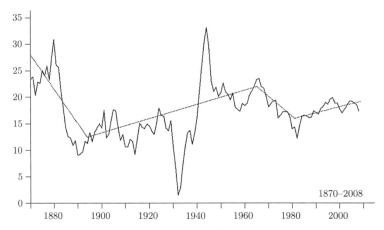

Figure 21.1 Secular profile of the profit rate: U.S. nonresidential private economy (percent, yearly). In the numerator, profits are measured in a broad definition, as the net domestic product minus total labor compensation. (A correction is made for self-employed persons.) The denominator is the stock of fixed capital, net of depreciation. Dotted lines are trend lines.

leading to the structural crisis of the 1970s, the second major crisis since the Civil War resulting from a decline of the profit rate and diminished profitability levels. One can finally observe a moderate upward movement during the neoliberal decades. (In the analysis of such historical trends, a complex of technical, organizational and, more generally, sociopolitical determinants must be considered, Box 21.2.)

The Depression occurred in a period of comparatively low profitability by historical standards, but in the initial steps of a recovery, an intermediate period between two downward trends. The Great Depression can be labeled a "structural crisis," but unlike the crises of the 1890s and 1970s, it was not the outcome of a fall of the profit rate.

Figure 21.1 echoes the analysis in Chapter 4. The detailed investigation of profit rates in Chapter 4 shows that the crisis of neoliberalism, as the Great Depression, cannot be interpreted as a profitability crisis.

The Paradoxes of Modernity and Globalization

A central aspect of the Great Depression is that it occurred during a phase of spectacular transformation of technical-organizational trends, the product of the corporate and managerial revolutions.

Box 21.2
Technical and Profitability Trends

The two downward trends of the profit rate in Figure 21.1 refer to distinct technical and organizational paradigms as analyzed by Marx. Marx imputed the tendency of the profit rate to fall to the historical features of technical change. The main such feature is the large cost of the mechanization required to enhance the productivity of labor.[1]

The intermediate period can be interpreted as a gradual transition between two such paradigms, as the new, more efficient sector of large corporations (bolstered by the financial sector and efficiently managed) emerged and gradually outgrew the traditional sector.[2] The new pattern of relations of production—in its two facets, ownership (as in the holding of corporate shares) and control (as in management)—allowed for a significant acceleration in the progress of labor productivity without excessive additional costly investment in fixed capital in comparison to the increase in output.[3] This favorable configuration of technical change in a broad sense (machinery and organization) came to an end when the new technology had been generalized to the sectors of the economy where it could be more efficiently implemented.

Underlying the upward trend after the crisis of the 1970s, one can also detect the benefits associated with an increased productive and managerial efficiency related to the new information technologies, in combination with the technical and organizational features proper to the extension of transnational corporations worldwide. Whether these tendencies can be interpreted as a transition toward a third paradigm remains to be determined. One specific aspect of the latter decades is, however, the impact of free trade, the cheapening of capital and consumption goods imported from countries where production costs are low. In the context of stagnating purchasing powers, the benefit of such diminished costs went entirely to corporations, and none to wage earners below the top wage brackets.

---

1. K. Marx, *Capital,* vol. 3 (1894; New York: Vintage Books, 1981), part 3.

2. G. Duménil and D. Lévy, "Technology and Distribution: Historical Trajectories à la Marx," *Journal of Economic Behavior and Organization* 52 (2003): 201–233.

3. The investment in the establishment of the assembly line was large, but the progress in productivity was tremendous.

When the new institutional framework of modern capitalism was established at the beginning of the twentieth century, all segments of the economy did not progress at the same pace. In the wake of the crisis of competition in the late nineteenth century and the ensuing tremendous wave of incorporation around 1900, the new sector of corporations, transformed by the managerial revolution, developed rapidly under financial hegemony. This sector benefited from the support of the new financial institutions and from the advance of management resulting from its delegation to the classes of salaried managerial and clerical personnel. This is how the upward trend of the profit rate was established. The traditional sector of individual ownership and management survived, though under considerable competitive pressure. It was, in particular, supported by the antitrust legislation, of which the Sherman Act of 1890 was the emblematic instrument, intending to limit the dominance of trusts and cartels (the first federal legislation to this purpose).[3] The act provided a degree of protection to the traditional sector. But, prohibiting agreements among independent enterprises, it also paved the way to the wave of incorporations at the turn of the twentieth century that the new corporate legislation made possible.[4]

Thus, a major feature of the first decades of the twentieth century was the coexistence of traditional and advanced segments within the same industries.[5] The auto industry was typical of these trends. Paralleling the rise of large automakers such as Ford and General Motors, small manufacturing workshops using obsolete methods of production remained active during the 1920s.[6] Though neglected in the literature this heterogeneous feature of technology and organization is a major explanatory factor of the severe character of the Depression.

A contraction of activity is a cumulative movement downward in which the initial steps in the reduction of demand provoke cuts in production that, in turn, diminish demand. When the recession began in 1929, the backward sector was all set to fall, and its collapse added to the cumulative contraction of output.

There are also nonfinancial roots to the crisis of neoliberalism. Mechanisms similar to the above, for example, the heterogeneous features between distinct segments of industry more or less adapted to the new pattern of globalization, might play a role in the contemporary crisis when the contraction of output deepens. The main nonfinancial factor of the crisis of neoliberalism was, however, the trajectory of disequilibrium of the U.S. economy that also mirrors growing heterogeneity worldwide.

While, in the case of the Great Depression, financial factors converged with the threats inherent in the heterogeneous character of the domestic production economy, the roots of the crisis of neoliberalism lie at the intersection of neoliberal financial-global trends and the unsustainable trajectory of the U.S. economy.

Bold Monetary and Financial Innovations

The comparison between the neoliberal decades and the period that stretches from the last decades of the nineteenth century to the 1920s shows that neoliberal financial trends had a major historical precedent.

It is hard to imagine more daring transformations than during this previous episode, a period of dramatic expansion of monetary and financial mechanisms.[7] Under the national banking system[8] in the United States, banks became major actors in the economy. That such an expansion of financial mechanisms ended up in the Great Depression is certainly not coincidental.

A straightforward and spectacular illustration of these trends is given in Figure 21.2. It shows the growth of the total financial assets (——) of banks in the United States. An increase from 26 percent of GDP in 1870 to 55 percent in 1910 is revealed.[9] A symmetrical aspect (the same expansion seen from the liability side of balance sheets) was the increase in the amount of money, whose major component became bank accounts. The second variable (-----) in Figure 21.2 is the stock of money, M2. Beginning with the Civil War, a steep upward trend in the quantity of money is observed, from 23 percent to 61 percent of GDP between 1870 and 1910. (It is easy to understand why the two variables move in tandem, since the source of money issuance is credit, the main activity of banks.) In those years, the activity of banks was less diversified than in contemporary capitalism. Their main functions were the management of deposits and the provision of loans.

During the neoliberal decades, a similar rise was observed for bank financial assets. Between 1980 and 2008, the percentage rose from 57 percent to 98 percent of GDP, in sharp contrast with the earlier period of also twenty-eight years, 1952–1980. During this latter period, the variable increased from 48 percent to 57 percent. No upward trend prevailed for M2 after World War II, due to a shift toward time deposits that are not included in M2.

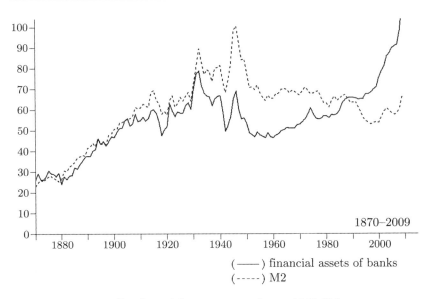

(——) financial assets of banks
(-----) M2

Figure 21.2 Assets of banks and finance companies, and M2: U.S. economy (percentage of GDP, yearly). The assets of banks and the stock of money grew in tandem up to World War I. The final rise of bank assets during the neoliberal decades is the expression of the diversification of the activity of banks and the treatment of the crisis.

The contents of the two waves of expansion of financial mechanisms are, however, significantly distinct. The latter decades of the nineteenth century and the early twentieth century were the period of formation of the modern framework of banking and monetary mechanisms. During the neoliberal decades, a new upward trend of bank financial assets was established, but the main aspect of financialization was the rise of pension and mutual funds, the growth of the GSEs devoted to the refinancing of mortgage loans, and the rise of private-label ABS issuers (Figure 7.1).

As shown in Figure 21.3 (——), another illustration of the expansion of monetary and financial mechanisms is the tremendous (and ephemeral) increase in the number of banks, culminating in 1920.

For a number of variables, the 1920s appear a decade of dramatic acceleration in financial trends as after 2000. An important aspect was the wave of loans financing the purchases of stocks. (In those years, the stock market was at the center of the financial structure, with loans directed to shareholders rather than enterprises themselves, while stock shares were given as collateral.) The final rise of stock prices was fueled by an explosion of credit

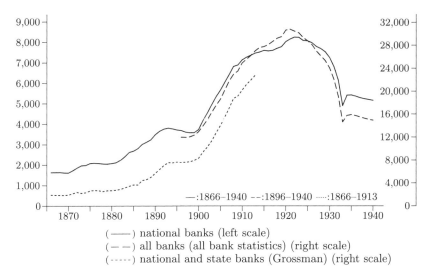

(——) national banks (left scale)
(— —) all banks (all bank statistics) (right scale)
(-----) national and state banks (Grossman) (right scale)

Figure 21.3 Number of banks: U.S. economy (yearly). The national banking system was created in the early 1860s (National Currency Act of 1863 and the National Bank Act of 1864), in which a number of banks (——, left scale), denoted as "National Banks," were conferred the right to issue national bank notes, with a guarantee by the federal government. These bank notes grew as a "national currency," up to the creation of the Federal Reserve in 1913. The profile of the number of all banks was similar, as shown in the two other estimates in the figure (— — and -----).

to investors, whose channel was the rise of loans to brokers and dealers in securities, themselves lending to their customers.[10] Figure 21.4 illustrates the dramatic rise of the two components of such loans to brokers and dealers, gathering momentum during the 1920s and finally soaring to October 1929. One can also observe the subsequent collapse into the Depression.

It is interesting to emphasize that a significant fraction (-----) of these loans was made by lenders other than banks, as the latter wave of financing after 2000 came from private-label ABS issuers and through devices such as CDOs. Thus, in each period, the final phase of expansion was not fueled by traditional institutions, through the usual channels, but via daring, innovative procedures. And "innovation" refers here to perilous and questionable developments.

Such historical coincidences are revealing. They do not imply, however, that the expansion of financial mechanisms can be interpreted as the exclusive or even fundamental cause of the ensuing crises, although

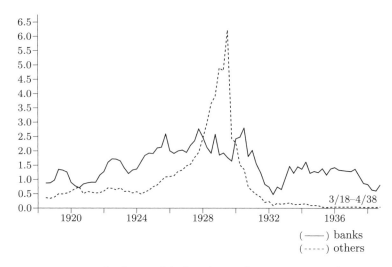

Figure 21.4 Loans to brokers and dealers during the interwar period: U.S. economy (percentage of GDP, quarterly).

financialization was certainly an important factor.[11] Even limiting the analysis to financial mechanisms, not only such waves are involved, but also the deliberate refusal of the implementation of regulatory frameworks and policies susceptible of counteracting the destabilizing effects of these developments.

A Deficient Determination to Regulate and Control

Was the Depression (up to the New Deal in 1933) the consequence of *laissez-faire?* A widely held view is that the sources of macro instability in the 1920s could probably have been checked, at least considerably dampened, by a parallel development of efficient macro policies and regulation on the part of central institutions. Clearly, the existing devices (given the refusal to confer important powers and means on the Federal Reserve) were not able to confront these trends. The observation of a lag in the establishment of central controls susceptible of checking the increased macro instability is a general feature of the dynamics of capitalism (Box 21.3).

At a broader level of generalization, one is led to interpret the Depression as the outcome of the combination on the part of capitalist classes, in the early twentieth century, of a tremendous capability to stimulate tech-

---

Box 21.3
The Tendency toward Increasing Instability

The thesis of the tendency toward increasing instability can be summarized in four propositions:[1] (1) the advance of managerial and financial mechanisms in capitalism gradually adds to the potential instability of the macroeconomy; (2) this tendency requires the gradual improvements of regulatory frameworks and of the efficiency of macro policies; (3) there is always resistance to the implementation of such devices; and (4) this is, finally, performed, but after the crisis, the violence of perturbations being the engine of the required adjustment beyond social resistance.

Two sets of factors, management and financial mechanisms, are involved in the first statement above. Enterprises' capability to adjust output to the signals of demand is a factor of efficiency according to their own objectives (maximizing the profit rate). It contributes, however, to macroeconomic instability since the signals of a rising or diminishing demand in each firm are transmitted rapidly throughout the economy, initiating cumulative movements as in overheatings or recessions.

The tendency toward increasing instability is much more general than the episode of the Depression, and harks back to the emergence of a sophisticated economy in the nineteenth century. The Great Depression was, however, the major event, and it created the conditions for the implementation of the regulatory framework of the New Deal, the Keynesian revolution at the end of World War II, and the corresponding macro policies. A similar advance is on the agenda within contemporary capitalism, both nationally and, even more so, globally. The main aspects are reregulation and macro policies.

---

1. G. Duménil and D. Lévy, *La dynamique du capital: Un siècle d'économie américaine* (Paris: Presses Universitaires de France, 1996), chap. 12.

---

nical, organizational, and financial innovation, on the one hand, and a staggering resistance to create the institutions and mechanisms required by the stabilization of the financial sector and the macroeconomy, on the other hand. There was a strong resistance to the creation of the central institutions susceptible of counteracting the destabilizing potential inherent in the formation of a modern credit and monetary framework, and there was no attempt at moderating the advance of financial mechanisms during the 1920s.

In the analysis of social processes, it is important not to refer to individual motivations in terms of mere "refusal" or "wills," as expressed in deliberate endeavors. But it is equally necessary to emphasize the often clear consciousness of the implications of social transformations on the part of the upper classes, segments of classes, or narrow-interest groups. There is a deep perception—although sometimes misguided and with possible diverging options—of the interests of such communities by their members. There is a typically rightist view of basic capitalist interests that constantly underlies ongoing controversies and decision making (as in neoliberalism). It manifests a strong aversion against excessive state intervention (except when required by the preservation of immediate interests), the defense of free markets (that is, the unlimited quest for high income), the assertion that the "discipline" of the market is sufficient to ensure the stability of the system, the necessary "flexibility" of markets (in particular the labor market), the alleged negative effects of worker organization, the fear of inflation, and so on. Leading intellectuals, politically oriented to the Right, give the appearance of scientific statements to these principles, and conferences and think tanks contribute to their constant refinement and renewal. Lobbyists act to convince government officials whenever necessary.

Historical investigation reveals the acute perception of the social stakes surrounding the progress of financial regulation, and centralized macro and financial policy. There was, in the United States, a strong and lasting opposition to the creation of a central bank. All the violence of recurrent crises was necessary. And when the bank was created, it went on acting on the basis of backward principles, such as the real bills doctrine, which linked the appropriate level of credits to the volume of trade. Even in contemporary capitalism, prior to the crisis, a strong opposition to regulation existed at the top of the administration (though the central role of the Federal Reserve was not questioned). Only a small number of ultrarightist thinkers still oppose the Federal Reserve or the GSEs, on behalf of the absence of financial responsibility vis-à-vis the consequences of decisions.

From the nineteenth century, in the name of the quest for unbounded profitability and high income, Finance balked at the implementation of the framework of control of the macroeconomy and regulation. The reason is that core capitalist mechanisms, such as the ability to "create" capital by credit, are involved. The much needed step forward was finally accomplished after World War II, but at the cost of a dramatic depression and, for the capitalist classes and financial institutions, decades of containment of their interests. It was a rehearsal of what the crisis of neoliberalism is about.

There was a central bank in the United States during the 1920s and the Depression. The Federal Reserve was created in 1913, after a long process initiated in the wake of the 1907 crisis. But the control of the financial structure was not on the agenda of the Reserve, and its action during the contraction of output remained dramatically insufficient. The same contrast between the determination to create a new framework, nationally and internationally, favorable to the class strategy expressed in neoliberalism, and the resistance to the establishment of the corresponding regulations and institutions susceptible of guaranteeing the stability of the construction, is a manifestation of a tendency inherent in the ambition of the upper classes that, sooner or later, had to lead to a major crisis. In this respect, history stubbornly repeats itself. The lessons from the Depression were forgotten, as manifest in the unstoppable march toward deregulation (Chapter 9). Financial authorities recovered memory when financial corporations fell.

The Relentless Dynamics of the Contraction

When the contraction of output began in the first stage of the Depression, the Federal Reserve diminished its interest rates. This move did not stop the deteriorating situation of banks. There was a demand for loans from the economy. But, in a context of price deflation, the risks of default were growing,[12] in particular, on the part of traditional small businesses. In addition, lending was no longer profitable given the prevailing low interest rates and the large ongoing uncertainty. Banks stopped lending, a dramatic example of the credit crunch. The process ended in the banking crisis that culminated in 1932 and the sharp contraction of output. Overall, central monetary institutions were not passive, diminishing interest rates, but the transmission belt was broken.

In comparison to the Great Depression, the action of monetary institutions since August 2007 appears far more ambitious and prompt. From the end of 2007, when the economy was not yet in recession (and more in the wake of each new deepening of the crisis), the Federal Reserve stepped in to bolster financial institutions by an active and innovative credit policy in its function of lender of last resort. Such policies were pushed far beyond the reduction of interest rates and standard open-market operations, in an attempt to avoid a cumulative banking crisis and, more generally, financial crash. A lot was done but the intervention of the Federal Reserve did not stop the financial collapse. It did not interrupt the implacable development of the credit crunch and the entrance into the Great Contraction.

These observations retrospectively question the interpretation of the Great Depression. Would more sophisticated and daring devices have checked the Depression? One may wonder what the real power of financial authorities is in front of a major financial crisis. The bottom line is, however, the same. Between October 1929 and March 1933, as between August 2007 and early 2009, the action of the Federal Reserve was unable to check the financial crisis. Beyond common aspects and differences, history repeated itself.

22

Policies and Politics of the New Deal

In many respects, the situation of the U.S. economy in 2009 is similar to the one prevailing in the early 1930s. If the downturn of output is considered, the parallel must be drawn between 1929 and 2008, almost an eightieth anniversary. Focusing on the treatment of the proper financial component of the crisis, the parallel is between 1930–1933 and 2007 for a still undetermined number of years.

The year 1933 marked the beginning of the New Deal.[1] (It is traditional to distinguish two New Deals, the first one between 1933 and 1935, and the second one, from 1935 to World War II.) Is it where the United States and the major capitalist countries stand in 2009, in the first steps of a "new New Deal"?

Emergency and Foundation

The Great Depression was a structural crisis. The challenge for governments during the 1930s and 1940s was not only to reverse the contraction of output, but also to lay the foundations of a new, sustainable social order. Neither the former nor the latter could be accomplished in a short span of time. More than fifteen years were necessary, and one may wonder how much time would have been required in the absence of the stimulation created by the war economy. The relationship between the two tasks, emergency and foundation, was tighter than could, a priori, be thought. Independent of the degree of consciousness on the part of politicians, the majority of the measures taken during the New Deal combined the two objectives.

The treatment of the contemporary crisis shares this double nature with the New Deal. The second objective, founding a new social order, will gradually become clearer as time passes. There is, apparently, still no clear consciousness of the dimension of the task. Historical experience can be helpful, but there is no preestablished plan to which politicians might resort. In the case of the Depression, the crisis of the 1890s was in all memories. The same is true concerning the crisis of neoliberalism. The determination to support financial institutions and the macroeconomy is clearly inspired by the New Deal. But the situation is also significantly distinct, and the contemporary crisis also reveals that all aspects of the Great Depression have not necessarily been thoroughly understood.

Besides the large uncertainty and the import of earlier experiences, the conduct of policies and reforms is deeply influenced by the ongoing political strife among social groups. In the 1930s, there was no consensus concerning either the measures supposed to stimulate demand and output or the features of the new economy and society. The conflicts of interests were sharp.

Under such circumstances, officials must manifest a real ability to govern beyond sectional interests, but they are also led by a political project. Underlying President Roosevelt's action, one can rather clearly identify the vision of a "tempered capitalism." The main principles were the moderation of the excesses of the financial sector and big business, a larger intervention of government, and a new role and new rights for the popular classes. This transformation meant a direct confrontation with the tenants (and beneficiaries) of the first financial hegemony.

The exact features of the new power configuration were not settled until the end of World War II, in particular concerning the relative roles of private enterprises (the so-called market), central institutions, and unions. Important components of the New Deal were, in a sense, consolidated after the war and this observation explains why the phrase "New Deal coalition" is sometimes used in the characterization of the postwar years, as if the action of the New Dealers had been unambiguously continued after World War II. Many among the basic traits of the New Deal, concerning the financial sector, the action of government, and labor, were certainly preserved. But there was also considerable adjustment, and a number of concessions were made in the direction of big business. Overall, a new social order was established, the combined outcome of the social turmoil of the 1930s and 1940s, and of the compromise found at the end of the war.

Protectionism

The Smoot-Hawley Tariff Act of June 1930 was the first major device implemented after the outburst of the crisis, prior to the New Deal. It raised tariffs to high levels on imported goods. Its relevance to the analysis of the contemporary crisis is obvious.

The debate around free trade and protectionism reflects the contradictory interests among various categories of corporations, and the concerns of a number of politicians. It also illustrates the tensions prevailing among countries, participants in the international division of labor. These divergent interests found a clear expression in the widespread opposition to the act, in the United States and outside. Many countries retaliated, notably Canada and European countries. More than 1,000 economists signed a petition to President Hoover against the act, and businessmen (H. Ford and Th. W. Lamont, chief executive of J. P. Morgan) intervened in an attempt to reverse the legislation. The effects of the act were somewhat alleviated by the Reciprocal Tariff Act of 1934, which gradually lowered tariffs with Canada, Great Britain, and a set of Latin American countries.

The Smoot-Hawley Tariff Act is blamed for having caused a sharp decline of foreign trade, accentuating the Depression. Concerning the United States, a preliminary observation is that U.S. foreign trade was quite limited during those years. The average of exports and imports (half of the sum) amounted to 4.6 percent of GDP in 1929. GDP reached its minimum in 1933, a decline by 27 percent in comparison to 1929. Imports and exports fell much more considerably, by 37 percent and 47 percent, respectively, between 1929 and their own minimum values in 1932. The effects on the U.S. economy were probably limited, but the blow was felt in a number of countries of the periphery more dependent on foreign trade.

Protectionism, in the strict sense, did not survive as such after World War II, but one feature of the first postwar decades was the distance taken from free trade. Keynes saw in free trade an obstacle to the conduct of monetary policy (Chapter 9), and tariffs were part of the new postwar framework. In those years, the obstacles to free trade were among the most controversial issues. The United States refused to ratify the Bretton Woods agreements concerning international trade and blocked the creation of the International Trade Organization. The U.S. government initiated the process that led to the GATT in 1947, the first step toward the restoration of free trade. Tariff and nontariff barriers remained, however, a feature of the first postwar decades.

The control of foreign trade during the Depression destabilized the previous international division of labor. Under such circumstances, a number of Latin American countries implemented import-substitution models, that is, development strategies centered on national industry. The action of governments in favor of industrialization, notably the protection from international competition, was central (Box 23.1). These frameworks played a crucial role in the development of these countries after World War II.

Moderating Competition

The Depression was imputed to the excesses of the financial sector but also, more generally, to big business considered responsible for the failure of many small enterprises, victims of excess competition.[2] (The memory of the Depression of the 1890s was in all minds, combined, on the part of the new administration, with a significant anti-big business inclination prolonged to the late 1930s.) Such perceptions inspired the passage of the National Industrial Recovery Act (NIRA), in June 1933, which created the National Recovery Administration (NRA), a pillar of the first New Deal.

The NRA tried to dampen the rigor of competitive pressures by agreements negotiated between enterprises under the aegis of government officials. A second aspect was the regulation of labor relations (with minimum wages and maximum hours worked). Business was divided into twelve industrial groups, and organized by codes. Their explicit purpose was to stop cutthroat competition, placing anti-deflationary floors on prices, and coordinating the management of wages, prices, and outputs. (One can, parenthetically, note that Keynes strongly criticized the reform program of the NRA.)[3] The entire device was declared unconstitutional in 1935,[4] marking the end of the first New Deal, but measures concerning labor were later included in labor legislation. This does not mean that the codes did not contribute to the stabilization of the macroeconomy.

It is hard to imagine the set of radical views that prevailed in the context of the Depression, notably the appeal of "planning" as a substitute for traditional competitive mechanisms (Box 22.1). The controversy around the action of the NRA raised very fundamental issues. What role should be conferred on market mechanisms? What place for central coordination? The repeal of the codes provided a first answer. There were limits to the questioning of "market mechanisms."

Box 22.1
The First New Deal and the Planners

A radical and lasting change of the U.S. economy was at issue in the definition of the first New Deal. In the words of Arthur Schlesinger:

> The essence of the first New Deal was affirmative national planning. The men of 1933 believed that, in a modern industrial society, the problem of price-wage-profit behavior and of the allocation of resources, could not be left to solve themselves. These problems could be handled, in their view, only by a considerable integration of private and public planning. . . . The first New Deal proposed to rebuild America through the reconstruction of economic institutions in accordance with technological imperatives.[1]

Gardiner Means was a typical planner:[2]

> He [Means] cogently argued that administered prices had superseded market prices in vital parts of the economy, and that this was a necessary phase in economic growth.[3]

Another symmetrical option was the return to smallness. The emblematic character was Justice Brandeis:[4]

> The fight of 1935 [at the end of the first New Deal] was essentially between the planners and the neo-Brandeisians, the devotees of bigness and the devotees of competition.[5]

---

1. A. M. Schlesinger, *The Age of Roosevelt,* vol. 3, *The Politics of Upheaval* (Boston: Houghton Mifflin, 1960), 389.
2. G. C. Means, "Industrial Prices and Their Relative Inflexibility," U.S. Congress, Senate, 74th Cong., 1st sess., 1935, S. Doc. 13.
3. Schlesinger, *Age of Roosevelt,* 3:218.
4. Brandeis was 79 years old in 1935. He presented himself as working in the tradition of Jefferson and Wilson (of whom he had been an adviser). His main contention was that concentration was a threat to the traditional democratic values of America and advocated the return to "small units." He was successful in animating a group of young followers.
5. Schlesinger, *Age of Roosevelt,* 3:398.

Besides tariffs, the antitrust measures of the postwar period are an interesting example of devices implemented during the treatment of the Depression that were somehow preserved, though under more moderate forms, after World War II.

Programs and Deficits

It is useful to recall that government deficits were not considered a central instrument in the treatment of the crisis (in sharp contrast with the situation prevailing in 2009), though they obviously played a role during the 1930s and 1940s.

Already, the Hoover administration had seen in public programs an emergency policy tending to support employment or remedy the effects of unemployment, but not a major demand device.[5] Such views remained those of President Roosevelt.[6] (One can recall here the creation of the Civilian Conservation Corps, a public works relief program for unemployed men, between 1933 and 1942, probably one of the most popular measures of the New Deal.)

There was no demand policy beyond the fact that infrastructure and building programs were devised to "prime the pump." Deficits were there, though moderate and not welcomed by President Roosevelt. They prevailed because they were unavoidable, acting as built-in stabilizers (the inertia of government expenses dampening business-cycle fluctuations). During the contraction of output in 1937, expenses were cut. President Roosevelt became more open to deficits after this unfortunate experiment, although his position remained ambiguous.[7]

Figure 22.1 shows government (federal, state, and local) receipts and expenditures as percentages of U.S. GDP. The distance between the two lines measures the balance of the budget. One can observe that both receipts and expenditures increased significantly during the Depression, beginning prior to the New Deal, but deficits remained limited, given the severe character of the Depression. Overall, the programs of the 1930s and 1940s can be interpreted as anticipating postwar demand policies, but not as a major and deliberate move aiming at the stabilization of the macroeconomy. The figure depicts the upward trend of both government receipts and expenditures—the economic size of government—as a crucial feature of the formation of the postwar economy. In 1929, government

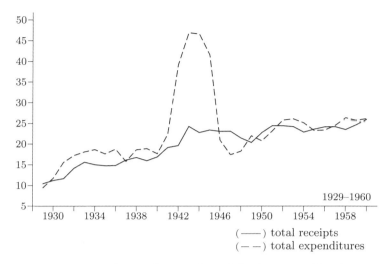

Figure 22.1 Receipts and expenditures of U.S. federal, state, and local governments (percentage of GDP, yearly).

receipts amounted to 9 percent of GDP. In 1952, they reached 26 percent (35 percent in 2008).

Tremendous deficits prevailed during World War II. They remained limited during the Keynesian decades and, finally, grew during the neoliberal decades, with the exception of the second half of the 1990s (Figure 19.4). This could be judged paradoxical, given neoliberal orthodox financial principles, but it is also coherent with the policy in favor of the wealthiest fractions of the population intending to diminish the taxation of the high income brackets and the existence of high interest rates on Treasury securities.

In the wake of three postwar decades of Keynesianism, the treatment of the contemporary crisis reveals that the lessons from the Depression have been learned. The support provided by the Federal Reserve to the financial sector, avoided a total collapse, but it was unable to prevent the credit crunch and the contraction of the macroeconomy. In a pure Keynesian vein, the emphasis moved to the direct stimulation of demand by deficits. It was clearly understood that a sharp contraction of output requires major spending much larger than receipts. This is the meaning of President Obama's spending plans. Not coincidentally, the size of the deficits for 2009 is similar to the contraction of loans to households and nonfinancial corporations (minus 14 percent of GDP between the second quarter of 2007 and the fourth quarter of 2008). Nothing proves, however, that the sums will be sufficient to stop the contraction and restore growth.

Macro Policies after World War II

The proper Keynesian framework of macro policy was implemented after the war. It confirmed the initiative of private corporations with respect to production and trade—alleged market mechanisms moderated by anti-trust legislation—while the control of the macroeconomy was placed in the hands of central institutions, basically the Federal Reserve. Keynesian macro policies meant the continuous control of macroeconomic mecha-nisms by monetary and fiscal policy, that is, much more than the use of large deficits in a depression.[8]

A symbolically important manifestation of the new trends that echoes the new relationship to labor was the vote of the Employment Act in 1946, defining the maintenance of full employment as a responsibility of the federal government, with explicit reference to Keynesian economics. (The act also created the Council of Economic Advisers.) The point was not only the stabilization of the macroeconomy, but the definition of a duty of the government, a political commitment.

The international component was established at Bretton Woods at the end of the war. The main aspects were fixed exchange rates, limits on the inter-national movements of capital, and the creation of the IMF to help coun-tries facing a temporary shortage of reserves in international currencies (Chapter 9). Nonetheless, the United States always fought to limit the role of the IMF and ensure its dominance, in particular the preeminence of the dollar.

In the contemporary crisis, the situation is distinct from that prevailing during the interwar period, since national frameworks of monetary policy have been established in each country. The same lack of stabilizing mecha-nisms is observed, however, when the global economy is considered. The action of the IMF is certainly not negligible, but the global financial crisis demonstrated that, up to now, the potential of the IMF did not measure up to the requirements of the stabilization of the world economy. The limits to macro policies inherent in neoliberal globalization pose serious problems.

Stabilizing and Taming the Financial Sector

Few components of the New Deal illustrate as convincingly the variety of measures taken under the pressure of events as the action concerning the financial sector.

A first, immediate measure was the Emergency Banking Act of March 9, 1933 (passed four days after President Roosevelt's inauguration), which declared the "bank holiday" at a federal level, the inspection of banks, and their possible return to activity. (Only two-thirds of banks reopened rather rapidly.) This spectacular measure was followed by the implementation of a broad regulatory framework and by the creation of the Federal Deposit Insurance Corporation (FDIC). These measures were intended to stabilize the financial sector, with a special concern on depository institutions. The most famous component was the Glass-Steagall Act, aimed at the limitation of speculation, and placing ceilings on interest rates on deposits (Regulation q). Central to the Glass-Steagall Act was the separation between investment and commercial banking. The Securities Act of 1933 and the Securities Exchange Act of 1934 regulated the issuance and secondary trading of securities. To this, one can add the regulation of broker-dealers in 1934.

Other devices were targeted to the support of mortgage borrowers facing difficulties and to the stimulation of new loans. A first legislative piece was passed in June 1933, the Homeowners Refinancing Act, supplemented by the National Housing Act of 1934, creating the FHA and the Federal Savings and Loan Insurance Company (FSLIC). It was followed by the Housing Act of 1937. Fannie Mae was created in 1938, as a government agency (Chapter 13). To this new approach to financial mechanisms one can add the Revenue Act of 1935, which increased taxes on high income, estates, and corporations, also known as the "soak the rich" tax.[9]

The regulatory framework of the New Deal survived to World War II. It defined, therefore, an important aspect of the U.S. economy during the postwar decades, a pillar of the containment of financial interests, up to the establishment of neoliberalism. There is no surprise in the fact that one of the first neoliberal objectives during the 1980s was the elimination of these constraints, but more than twenty years were necessary to perform the task (Chapter 9).

The contemporary crisis will, obviously, mean reregulation. The existence of subprime loans, securitization, off-balance sheet entities, and derivative markets is questioned. On February 4, 2009, in testimony before the Senate Banking Committee, Paul A. Volcker (former chairman of the Federal Reserve and member of President Obama's Economic Recovery Advisory Board) outlined the contours of a new regulation and overseeing framework for the U.S. financial sector. A first aspect was the transformation into government agencies of Fannie Mae and Freddie Mac, whose status prior to the crisis was ambiguous (Chapter 13). (This actually means a return to the situation prevailing before 1970.) Second, Volcker suggested the registration of hedge and equity firms, and their periodic reporting. Concerning large financial corporations, he advocated "particularly close regulation and supervision, meeting high and common international standards," pointing to the creation of a super regulatory agency, possibly part of the Federal Reserve. In another declaration, on February 20, 2009, Volcker referred to the outright suppression of a number of new instruments (such as CDOs or CDSs), moving one step further in the direction of a post-neoliberal finance.

The Relationship with Labor

The measures taken during the New Deal meant much more than regulation and policies. The new attitude of the administration toward labor, notably on the part of the president, established the bases of a new broader relationship with the popular classes, the compromise to the Left of Chapter 6, at least in a first crisis configuration. To this legislation, one can add the constantly favorable attitude of President Roosevelt toward the purchasing power of workers.

The issue of the social basis of the new attitude toward labor prior to World War II remains controversial. Was a segment of big business in favor of a compromise or did it strongly opposed it? Can the new course be interpreted as a form of alliance between officials and workers in front of business in general and the financial sector in particular?

One thing is sure, the early twentieth century was a period of intense class confrontation in the United States in the context of the rise of the worker movement worldwide, and the creation of the Socialist Party of America in 1900. One can recall the large strikes, the famous Ludlow massacre in April 1914, and the creation of the U.S. Department of Labor and the Commission on Industrial Relations (CFI) in 1913.[10] According to James Weinstein, this situation led to a new stand favorable to concessions toward labor on the part of a fraction of big business (as in the National

Civil Federation [NCF]) concerning minimum wages, workmen's compensation, industrial insurance, and social security (as in voluntary systems but without legislation). The prevalence of such trends does not change the fact that World War I was a period of intense repression in the name of patriotism. Thousands of Socialists and radicals were convicted and jailed under the Espionage Act. During the 1920s, the capacity of labor to organize was limited by antitrust legislation. During the Depression, a new wave of strikes developed in 1933 and 1934, with general strikes in a number of cities and the takeover of factories.

Concerning the relationship between labor and capital during the New Deal, the main piece of legislation was the National Labor Relations Act, known as the Wagner Act, signed in July 1935. This act reintroduced a number of measures that had been declared unconstitutional within the NRA. (The act concerned most, though not all, of the private sector.) It protected the rights of workers in the organization of unions, collective bargaining, and strikes. It also established minimum wage, maximum numbers of hours worked, and created the National Labor Relations Board (NLRB). As could be expected, it met strong opposition on the part of business, in the name of "free markets." It was, finally, supplemented in 1938 by the Fair Labor Standards Act, establishing a national minimum wage with "time-and-a-half" remuneration for overtime, and regulating child labor.

Welfare measures, such as the Social Security Act of August 1935, were added to this framework. Their purpose was to provide support to retirees, unemployed people, families, and to provide health services. (Not all social categories were covered, notably women and a large fraction of African Americans.) These measures were basically maintained after World War II, in particular social security that, in 2000, still provided 38 percent of the income of people 65 years old and above.[11]

The pro-labor legislation was continued to the end of World War II, despite repeated attempts at limiting its impact. In 1946, there was a new wave of large strikes. The Labor-Management Relations Act, or Taft-Hartley Act, was passed in June 1947, with the collaboration of a number of Democrats and despite President Truman's veto. The act represented an important setback for the worker movement. It amended the Wagner Act, defining, in particular, "unfair labor practices" on the part of unions.

The succession of the Wagner Act and the Taft-Hartley Act, separated by a period of twelve years, is typical of the overall process of formation of the postwar compromise. Under the extreme circumstances of the Depression,

President Roosevelt confronting Finance, big business, and the double threat of communism and fascism, adopted an attitude clearly favorable to labor, one of the bases of the forthcoming social order. A significant adjustment occurred at the end of the war, but the welfare framework and much of the legislation more favorable to labor was prolonged to the first postwar decades.

These lessons concerning the consequences of the Great Depression must be kept in mind in the discussion of the possible impact of the contemporary crisis. Much can be gained on the part of the popular classes, but such conquests must be actively preserved.

The War Economy

The direct involvement of the government in the war economy was another expression of what central intervention in economic affairs can be, with the prevalence of dramatic deficits (Figure 22.1). The war economy simultaneously meant very large flows of demand from the government, direct organization of production, dramatic macro policies such as the control of prices and wages, and the direct involvement of the government in investment in equipment and structures with the purpose of increasing production.

During the three years 1943–1945, military outlays amounted to about 40 percent of GDP. In 1943, more than 60 percent of total enterprises' investment was financed by the government and managed by the private sector. This investment is known as "government owned and privately operated" (GOPO).[12] After World War II, the corresponding assets were sold at a very low price to the enterprises in charge of their management, and the government put an end to this direct involvement. This investment played a central role in the development of basic industries such as aluminum and rubber, important components of the postwar economy.

In January 1942, President Roosevelt created the National War Labor Board (NWLB) to arbitrate conflicts between labor and management in order to avoid interruptions in production. The board, active to 1945, came to control wages and prices. The decisions favored lower wages, with a practical freezing of the salaries of executives.[13] These measures explain the sharp reduction in wage inequality discussed in Chapter 5.[14] The most interesting observation is, however, the preservation of such income patterns after World War II, which were only gradually reversed (Figure 5.1).

"Tempered Capitalism" as of the End of World War II

Seen from the viewpoint of their genesis during the 1930s and 1940s, the main features of the new postwar capitalism can be summarized as follows. The market is there, in the sense that private enterprises decide on investment, output, and prices. The state is large. The financial sector is regulated. Serious limits have been placed on free trade and the free international movements of capital. The control of the macroeconomy is in the hands of central institutions. The right of labor to organize is, to some extent, guaranteed. The concentration of wages and, more generally, income to the benefit of the upper income brackets has been reduced. A limited fraction of profits is paid out as dividends, and the stock market increases moderately. A degree of welfare protection is ensured.

Beyond the correction of the contraction of output, it took about a decade and a half—a depression and a war—to the U.S. economy and society in general to accomplish this metamorphosis. A strong political leadership and all the muscles of the labor movement were required, a program for the coming decades in an optimistic scenario.

A New Social and Global Order:
The Economics and Politics of the Postcrisis

The credits (loans to the financial sector and securities purchased by the Federal Reserve) and government spending were the first measures to be taken to confront the manifestations (defaults, bankruptcies, and the contraction of output) of the crisis and avoid further deterioration. The treatment of the main causes of the crisis defines more basic but also urgent tasks to be performed. Financialization, accumulation, disequilibria, and globalization are involved. If such adjustments were not realized, there would be no actual recovery or only ephemeral recovery. The crisis also revealed the severity of the threats posed on the continuation of U.S. international hegemony. After the fall of the Soviet Union, the world was dominated by a single country, but a new period is now opened. The establishment of the new network of international power relations is already under way.

The course of history during the coming decades will be determined within such a complex of interacting factors, which condition the adjustment of the U.S. macroeconomy and the continuation of the international hegemony of the country. But the urgency of corrections (such as financial regulation and the rectification of the U.S. macro trajectory) is not, in itself, sufficient to guarantee that the transformations will be undertaken. If they are, it is impossible to foretell whether they will succeed or fail.

The dimension of the task is tremendous (Chapter 23). One can surmise that the "national factor," that is, the concern for the preservation of U.S. hegemony, will play a crucial role (Chapter 24). To this, one must add the proper political determinants, meaning the cooperation and rivalry among the upper classes, between these classes and the popular classes. The outcome of these confrontations will probably be the establishment of a new social order beyond neoliberalism in which managerial trends will be strengthened, though not in the short run. One can also expect the reconfiguration of international relationships within a multipolar world, possibly a new Atlantic-Asian bipolar framework (Chapter 25).

It must be understood that the present part discusses the nature of the social order that might result from prevailing historical trends and the shock of the crisis. Which reforms could a government—politically oriented Right or Left, and committed to the rectification of the present situation—implement? Which new international hierarchies will prevail? The issue here must not be mistaken with the definition of the new society and world that would be judged more desirable.

23

Economic Requirements

A first approach to alternative postcrisis domestic and international scenarios is to consider the factors that led to the crisis sequentially, and discuss the measures that could avoid the repetition of the chain of events that led to the contemporary stalemate. For example, the trends toward financialization, considered independently from other mechanisms, suggest new regulations that might contribute to the stability of the financial system. This is the straightforward viewpoint adopted in the present chapter, a broad spectrum of mild or more radical reforms as they could be implemented by a government committed to the restoration of the situation.

Diagram 2.1 distinguishes between two sets of determinants of the crisis. The upper strand emphasizes the role played by the quest for high income on the part of the upper classes in combination with the processes of financialization and globalization implemented to this end. The second set of determinants, in the lower part of the diagram, is the trajectory of the U.S. economy, the declining trend of accumulation and the cumulative disequilibria. The two first sections below are devoted to these financial and macro mechanisms. The third section discusses the possible occurrence of a crisis of the dollar, a development that would radically transform the present course of the crisis. The last section is devoted to the future of neoliberal globalization.

Rebuilding the Financial Sector

The most daring neoliberal endeavors, expressions of the quest for high income, were undertaken within financial institutions and pushed to the extreme in this sector. During the neoliberal decades, however, there was apparently no concern for the risks involved in this expansion. The sector was finally devastated by the crisis and destabilized the overall economy. On the agenda for the coming years and decades is, therefore, the rebuilding of the financial sector under sustainable conditions, both domestically and internationally.

The list below begins with the milder criticisms and favorite self-criticisms within financial circles. Four types of mechanisms are considered: (1) increased transparency, (2) diminished risk taking, (3) the control of indebtedness, and (4) the moderation of high income. Concerning such measures, the problem is one of degrees and acceptance of the actual implications. At the other extremity of the spectrum is the establishment of a new relationship between the financial sector and the real economy in favor of nonfinancial accumulation, a much more radical transformation (5). A financial sector in the service of the real economy is another financial sector, at odds with the unbounded quest for high income in these spheres. A last issue is the lack of stabilizing procedures at the level of the global economy (6).

1. *Transparency.* Among the measures more frequently mentioned is increased information. The lack of transparency played an obvious role in the contemporary crisis and should be corrected. But this rectification has institutional implications. The reference to transparency independent of structural rearrangement is, at best, a myth, actually mere propaganda. "Externalization" in OBSEs conceals the actual situation of financial institutions and deprives ratios such as the tier capital ratios of the Basel accords of any significance (Box 9.4). The same is true of off-shore centers, also known as tax havens,[1] where information purposely disappears. OTC transactions must be prohibited. In addition, all financial institutions must abide by the same rules concerning information and, more generally, be subject to the same type of regulations. Hedge funds, private equity firms, and so on must fulfill the requirements of the SEC as public corporations do.

2. *The limitation of risks.* Another major factor of the crisis was the involvement of financial institutions into risky operations, often the result of financial innovation. It is also common sense that barriers must be placed to such developments. But here, again, structural reforms are implied. One can first think of the Glass-Steagall Act of the New Deal, whose purpose was the separation between the management of deposits and the more perilous operations of investment banking. The crisis demonstrates that such boundaries are necessary and should be extended to the insurance of

financial products (to be isolated from traditional insurance). To limit the risks incurred by households, drastic measures must be taken to suppress or control dubious loans. The list of such limitations is long, from subprime loans (impossible in some other countries) to nontraditional mortgages such as "interest only," "negative amortization," and ARMs. The source of profit of large segments of the financial sector would run dry. Securitization and ABSs are another all too famous example of perilous instruments in the hands of private-label issuers. A whole pyramidal structure was built on the basis of original securitization, from MBSs to CDOs and CDO-square. Regulation should stretch from straightforward prohibition (in particular concerning the most sophisticated instruments) to limitation to controlled institutions or government agencies.

If the practice of hedging in its original concept of "protection" (as a form of insurance against, for example, the fluctuation of the price of raw materials or defaults on credits) may find economic justification in the logic of contemporary capitalist mechanisms, derivative markets are used to the end of speculation at a considerable distance from such original purposes. Some among these mechanisms could be regulated, and others suppressed, notably on OTC markets. Arbitrage aroused by differences in interest rates, as in SIVs, define another broad set of highly risky mechanisms. Such devices exploit the heterogeneous features of financial mechanisms, under the constant threat of reversal, as in the difference between the interest rates on short- and long-term securities. This appears as an additional reason to eliminate OBSEs.

3. *The control of the indebtedness of the financial sector.* Another important issue is the limitation of leveraging. The crisis shows that the self-discipline of the Basel Accords was not effective. It is urgently needed to set limits on the borrowings of hedge funds, private equity firms, family offices, and so on. Besides regulation there is also potential for a policy component. Monetary policy intends to control only one category of financial mechanisms, the loans to households and nonfinancial corporations, since these loans have an impact on demand, production, and investment. There is no such policy instrument aiming at the control of the masses of liabilities as in securitization, insurance, derivative markets, leveraging, and so on. They are urgently needed.

4. *The limitation of high income and accounting procedures.* Chapter 9 stresses the risks inherent in the unrestrained quest for high income. These practices led to unreasonable expansion, risky innovation, and

straightforward dissimulation, and the production of a fictitious surplus. Mark-to-market accounting was at the origin of an upward bias in the assessment of profits and capital gains, justifying the payment of huge masses of income that encroached on the own funds of corporations. Directly involved are the modes of remuneration of top managers and traders, as in stock options and bonuses, which can be deemed direct inducements to dissimulation and postponement in the reporting of losses. (There are no negative stock options or bonuses.)

5. *A financial sector in the service of the real economy.* The crisis questions the relationship between banks and nonfinancial corporations. Anticipating the discussion below of the corrections required by the straightening of the U.S. macro trajectory, one may wonder whether profit maximizing within the financial sector is compatible with the maintenance of the strong dynamics of accumulation within nonfinancial corporations. Neoliberal trends made the opposite demonstration. A striking observation in Chapter 10 is that the masses of income paid out are not compensated by corresponding capital flows to the benefit of nonfinancial corporations to finance accumulation. A process of negative accumulation is under way in the practice of buybacks (Chapter 4). The intervention of central financial institutions, such as government agencies in charge of securitization or active in perilous sectors such as insurance against defaults, would be a central component of a financial sector redirected toward economic development.

6. *The global control of a global finance.* There is, obviously, an international aspect inherent in all of these mechanisms. In neoliberalism, capitals enjoyed a total freedom of circulation around the globe. ABSs were sold internationally without restrain. A large fraction of vehicles and instruments was domiciliated in tax havens. When operations such as arbitrage were performed internationally, as in carry trade, the risk took a global character. In the new context created by the crisis, a considerable role should be conferred on international institutions in the control of capital movements and global regulation.

Straightening the Trajectory of the U.S. Economy

The second set of factors of the crisis points to the restoration of the trends of domestic accumulation in the United States, which conditions the ability to grow of the country. Then in the list of the problems affecting the U.S. economic trajectory comes the unsustainable degrees reached by the debt of households, and the rising dependency of the U.S. economy on foreign financing, in particular the "debt" component of this financial support that threatens the exchange rate of the dollar. The two debts, internal and external, are the two sides of the same coin, and they must be simultaneously curbed (Chapter 11). Here the task appears so difficult that it can be judged almost impossible to realize.

1. *Growth and investment.* The restoration of growth rates requires a deep transformation of corporate governance susceptible of inverting neoliberal trends toward dis-accumulation. The objective of this new management must be productive investment. Profits must be conserved within corporations to this end, that is, much less paid out as interest, dividends, and high wages to the upper fractions of wage earners. Another option is borrowing, at moderate interest rates, on the part of nonfinancial corporations to support their investment. The issuance of new shares is an alternative channel. It would mean a complete about-face with the practice of buybacks. Modes of taxation favorable to the conservation of profits for domestic investment could contribute to these corrections.

Independent of the method used, it is easy to understand that such procedures are at odds with the maximization of shareholders' value and, more generally, neoliberal objectives.

2. *Curbing external deficits and indebtedness.* Another urgent and difficult task is the creation of the conditions of a re-territorialization of production and demand, in order to stop the growing trade deficit. A drastic enhancement of competitiveness, the establishment of trade barriers, the limitation of consumption, a lower rate of exchange of the dollar or, obviously, a combination of these mechanisms are required.

There are many obstacles on the road to such adjustments. The establishment of trade barriers raises the problem of the likely retaliation on the part of other countries. The entire system of transnational corporations and capital exports is the basis of U.S. dominance worldwide. Protectionism would radically question the foundations of the U.S. economic empire. An interruption of the flows of cheap goods toward the U.S. economy would have a potentially dramatic impact on the purchasing power of workers if nominal wages were maintained or on the profitability of enterprises if wages were adjusted upward. (In the first, broad, definition of Figure 4.1, the massive imports of commodities—consumption and production goods—cheaper than those manufactured in the United States, was a factor in the slight increase of the profit rate after the crisis of the 1970s.)

Finally, a downward trend of the dollar would be a perilous development, threatening the international position of this currency. As is well known, a cheap currency is an obstacle to an efficient strategy of investment abroad and would encourage the penetration of foreign capital.

A way of limiting imports and stimulating exports would be a large increase in the ability of the country to produce efficiently on U.S. territory. Given ongoing economic conditions, increased competitiveness would require a large commitment on the part of the government to support research and development, albeit a time-consuming process. But there are two additional problems. One is the ability on the part of transnational corporations to transfer large segments of production to the rest of the world, and the second, the rise of increasingly competitive challengers entering into the same fields with increasing efficiency.

3. *Domestic indebtedness.* As shown in Chapter 11, if the overall trajectory of the U.S. economy is not rapidly reversed, in particular if the United States does not successfully limit its external deficit and the corresponding use of foreign financing, the maintenance of a normal use of productive capacity can only be ensured at the cost of the upward trend of domestic indebtedness. Who will borrow to stimulate demand? Households and government are the two potential agents. Between 1982 and 1993, the "burden" was on the state. It was, then, passed on to households (as strikingly illustrated in Figure 10.5). The next step is the return to more borrowings by the state, already under way.

The rise of either debt is problematic. In the short run, the situation combines a credit crunch concerning loans to households and a dramatically soaring government debt. A possible stimulation of borrowings by households assumes a restoration of the situation of the financial sector, in particular of institutions such as Fannie Mae and Freddie Mac, and an ability on the part of borrowers to pay back. The episode of the mortgage boom shows that the rise of the debt of households was fueled by the indebtedness of social categories that did not have the ability to repay. These groups are presently, and for an undetermined number of years, overindebted. Concerning government debt, the problem is the potential origin of the lending. Who is going to lend? The rest of the world? The central bank? The Federal Reserve certainly has the capability to increase its loans to the U.S. government (either directly or by helping banks or other financial institutions to buy Treasury securities), and it is easy to predict a new wave of the expansion of government debt through such channels.

4. *Monetary policy.* A final point is the ability to recover real control of the macroeconomy on the part of the Federal Reserve. As contended in Chapters 9 and 14, a few years prior to the crisis, U.S. monetary authorities lost the control of long-term interest rates. The cause lies in the trends of globalization (whose effects were multiplied by the prevalence of U.S. trade deficits). How should this aptitude be recovered? Would direct quantitative control of the masses of loans provide a way out? Or is the time ripe for global macro management? There is still a long way to go.

A Currency Crisis? Government Debt

As of late 2009, the main threat the accumulating disequilibria of the U.S. economy poses on the country is a possible devaluation of the dollar. Before entering into this discussion, it is interesting to examine the long-term profile of the exchange rate of the dollar.

The variables in Figure 23.1 are two price-adjusted dollar indices of the Federal Reserve. They are weighted indicators of the exchange rate of the dollar against the currencies of a large group of trading partners. (The weights mirror U.S. export shares. and foreign import shares.) The major currencies index is limited to the seven currencies that circulate widely

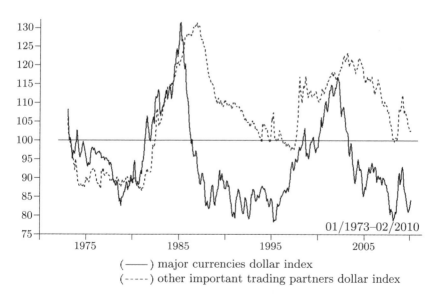

(——) major currencies dollar index
(-----) other important trading partners dollar index

Figure 23.1 Price-adjusted dollar indices (March 1973 = 100, monthly).

outside of the country,[2] while the other important trading partners (OITP) index is determined against a subset of other currencies.

Although there is no clear historical trend downward, the figure shows that after 2002, the dollar entered into a new phase of devaluation against other currencies. As of the end of 2009, the major currencies index returned to the low values observed in the late 1970s and early 1990s. The OITP index can be judged comparatively high. The sharp correction of the exchange rate after the peak in 1985 was not as strong for the countries considered in this latter index as for the major currencies. A number of currencies were, more or less rigorously, pegged to the dollar.

As an effect of the trade deficit, foreigners receive large flows of dollars. The confidence in U.S. government and corporations was such that, to date, the foreign holders of these balances of dollars agreed to invest them in U.S. securities. It is certainly difficult to imagine that the U.S. government would default on its debt, but this does not solve the entire issue. It is easy to understand that in the coming decades, it will be difficult to correct for the rising government debt without a degree of inflation and diminished or, possibly, negative real interest rates. (As of late 2009, the real interest rate on short-term government securities is already negative.) When such circumstances prevail or only appear likely to the holders of U.S. securities, the pressure on the exchange rate of the dollar will be strong. The risk is that along the ensuing trend downward of the exchange rate, a threshold will be reached, and U.S. monetary authorities will lose the control of their currency. The outcome would be a collapse of the exchange rate.

Large portfolios of public securities are held outside of the country, notably, China engaged in massive purchases of Treasury securities after 2000. Analysts point to the fact that China would lose considerably in a devaluation of the dollar and, therefore, will not seek such a development. This assessment is also ambiguous. Such an alternative—going on lending and risking more, stopping and loosing considerably—is typical of situations in which no smooth adjustment can settle a cumulative problem. China might decide, at some point, that a threshold has been reached. There is no way of assessing the location of such a threshold, and there is no historical precedent measuring up to contemporary degrees.

Figure 23.2 shows a measure of the debt of the government, as a percentage of GDP since the late nineteenth century. It illustrates the role played by World War I, although the effect of World War II appears much more dramatic. Directly relevant to the present analysis is the sharp con-

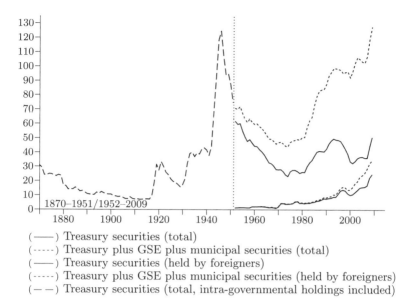

(——) Treasury securities (total)
(-----) Treasury plus GSE plus municipal securities (total)
(——) Treasury securities (held by foreigners)
(-----) Treasury plus GSE plus municipal securities (held by foreigners)
(— —) Treasury securities (total, intra-governmental holdings included)

Figure 23.2 Debt of government (percentage of GDP, yearly). The third and fourth variables are the same as, respectively, the first and second, but the amounts are limited to securities held by foreigners.

trast between the first postwar and neoliberal decades. The low real interest rates and high growth rate after World War II allowed for the repayment of a large fraction of the debt, while the neoliberal decades stand out as a period of rise to 1995, a consequence of the outstanding levels of real interest rates (while non-interest expenses were more or less contained as a percentage of GDP). Abstracting from major wars, it is worth emphasizing that since the late nineteenth century, neoliberalism is the single period in which such dramatic trends prevailed. In the last observations, the crisis is at the origin of a sharp upward trend of government debt, as had been the case during the 1930s. But the rise will be comparatively much larger.

To Treasury securities, one can add municipal securities and the bonds issued by GSEs such as Fannie Mae and Freddie Mac (traditional bonds and MBSs). GSEs' MBSs are backed by loans, mostly due by households and other securities and, in this respect, differ from Treasury securities. The responsibility of the U.S. government is, however, engaged (in particular since the nationalization of Fannie Mae and Freddie Mac in 2008). One can also notice the spectacular rise of these sums during the neoliberal decades. At the end of 2009, the total debt (the sum of the two components -----)

amounts to a percentage of GDP larger than at the peak reached during World War II.

The fraction of the government debt held by the rest of the world is of particular relevance to the discussion here of the exchange rate of the dollar. This is shown in the two other variables in Figure 23.2. The definitions are the same as above but the amounts are limited to securities held by foreigners. The upward trends are steep. Given U.S. disequilibria, the two variables will continue to grow. These observations point to a contradiction between the defense of the dollar by possibly rising interest rates (to attract foreign investors) and a reversal of the trend of the government debt, and there is no clear way out.

Overall, the large involvement of foreigners in the financing of the U.S. economy basically questions the stability of the dollar in a time frame that is impossible to define. It is hard to believe that ways out will be found if the dynamics of neoliberalism and neoliberal globalization are continued.

Free Trade and the Free Movements of Capital

Besides the above consequences concerning the increasing difficulties met in the conduct of macro policies, forgotten since Keynes's times, free trade and the free international movements of capital have been the objects of permanent controversies in the history of capitalism. Many contend that trade barriers are detrimental to all. Others contend that protections are necessary requirements for the rise of less developed countries. In the general case, at least up to neoliberal globalization, the most advanced countries acted in favor of the opening of trade and financial frontiers (or, rather, imposed it, sometimes not reciprocally), while developing countries favored limitations.[3] What trends will prevail in the coming decades?

The difficulties met by the United States will certainly have an important impact on its international trade and financial policies. The dimension of the task to be performed to stabilize the financial sector and to correct for the trajectory of the U.S. economy is such that one may wonder whether this correction can be conducted successfully in the framework of neoliberal globalization. And the enthusiastic declarations of political leaders in favor of free trade and free capital movements will not diminish the rigor of these requirements.

Can the U.S. disequilibrium of trade be corrected without resorting to protections? Can a new trajectory of domestic accumulation be estab-

Box 23.1
Import-Substitution Models

At the beginning of the twentieth century, most Latin American countries were deeply inserted within the imperialist international division of labor based on the exports of agricultural products and raw materials, and the imports of industrial goods. These countries, such as Argentina, Brazil, and Mexico, were profoundly affected by the dislocation of international trade during the Depression and World War II. This situation led to the development of the so-called import-substitution industrialization (ISI) model intending to diminish the dependency from the international economy, with an important role of the state.

The theoretical foundations of these policies were laid after World War II, as in the work of Raúl Prebisch, Hans Singer, and Celso Furtado, and the creation of the United Nations Economic Commission for Latin America and the Caribbean (UNECLAC or CEPAL) in 1948 of which Prebisch was appointed director. These economists are known as "structuralists" because of the emphasis placed on the social and economic "structures" of developing countries (as opposed to the "abstract" framework of Ricardian comparative advantages). The Singer-Prebisch hypothesis stressed the deterioration of the terms of trade to the detriment of the periphery.[1]

The balance of ISI is controversial and unequal according to the countries and periods. ISI culminated in the episodes of hyperinflation during the 1970s. It is, however, unquestionable that the major countries of Latin America grew rapidly from World War II to the debt crisis in 1982, with a sharp break in the trend of GDP with the entrance into neoliberalism. (For the seven major countries of Latin America, the average growth rate between 1951 and 1980 was 5.7 percent, to be compared to 2.7 percent between 1980 and 2005 with major crises as in 1995 in Mexico and 2001 in Argentina.)

1. R. Prebisch, *The Economic Development of Latin America and Its Principal Problems* (New York: United Nations, 1950).

lished without serious limitations of U.S. direct investment abroad? If the straightening of the situation of the United States is not realized by other means, there will be "no alternative." Restrictions to free trade and free capital movements will be unavoidable. But the fate of transnational corporations is involved, as well as the future of the economies of the rest of the world.

Concerning a likely rise of protections, the experience of Latin America during the Great Depression and after is worth consideration. These countries moved to development strategies, relying on their own economic potential, known as import-substitution industrialization (Box 23.1). These experiences show that a clear distinction must be made between the damaging short-term effects of protections, and a possible positive long-term impact on development strategies. In the contemporary crisis, the contraction of international trade will have severe consequences on countries or regions of the world that entered into neoliberal globalization with a development strategy turned toward exports—be they exports of raw materials and energy, highly labor-intensive goods or, gradually more, high technology. The same is true of countries like Germany and Japan, whose economies are highly dependent on exports. U.S. corporations and shareholders would also be affected by increased protection. (U.S. transnational corporations and the upper classes took tremendous advantage of neoliberal globalization.) In the longer run, the crisis might, however, induce all countries to opt for strategies of more autonomous development (a re-territorialization of *production* for the United States, or *demand* as in China) with positive effects—the much needed alternative to neoliberal globalization.

The National Factor

The emphasis in the previous chapter is on the correction of the consequences of neoliberal trends. A second crucial issue is the maintenance of
U.S. international hegemony. Actually, these two elements must be considered jointly as in the phrase "neoliberalism under U.S. hegemony," certainly the most accurate characterization of the situation of international
capitalism prior to the crisis.

Given the prevailing neoliberal trends in the country and the advance
of challengers around the globe, the economic preeminence of the
United States is diminishing at considerable speed. To distinct degrees,
depending on the course of events during the forthcoming decades, a
multipolar pattern of international hierarchies will gradually replace the
contemporary unipolar configuration. Such trends raise the issue of a
potential "global economic governance" to be substituted for U.S. international hegemony.

Obviously, the two sets of issues—the preservation of the strength of the
domestic economy and the international leadership of the country—
cannot be considered independent endeavors. A large country dominating
in fields such as technology and organization, as was the case of the United
States since the early twentieth century, is a likely candidate for international hegemony. This is where the "national factor" could become determinant. The United States demonstrated in the past a large potential for
reaction within dramatic historical junctures such as the two world wars
or the Great Depression.

The difficulty from the viewpoint of U.S. preeminence is, however, that the
United States has no exclusivity in terms of patriotism or nationalism. One
can think here of China, now engaged in a historical process of restoration of

its bright historical past. Last, one can surmise that the peoples of the other less advanced countries will play an increasing role in the coming decades. The pattern of an Atlantic-Asian bipolar world is reminiscent of post-World War II developments, creating circumstances favorable to the emancipation of these less favored countries. The condition is that their governments manifest a real ability to organize and cooperate. There would be a feedback effect on social orders in each country, as such trends would allow for an enhance diversity around the globe.

Losing Economic Preeminence

The amplitude of the problem is tremendous and the situation is evolving rapidly. Table 24.1 shows the comparative outputs in various regions and countries of the world in 2008, using PPP GDPs. The table distinguishes between "advanced," and "emerging and developing countries" (EDC). (The data and terminology are from the IMF.) One can observe that advanced economies still account for almost 55 percent of global GDP, with slightly more than 20 percent each for the European Union and the United States. China reaches almost 12 percent.

Beyond this preliminary, static approach, the mere consideration of GDP trends worldwide points to the ongoing reshuffling of international comparative masses. The growth of countries like China and India is a

Table 24.1 GDP in 2008 (PPP trillions of dollars)

	GDP	Percent
Advanced economies	37.86	54.7
United States	14.33	20.7
European Union	15.29	22.1
Other advanced	8.23	11.9
Emerging and dev. economies	31.37	45.3
China	8.2	11.8
India	3.31	4.8
Russia	2.29	3.3
Brazil	1.98	2.9
Mexico	1.55	2.2
Korea	1.28	1.8
Other emerging and dev. economies	12.77	18.5
World	69.23	100.0

well-known phenomenon initiated during the late 1970s, but another interesting observation is the significant break in global trends around 2000. Not only the growth of the periphery is at the origin of this new tendency, but also the dwindling performances of the countries of the center (an effect of diminished growth rates in the United States, slow growth in Europe, and stagnation in Japan).

This is clearly illustrated in Figure 24.1, which describes the values of GDPs for various groups of EDCs in comparison to the GDP of advanced countries. The variables are the ratios of the GDP in PPPs of each zone (as in Table 24.1) to the GDP of advanced countries. The figure breaks down all EDCs (——) into China and India (— —), and other EDCs (-----). For the entire group of EDCs, one can observe the horizontal trend of the ratio prior to 2000, followed by the sharp rise to 2008. During the plateau prior to 2000, the GDP of EDCs amounted to 58 percent of the GDP of advanced countries (average ratio for 1980–1999). (Interestingly, this plateau hides the diverging trends of China and India in comparison to the other countries of the group.) But the percentage reached 81 percent in 2008! One can surmise that the contemporary crisis and the new trends apparent in the United States will add to this effect during the coming years. If such tendencies are prolonged, as is likely, a major reconfiguration will occur in a not too distant future.

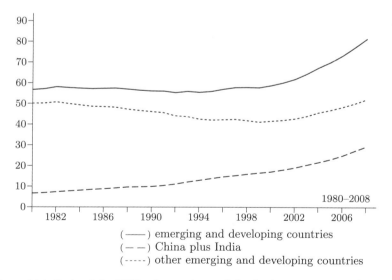

(——) emerging and developing countries
(— —) China plus India
(-----) other emerging and developing countries

Figure 24.1 Ratio of the GDPs of emerging and developing countries to the GDP of advanced countries (percentage, yearly).

The data concerning the production of steel in various regions of the world (Figure 20.4) further illustrate these new hierarchies, notably the volume of Chinese output in comparison to the United States, and the upward trend prevailing in China. The last observation in Figure 20.4 shows a production of steel in China almost ten times larger than in the United States, while it was about equal ten years earlier. In addition, China is now massively investing in the sources of raw materials worldwide and beginning to export capital (purchasing existing corporations, a form of direct investment).

The most alarming observation concerning the preeminence of the United States among large economies is, however, the process of negative *domestic* accumulation typical of U.S. nonfinancial corporations. This process has already been described in the tendency of these corporations to buy back their own shares, in particular during the later phase of neoliberalism prior to the crisis (Figure 4.4). Not only must the accumulation of capital *on U.S. territory* be considered, but also the accumulation of U.S. capital *in the global economy*. The same process of comparative decline is apparent. Figure 24.2 provides a striking image of this tendency. The variable is the percentage of the new capital raised in stock markets by U.S. corporations in the total of such capital raised worldwide. The percentage culminated at almost 50 percent as recently as in 1997, and fell to hardly more than 15 percent in 2007. These movements signal a comparative regression in the global deployment of U.S. transnational corporations.

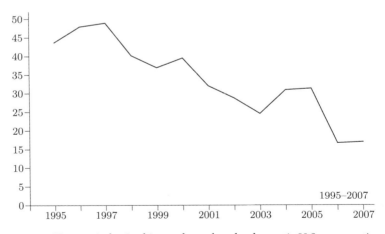

Figure 24.2 New capital raised in stock markets by domestic U.S. corporations (percentage of total such capital raised worldwide, yearly).

Moving to international monetary relations, despite the continuing leadership of the dollar, the currencies in which bonds are issued testify to the rising role of the euro vis-à-vis the dollar after 2000. In spite of the preeminence of European markets in the issuance of bonds during the second half of the 1990s, only one-quarter of these bonds was denominated in the currencies that later formed the euro. The issuances in euros became larger than in dollars after 2003.[1] The pound does not seem to offer an alternative option. (In the interpretation of these movements, one must be aware that the variations of exchange rates play a significant role.)

One feature of the contemporary world economy is the concentration of capital in the hands of the U.S. and European capitalist classes, as well as the dominance of their financial institutions, at least to the crisis. In a number of fields, Europe is leading over the United States and already represents a second center across the Atlantic. But ongoing trends point to the rise of challengers worldwide, both with respect to the capitalist classes and financial institutions.[2]

In 1990, it was possible to ascribe the comparative decline of the U.S. economy to the strategy of global deployment of the national capitalist classes to the detriment of the U.S. domestic economy. The global trends prevailing after 2000 demonstrate, independent of the comparative position of country, that this strategy does not preserve the global preeminence of the U.S. capitalist classes and transnational corporations internationally.

Overall, the assessment of ongoing trends is straightforward. The rest of the world is progressing. The U.S. economy and U.S. capital in the world are comparatively shrinking. And the speed of this decline is faster than is often thought. Will the United States have the capability to reverse such trends in the coming decades?

A Multipolar World

One must certainly be careful in the formulation of predictions concerning the decline of U.S. economic dominance. Already during the 1970s, the thesis had been advanced for the formation of a "triad" as a substitute for U.S. unchallenged leadership in the capitalist world of the time. Japan failed in its transition to neoliberalism, growth in Europe was slower than in the United States and, to the end of the long boom during the second half of the 1990s, neoliberalism strengthened the power of the U.S. economy in comparison to other major capitalist countries. The problem is that the continuation of this apparently favorable course of events after 2000 was achieved only at the cost of rising indebtedness, wild financialization, and the fictitious access to very high rates of return. The years preceding the crisis, actually, meant a reprieve. Even if, during the coming years, the United States shows a large capability to confront the contemporary crisis, to establish a new social order, and to maintain a sustainable macro trajectory, it is unlikely that the unchallenged position of the country will be preserved as it prevailed to 2008.

Despite the financial importance of Europe in the world, it is hard to imagine that the continent could become a new leader on its own, with the euro replacing the dollar as international currency. As is well known, the European Union is politically weak, and there is no sign that the situation will evolve rapidly toward the establishment of a strengthened political entity. As of late 2009, the crisis does not seem to stimulate such trends.

The network of financial relationships between the United States and Europe is very tight.[3] An option for coming decades could, thus, be a consolidated transatlantic superpower. This would require enhanced cooperation between the two zones (economic cooperation, as in a more advanced Transatlantic Economic Partnership [TEP], or political and military collaboration, as within NATO). Will this opportunity be seized? Ambition on one side of the Atlantic and the lack of cohesion on the other side are the two key political factors blocking such an alternative to the U.S. rather solitary leadership.

The future of a potential hegemony of the United States and Europe cannot be assessed, however, independent of the ambitions and actions of potential challengers from the periphery. Concerning economic growth in general (the growth rate of GDP), ongoing trends are clearly in favor of China and India.[4] The hypothesis that China might emerge as a new hegemonic financial center as a substitute for the United States is sometimes put forward. Two aspects of this development must be considered. On the one hand, during the first phase of the contemporary crisis, countries of the periphery clearly seized the opportunity to enter into the capital of the ailing world leaders. Sovereign wealth funds (SWFs) from the periphery, seeking higher returns, gradually changed their investment strategy from riskless government securities to more demanding investments. There was a clear determination on the part of the corporations and SWFs of these countries to take stakes in the financial institutions of the United States. In this first stage, U.S. corporations were actually seeking financial support on the part of Asian countries or countries benefiting from the high price of oil, as in the Middle East. The deepening of the crisis and the decision of the U.S. government to enter into the capital of falling institutions limited this movement. On the other hand, the challengers to U.S. financial hegemony also developed their own financial institutions. Despite the stock-market downturn that affected Chinese financial centers, as in Shanghai and Hong Kong, it appears striking that large financial institutions in this part of the world are gaining considerable importance. Such developments foreshadow the establishment of a towering financial center in Asia, which will supplement the tremendous industrial power of China.

There is still a long way to go for China in these fields to emerge as a new leader. A currency ambitious to dominate internationally must be convertible into other currencies, and its rate of exchange cannot be managed with the objective of serving the development of the country, as in the case of the yuan. This difficulty probably explains why, at least in a first stage, China is seeking an increased role for the IMF.

In contemporary world capitalism, more than the emergence of a candidate to the succession, there is considerable potential for the constitution of regional entities under the hegemony of regional leaders. In the European Union, it would be around Germany and France; in Asia, around China, Japan, and India, or a combination; in Latin America, around Brazil; in central Europe and Asia, around Russia; and, possibly, in Africa, around South Africa. (Such perspectives are contemplated at Davos, Box 24.1.) But the world might again become bipolar, as in the past, with a consolidated Atlantic economy on one side, and a powerful Asian pole on the other side.

Global Governance

The progression in global trends also adds to the necessity for global governance, a political issue. In the very likely establishment of a multipolar world, and in the absence of the emergence of a new hegemonic power, a strengthened global exercise of power will be required. Again, "there is no alternative," global governance or disorder.[5] In the field of monetary and financial mechanisms, much needed transformations are the creation of a truly international currency, the regulation and overseeing of financial mechanisms internationally, the provision of credit to countries facing difficulties, and a form of control of global macroeconomic trends.

Box 24.1
New Concerns at Davos (The 2008 and 2009 Reports)

The awareness of the shifting pattern of power is clearly expressed in the 2008 Davos report:[1]

> The global business climate continues to be profoundly affected by shifts in power from developed economies to emerging markets including Brazil, Russia, India and China, which are spawning multinational companies of their own that are effectively competing against established corporations from the West.

Or:

> Perhaps the best indication of the changing balance of economic power, though, is the list of who has been bailing out the big banks wounded by the subprime fiasco. Swollen with revenues from oil, electronics and public savings, sovereign wealth funds have become the latest global financial force, sparking concern that they may have more than profits in mind as they buy up strategic assets in developed countries.

In 2009, the establishment of a multipolar world is explicitly considered in this respect with four distinct scenarios that combine the more or less rapid decline of the U.S. hegemony, and the prevalence of more or less order or disorder:[2]

(continued)

It is useful to return here to the experience of the Bretton Woods negotiations and agreements. As originally contemplated by Keynes, the institutions that emerged in 1944 would have been much closer to the truly supranational institutions that they finally were. Such institutions should have enjoyed a larger ability to decide on behalf of global interests and to enforce their decisions (Box 24.2). But the United States opposed the establishment of an institution such as the International Trade Organization, more sophisticated and with distinct functions than the IMF. They also vetoed the creation of a new international currency, such as Keynes's bancor. They assumed themselves the international leadership that should have been in the hands of international institutions. In particular, the role of international currency was conferred on the dollar.

Despite the recurrent meetings of the G20, the circumstances of the contemporary crisis stress the risks associated with the lack of such in-

---

(continued)

1. Financial regionalism is a world in which post-crisis blame-shifting and the threat of further economic contagion create three major blocs on trade and financial policy, forcing global companies to construct tripartite strategies to operate globally.

2. Re-engineered Western-centrism is a highly coordinated and financially homogeneous world that has yet to face up to the realities of shifting power and the dangers of regulating for the last crisis rather than the next.

3. Fragmented protectionism is a world characterized by division, conflict, currency controls and race-to-the bottom dynamic that can only serve to deepen the long-term effects of the financial crisis.

4. Rebalanced multilateralism is a world in which initial barriers to coordination and disagreement over effective risk management approaches are overcome in the context of rapidly shifting geo-economic power.

---

1. World Economic Forum, "The Power of Collaborative Action" (Annual Meeting at Davos, 2008), 5 and 7.
2. World Economic Forum, "The Future of the Global Financial System: A Near-Term Outlook and Long-Term Scenarios" (Annual Meeting at Davos, 2009), 47.

---

ternational institutions susceptible of regulating and somehow governing the world economy. The crisis demonstrates that the most important institution, the IMF, did not enjoy the necessary ability to carry out such urgently needed tasks, neither the power nor the funding. During the previous decades, the IMF zealously contributed to the imposition of neoliberalism on countries of the periphery, but never acted to enforce any form of discipline among advanced capitalist countries. In the treatment of the propagation of the crisis to the world economy at the end of 2008, the Federal Reserve clearly chose to perform the work on its own (with the collaboration of other central banks, as in currency swaps). The other option was the delegation of the task to the IMF. Such a transfer implied that the IMF be given the means to intervene. The refusal to do so, to the present, is a clear expression of the determination on the part of the United States to prolong their monetary hegemony worldwide despite the ongoing financial storm.

Box 24.2
Global Governance

It is important to stress that reference is made here to the embryonic forms of an actual world state.[1] At issue is not the ideal "democracy of the citizens of the world" but a supranational state as it could exist in a world of class and imperialist hierarchies. States, be they national or global, are not autonomous entities. As has been amply demonstrated by the action of the existing weak forms of such institutions internationally, there is, to date, no power transcending such class and imperial relationships. The action of these institutions mirrors prevailing class and international hierarchies.

As in the case of any state in a given country concerning classes, such institutions are the frameworks in which the powers and compromises among major countries are established. This is where the contents of the prevailing international order are defined. The history of the postwar decades clearly illustrates the nature of these international institutions. The negotiations of the Bretton Woods agreements were marked by a degree of rivalry between the United Kingdom and the United States. Neither party could completely impose its views. A compromise was struck. During the Cold War, none of the two superpowers could dominate, and the United Nations played a more important role. The situation, again, changed during neoliberalism under U.S. hegemony. The IMF, the WB, the OECD, and the WTO worked during these decades as the agents of the class objectives inherent in the new social order, imposing free trade and the free mobility of capital worldwide, "adjusting" national economies to the arrival of international capital (notably by the deregulation of labor and the financial markets, and privatization). The IMF was, thus, the active agent of the imposition of the so-called "Washington consensus" in the periphery, that is, the establishment of neoliberalism, sometimes under extreme and unsustainable configurations as in Argentina during the 1990s (with the collaboration of the local upper classes). These new social configurations sometimes destabilized highly performing development models as in Asia.

---

1. J. Bidet and G. Duménil, *Altermarxisme: Un autre marxisme pour un autre monde* (Paris: Presses Universitaires de France, 2007), chap. 8.

There are, however, symptoms that new trends are under way, meaning new power hierarchies. As of 2009, Russia and China are already pushing in the direction of the creation of a new international currency under the aegis of the IMF, a substitute for the dominance of the dollar. Brazil is seeking alliance with oil-producing countries and tends to limit the use of the dollar in its exchanges with its neighbors. Such initiatives multiply, testifying to new political trends internationally. The president of the IMF, Dominique Strauss-Kahn, declared that he wanted to double the resources of the IMF to $500 billion. Japan signed an agreement to lend an extra $100 billion. As of early 2009, European leaders made declarations in favor of increased IMF funding. Zhou Xiaochuan, the governor of the Chinese central bank, suggested the use of the IMF's special drawing rights to create a synthetic currency. The declaration made during the G20 meetings, in April and September 2009, confirmed these trends. A new crisis, questioning U.S. hegemony, was probably necessary. Will it be sufficient to impose new arrangements measuring up to the task to be performed? Possibly, a crisis of the dollar.

Being Domestically Strong and Leading Internationally

In the context created by the crisis and the rise of competitors, considerable pressure is placed on the United States to create conditions conducive to an economic restoration. "Mediocre" performances would condemn the country to rapid comparative decline.

In the analysis of the potential demise of U.S. international hegemony, one should not forget the lessons taught by the circumstances of the historical establishment of the dominance of the country. The conviction of the international superiority of the United States, as of the end of World War I, was deeply rooted in the advance acquired by the country in the implementation of the system of large and highly performing corporations, backed by the new financial sector, and at the cutting edge of managerial practices.[6] This leadership was clearly expressed in the prominent position of the national industry within the main segments of manufacturing worldwide.

Having successfully pushed to their limits the implications of the "manifest destiny" of the country to dominate North America to the Pacific and far enough to the South, there was a clear consciousness of the correspondence between the early access, at the beginning of the twentieth century, to the institutional framework of modern capitalism—being the best in these fields—and the vocation of the country to rule the world. In a Wilsonian perspective, it was understood that, among vying countries, the most "efficient," in a broad sense of the term, enjoyed a larger aptitude to lead. The

United States had acquired this preeminence. Reciprocally, the gradual enforcement of this new international leadership was a crucial factor in the consolidation of the technical and organizational advance of the country.

This historical precedent shows that it is impossible to separate the historical advance of the relations of production—notably the corporate, financial, and managerial revolutions—and the network of inter-imperialist hierarchies worldwide. A large country, leading in the first field, enjoyed a central position in the second. Within the phase capitalism is now entering, the challenge for the U.S. upper classes is to invent and implement such a renewed framework.

The comparison between the dangers threatening the U.S. hegemony and the effects of World War I on the dominance of the United Kingdom is also telling. After World War I, this latter country attempted to recover its earlier financial leadership by the restoration of the convertibility of the pound at a high exchange rate, with detrimental effects on the macroeconomy of the country during the 1920s, as analyzed by Keynes.[7] U.K. corporations were not adjusted to the new managerial standards.[8] To the contrary, the United States emerged from World War I as the new rising power, "institutionally" the most efficient. The country abandoned the temptation of the construction of the traditional, *formal,* empire that it had initiated at the end of the nineteenth century, and moved along the new lines of the Wilsonian *informal* imperialism.[9]

The transition between the hegemony of the United Kingdom and the United States was accomplished gradually.[10] Although the Great Depression originated in the United States, the country—consolidated by the war economy and its late but victorious participation in the war—emerged as the unquestioned leader of the so-called free world in front of the Soviet Union. The same will be true of the contemporary crisis. Among the major powers, the most performing countries in the implementation of the new social framework—including management, education, technology, research and development policies, and so on—will gradually acquire the ability to lead, at least regionally, and occupy a towering position within the international hierarchies.

A Potential for Reaction?

It is hard to imagine that the United States will abandon its preeminence without fighting back. Since World War I and World War II, the country demonstrated a truly astounding capability to lead at least part of the world. The instruments of this domination were varied including technical, organizational, and financial leadership, and massive foreign investment, as well as the engagement within the two world wars and the day-to-day practice of corruption, subversion, and military operations in the rest of the world. Abstracting from the trauma of the defeat in Vietnam, none of the wars or crises destabilized this hegemony. In particular, an important lesson from the past is that the Great Depression did not unsettle U.S. international leadership.

One can surmise that the consciousness of an incipient decline, or the mere threat of such a decay, will play a major role during the coming decades. The fate of U.S. hegemony must, thus, be considered not only a *consequence* of social and economic developments, but also a *factor* that will weigh on the politics of both the treatment of the crisis and the establishment of a new social order. The political and ideological determination to preserve the position of the country worldwide will count among the main forces susceptible of imposing the choice of organization and efficiency, as opposed to the unchecked dynamics of the quest for income in a "free (capitalist) market" on the part of a privileged minority. The same conviction could feed a growing sense of the necessary containment of financial interests. Only the apparent temporary convergence of the two objectives in neoliberalism ("what is good for Finance is good for the United States") created the illusion of their compatibility, and ensured the political conditions for the continuation of the neoliberal class strategy. This period is probably over.

Clearly, the United States demonstrated during earlier dramatic episodes of history (such as the New Deal and wars) large organizational capabilities and, under the leadership of a strong state, the national commitment to the defense of the preeminence of the country worldwide. But there is also a threatening facet to this national factor. Its name is "nationalism," a perilous development in the context of a far-Right alternative.

In the coming decades, in a framework of increased international competition, the key element will be the capability to organize. The national factor will play a central role in the ability of the candidates to leadership to realize their ambitions. But this field is one of rivalry, not the solitary race of a single threatened leader.

The Chinese Challenge

In this discussion of a U.S. national factor, one must keep in mind that the United States has no exclusivity in this respect. The country is not the single one around the world in which a strong state may take the fate of the country in its hands when necessary. Though in a quite distinct historical context, the historical trajectory of Meiji Japan is now being repeated by China, with a tremendous potential. China was deeply humiliated by imperialist powers during the nineteenth century and the early twentieth century, notably by the Opium Wars and by the Versailles Treaty of 1919. Seven years after the foundation of the ephemeral Republic of China, the treaty sparked the famous May Fourth Movement, opening a long cultural and political process, and leading to the restoration of national pride in the victory of Communist forces in 1949 under the leadership of President Mao Zedong. Beyond the radical change in the social order, the new Chinese leaders share with Mao Zedong, whose image was consequently preserved, the ambition to restore the towering position China enjoyed in the past.

The exact content of the transformation of the Chinese economy and society to the present day remains to be determined. China took advantage of the neoliberal international division of labor, with a cheap labor power and a strong organizational capability, and simultaneously followed a much broader strategy of both self-centered development and expansion around the globe. That, to date, the movement was conducted in a world dominated by neoliberalism certainly had a large impact on the trajectory of China, as was earlier the case in Russia.

Seen from the viewpoint of the integration into a neoliberal world, the country is engaged in a twofold process, under the aegis of a very strong government inherited from the previous social order. The key element is primitive accumulation within a capitalist sector, paralleling a still important sector of public corporations. Private wealth is accumulating in China (with already forty-two billionaires, in dollars, in China proper, and twenty-six in Hong Kong in 2008). Within academic circles in this country, neoliberal ideology had a devastating impact. On the other hand, in several important respects, notably the control of its currency and of its financial institutions, China did not comply with all the requirements of neoliberal globalization, and this represents a major exception to the diffusion of the neoliberal model around the world.

The conditions created by the contemporary crisis might considerably alter ongoing directions to the benefit of the prolongation or extension of managerial trends, stimulated by a very strong national factor. In the short run, this explains why the country was much better prepared to the adverse conditions of the crisis. The first measures taken testify to a determination to preserve the spectacular development trajectory. In the longer run, one can surmise that a "Chinese way," somehow transformed in the wake of the contemporary crisis, will be prolonged during the coming decades. This trajectory will add to the probably increasing diversity of configurations around the world. But how to resist the rising power of "money," actually, capital accumulation?

Peoples' Struggles: Increasing Diversity

Thirty years of neoliberal globalization under U.S. hegemony gradually imposed the view of the convergence of all social orders to a single configuration. The sufferings in the countries subjected to the new neoliberal order, as in Africa, Asia, and Latin America, were presented by the tenants of neoliberalism as the unfortunate effects of a deficient ability to adapt to an inescapable common fate. The same is true of the fractions of the population specifically hurt by neoliberalism in every country. The entire world was allegedly programmed to converge to the common model, even China. This was performed, but also with some limitations that might play a significant role during the coming decades:

1. In the first place, the domestic rules of neoliberalism had to be implemented in all countries, which was, to a large extent, done successfully. Everywhere, the "market" (another name for the freedom to act by the upper classes and the most powerful countries) would dominate. This framework would combine a minimum support to the weakest fractions of the population, private health insurance and pension funds, but no welfare system that could manifest a threatening solidarity within the popular classes.

This "rosy" picture of the global adjustment to neoliberal trends, as in the minds of the neoliberal leaders, never fully corresponded to the prevailing social arrangements. In most countries, the neoliberal compromise among the upper classes is less advanced than in the United States. In Europe (with distinct situations among countries) and Japan, earlier social patterns were never totally offset, even in the United States. European societies or the Japanese society are still penetrated by the experience of the postwar decades, with a stronger involvement of government in economic affairs and welfare systems. Although major political parties traditionally considered as left entities moved in the direction of the neoliberal compromise (as in the alleged "middle ways" of the 1980s and 1990s), a segment of the popular movement, as in unions and radical left organizations, are still inspired by the memory of an alternative power configuration.

2. Concerning international relationships, each country was supposed to occupy its own specific place in the international division of labor, within large zones of free trade or a world totally open to the international flows of commodities and capitals. Countries of the periphery were expected to specialize in activities in which they are more performing. ("Performance" is understood here in comparison to other activities, a rate of exchange allowing for their international competitiveness and the equilibrium of foreign trade, as in the theory of comparative advantages.) Thus, the periphery would be able to supply cheap commodities to the center and offer profitable opportunities to investors—in other words, the best of the neoliberal imperial worlds. More complex national development strategies are, however, implemented, and not only in China, and the resistance to imperialist pressures is sometimes strong.

After more or less twenty years of adjustment (sometimes dramatic as in dictatorships, or in the crises of the 1990s in Mexico, or of 2001 in Argentina), Latin America is the first region of the world in which popular struggles, votes, and new policies manifested a refusal of the imperialist neoliberal order. The North American Free Trade Agreement (NAFTA, effective in January 1994) was imposed on Mexico when neoliberalism was still on the offensive. But the projected Free Trade Area of the Americas (FTAA), better known as Área de Libre Comercio de las Américas (ALCA), initiated in 2001, missed the deadline of 2005, in the wake of the failure of the Doha Round of the WTO. (As of late 2009, the process is still under negotiation but with little chances of success.) The Alternativa Bolivariana para los Pueblos de nuestra América (ALBA) was created beginning in 2004 with Venezuela and Cuba and, as of 2010, including also Nicaragua, Bolivia, Ecuador, and three small Caribbean islands. The election of governments oriented to the Left in South America signaled a similar tendency (with the exception of Colombia and Peru).

Already after World War II, the prevalence of a bipolar world allowed for a degree of autonomy of what was known as the "third world," vis-à-vis the two superpowers of the time. Emblematic of the period were the

Bandung Conference in 1955, import-substitution industrialization in Latin America, and a strong involvement of governments in the development of many countries (inspired by the European industrialization in the nineteenth century and Sovietism in those years). The crisis of neoliberalism is creating such an opportunity for developing countries to be seized. The exact configuration remains, however, to be found and the transition to be managed.

To sum up, a crucial issue in the coming decades will be the economic and political trajectories in other regions of the world. What trends will prevail? It is hard to imagine a world dominated by neoliberal dynamics and the United States drawn to new logics. Europe does not need to confront the constraints of an unsustainable trajectory as in the United States. The European situation is much less severe, only mediocre. The main point is what will become of the social orders prevailing in countries like China, Russia, India, and Brazil. The continuation of the move toward neoliberalism or innovative paths? The same is true of the social democratic trends now prevailing in Latin America.

Thus, the fate of neoliberalism on a world scale is not strictly in the hands of the United States and Europe and, in the coming decades, it might gradually become less so. This fate will be largely determined in the long run by the path followed by challengers from other regions of the world. After thirty years of neoliberal globalization, this situation opens new perspectives. Key to these historical trends will be the political trends in China and South America.

25

Beyond Neoliberalism

When things are considered from the viewpoint of historical dynamics—
the succession of various social orders in the history of capitalism, separated by structural crises—the occurrence of the contemporary crisis suggests a transition to a new social order, a new phase of modern capitalism
beyond neoliberalism. But the mere repetition of historical events is not a
convincing argument.

Only limited adjustments have been performed in the United States during the first stages of the crisis. The hypothesis here is, however, that major
corrections must be expected in the longer run. Such rectifications should
take the form of strengthened managerial trends, in the broad sense of
corporate management and policies. This could be done within a new social arrangement to the Right or to the Left, but, ongoing political circumstances suggest a bifurcation along the first branch of the alternative, to the
Right, what the present study denotes as a "neomanagerial capitalism."

Time Frames and the Constraint of Events

It would be naive to imagine that the return to positive growth rates in
2010 or in any subsequent year could autonomously open a new era in
which the upper classes and governments—suddenly aware of the risks
inherent in the continuation of neoliberal objectives—would deliberately
lay the foundations of a new social order. The consciousness of the necessity of dramatic adjustments will only be acknowledged gradually, as a result of accumulating difficulties. None of the necessary changes will be
undertaken if not under the stubborn pressure of events. A likely list of
the developments that could stimulate new dynamics is as follows: (1) the

weakness of the economic recovery and the likelihood of a new contraction of GDP, (2) the threat of the repetition of a new episode of financial
perturbation, (3) a crisis of the dollar, and (4) the multiplication of new
symptoms of the lost economic preeminence of the United States.

How long would it take? The historical perspective of the first chapter
points to the significant duration of structural crises and to the diversity of
the mechanisms involved. One thing is clear, as of late 2009, the crisis is
not over. New dramatic episodes can be expected. The example of the
Great Depression and World War II (the period that stretches between 1929
and 1945) is telling. The contemporary crisis will probably be no exception. A crucial issue is also what is meant by "recovery." How will the
growth of the U.S. economy be sustained in the coming years? By a daring
credit policy toward households? By expanded government expenses? All
of these options are risky. Will a new investment boom reminiscent of the
long boom of the second half of the 1990s appear center stage as a *deus
ex machina*? How long will it last? Overall, what will be the course of the
U.S. macroeconomy in the coming ten or twenty years?

The conclusion reached here is that the chances of neoliberalism are
rather limited, but that this outcome will only be determined in a time
frame whose duration is difficult to foretell. The objectives of neoliberalism are incompatible with the maintenance of U.S. hegemony or, more
rigorously, incompatible with the determination to slow down its decline.
They are also at odds with the correction of the U.S. macro trajectory. And
the two sets of issues are related. One can surmise that the determination
to preserve the comparative power of the country will play a central role.
Though not tomorrow.

Strengthened Managerial Trends

What are the alternatives to neoliberal dynamics? The dilemma is traditionally formulated as between market and organization, or market and state
intervention. We are told that the correction of ongoing trends requires enhanced state intervention and a comparative setback of allegedly autonomous market mechanisms. These words are those of straightforward
Keynesian replies to neoliberal propaganda. They do not acknowledge, however, the social nature of underlying relationships. In terms of class patterns
and hierarchies, the crucial point is the role conferred on *managerial classes*
in comparison to *capitalist classes,* and the relationship between the two.

The divergence between the preservation of the power of the United States as a country and the interests of the upper classes is the product of the objectives and practices of capitalist classes, financial managers, and top managers. There is intrinsically no such divergence concerning nonfinancial managers. This property is an important factor working in favor of the strengthening of the comparative social positions of nonfinancial managers. Given the challenge of economic governance for the coming decades, an increased role must be conferred on managers in charge of technology and organization within nonfinancial corporations and government institutions, actually a leadership—a management freed, at least to a significant extent, from the objectives and biases proper to neoliberalism.

The main aspects of this strengthened managerial leadership are rather intuitive. A first aspect is the requirement of the conservation of profits within nonfinancial corporations to the end of investment. In the urgently needed new corporate governance, the "creation of shareholders' value" cannot remain the almost exclusive objective of management. Tremendous gains in the stock market would no longer be expected. Policies constitute a second component. They must aim at efficiency, as in education, research, or the development of infrastructures, and so on, not simply deregulation. A third element is inflation and taxation. They are equally dreadful to the holders of large portfolios of financial assets. Both would, however, be necessary in the coming years and decades to correct for the rising indebtedness of the government, a lesson from history. As is already evident in the treatment of the contemporary crisis, a corresponding threat is placed on tax havens, which were a key instrument in tax evasion, and allowed for the corresponding concentration of wealth at the top of the social hierarchies in neoliberalism. Given the diverging interests among the various fractions of the upper classes in the above respects, one can expect the initiative of a fraction of officials and nonfinancial managers in favor of such developments, but there will be a strong resistance on the part of those who more strongly benefited from neoliberal trends, that is, capitalists, financial managers, and the upper fractions of management involved in the hybridization process described in Chapter 5.

In order to restore the situation of the U.S. economy, it will be necessary to place severe limitations on the transfer of large flows of income toward the upper fractions of income brackets. Not only capital income (interest and dividends) is involved in such a rectification, also the high "surplus labor compensation" that accounted for the major drain on the surplus generated within corporations during the neoliberal decades, a pillar of the neoliberal compromise. A problem is how these reductions would be shared within the upper classes.

Managerial Efficiency and Social Inclinations: To the Left or to the Right?

The investigation of scenarios at the top of the social hierarchies for the coming decades harks back to the pattern of configurations in Table 6.1. The typology there emphasizes the political orientation of power configurations, "toward the Right" or "toward the Left." The compromise to the Right refers to the alliance between the capitalist and managerial classes; the compromise to the Left refers to the alliance between the managerial and popular classes. This first criterion is combined with a second, depending on the class that assumes the leadership in each instance. The social basis of neoliberalism can, thus, be described as manifesting the compromise between the capitalist and managerial classes, under the leadership of the capitalists, that is, to the Right [1]. The social compromise that prevailed during the first postwar decades is interpreted as between the managerial and popular classes, under the leadership of the managerial classes [2]. It is denoted as "Center Left." But another configuration, to date without precedent, is also introduced in the table. It is a compromise to the Right, as in neoliberalism, but under the leadership of the managerial classes instead of the capitalist classes [3].

In the interpretation of this classification, it is important to distinguish between (1) *organization and efficiency* in the sense of corporate governance, government intervention, regulation, and policies; and (2) the *fate of popular classes,* according to the political orientation of the prevailing compromise, to the Left or to the Right. This second aspect is central in the distinction between the Center-Left compromise and neo-managerial capitalism, where the social compromise is at the top of the social hierarchies.

Two bifurcations are, thus, involved in the analysis of possible scenarios as suggested in Diagram 1.4:

1. In the first bifurcation, one option is the continuation of neoliberalism, given limited adjustments supposedly sufficient to avoid the repetition in the short run of an event such as the contemporary crisis. The configuration is that denoted [1] above. This is where the United States

stands, as of late 2009. Limited measures are considered as stricter Basel ratios or the creation of institutions in charge of the supervision of financial mechanisms. In other words, nothing serious.

2. The second branch of the alternative is the establishment of a managerial leadership susceptible of handling more efficiently the difficult situation to which the United States is confronted. Both the unsustainable trajectory of the country and its declining international hegemony require a new corporate management, new policies, and limitations to globalization.

The political orientations to the Right or Left are determined by the second bifurcation. Managerial classes can ally either with the capitalist classes or the popular classes. Thus, two variants of managerial leadership are defined:

1. The first configuration, to the Right, as in [3] above, has no historical precedent. It is denoted here as a "neomanagerial capitalism," meaning a compromise among the upper classes under managerial leadership. The main difference with the compromise to the Left below is that there is no room for the welfare component of the postwar decades.

2. The second branch points to the alliance to the Left, in [2], as in the Center-Left compromise of the postwar decades. The managerial leadership is still there, but the situation made to popular classes is more favorable.

Income distribution is a key element in the definition of these social arrangements. The containment of high income is congenial to the compromise to the Left [2]. The situation would be distinct in the event of the prevalence of a neomanagerial capitalism [3]. Three features of such a social order must be emphasized:

1. The alliance being at the top, there would be no "intrinsic reasons"— that is, no reasons inherent in the social foundations proper to this social order—to observe a severe containment of high incomes. A managerial leadership implies, however, a new balance of power between managerial and capitalist classes in favor of managers, with a corresponding rearrangement of income hierarchies. Among other things, financial regulation, a necessary ingredient of neomanagerial capitalism, would place limits on the expansion of capital income. One could, thus, expect a moderate containment of capital incomes (interest, dividends, and capital gains in the stock market), and a continuation of the payment of high wages at the top of income hierarchies, to various degrees depending on the components of management. In neoliberalism, even in the nonfinancial sector, top management is directly aimed at stock-market performances and re-

munerated as such. The new social order would naturally impose limitations on these practices. Straightforward financial management would be even more affected.

2. It is important to return here to the consequences of the process of hybridization among the upper classes, typical of contemporary capitalism. Gradually more, the same upper brackets tend to benefit from very high wages and capital income. Thus, for capitalist families, at least their most dynamic segments, diminished capital income could be compensated by an even larger access to high wages as is already the case.

3. There is, however, another set of factors, specific to the contemporary situation of the U.S. economy, which lies beyond these reasons "intrinsic" to the social arrangement in neomanagerial capitalism. It is the rapid decline of U.S. international hegemony and the requirement to curb the unsustainable features of the trajectory of the U.S. economy. Actually, these factors are those that create the urgency of the abandonment of neoliberal trends and of the transition to the new social order. But more than that is involved. At the top of the social hierarchies, the upper classes—their capitalist as well as managerial segments, or more or less so—must impose on themselves a containment of their incomes, at least during a lasting transition. This is a basic requirement intending to limit consumption, restore domestic accumulation trends, and correct for the disequilibrium of foreign trade. Nothing proves, however, that the upper classes will be able to subject themselves to such discipline.

The Economics and Politics of Social Change

Does a structural crisis, such as the crisis of neoliberalism, favor one of the branches of the bifurcations above?

Structural crises are conducive to social change, but it would be difficult to find a more telling illustration of their potentially diverging effects on the succession of power configurations than the comparison between the Great Depression and the crisis of the 1970s. Both crises stimulated waves of social confrontation between the same social actors. The antinomy is, however, remarkable between the two historical junctures, at a distance of about forty years. The outcomes—the contention of capitalist interests after the Great Depression and their restoration after the crisis of the 1970s—were opposite. The first crisis was a crisis of hegemony and, the second, a profitability crisis, and there is certainly a relationship between the circumstance of a crisis and its potential consequences, but nothing mechanical.

During the Depression a link was established between officials in administration and the popular classes, under the pressure imposed by a strong worker movement worldwide. Financial interests were contained. The technical and organizational trends that prevailed in the wake of the Depression created favorable underlying conditions, with a rising productivity of capital, a preservation of profit rates, a rise of the purchasing power of wage earners, and rising government revenue.

During the crisis of the 1970s, the social forces supporting the postwar compromise were not able to successfully deal with the crisis. The postwar compromise was destabilized because it was politically weak and because the underlying economic conditions that had supported its establishment vanished during the 1960s (Chapter 5). Keynesian policies failed in a situation of deficient profitability, not insufficient demand. The conflict over income distribution was never superseded. The crisis stimulated a resistance to the deterioration of their situation on the part of the popular classes, as manifest, notably, in the multiplication of major strikes. But, from 1980 onward, the history of the labor movement was basically one of setbacks, although resistances certainly diminished considerably the impact of neoliberal trends. Simultaneously, the capitalist classes were gradually acting with increasing efficiency, seeking the full restoration of their earlier privileges with the increasing support of higher management. The popular classes lost. Thus, not only Sovietism, unable to reform itself, was disarticulated, also the social democratic compromise, paving the way to the new financial hegemony in a unipolar world.

A parallel can be drawn between the dilemma to which the upper classes are confronted in the coming decades and the failure of the postwar compromise. In the context of the present crisis, if the tasks listed in Chapter 23 were not accomplished because of an excessive resistance to change on the part of the capitalist classes and a fraction of management, the historical juncture would be highly reminiscent of the situation in the late 1970s but at the top of the social hierarchies. The outcome would be identical: the end of a power configuration.

The Road to the Center Right

Despite quite distinct historical circumstances, the contemporary crisis creates a major historical opportunity for popular struggles, reminiscent of the Great Depression. Mastering the present situation of the U.S. economy—

the rebuilding of the financial system, the restoration of the trends of accumulation, and the correction of disequilibria—requires the containment of the interests of Finance. There is potential in the crisis to destabilize the cohesion among the upper classes, as was the case during the 1930s.

Thus, an optimistic scenario is that the situation created could work in favor of a transition evocative of the New Deal, in which a large segment of the upper fractions of wage earners seeks and, actually, finds the support of the popular classes. The switch in leadership would be accomplished *OPTIMISTIC SCENARIO* under the pressure of a popular movement. Such trends would create conditions favorable to the demands of the popular classes, since managers would need the support of these classes to realize the new objectives. In other words, there would be no other option to tame capitalist interests than this reliance on the popular classes. Government officials, in alliance with the fractions of management (components other than financial management, technical and lower segments of management, etc.) that are not irreversibly committed to the defense of the interests of the wealthiest fraction of the population, would have no other choice than the reliance on popular support.

The first timid symptoms of such a move on the part of one fraction of the upper classes were apparent in the early treatment of the contemporary crisis in the United States by the Obama administration, notably concerning high incomes, taxation, regulation, and welfare. As of late 2009, the new course of events does not manifest, however, the prevalence of such political trends.

A pessimistic scenario is that, in the absence of an impetuous popular movement, an opportunity would be created for a far-right alternative, the worst of all outcomes, but which cannot be ruled out. This is what the popular struggle, underpinning the action of President Roosevelt, prevented *PESSIMISTIC SCENARIO* during the interwar years, while, in other countries, as in Nazi Germany, the Far-Right option prevailed. The consequences would be dreadful, meaning repression nationally and propensity to perilous military undertakings internationally, worse than neoconservative trends, in a sense, that would mark their culmination.

Neomanagerial capitalism defines a third, more realistic, scenario. A *NEOMANAGERIAL CAPITALISM* structural feature of social relationships in the United States, significantly distinct from other countries, is the close relationship between the components of the top layers of the social pyramid. Already, the containment of capitalist interests during the postwar compromise had been significantly less acute in the United States than in Europe or Japan. Such traits are manifest in the neoliberal compromise and the hybridization process at the top, as the savings of the upper wage brackets are already largely invested in securities, and owners are also engaged in upper management and lavishly remunerated as such.

In post-neoliberalism, such privileged links could work, in the short run, to delay the implementation of the radical changes urgently needed, as managers and officials could balk at hurting the interests of their social "cousins," capitalist owners, by drastic measures. As of late 2009, such arrangements seem to prevail. But, in the longer run, these underlying configurations at the top of U.S. social hierarchies also provide robust foundations for a joint strategy of the upper classes, whatever the exact distribution of powers and the consequences on income patterns. This means a significant potential for change, though not in favor of the popular classes.

Thus, overall, social trends point to the establishment of a new compromise to the top of the social hierarchies, a Center-Right rather than Center-Left social arrangement. Given what the previous chapter denotes as a "national factor" and the weakness of the popular struggles, this neomanagerial capitalism strategy appears as the most likely outcome of the crisis of neoliberalism for the coming decades.

APPENDIXES

NOTES

INDEX

Appendixes

Appendix A introduces the model underlying the analysis in Chapter 11. Appendix B and Appendix C are devoted to sources and acronyms, respectively.

Additional materials are presented on the webpage of the authors (www.jourdan.ens.fr/levy/dle2010b.htm):

M1. A North Atlantic Financial Hegemony?
   Capitalist classes: A joint U.S.-European leadership I
   Large financial institutions: A joint leadership II
   The cutting edge of financial mechanisms: U.S. leadership
   Direct investment abroad: A joint leadership III
   Currencies: The dominance of the dollar
   Partners across the Atlantic
   The rise and decline of Japan
M2. The Emerging Financial Periphery.
   Capitalism in the periphery
   Financing the U.S. economy: Asia and oil-producing countries
   More demanding foreign investors
   The rise of sovereign funds
   The "third-world debt": The IMF's lost stick

The Dynamics of Imbalance:
A Model

This appendix introduces a model of the U.S. economy, allowing for the interpretation of the basic macro mechanisms characteristic of the neoliberal decades. The purpose of the model is to study long-term trajectories, not business-cycle fluctuations.

A number of simple assumptions are made on issues that could be treated in a more sophisticated framework. In particular, an explicit treatment of the relationship between flows and stocks would not alter the results of the model. Under the assumption of given parameters, this treatment of flows and stocks leads to a model in which a homothetic trajectory is reached. (Results are given in a footnote.)

The framework is that of Chapter 11. Four agents are considered: nonfinancial enterprises, consumers, the financial sector, and the rest of the world. "Consumers" jointly refers to households and government, and the demand emanating from these agents is denoted as "consumption." Monetary policy controls the general level of consumption, as more or less loans are granted to consumers. Enterprises adjust the use of their productive capacity according to the level of demand in a Keynesian fashion. This demand is the sum of consumption and investment that are purchased domestically, plus exports.

The value of the stock of fixed capital is set equal to 1, as well as the productive capacity corresponding to the "normal" or "target" capacity utilization rate, $u = 1$. All variables are expressed as shares of this stock of fixed capital or, equivalently, the corresponding "normal GDP," that is, output when $u = 1$. Thus, the capacity utilization rate measures the actual GDP (output or total income), which can be smaller or larger than one. Greek letters denote parameters, and Roman letters, endogenous variables.

A Macro Framework

The basic relationships are represented by arrows in Diagram A.1.

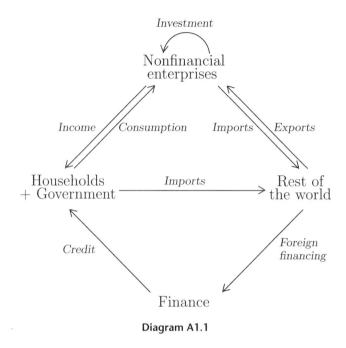

Diagram A1.1

1. An income flow is paid to consumers as wages, capital income, or taxes. When the capacity utilization rate is normal, this income is equal to α, otherwise, it varies with u:

$$R = \alpha + \beta(u - 1) = \alpha - \beta + \beta u \quad \text{with} \quad 0 < \beta < \alpha < 1.$$

2. Since the capital stock is equal to 1, enterprises' investment, I, which is expressed as a fraction of this stock, also measures the potential growth rate, ρ, of the economy. Investment is self-financed, that is, enterprises do not borrow. After paying the income flow above, they use the remaining fraction of their income to buy investment goods. One has

$$\rho = I = u - R = -(\alpha - \beta) + (1 - \beta)u.$$

Since $\alpha > \beta$, R/u, the share of distributed income in GDP diminishes with u and I/u, the share of investment is, conversely, procyclical.

3. A financial system provides consumers with a flow, φ, of new loans net of their deposits. The flow (positive or negative) of new loans is monitored by the central bank.

4. The demand emanating from consumers is equal to the sum of their income and net new loans: $C = R + \varphi$. Thus, consumers' savings are $-\varphi$.

5. Total demand from domestic agents is the sum of consumption and investment:

$$D = C + I = u + \varphi.$$

6. A given fraction, $m = \lambda D$, of this demand is imported, and the remaining fraction, $(1 - \lambda)D$, is directed toward domestic producers.

7. The economy exports goods to the rest of the world, amounting to a given fraction, ε, of the potential output of the country.

8. Foreign financing is entirely channeled to the domestic economy *via* the financial sector.

Determination of the Main Variables

The other variables can be derived from the above. The balance of trade, denoted as a "deficit" (imports minus exports), is $d = m - \varepsilon$. The flow, f, of foreign financing from the rest of the world is equal to this deficit, an accounting identity:

$$\text{(A.1)} \qquad\qquad\qquad f = d.$$

A positive trade deficit means positive financing from the rest of the world.

Enterprises set output to the sum of all components of demand—investment and consumption purchased from domestic producers, plus exports—that is, $u = (1 - \lambda)D + \varepsilon$, an implicit equation in u, whose root is

$$\text{(A.2)} \qquad\qquad\qquad u = 1 + \frac{1 - \lambda}{\lambda}\varphi - \frac{\delta}{\lambda}.$$

The auxiliary notation δ is

$$\text{(A.3)} \qquad\qquad\qquad \delta = \lambda - \varepsilon.$$

Note that δ is formally a deficit. Assuming $u = 1$, the first term, λ, measures the imports of enterprises and households, abstracting from the effect of net loans, while the second term, ε, measures exports. Thus, δ is denoted as a "structural propensity to run a deficit."

Substituting the value of u, as in equation A.2, into the expressions for demand and imports, one obtains

$$\text{(A.4)} \qquad\qquad D = \frac{\varphi + \varepsilon}{\lambda} \text{ and } m = \varphi + \varepsilon.$$

Combining equations A.1 and A.4, and the definition of the trade deficit, $d = m - \varepsilon$, one has

$$\text{(A.5)} \qquad\qquad\qquad f = d = \varphi.$$

This equation means that the trade deficit, d, and the flow, f, of financing from the rest of the world are equal, and also equal to the flow, φ, of net domestic loans, equivalently, minus consumers' savings.

The same analysis could be conducted in a model articulating flows and stocks.[1]

Monetary Policy: Capacity Utilization vs. Deficit and Indebtedness

The discussion in this section is valid independent of the sign of δ. For simplicity, only the case $\delta > 0$ that corresponds to the situation of the U.S. economy is explicitly considered.

The level of borrowings is under the control of the central bank. The normal utilization of productive capacity obtains for a particular flow of new borrowings:

$$(A.6) \qquad u = 1 \leftrightarrow \varphi = \varphi_1 \quad \text{with} \quad \varphi_1 = \frac{\delta}{1 - \lambda}.$$

This level of borrowings is all the more elevated because δ (a country with a large propensity to deficit) and λ (a country with a large propensity to import) are large.

A flow of new borrowings equal to zero implies the prevalence of a given capacity utilization rate a priori distinct from 1:

$$\varphi = 0 \leftrightarrow u = u_0 \text{ with } u_0 = 1 - \frac{\delta}{\lambda}.$$

The two objectives, the control of borrowings and the prevalence of a normal capacity utilization rate, are not only distinct but contradictory. A larger capacity utilization rate requires more borrowings on the part of consumers. Larger such borrowings mean larger deficits of trade and also larger foreign financing.

Two Types of Countries and Four Configurations

Two types of countries can be distinguished depending on the value of δ. Countries with a negative propensity to run a deficit, that is, a propensity to run a surplus, say Germany or China (configuration 1), and countries with a positive propensity to run a deficit such as France or the United States (configurations 2, 3, and 4):

1. *Countries with a propensity to run a surplus.* In this first instance $u = 1$ can be reached with a surplus of foreign trade, that is, $f = \varphi_1 < 0$ (positive consumers' savings). An equilibrium of trade $(f = \varphi = 0)$ would imply $u > 1$, a configuration that is not sought by monetary authorities because of the fear of inflation.

The three following configurations correspond to the second category of countries.

2. *Countries with an unlimited ability to expand the debt of consumers and foreign financing.* In this second instance $u = 1$ can be reached. The condition is to provide consumers with a flow of new loans: $\varphi = \varphi_1$.

3. *Countries with a limited ability to expand the debt of consumers.* If φ is limited ($\varphi < \varphi^+$ with $\varphi^+ < \varphi_1$), the capacity utilization rate will be smaller than one, and given by equation A.2.

4. *Countries with a limited ability to expand foreign financing.* The same situation as above prevails if f is limited ($f < f^+$ with $f^+ < \varphi_1$).

In configurations 3 and 4, the limitation can be absolute ($\varphi^+ = 0$ or $f^+ = 0$) or relative (if the flow of borrowings can be increased but not at a level sufficient to guarantee $u = 1$).

Configuration 2 corresponds to the U.S. economy during the neoliberal decades (up to 2005). Configuration 3 describes the U.S. economy during the last phase of tremendous expansion of financial mechanisms (since 2005). There was, obviously, a limit, but it was crossed. Configuration 4 is typical of European economies, such as France, in the situation of deficient demand discussed in Chapter 11.

Application to the U.S. Macro Trajectory

The model can be used to analyze the historical trajectory of the U.S. economy (where $\delta > 0$), by allowing for the variation of parameters α, λ, and ε, with $\delta = \lambda - \varepsilon > 0$ (assuming β constant). The situation considered is the second configuration, at least, to 2005. The objective of monetary policy is the maintenance of the utilization of productive capacity ($u = 1$) and decent growth rates.

Two important developments, the shifts introduced in Chapter 11 and documented in Chapter 10, had converging effects. The distributional shift refers to the lavish distribution of income as interest, dividends, and high wages at the top, that is, a rise of α. The free-trade shift refers to the insertion of the U.S. economy into the global economy. In this latter respect, two straightforward trends are involved: (1) the growing attractiveness of imports (given the general liberalization of trade flows with countries where labor costs are comparatively low), that is, a rise of λ, and (2) the upward trend of exports, that is, the rise of ε. It is not necessary to assume, however, an increasing exposition of the U.S. economy to foreign trade deficit, only the gradual opening to foreign trade is required. (The propensity to run a deficit, δ, is assumed constant.)

The equations of the model show that the five "U.S. neoliberal trends" follow from the rises of α and λ (the two shifts):

1. In a straightforward manner, a diminishing accumulation and growth rate: $\rho = 1 - \alpha$.

2. The rise of the flow, φ, of domestic net loans to consumers, households, and government (equation A.6). This is what Chapter 11 denotes as the "diminishing efficiency of credit as macro stabilizer."

3. An increased share of consumption in total output:

$$C = \alpha + \varphi.$$

4. and 5. The rise of the trade deficit, d, and of external financing, f, from the rest of the world (equation A.5).

Sources

List of Main Sources

BIS: Bank of International Settlement, www.bis.org/statistics/.

BOE: Bank of England, www.bankofengland.co.uk.

EURO: Eurostat, epp.eurostat.ec.europa.eu.

FAA: Fixed Assets Accounts Tables (BEA),
www.bea.gov/national/FA2004/index.asp

FED: Federal Reserve, Statistics and Historical Data,
www.federalreserve.gov/econresdata/releases/statisticsdata.htm.

FOF: Flow of Funds Accounts (Federal Reserve),
www.federalreserve.gov/Releases/Z1/Current/data.htm.

FORBES: Forbes, Lists, www.forbes.com/lists/.

IFSL: International Financial Services London, www.ifsl.org.uk.

ITA: International Transactions Accounts (BEA),
www.bea.gov/international/index.htm.

MBA: Mortgage Bankers Association, www.mbaa.org/.

NIPA: National Income and Product Accounts (BEA),
www.bea.gov/national/index.htm.

PS: T. Piketty and E. Saez, "Income Inequality in the United States, 1913–1998,"
Quarterly Journal of Economics, vol. 118, no. 1 (2003): 1–39,
www.econ.berkeley.edu/~saez.

WEO: World Economic Outlook (IMF), www.imf.org/external/ns/cs.aspx?id=28.

WFE: World Federation of Exchanges, www.world-exchanges.org/statistics.

WWR: World Wealth Report of Capgemini–Merrill Lynch, Archives,
www.us.capgemini.com/worldwealthreport08/wwr_archives.asp.

Yahoo: Yahoo Finance, finance.yahoo.com/.

Sources of Figures and Tables

Repeated use is made of U.S. GDP, the GDP deflator, and the GWP. The sources for the three variables are:

—U.S. GDP: NIPA, table 1.1.5.
—U.S. price index for GDP: NIPA, table 1.1.4.
—GWP: WEO and Penn World Tables, pwt.econ.upenn.edu/.

Figure 3.1: PS, table A3.
Table 3.1: WWR.
Figure 3.2: PS, table A1.
Figures 3.3, 3.4, and 3.5: NIPA, table 1.14; PS, table B2.
Figure 4.1: NIPA, table 1.14; FAA, table 6.1; FOF, tables L.102 and B.102.
Figure 4.2: FED, table H.15.
Figure 4.3: NIPA, tables 1.14 and 7.10.
Figure 4.4: FOF, tables F.102 and B.102.
Figure 4.5: NYSE, Composite index, www.nyse.com/about/listed/nya_resources.shtml; NIPA, table 1.14.
Figure 4.6: FAA, table 6.1ES; NIPA, tables 1.5.4, 1.14, 6.19, and 7.10; FLOW, tables B.102, R.102, F.xxx, and L.xxx with xxx = 102, 109, 114, 115, 116, 117, 127, and 129.
Figure 4.7: FDIC, Historical Statistics on Banking, www2.fdic.gov/hsob/.
Figure 5.1: PS, table B2.
Table 5.1: PS, table A7.
Table 7.1: [1] FOF; [2] NIPA; [3] WFE; [4] WWR; [5] Sovereign Wealth Funds Institute, swfinstitute.org/funds.php; [6] WEO; [7] McKinsey Global Institute; [8] Pensions & Investments—Warson Wyatt World 500 largest Managers; [9] CBS fund management; [10] The Banker, www.thebanker.com; [11] BIS, Banking statistics, table 6A.
Figure 7.1 and Tables 7.2 7.3: FOF, table L.1.
Figure 7.2: FED, Commercial paper.
Figure 7.3: The Boston Consulting Group, "Get Ready for the Private-Equity Shakeout. Will This Be the Next Shock to the Global Economy?" (Heino Meerkatt, Heinrich Liechtenstein, December 2008).
Figure 7.4: BIS, Semiannual OTC derivative markets statistics.
Figure 8.1: World Trade Organization (WTO), Total merchandise trade, stat.wto.org/StatisticalProgram/WSDBStatProgramHome.aspx.
Tables 8.1 and 8.2: IFSL.
Figure 8.2: United Nations Conference on Trade and Development, stats.unctad.org/FDI/ReportFolders/ReportFolders.aspx.
Figure 8.3: NIPA, tables 1.7.5 and 6.16; ITA, table 1.

Table 8.3: BIS, Triennial Central Bank Survey of Foreign Exchange and Derivatives Market Activity, table 1.

Figure 8.4: FOF, tables L.209 and L.212.

Figure 8.5: EURO, Balance of payments statistics and international investment positions.

Figure 8.6: BIS, Banking statistics, table 6A.

Figure 8.7: BIS, Banking statistics, table 2A.

Figure 9.1: EURO, ten-year government bond yields, secondary market.

Figures 9.2 and 9.3: FED, table H.10; Yahoo.

Figure 10.1: NIPA, table 1.1.5; FED, table H10.

Figure 10.2 and Table 10.1: FOF, table L.107.

Figure 10.3: NIPA, tables 2.3.5 and 7.4.5; FOF, table F.100.

Figure 10.4: NIPA, table 7.4.5; FOF, table F.100.

Figure 10.5 and Table 10.1: FOF, table L.1.

Figure 10.6: FOF, tables L.100 and B.100.

Figure 10.7: NIPA, table 1.14; FOF, tables F.102, L.102, and B.102.

Figure 10.8: FOF, table L.107; EURO, Balance of payments statistics and international investment positions.

Table 11.1: NIPA, table 2.1.

Table 11.2: NIPA, tables 2.1, 3.1, and 1.14.

Figure 12.1: NIPA, table 1.7.6.

Table 12.1: A. B. Ashcraft and T. Schuermann, *Understanding the Securitization of Subprime Mortgage Credit* (New York: Federal Reserve Bank, 2007).

Figure 12.2: NIPA, table 5.3.5.

Table 12.2: MBA, News and Media, Press Center.

Figure 12.3: MBA, Research and Forecasts, Economic Outlook and Forecasts.

Figure 12.4: FOF, table F.212.

Figure 12.5: Consumer expenditure survey, Bureau of Labor and Statistics.

Figure 12.6: Standard & Poor's, Alternative Indices, Case-Shiller Home Price Indices, www2.standardandpoors.com/.

Figure 12.7: U.S. Census Bureau, New Residential Construction, www.census.gov/ftp/pub/const/permits_cust.xls.

Figure 13.1: FOF, tables L.210 and L.126.

Figure 13.2 and Tables 13.1 and 13.3: Asset-Backed Alert, ABS Market statistics, www.abalert.com.

Figure 13.2: FOF, table F.212.

Table 13.2: FOF, tables L.102, L.126, L.209, L.210, L.211, and L.212.

Figure 14.1: FED, table H.15; Freddie Mac, Primary Mortgage Market Survey, www.freddiemac.com/pmms/.

Figure 15.1: FED, Factors Affecting Reserve Balances, table H.4.1.

Figure 16.1: FED, Charge-off and Delinquency Rates.

Figure 16.2: Markit CDX Indices, www.markit.com/information/products/ category/indices/cdx.html.

Figure 16.3: FED, table H.15; British Bankers' Association, Historic LIBOR rates, www.bba.org.uk/bba/jsp/polopoly.jsp?d=141&a=627.

Table 17.1: IMF, Global Financial Stability Report, April and October 2008.

Figure 17.1: NYSE, Composite and financial indices, www.nyse.com/about/listed/ nya_resources.shtml, www.nyse.com/about/listed/nykid_resources.shtml.

Figure 17.2: Yahoo.

Figures 18.1, 18.2, 18.3, and 18.4: FED, Factors Affecting Reserve Balances, table H.4.1.

Figure 19.1: FOF, tables F.100 and F.102.

Figure 19.2: FED, table G.17.

Figure 19.3: U.S. Census Bureau, Monthly Retail Sales, www.census.gov/marts/ www/timeseries.html.

Figure 19.4: NIPA: table 3.1.

Figure 20.1: Yahoo.

Table 20.1: BOE, Financial Stability Report, October 2008.

Figure 20.2: FED, table H.10.

Figure 20.3: FED, table H.10; Yahoo.

Figure 20.4: World Steel Association, Crude Steel Production, www.worldsteel.org/.

Figure 20.5: OECD, stats.oecd.org/wbos/Index.aspx?datasetcode=MEI_TRD.

Figure 20.6: ECB, sdw.ecb.europa.eu/browse.do?node=bbn131; BOE, www .bankofengland.co.uk/statistics/rates/baserate.xls; FED, table H.15; Bank of Japan, www.boj.or.jp/en/theme/research/stat/boj/discount/index.htm.

Figure 20.7: FED, table H.4.1; ECB, www.ecb.int/mopo/implement/omo/html/ tops.zip.

Figure 21.1: G. Duménil and D. Lévy, *The U.S. Economy since the Civil War: Sources and Construction of the Series* (Paris: Cepremap, Modem, 1994), www.jourdan.ens.fr/levy/.

Figure 21.2: FED: table H6; FOF: tables 109 and 127; R. J. Gordon, The American Business Cycle: Continuity and Change, (1986), Appendix B; Federal Reserve, *All Bank Statistics, United States, 1896–1955* (Washington, D.C.: Board of the Federal Reserve, 1959), fraser.stlouisfed.org/publications/ allbkstat/; R. Grossman, "U.S. Banking History, Civil War to World War II," in R. Whaples, *EH.Net Encyclopedia* (2008), eh.net/encyclopedia.

Figure 21.3: Annual Report of the Controller of the Currency (Washington, D.C.: U.S. Department of the Treasury, 1931), 6 and 8; O. M. W. Sprague, *History of Crises under the National Banking System* (Washington, D.C.: Government Printing Office, National Monetary Commission, 1910), table 24; Grossman, "U.S. Banking History."

Figure 21.4: Federal Reserve, *Banking and Monetary Statistics, 1914–1941*
   (Washington, D.C.: Board of the Federal Reserve, 1943), fraser.stlouisfed.org/
   publications/bms/.
Figure 22.1: NIPA, table 1.1.6.
Figure 23.1: FED, table H.10.
Figure 23.2: FOF, tables 209, 210, and 211; TreasuryDirect, www.treasurydirect
   .gov/govt/reports/pd/histdebt/histdebt.htm.
Figure 24.1 and Table 24.1: WEO.
Figure 24.2: WFE.

Acronyms

ABCP:	asset-backed commercial paper
ABS:	asset-backed security
AIG:	American International Group
AMLF:	ABCP MMMF Liquidity Facility
ARM:	adjustable rate mortgage
ARRA:	American Recovery and Reinvestment Act
BIS:	Bank of International Settlements
BLS:	Bureau of Labor Statistics
BRIC:	Brazil, Russia, India, and China
CDO:	collateralized debt obligation
CDS:	credit default swap
CLO:	collateralized loan obligation
CMBS:	commercial mortgage-backed security
CPFF:	Commercial Paper Funding Facility
DIA:	direct investment abroad
EDC:	emerging and developing countries
Fannie Mae:	Federal National Mortgage Association
FDIC:	Federal Deposit Insurance Corporation
FHA:	Federal Housing Administration
FHFA:	Federal Housing Finance Agency
FHLB:	Federal Home Loan Bank
Freddie Mac:	Federal Home Loan Mortgage Corporation
FSLIC:	Federal Savings and Loan Insurance Company
GATT:	General Agreement on Tariffs and Trade
GDP:	gross domestic product
Ginnie Mae:	Government National Mortgage Association
GOPO:	government owned and privately operated
GSE:	government-sponsored enterprise

GWP:	gross world product
HEL:	home equity loan
HELOC:	home equity line of credit
HNWI:	high net worth individual
IBF:	International Banking Facility
IMF:	International Monetary Fund
IRS:	Internal Revenue Service
ISI:	import-substitution industrialization
JOM:	Japan offshore market
LBO:	leveraged buyout
LIBOR:	London interbank offered rate
MBS:	mortgage-backed security
MMIFF:	Money Market Investor Funding Facility
MMMF:	money market mutual fund
MTN:	medium-term note
NATO:	North Atlantic Treaty Organization
NIPA:	national income and product account
NIRA:	National Industrial Recovery Act
NRA:	National Recovery Administration
NYSE:	New York Stock Exchange
OBSE:	off-balance-sheet entity
OECD:	Organization for Economic Cooperation and Development
OITP:	other important trading partners
OTC:	over the counter
PDCF:	Primary Dealer Credit Facility
PPP:	purchasing power parity
RMBS:	residential mortgage-backed security
ROE:	rate of return on equity
SEC:	Securities and Exchange Commission
SIV:	structured investment vehicle
SNB:	Swiss National Bank
SWF:	sovereign wealth fund
TAF:	Term Auction Facility
TALF:	Term Asset-Backed Securities Loan Facility
TSLF:	Term Securities Lending Facility
WB:	World Bank
WTO:	World Trade Organization

Notes

1. The Historical Dynamics of Hegemony

1. G. Duménil and D. Lévy, *Capital Resurgent: Roots of the Neoliberal Revolution* (Cambridge, Mass.: Harvard University Press, 2004). This interpretation making neoliberalism a *class* phenomenon was first published in English in G. Duménil and D. Lévy, "Costs and Benefits of Neoliberalism: A Class Analysis," *Review of International Political Economy* 8–4 (2001): 578–607.
2. G. Duménil, M. Glick, and D. Lévy, "The History of Competition Policy as Economic History," *Antitrust Bulletin* 42–2 (1997): 373–416.
3. K. Marx, *Capital*, vol. 3 (1894; New York: Vintage Books, 1981).
4. T. Veblen, *The Theory of the Leisure Class* (London: Macmillan, 1899).
5. The period also witnessed weak attempts on the part of the banking system and the government to implement the first centralized procedures targeted at the stabilization of monetary and financial mechanisms, up to the establishment of the Federal Reserve in 1913.
6. In relation to the Great Depression, the phrase "Great Contraction," as in Milton Friedman's and Anna Schwartz's study, could be judged euphemistic (M. Friedman and A. Schwartz, *Monetary History of the United States* [Princeton, N.J.: Princeton University Press, 1963]). It is used here under the assumption that the fall of output in the contemporary crisis will remain less severe than during the 1930s.
7. Had the downward trend of the profit rate been checked in a timely manner, the structural crisis of the 1970s would not have paved the way for the establishment of neoliberalism. Had not this trend been, to some extent, reversed during the neoliberal decades, the course of history would also have been profoundly altered.

II. The Second Reign of Finance

1. The emphasis in this part is on the U.S. economy and society. Information concerning the capitalist classes of other countries is given in G. Duménil and D. Lévy, Additional Materials 1 (2010), www.jourdan.ens.fr/levy/dle2010b.htm.

3. The Benefit of Upper Income Brackets

1. T. Piketty and E. Saez, "Income Inequality in the United States, 1913–1998," *Quarterly Journal of Economics* 118, no. 1 (2003): 1–39.
2. E. Wolff, *Top Heavy* (New York: New Press, 1996).
3. In France, for example, the share of incomes others than wages fluctuated around 20 percent of total income between 1959 and 1973. It lost seven percentage points during the structural crisis of the 1970s, recovered eleven points, and stabilized around 24 percent.
4. Conversely, the share of the 90–95 fractile increased prior to neoliberalism.

4. The Apotheosis of Capital

1. In this chapter, "financial corporations" exclude pension or mutual funds, as well as GSEs or their mortgage pools and private-label issuers.
2. A first compromise (as symbolically expressed in the Sherman Act) was struck with the capitalist owners of smaller and traditional firms (later eliminated during the Great Depression).
3. K. Marx, *Capital*, vol. 3 (1894; New York: Vintage Books, 1981).
4. G. Duménil and D. Lévy, "The Profit Rate: Where and How Much Did It Fall? Did It Recover? (USA 1948–2000)," *Review of Radical Political Economy* 34 (2002): 437–461; G. Duménil and D. Lévy, *Capital Resurgent: Roots of the Neoliberal Revolution* (Cambridge, Mass.: Harvard University Press, 2004).
5. It would be possible to consider total tangible assets, including inventories, instead of fixed capital.
6. Due to the increase of taxation during the war, after-tax profitability levels during the first postwar decades remained about at levels reached in 1929, despite the dramatic restoration of profit rates *à la Marx*. G. Duménil and D. Lévy, *La dynamique du capital: Un siècle d'économie américaine* (Paris: Presses Universitaires de France, 1996), chap. 19, fig. 19.1.
7. The measure of enterprises' own funds is difficult within Flows of Funds data, and there is a significant degree of uncertainty concerning this variable. The introduction of this new variable is, however, important in the consideration of the comparative profitability of the nonfinancial and

financial sectors at the end of this chapter. Besides the problems posed by deficient information, one aspect of the difficulties raised by the measure of the own funds of corporations is the consideration of "goodwill," that is, the difference between the account value of a firm that has been bought and the price at which it has been purchased. This difference is treated on the asset side of balance sheets as an intangible asset (and classified in the account as "Other miscellaneous assets" in Flow of Funds). The reports of the FDIC show that this component is relatively important in comparison to own funds for insured deposit banks and has been consistently increasing. Federal Deposit Insurance Corporation, Quarterly Banking Profile (Washington, D.C.: FDIC, 2008).

8. The percentage peaked slightly above 100 percent after 2000, a practice that is not without precedent (for example, during the Great Depression), meaning that corporations are using their depreciation allowance, drawing on their liquidities, or selling financial assets.

9. Duménil and Lévy, *Capital Resurgent*, chap. 14, notably, 120.

10. H. Sylverblatt and D. Guarino, "S & P 500 Buybacks: Three Years and $1.3 Trillion Later," *The McGraw Hill Companies*, December 13, 2007.

11. The profile observed reflects both the variations of indices and of the GDP deflator.

12. This is what Costas Lapavistas calls "direct exploitation" (C. Lapavistas, "Financialized Capitalism: Direct Exploitation and Periodic Bubble" [Working paper, Department of Economics, School of Oriental and African Studies (SOAS), London, 2008]).

13. It is important to recall that households also receive interest. This interest remained larger than interest paid. Obviously, one category of households receives interest, while another pays, though neither is exclusive.

14. Duménil and Lévy, *Capital Resurgent*, chap. 11, fig. 11.3.

15. FDIC, Quarterly Banking Profile.

5. The Managerial and Popular Classes

1. The rise of wages at the top of the income hierarchies is now broadly acknowledged. The summary of the working paper by Anthony Atkinson, Thomas Piketty, and Emmanuel Saez states unambiguously: "Over the last 30 years, top income shares have increased substantially in English speaking countries and India and China but not in continental Europe countries or Japan. This increase is due in part to an unprecedented surge in top wage income." A. Atkinson, T. Piketty, and E. Saez, "Top Incomes in the Long Run of History" (Working paper series, National Bureau of Economic Research [NBER], 15408, October 2009), www.nber.org/papers/w15408.

2. J. Weinstein, *The Corporate Ideal in the Liberal State, 1900–1918* (Boston: Beacon Press, 1968).

3. A well-known example is Joseph Schumpeter, who raised the question of the possible survival of capitalism and answered negatively. J. Schumpeter, *Socialism, Capitalism and Democracy* (New York: Harper and Brothers, 1942).

4. The phrase was, however, coined in reference to this country. R. I. McKinnon, *Money and Capital in Economic Development* (Washington, D.C.: Brookings Institution, 1973); E. Shaw, *Financial Deepening in Economic Development* (New York: Oxford University Press, 1973).

5. G. Duménil and D. Lévy, "Finance and Management in the Dynamics of Social Change: Contrasting Two Trajectories—United States and France," in L. Assassi, A. Nesvetailova, and D. Wigan, eds., *Global Finance in the New Century: Beyond Deregulation* (New York: Palgrave Macmillan, 2007), 127–147.

6. E. Helleiner, *States and the Reemergence of Global Finance: From Bretton Woods to the 1990s* (Ithaca, N.Y.: Cornell University Press, 1994).

6. A Theoretical Framework

1. J. Burnham, *The Managerial Revolution* (Harmondsworth, U.K.: Penguin Books, 1945); R. L. Marris, *The Economic Theory of Managerial Capitalism* (London: Macmillan, 1964); J. K. Galbraith, *The New Industrial State* (New York: New American Library, 1967); A. D. Chandler, *The Visible Hand: The Managerial Revolution in American Business* (Cambridge, Mass.: Harvard University Press, 1977); D. Stabile, "The New Class and Capitalism: A Three-and-Three-Thirds-Class Model," *Review of Radical Political Economics,* 15, no. 4 (1983): 45–70; M. Zeitlin, *The Large Corporation and Contemporary Classes* (New Brunswick, N.J.: Rutgers University Press, 1989); J. McDermott, *Corporate Society: Class, Property, and Contemporary Capitalism* (Boulder, Colo.: Westview Press, 1981); E. Olin Wright, *Class Counts: Comparative Studies in Class Analysis* (Cambridge: Cambridge University Press, 1997); J. Lojkine, *Adieu à la classe moyenne* (Paris: La Dispute, 2005).

2. As later expressed in the study: A. Berle, *Power without Property* (New York: Harcourt, Brace, 1960).

3. Within a strictly defined Marxian framework of analysis (the concepts of Marx's *Capital*), there is no better option than to locate managerial and clerical personnel as a new petty bourgeoisie. But this interpretation simultaneously underlies the limits of Marx's perspective, and suggests the definition of a new framework compatible with the features of modern capitalism. This is the viewpoint adopted in G. Duménil, *La position de classe des cadres et employés* (Grenoble, France: Presses Universitaires de Grenoble, 1975). Nicos

Poulentzas remained faithful to the strictly defined Marxian approach. *Pouvoir politique et classes sociales* (Paris: Maspero, 1972). The interpretation of class patterns in terms of a broad proletarian class is common within Trotskyist circles, in reference to the work of Ernest Mandel. *Les étudiants, les intellectuels et la lutte de classes* (Paris: La Brèche, 1979), www.ernestmandel .org/fr/ecrits/txt/1979/etudiants/index.htm), defended such views and, indirectly, to the work of Leon Trotsky himself. (The society Soviet Union was not a class society, but a bureaucratically degenerated workers' state.) See also M. Löwy, *Pour une sociologie des intellectuels revolutionnaires* (Paris: Presses Universitaires de France, 1976).

4. K. Marx, *Capital,* vol. 3 (1894; New York: Vintage Books, 1981), chap. 52. See also chap. 48, "The Trinity Formula."

5. The "agent" and the "principal" in contemporary terminology.

6. J. Lojkine, *La classe ouvrière en mutations,* Messidor (Paris: Éditions sociales, 1986).

7. Concerning popular classes, the ambiguous nature of their somehow converging social positions was already discussed in Hilferding's book in 1910 and is still the object of sociological investigation in contemporary capitalism given the transformation of production labor.

8. Present-day China could be interpreted as an example of the third configuration, in a very specific context.

9. G. Duménil and D. Lévy, *Au-delà du capitalisme?* (Paris: Presses Universitaires de France, 1998); J. Bidet and G. Duménil, *Altermarxisme: Un autre Marxisme pour un autre monde* (Paris: Presses Universitaires de France, Quadrige, Essais-Débats, 2007); G. Duménil and D. Lévy, "Cadres et classes populaires: Entre gauche traditionnelle, altermondialisme et anticapitalisme," *Actuel Marx* 44 (2008): 104–116.

7. A New Financial Sector

1. Financialization is addressed in this chapter from the viewpoint of the U.S. economy. A more global information is provided in G. Duménil and D. Lévy, Additional Materials 1 and 2 (2010), www.jourdan.ens.fr/levy/dle2010b.htm.

2. The sectors have been determined according to the classification in Flow of Funds accounts. This classification is sometimes misleading. For example, "mortgage pools" and "issuers of asset-backed securities" are not new institutions, but new tools in the hands of GSEs and commercial banks, respectively (see Table 13.2).

3. "Closed-end" refers to the limited number of shares.

4. Then, in the list: finance companies, funding corporations, open-ended investment companies, and real estate investment trusts.

5. The majority of the financing of banks does not result from borrowings but deposits, and this is what allows them to lend extensively.

6. A study by the rating agency Fitch of the SIVs that it rates provides information on their basic features (S. Bund, G. Moore, and K. Vladimirova, "Rating Performances of Structured Investment Vehicles (SIVs) in Times of Diminishing Liquidity for Assets and Liabilities," Structured Credit Special Report [New York and London: Derivative Fitch, September 20, 2007]). Fitch-rated SIVs are financed up to 29 percent by commercial paper and 62 percent by MTNs, with a weighted-average life of 0.71 year. The securities they hold have a weighted-average life of 3.62 years.

7. International Monetary Fund, Global Financial Stability Report. *Market Developments and Issues* (Washington, D.C.: IMF, April 2008), 69.

8. More precisely, the amount used to calculate payments made on swaps and other risk-management products. This amount generally does not change hands and is thus referred to as notional.

9. They were invented in Chicago in the middle of the nineteenth century concerning the prices of crops.

8. Free Trade and the Global Financial Boom after 2000

1. In particular, within the 1986–1994 Uruguay Round.

2. See G. Duménil and D. Lévy, Additional materials 1 (2010), Figure M1.2, www.jourdan.ens.fr/levy/dle2010b.htm.

3. The Bank of International Settlements publishes statistics on "reporting banks," an almost exhaustive sample of the global banking system, concerning their activity in foreign countries or in foreign currencies. Two criteria are used: (1) the nationality of ownership of banks, whose branches can be established anywhere in the globe; and (2) their territorial location (for example, banks established on U.S. territory instead of banks of U.S. nationality). Some ambiguity arises from the fact that U.S. IBFs are "offshore" entities located on U.S. territory. They are considered as offshore. The same is true of JOMs.

4. Jointly developed by the BIS, the IMF, the OECD (Organization for Economic Cooperation and Development), and the WB (World Bank).

5. M. R. King and P. Maier, "Hedge Funds and Financial Stability: The State of the Debate" (Bank of Canada Discussion Paper, 2007–2009, September 2007).

6. As many other financial operations, carry trade can be highly leveraged. If, for example, equity amounts to 10 percent of the investment and 90 percent is borrowed, and money is borrowed at 2 percent and lent at 5 percent, assuming a constant exchange rate, the return on own funds amounts to 30 percent. The purpose of borrowing in the currency of another country with low

interest rates can simply be to finance an asset under more favorable conditions (for example, households of Eastern Europe borrowing in Switzerland to buy a house) but the exchange risk is there.

9. A Fragile and Unwieldy Structure

1. E. Helleiner, *States and the Reemergence of Global Finance: From Bretton Woods to the 1990s* (Ithaca, N.Y.: Cornell University Press, 1994).
2. "Unanimity is required" to restrict the mobility toward countries outside of the Union (Article 73c).
3. J. M. Keynes, *Bretton Woods and after, April 1944–March 1946: The Collected Writings of John Maynard Keynes,* vol. 26, *1946* (London: Macmillan, St. Martin's Press for the Royal Economic Society, 1980), 17.
4. J. Nembhard, *Capital Control, Financial Regulation, and Industrial Policy in South Korea and Brazil* (Westport, CT: Praeger, 1996), chap. 2.
5. J. M. Keynes, *Writings of John Maynard Keynes,* vol. 20, *1933* (London: Macmillan, St. Martin's Press for the Royal Economic Society, 1982), 598–609.
6. Federal Reserve Bank of San Francisco Economic Letter, November 2006.

10. Declining Accumulation and Growing Disequilibria

1. About equal, since the balance of income is almost null in the United States.
2. The analysis in this part draws on the previous investigations: G. Duménil and D. Lévy, "Le néolibéralisme sous hégémonie états-unienne," in F. Chesnais, ed., *La finance mondialisée: Racines sociales et politiques, configuration et conséquences* (Paris: La Découverte, 2004); G. Duménil and D. Lévy, *The New Configuration of U.S. Imperialism in Perspective,* www.jourdan.ens .fr/levy/dle2004l.doc; G. Duménil and D. Lévy, "Néolibéralisme: Dépassement ou renouvellement d'un ordre social," *Actuel Marx* 40 (2006): 86–101.
3. The contribution of the various regions of the world to the financing of the U.S. economy is discussed in G. Duménil and D. Lévy, Additional Materials 1 and 2 (2010), www.jourdan.ens.fr/levy/dle2010b.htm.
4. Within the consumption of households in NIPA, "housing" is treated as the purchase of a service. Besides other components, the price of this service includes the depreciation of fixed capital (the price of homes outstanding). Thus, when consumption in the strict sense and the residential investment of households are aggregated, this component must be subtracted from "housing services."
5. The savings of the entire economy are defined as national income minus the consumption and investment of households and government. They are equal to the net investment of private business minus the net borrowings to the rest of the world.

6. One must distinguish between "government consumption expenditures," which includes wages paid and the depreciation of government-fixed capital, and the "purchase of goods and services," which includes government investment. This is the variable used here.

7. "Credit market instruments" exclude the assets in pension or other funds, the corporate equities directly held by households, the equities in noncorporate business, and deposits.

8. Freddie Mac, Cash-Out Refinance Report (Tysons Corner, Va.: Freddie Mac, 2008).

9. D. Maki and M. Palumbo, "Disentangling the Wealth Effect: A Cohort Analysis of the Household Saving in the 1990s" (Working paper, Federal Reserve, 2001).

10. Empirical measures based on Flows of Funds accounts are difficult to conduct due to the presence of accounts of unidentified "miscellaneous assets" and "miscellaneous liabilities." Important breaks are apparent in the data in the early 1970s and, then, an upward trend in miscellaneous assets is manifest, reaching more than 50 percent of tangible assets. Such observations question the reliability of the data. In a calculation, these accounts can be either conserved or set aside. Given the overall sizes of tangible assets and net worth, a likely approximation is that these two variables remained about equal over the entire period.

11. Contrary to other countries, such as France, where, prior to neoliberalism, loans were broadly used to finance real accumulation. G. Duménil and D. Lévy, *Capital Resurgent: Roots of the Neoliberal Revolution* (Cambridge, Mass.: Harvard University Press, 2004), chap. 14.

11. The Mechanics of Imbalance

1. One could equivalently assume, as is traditional in Cambridgian models, that (1) enterprises distribute total income to households, as wages and profits; (2) a fraction of income is saved and deposited (financial investment) within financial institutions; and (3) these institutions make loans to enterprises to finance investment and, possibly, to households. (In this latter case, the new borrowings must be added to the component of households' income that is not invested within financial institutions, to constitute the purchasing power that households use to consume.)

12. The Second Reprieve: The Housing Boom and Crash

1. A recession is generally defined by the occurrence of two successive quarterly declines in GDP.

2. In the metrics of this figure, the NYSE index peaked in the third quarter of 2000, fell to the first quarter of 2003, and recovered. Profits culminated in the third quarter of 1997, fell to the third quarter of 2001, and recovered.

3. Consumer expenditure survey (Washington, D.C.: U.S. Department of Labor, Bureau of Labor Statistics, 2008), www.bls.gov/cex/.

4. Credit and housing markets are highly discriminated and these discriminations played a role in the wave of subprime loans. G. Dymski, *Discrimination in the Credit and Housing Markets: Findings and Challenges* (Riverside, Calif.: University of California, 2009).

5. Acronym of Fair Isaac Corporation, the creator of the FICO.

6. National Association of Realtors, Existing-Home Sales and Prices Overview, 2009, www.realtor.org/research/research/ehsdata.

13. Feeding the Mortgage Wave

1. Federal Deposit Insurance Corporation, Quarterly Banking Profile (Washington, D.C.: FDIC, 2008).

2. Bank of International Settlements, Semiannual OTC Derivative Markets Statistics (Basel, Switzerland: BIS, 2008).

14. Losing Control of the Helm in Times of Storm

1. Freddie Mac, Primary Mortgage Market Survey (Tysons Corner, Va.: Freddie Mac, 2008).

2. A. Greenspan, Federal Reserve Board's Semiannual Monetary Policy Report to the Congress (Washington, D.C.: Federal Reserve Board, July 20, 2005), www.federalreserve.gov/boarddocs/hh/2005/february/testimony.htm.

3. Contrary to John Taylor's assertion, it is difficult to pin responsibility for the crisis on Alan Greenspan with respect to his management of interest rates. *Getting Off Track: How Government Actions and Interventions Caused, Prolonged, and Worsened the Financial Crisis* (Stanford, Calif.: Hoover Press, 2009). Greenspan chose to sustain the U.S. macroeconomy in the short run. If the Federal Funds rate had been strongly increased earlier than it was, the U.S. economy would not have recovered from the recession or the recovery would have been very weak. There was no straightforward way out. One option was a stimulative monetary policy, accompanied by a degree of regulation of mortgage markets and securitization. This is where Greenspan's responsibility could be more straightforwardly involved, since such practices were at odds with his views concerning the self-discipline of markets. But the path was narrow.

4. Reply to Congressman Henry Waxman of the House Oversight and Government Reform Committee on October 23, 2008.

15. A Stepwise Process

1. Chicago Fed Letter, August 2007. S. Agarwal and C. T. Ho, "Comparing the Prime and Subprime Mortgage Markets," www.chicagofed.org/digital_assets/publications/chicago_fed_letter/2007/cflaugust2007_241.pdf.

16. The Seismic Wave

1. One can observe that delinquency rates on mortgages increased only to a limited extent during the 2001 recession, peaking in the last steps of Phase I, prior to a new decline toward the low plateau reached between 2004 and the beginning of 2006 at about 1.6 percent, to be compared to the peaks at 2.4 percent in 2001 and 3.4 percent in 1991.
2. RealtyTrac U.S., 2009, www.realtytrac.com/.
3. Mortgage Bankers Association, "Delinquencies Continue to Climb, Foreclosures Flat in Latest MBA National Delinquency Survey" (Washington, D.C.: Mortgage Bankers Association, 2009), www.mortgagebankers.org/.
4. First American CoreLogic "The Negative Equity Report," February 2010, www.facorelogic.com/newsroom/marketstudies/negative-equity-report/download.jsp. See also L. Ellis, "The Housing Meltdown: Why Did It Happen in the United States?" (Working paper, Bank for International Settlements, 2008, no. 259).
5. Markit collects data on CDSs from a large set of financial institutions worldwide, and builds indices that it sells to 1,000 financial firms worldwide (commercial banks, investment banks, hedge funds, asset managers, insurance companies, auditing firms, regulatory agencies, rating agencies, and fund administrators). These indices are used as estimates of the price of CDOs for which there is no market. "Markit owns and administers the ABX.HE, which is a liquid, tradeable tool allowing investors to take positions on subprime mortgage-backed securities via CDS contracts. The index has become a benchmark for the performance of subprime RMBSs. Its liquidity and standardization allows investors to accurately gauge market sentiment around the asset-class, and to take short or long positions accordingly," "Markit CDS Pricing" (London: Markit, 2009), www.markit.com/en/products/data/cds-pricing/cds-pricing.page.

17. The Financial Structure Shaken

1. See Box 9.4.
2. Bank of England, Financial Stability Report (London: Bank of England, October 2008), 17, no. 24.
3. See section titled Fictitious Gains and Real Income Flows.
4. On these issues, one can consult S. Bergstresser and T. Philippon, *CEO Incentives and Earnings Management* (Boston, Mass.: Harvard Business School, 2004).

18. The State to the Rescue of the Financial Sector

1. Board of Governors of the Federal Reserve System (Washington, D.C.: Federal Reserve, April 17, 2007), www.federalreserve.gov/newsevents/press/bcreg/20070417a.htm.
2. Former Federal Reserve governor in Kansas, and member of the Council of Economic Advisers.
3. Earlier chairman of the Council of Economic Advisers and chief economic adviser to President Ronald Reagan.
4. In case of default, the lender is not protected beyond the value of the collaterals.
5. Trouble Assets Relief Program (Washington, D.C.: U.S. Department of the Treasury, 2009), www.financialstability.gov/.
6. The following commentaries by the Federal Reserve Bank of New York are helpful: "Why is the payment of interest on reserve balances, and on excess balances in particular, especially important under current conditions? Recently the Desk has encountered difficulty achieving the operating target for the federal funds rate set by the FOMC, because the expansion of the Federal Reserve's various liquidity facilities has caused a large increase in excess balances. The expansion of excess reserves in turn has placed extraordinary downward pressure on the overnight federal funds rate. Paying interest on excess reserves will better enable the Desk to achieve the target for the federal funds rate, even if further use of Federal Reserve liquidity facilities, such as the recently announced increases in the amounts being offered through the Term Auction Facility, results in higher levels of excess balances. What other methods does the Federal Reserve have at its disposal to facilitate the implementation of monetary policy when the use of its various liquidity facilities contributes to high levels of excess balances? Initially, the Federal Reserve was able to prevent excess balances from expanding as the use of its new liquidity facilities grew by reducing other assets it held on its balance sheet, notably holdings of U.S. Treasury securities. But many of its

remaining holdings of Treasury securities are now dedicated to support the Term Securities Lending Facility and other programs. More recently, the Supplemental Financing Program has been invaluable in helping to limit the growth in excess balances as use of the Federal Reserve's liquidity programs has continued to expand. Under the Supplemental Financing Program the U.S. Treasury has issued Treasury bills in the market and deposited the proceeds in an account at the Federal Reserve. But payment of interest on excess balances could enable the Desk to achieve the operating target for the federal funds rate even without further use of these other measures and in principle with any level of excess balances. And in addition to remunerating excess balances, the Federal Reserve is exploring other methods to manage reserve levels for the purpose of implementing monetary policy with its authority to pay interest on reserves." FAQs about interest on reserves and the implementation of monetary policy (New York: Federal Reserve Bank of New York, 2009), www.newyorkfed.org/markets/ior_faq.html.

19. The Great Contraction

1. The debt held by the public is equal to the total federal debt held by individuals, corporations, state or local governments, foreign governments, and other entities outside the United States, *minus* government federal financing bank securities. The securities held by the public include (but are not limited to) Treasury bills, notes, bonds, Treasury Inflation-Protected Securities (TIPS), U.S. savings bonds, and state and local government-series securities.

20. World Capitalism Unsettled

1. Flow of Funds accounts.
2. Federal Reserve, *News and Events* (Washington, D.C.: Federal Reserve, October 13, 2008). Emphasis added.

21. Eighty Years Later

1. K. Marx, *Capital,* vol. 3 (1894; New York: Vintage Books, 1981), Part 3: The Law of the Tendential Fall of the Rate of Profit.
2. G. Duménil and D. Lévy, *Capital Resurgent: Roots of the Neoliberal Revolution* (Cambridge, Mass.: Harvard University Press, 2004), chap. 15.
3. The act states: "Every person who shall monopolize, or attempt to monopolize, or combine or conspire with any other person or persons, to monopolize any part of the trade or commerce among the several States, or with foreign

nations, shall be deemed guilty of a felony" (Sherman Act, 15 U.S.C. § 2). (Washington, D.C.: U.S. Department of Justice), www.usdoj.gov/atr/foia/ divisionmanual/ch2.htm#a1).

4. G. Duménil, M. Glick, and D. Lévy, "The History of Competition Policy as Economic History," *Antitrust Bulletin* 42, no. 2 (1997): 373–416.

5. G. Duménil and D. Lévy, "Stylized Facts about Technical Progress since the Civil War: A Vintage Model," *Structural Change and Economic Dynamics* 5, no. 1 (1994): 1–23.

6. T. F. Bresnahan and M. Raff, "Intra-industry Heterogeneity and the Great Depression: The American Motor Vehicles Industry, 1929–1935," *Journal of Economic History* 51, no. 2 (1991): 317–331. The mushrooming of banks prior to 1920 provides another illustration of the heterogeneity of the U.S. economy: a multiplication of small banks besides large banks. The concentration of the industry during the 1920s also testifies to the underlying trends toward the new structure of large corporations.

7. G. Duménil and D. Lévy, *La dynamique du capital: Un siècle d'économie américaine* (Paris: Presses Universitaires de France, 1996), chap. 22.

8. Duménil and Lévy, *Capital Resurgent*, fig. 20.3, box 18.1.

9. Federal Reserve, *All Bank Statistics, United States, 1896–1955* (Washington, D.C.: Board of the Federal Reserve, 1959), fraser.stlouisfed.org/publications/ allbkstat/.

10. Federal Reserve, *Banking and Monetary Statistics, 1914–1941* (Washington, D.C.: Board of the Federal Reserve, 1943), table 139: Brokers' loans by group of lenders, fraser.stlouisfed.org/publications/bms/.

11. In the analysis of long waves by Immanuel Wallerstein and Giovanni Arrighi, financialization coincides, after the culmination of a Phase A, with the entrance into Phase B, as investments are redirected toward the financial sphere. G. Arrighi, *The Long Twentieth Century: Money, Power and the Origins of Our Times* (London: Verso, 1994); I. Wallerstein, "Globalization or the Age of Transition? A Long-Term View of the Trajectory of the World-System," *International Sociology* 15, no. 2 (2000): 250–268.

12. I. Fisher, "The Debt-Deflation Theory of Great Depressions," *Econometrica* 1 (1933): 337–357.

22. Policies and Politics of the New Deal

1. A vast literature has been devoted to the New Deal. Among the studies treating specifically this issue, one can mention the following: W. E. Leuchtenburg, *Franklin D. Roosevelt and the New Deal, 1932–1940* (New York: Harper and Row, 1963); R. Levine, *Class Struggle and the New Deal: Industrial Labor, Capital and the State* (Lawrence: University Press of

Kansas, 1988); and S. Fraser and G. Gerstle, *The Rise and Fall of the New Deal Order, 1930–1980* (Princeton, N.J.: Princeton University Press, 1989).

2. The expression of what the previous chapter denotes as the "heterogeneous features of technology and organization."

3. R. Skidelsky, *John Maynard Keynes,* vol. 2, *The Economist as Savior, 1920–1937* (London: Macmillan, 1992), 492–493.

4. On the grounds of the violation of the separation of powers.

5. According to Stein: "The stimulating effect of the fiscal policy of all Governments—Federal, State, and Local—was larger in 1931 than in any other year of the 1930's." H. Stein, *The Fiscal Revolution in America* (Chicago: University of Chicago Press, 1969), 26.

6. Ibid., 117.

7. Ibid., 99–100.

8. Although the phrase "monetary and fiscal policies" had not been forged, Keynes's basic policy framework had already been defined in 1933. J. M. Keynes, "The Means to Prosperity" (1933), in *The Collected Writings of John Maynard Keynes* (London: Macmillan, St. Martin's Press for the Royal Economic Society, 1972), 335–366.

9. J. A. Henretta, D. Brody, L. Duménil, and S. Ware, *America's History,* vol. 2, *Since 1865* (Boston: Bedford / St. Martin's, 2004).

10. Weinstein tells the story of the Colorado Coal Strike of 1913–1914 as follows: "Strike tactics on both sides resembled preparations for war. Under CFI direction, sheriffs recruited large numbers of guards and deputies from out of state; they were armed and paid by the company, deployed in trenches around mining properties, and equipped with huge searchlights and machine guns.... Violence began immediately and grew in intensity, with the union retaliating for each killing perpetrated by the company and its sheriffs. Individual killings soon developed into pitched battles involving hundreds of strikers and company police; the miners held their own in widespread guerrilla warfare." J. Weinstein, *The Corporate Ideal in the Liberal State, 1900–1918* (Boston: Beacon Press, 1968), 193. "The clashes between strikers and the Guard culminated in a pitched battle at the miner's Ludlow tent colony. There, after a day-long battle, Guardmen burned the colony to the ground, killing two women and eleven children who were trapped under the burning tents" (ibid., 194).

11. G. Duménil and D. Lévy, "Neoliberal Income Trends: Wealth, Class and Ownership in the USA," *New Left Review* 30 (2004): 105–133.

12. R. J. Gordon, "$45 Billion of U.S. Private Investment Has Been Mislaid," *American Economic Review* 59, no. 3 (1969): 221–238.

13. W. Lewellen, "Executive Compensation in Large Industrial Corporations" (Working paper, National Bureau of Economic Research, 1968).

14. T. Piketty and E. Saez, "Income Inequality in the United States, 1913–1998," *Quarterly Journal of Economics* 118, no. 1 (2003): 1–39.

23. Economic Requirements

1. They are sometimes presented as distinct entities but the separation is not convincing.
2. Euro area, Canada, Japan, United Kingdom, Switzerland, Australia, and Sweden.
3. P. Bairoch, *Economics and World History: Myths and Paradoxes* (Chicago: University of Chicago Press, 1993).

24. The National Factor

1. These variables are presented in figure M1.3 in G. Duménil and D. Lévy, Additional Materials 1 (2010), www.jourdan.ens.fr/levy/dle2010b.htm.
2. G. Duménil and D. Lévy, Additional Materials 1 and 2 (2010), www.jourdan .ens.fr/levy/dle2010b.htm.
3. G. Duménil and D. Lévy, Additional Materials 1 (2010), www.jourdan.ens.fr/ levy/dle2010b.htm.
4. G. Duménil and D. Lévy, Additional Materials 2 (2010), www.jourdan.ens.fr/ levy/dle2010b.htm.
5. This is the thesis put forward by Charles Kindleberger. C. Kindleberger, *The World in Depression, 1929–1939* (Berkeley: University of California Press, 1993).
6. A. D. Chandler, *Scale and Scope: The Dynamics of Industrial Capitalism* (Cambridge, Mass.: Harvard University Press, 1990).
7. J. M. Keynes, "The End of Laissez-Faire: Essays in Persuasion" (1926), in *The Collected Writings of John Maynard Keynes,* vol. 9 (London: Macmillan, St. Martin's Press for the Royal Economic Society, 1972), 272–294.
8. Chandler, *Scale and Scope.*
9. N. Gordon Levin, *Woodrow Wilson and World Politics* (Oxford: Oxford University Press, 1968).
10. During the 1920s, central banks were accumulating balances of dollars, besides reserves in pounds. B. Eichengreen and M. Flandreau, "The Rise and Fall of the Dollar, or When Did the Dollar Replace Sterling as the Leading Reserve Currency?" (Genoa, Italy: Past, Present and Policy Panel, 2008).

Appendix A

1. In such a model, a subscript, t, must be introduced to denote the period considered. The two following equations are used:

$$K_{t+1} = K_t + I_t \text{ and } \Phi_{t+1} = F_t + \varphi_t.$$

K and Φ are the stock of fixed capital and the stock of debt, respectively. On the homothetic trajectory, the growth rate common to all variables is

$$\rho = b\left((1-\beta)\frac{(1-\lambda)\varphi + \varepsilon}{\lambda} + \beta - \alpha\right).$$

The rate of indebtedness, measured as the stock of debt over the stock of fixed capital, is $\frac{b\varphi}{\rho}$.

Index

1920s: financial expansion and instability in, 272–277; labor organization, 291; United Kingdom in, 320

1960s. *See* Euromarkets; Managerial capitalism; Policies; Welfare state and social protection

1970s, 15, 46, 47. *See also* Crisis of 1970s; Crisis of the dollar; Income; Inflation; Managerial capitalism; Regulation

1979 coup, 8, 60–62, 132, 150, 200. *See also* Interest rates; Neoliberalism

1980s. *See* Crisis of banking and thrift institutions (late 1980s and early 1990s); Neoliberalism: phases of; Third world

1990s, 28, 39, 324. *See also* Boom: of information technologies (long boom of second half of 1990s); Investment abroad

1991 recession, 39, 62, 144, 173, 175, 214

2000, period following: break in global trends, 311, 313; explosion of financial mechanisms, 23, 33, 36, 107, 112, 113–124. *See also* Convergence of long-term interest rates

2001 recession, 33, 39, 65, 116, 173–174, 176–177, 202, 208, 214–215, 244, 249

2008 recession. *See* Great Contraction

Accounting procedures. *See* Mark to market

Accumulation: downward trend of, 24, 36, 37, 63, 151–152, 174; primitive, 88, 322; rate of, 151–152. *See also* Disaccumulation; Investment (real); Overaccumulation

Acts. *See* American Recovery and Reinvestment Act; Commodity Futures Modernization Act; Commodity Futures Trading Commission Act of 1974; Commodity Futures Trading Commission Act of 1936; Community Reinvestment Act (CRA); Depository Institutions Deregulation and Monetary Control Act; Economic Stimulus Act; Emergency Banking Act; Emergency Economic Stabilization Act; Employment Act; Espionage Act; Fair Labor Standards Act; Federal Housing Enterprises Financial Safety and Soundness Act; Futures Trading Practices Act; Garn–St. Germain Act; Glass-Steagall Act; Homeowners Refinancing Act; Housing Act; Housing and Economic Recovery Act; National Bank Act; National Currency Act; National Housing Act; National Industrial Recovery Act; National Labor Relations Act; Revenue Act; Securities Act; Sherman Act; Smoot-Hawley Tariff Act; Social Security Act; Taft-Hartley Act; Wagner Act

Adjustable rate mortgages (ARMs), 39, 181, 198–199, 215–216, 247, 299

Administered prices, 285

Advanced economies, 310. *See also* Emerging and developing countries

Advisory boards, 86, 290

Divorce between upper classes and countries: Chinese honeymoon, 27; United States, 26–27

Doha round, 324

Dollar: exchange rate of, 143, 301; exchange rate of, and U.S. trade deficit, 158–159; international role (dominance) of, 9, 29, 164, 289, 314, 316, 337; price-adjusted dollar indices, 303. *See also* Crisis of the dollar; Currencies; Dollarization; Major currencies index; Other important trading partners index; U.S. hegemony

Dollarization, 137

Domestic debt. *See* Indebtedness

Duménil, Gérard, 66n1, 318n1, 356n3 (Chap. 6), 357n9

Duménil, Gérard, and Dominique Lévy, 57n2, 66n2, 86n1, 364n2 (Chap. 21), 269n2, 271n2, 277n1, 348, 353n1, 353n2, 354n1 (Chap. 3), 354n4 (Chap. 4), 354n6, 355n9, 355n14, 356n5, 357n1, 357n9, 357n1, 358n2, 359n2 (Chap. 10), 359n3 (Chap. 10), 360n11, 365n4, 365n5, 365n7, 365n8, 366n11, 367nn1–4 (Chap. 24)

Dymski, Gary, 361n4

Economic Recovery Advisory Board, 290

Economic Stimulus Act, 78, 250, 328

Education, 16, 22, 78, 83, 320, 328

Efficacy of monetary policy, 172, 240, 246. *See also* Credit: efficiency of, as macro stabilizer; Greenspan, Alan; Monetary policy

Emergency Banking Act, 289

Emergency Economic Stabilization Act, 236, 237

Emerging and developing countries, 310–311, 316

Emerging markets, 135, 316

Employment Act, 80, 288

Enron, 131, 133

Espionage Act, 291

Euro. *See* Currencies

Euro area. *See* Europe

Euromarkets, 132

Europe, 109, 132, 139–140, 324; and international hegemony, 31, 314; as neoliberal stronghold, 31; weakness of, 9

European Central Bank (ECB), 261–263

European hegemony, 314

European Union. *See* Europe

Exchange rates, 136–137; cheap currencies, 301, 302; fixed, 136, 288; floatation of, 7, 132; fluctuation of, 123, 139–140; and international trade, 137–138, 144, 158–159; pegged to the dollar, 304; and stock-market indices in carry trade, 138–140

Exchanges (currencies). *See* Currencies: currency exchanges

Exports. *See* Foreign trade; Imports

Exports of capital, 52. *See also* Investment abroad

External debt, 119. *See also* Deficits of U.S. economy: of balance of trade; Foreign financing

External disequilibria. *See* Deficits of U.S. economy: of balance of trade; Foreign financing; Trajectory of U.S. economy

Externalization, 128, 130, 298. *See also* Off-balance-sheet entities (OBSEs)

Extraction of a surplus. *See* Capitalism; Surplus labor compensation

Failure of monetary policy, 23, 195–196, 198, 199. *See also* Credit: efficiency of, as macro stabilizer; Efficacy of monetary policy; Monetary policy

Fair Isaac Corporation (FICO), 180, 361n5

Fair Labor Standards Act, 291

Family offices, 56, 120, 299

Fannie Mae. *See* Federal National Mortgage Association (Fannie Mae)

Far-Right. *See* Right and Left

Fascism, 82, 292

Federal agencies, 41, 103, 207, 212, 229, 232, 238, 241–242; reference to Fannie Mae, Freddie Mac, and Ginnie Mae as "agencies," 207. *See also* Government-sponsored enterprises (GSEs); Securitization: by agencies and GSEs

Income: bias in income distribution,
45–48, 48–52; diminishing capital
income and rising wages within upper
classes, 330; high percentage of wages in
upper income brackets, 73–74; inequalities, 45, 75, 292; limitation of high
income, 30, 45–46, 299–300, 328–329;
patterns (in the postwar compromise
and neoliberalism), 166–167; of top
managers and traders, 300; wages and
capital income, 72. *See also* Bonuses;
Capital income; Dividends; Fictitious
gains; Inflation; Interest; Labor
compensation; Profits; Quest for high
income; Share of profits; Stock options;
Surplus labor compensation; Wages
Incorporation (wave of). *See* Corporate
revolution
Increasing instability (thesis of). *See*
Tendential instability
Indebtedness: curbing of, 199, 301; domestic
debt, 302; foreign debt, 162; growing debt
of U.S. sectors (gross and net), 104–106;
of financial sector, 104–106, 299; by
income brackets, 178–181; twin (domestic
and foreign debts as two sides of same
coin), 159–163, 168, 301. *See also* External
debt; Financial institutions; Government;
Households; Investment abroad; Third
world
India, 2, 26, 118, 119, 310, 311, 314, 315, 316,
325, 355n1
Industrial capital. *See under* Marx, Karl
Inflation, 140, 278, 304, 328; aversion
toward, 60, 278; cumulative, 17, 60;
devaluation of assets or debt by (income
transfer), 60, 67–68; fight against, 8, 53,
132, 196, 278; hyperinflation, 307; low
inflation in neoliberalism, 62
Information technologies. *See* Boom: of
information technologies (long boom of
second half of 1990s)
Infrastructures, 328
Instability. *See* Destabilization; Financial
structure, fragile and unwieldy nature
of; Tendential instability
Insurance against defaults. *See* Credit
default swaps (CDSs)

Insured banks. *See* Federal Deposit
Insurance Corporation (FDIC); Profit
rates
Intellectual property, 23
Intellectuals, 278
Interbank market. *See* Crisis of interbank
market
Interest, as source of capital
income, 65
Interest-bearing capital. *See under* Marx,
Karl
Interest only, 181, 299
Interest rates, 60, 62, 123, 132, 136, 138,
261, 304; comparison of central banks'
rates, 261; decline after 2000, 62, 70, 200,
202; London Interbank Offered Rate
(LIBOR), 219, 224, 230–234, 238;
long-term, 60–61, 160–161, 196, 199–203,
258, 303; real, 16–17, 46, 60–62, 68, 83,
138, 153, 160, 200, 304–305; short-term,
60–61, 137, 197–198, 201. *See also* 1979
coup; Adjustable rate mortgages (ARMs);
Convergence of long-term interest rates;
Credit: efficiency of, as macro stabilizer;
Efficacy of monetary policy; Federal
Funds rate; Greenspan, Alan
Intermediate classes. *See* Managers / mana-
gerial classes
Intermediate period, 47, 78, 270–271.
See also Capitalism; capitalism
International differences in social orders,
17, 27, 79, 80, 83, 322
International division of labor, 25, 31, 283,
284, 307, 322, 324
International hegemony, 7, 31, 37, 295, 309,
319, 330–331; domestic conditions to,
319–320. *See also* Atlantic; China; Class
hegemony and compromise; Europe;
Imperialism; U.S. hegemony
International institutions, 9, 31, 56, 94,
126, 133, 269, 300, 316, 318. *See also*
International Monetary Fund (IMF);
North Atlantic Treaty Organization
(NATO); United Nations; World Bank;
World Trade Organization (WTO)
International Monetary Fund (IMF), 9, 56,
133, 288; and imposition of neoliberal-
ism, 317, 337; and debt of the periphery,

Phases of crisis of neoliberalism, 38–41;
phase A (A1 and A2), 213, 216, 220, 230,
365n11; phase B (B1, B2, and B3), 211, 216,
219–220, 225, 230–234, 239, 241, 245,
365n11; phase C, 211, 219–220, 224–226,
228, 234–237, 239, 241, 244, 246, 250, 252,
256, 258, 260, 262; phase D, 212, 229,
237–238, 240–241; phase I, 176, 177, 197,
199, 362n1 (Chap. 16); phase II, 176, 177,
197, 199; phase III, 177, 178, 198, 199, 202;
phase IV, 177, 198, 199, 208, 213, 214, 215;
phases A to D, 208–209; phases I to IV,
173–174; phases I to IV and A to D, 214
Phases of modern capitalism. *See* Modern
capitalism: phases of
Phases of neoliberalism. *See* Neoliberalism: phases of
Piketty, Thomas, 45, 354n1 (Chap. 3),
355n1 (Chap. 5), 367n14
Planning and planners. *See* Great
Depression
Plihon, Dominique, 127n1
Policies: ability to stimulate demand by
credit, 302; control of indebtedness of
financial sector, 299; credit, 38; in
globalization, 134–137; Keynesian policies
in crisis of 1970s, 79, 332; macro stabilizers
(built-in stabilizers), 156, 168, 195, 286;
resistance to the use of macro policies,
278. *See also* Credit: efficiency of, as macro
stabilizer; Development; Efficacy of
monetary policy; Fiscal policy; Import-
substitution models; Keynesian economics (Keynesianism); Monetary policy
Popular classes: alliance with managerial
classes, 17–19, 78, 80–82, 87, 329, 330;
clerical workers (personnel) and
production workers, 78, 81–82, 90;
leadership in socialism, 98; and proletarian classes, 95, 357n7; in social orders, 78,
95–98, 282; role in social change, 30–32,
39, 290, 333–334; solidarity within
popular classes, 323; in the tripolar class
configuration (definition), 13–14, 90, 95.
See also Class struggle; Income; New
Deal; Purchasing power; Right and Left
Postwar compromise: class foundations,
17, 30, 78, 80, 95–98; collapse (eco-

nomic and political weakness) of, 83,
332; differences among countries, 17,
77; Keynesian compromise, 15–17, 77;
to the Left, 30; as less a capitalism, 80;
managerial leadership, 29–30, 80–81,
87, 96; mixed economies, 17, 31, 77;
New Deal and, 87, 97, 282, 289, 291;
origins of, 15, 82–83, 282, 332; social
component of, 78; social-democratic
compromise, 15, 82; tempered
capitalism, 78, 282, 293; three components of, 77–82; underlying economic
conditions, 83, 332. *See also* Containment of capitalist interests (in the
postwar compromise); Managerial
autonomy in the postwar compromise;
New Deal; Right and Left; Social
orders / power configurations
Postwar decades. *See* Postwar compromise
Poulentzas, Nicos, 357n3 (Chap. 6)
Pound Sterling. *See* Currencies
Power configurations. *See* Social orders / power configurations
Prebish, Raul, 307
Prices. *See* Control of prices and wages; Oil
and oil prices
Primitive accumulation. *See* Accumulation
Private equity firms, 56, 86, 109, 121,
125–126, 298, 299
Private-label ABSs, 187, 193, 200, 216;
issuers of, 103, 104, 107, 187, 188–189,
196, 217, 241, 274, 275, 299. *See also*
Asset-backed securities (ABSs)
Production labor (transformation of), 95
Production workers. *See* Popular classes
Productive capacity. *See* Capacity
utilization rate
Productive capital. *See under* Marx, Karl
Productivity of capital, 59, 152, 332
Productivity of labor, 271
Profitability. *See* Profitability crises; Profit
rates; Profits; Structural crises
Profitability crises, 17, 19–21, 33, 270,
331–332. *See also* Crisis of 1890s; Crisis
of 1970s; Marx, Karl: and the conse-
quences of profitability crises
Profit rates: and accumulation, 152–153;
and capital gains, 67–68; comparison

between nonfinancial and financial corporations, 66–69; effect of inflation on, 67–68; effect of interest payment, 59, 152–153; effect of taxation on profit rates, 59; effects of business-cycle fluctuations on, 267; on enterprises' own funds, 58–59, 67–69; of financial corporations, 69–70; historical profile, 267–270; of insured banks, 69; à la Marx, 57, 59, 60, 68, 270, 354n6; of nonfinancial corporations, 57–60, 66–69, 152–153; rate of retained profits, 59–60, 83, 152–153; rate of retained profits and accumulation, 152–153; rate of return on equity (ROE), 67, 69–70, 128, 221; recovery and restoration ratios, 58–60; trends of, 11, 19, 20, 59, 269. *See also* Profitability crises; Structural crises

Profits, 301, 306, 317; conservation of profits within corporations, 79, 293, 328; dubious, 8; paid out, 50, 301; retained, 50; and taxes, 50; and upper wages, 52. *See also* Dividends; Profit rates; Share of profits; Transnational corporations

Proletarian class, 91

Propensity to run a deficit/surplus, 164–165, 166, 168; model, 341–343

Protectionism, 301, 306–308, 317; effects in the short and long run, 308; Keynes and, 136–137, 283; in the New Deal, 283–284; retaliation, 301. *See also* Free trade; Import-substitution models

Public sector, 25, 79, 82, 322

Purchasing power, 18, 29, 34, 46–47, 78, 82, 83, 271, 290; after neoliberalism, 29; deficient purchasing power and crises, 34, 268; in neoliberalism, 18, 53, 78, 85, 166, 271, 301; in the postwar compromise, 16, 82–83, 332; profile over time, 46–49

Purchasing power parity (PPP), 102, 310–311

Quantity of money. *See* M2

Quest for high income, 22–24, 36, 125–127, 168–169, 297–299. *See also* Fictitious surplus; Income; Neoliberalism

Radical and left organizations or views, 82, 98, 284, 297, 322, 324

Rate. *See* Accumulation: rate of; Federal Funds rate; Growth rates; Interest rates; Investment (real): rates of; Profit rates; Savings: saving rates

Rate of profit or return. *See* Profit rates

Rating agencies, 130, 135, 216, 218, 223, 358n6 (Chap. 7)

Reagan, Ronald, 17

Real bills doctrine, 278

Real income. *See* Purchasing power

Real income flows (as opposed to fictitious gains), 127–131

Real interest rates. *See* Interest rates

Recession, 22, 24, 61, 173, 196, 245–247, 277, 360n1 (Chap. 12). *See also* 1991 recession; 2001 recession; Business cycle; Great Contraction; Great Depression

Reciprocal Tariff Act, 283

Recovery ratio. *See* Profit rates

Regional entities or leaders, 31, 315, 317

Regulation, 16, 297; financial, 16, 28, 83, 126, 278, 297–300, 330; in 1970s, 133; Regulation q, 289. *See also* Acts; Deregulation; Glass-Steagall Act; Great Depression; Neomanagerial capitalism; New Deal; Regulation School

Regulation School, 268

Related markets, 38, 208, 216–218

Relations of production. *See* Capitalism; Marx, Karl

Renminbi. *See* Yuan

Rentiers, 13

Repression, 82–83, 291, 333

Research and innovation, 9, 23, 301, 328

Reserves. *See* Central banks; Federal Reserve

Residential. *See* Boom: in residential investment (housing boom); Mortgage-backed securities (MBSs); Mortgages

Rest of world. *See* United States and rest of world

Restoration ratio. *See* Profit rates

Retail sales, 249–250

Re-territorialization, 29, 301, 308. *See also* De-territorialization

Retirement, 16, 78, 86

Technical and organizational paradigm, 271

Temin, Peter, 269

Tempered capitalism. *See* Postwar compromise: tempered capitalism

Tendential instability, 276, 277

Term Auction Facility (TAF). *See* Federal Reserve instruments

Terms of trade, deterioration of, 307

Thatcher, Margaret, 17, 23

Third world, 324; debt and debt crisis, 61, 307, 324, 337

Time frames, 33, 326–327

Trade. *See* Foreign trade

Trajectory of U.S. economy, 24, 28, 33, 36, 143–155, 272, 300–303; external trade, 24; financing by rest of world, 144–146, 337; model, 343; straightening of, 300, 303; unsustainable, 34. *See also* Accumulation; Alternatives to neoliberalism: correcting disequilibria; Deficits of U.S. economy; Historical tendencies; Indebtedness; Trends

Tranches, 135, 190–191, 216–217

Transatlantic Economic Partnership (TEP), 314

Transatlantic hegemony, 314, 337

Transnational corporations, 18, 29, 84, 116, 271, 301; profits retained abroad by, 52

Transparency. *See* Alternatives to neoliberalism: increased transparency

Transportation and communication, 12

Treasury, 40, 188, 207, 229, 235–242, 252

Treasury securities, 41, 190, 232, 239, 241, 287, 302, 305, 363n6; held by rest of world, 116, 118, 168–169, 304

Treatment of crisis of neoliberalism, 40, 41, 228–243; consciousness of necessity of adjustment, 41, 265, 281–282, 321, 326; curbing external deficits, 301; curbing indebtedness, 301–302; duration of adjustment in United States, 22, 25, 41, 327. *See also* Capital financing; Credit: financing of; Deficits of U.S. economy: government; Federal Reserve; Guarantees (deposit, loans, notes, securities)

Trends, 143–155, 167. *See also* Tendential instability; Trajectory of U.S. economy

Triad, 313

Trigger vs. cause, 38

Tripolar class configuration, 13, 73, 90, 92, 95. *See also* Capitalists; Managers/managerial classes; Popular classes

Trusts, pools, and cartels. *See* Competition

Typology of social orders. *See* Social orders/power configurations

UBS, 128–129, 131, 227

Underconsumption, 37

Unions, 282, 291, 324, 366n10

United Kingdom, 82, 253–254, 259; and neoliberalism, 8, 117, 132, 137–138, 154–155; and U.S. hegemony, 269, 318, 320

United Nations, 318

United Nations Economic Commission for Latin America and the Caribbean. *See* CEPAL

Upper classes. *See* Classes

United States and rest of world, 144–146, 157; debt held by rest of world, 162; profits and capital income from rest of world, 115–116; U.S. securities held by rest of world, 116, 118, 305. *See also* Trajectory of U.S. economy: financing by rest of world

U.S. hegemony, 143, 309–325; Chinese challenge to, 322–323; decline of, 9, 26–28, 31, 295, 310–313, 316, 327, 331; manifest destiny, 319; and neoliberal trends, 154–155, 327; potential for reaction to, 320–321; strengthened by neoliberalism, 313; and World War I, 319. *See also* Dollar; Imperialism

Veblen, Thorstein, 13

Vehicles: special-purpose, 105–108; structured investment (SIVs), 106–107, 130, 218, 233, 299, 358n6 (Chap. 7)

Venezuela, 324

Versailles Treaty, 322

Vietnam, 88, 321

Vladimirova, K., 358n6

Volcker, Paul, 61, 133, 290

"Vulgar economy," 91

Wage earners: breaking wage-earning homogeneity, 49–50, 71–98; hierarchies,